REPRODUCTION, MEDICINE AND THE SOCIALIST STATE

By the same author

WOMEN AND STATE SOCIALISM: Sex Inequality in the
Soviet Union and Czechoslovakia

REPRODUCTION, MEDICINE AND THE SOCIALIST STATE

Alena Heitlinger

Associate Professor of Sociology
Trent University, Ontario

St. Martin's Press   New York

First published in the United States of America in 1987

Printed in Hong Kong

ISBN 0–312–67403–1

Library of Congress Cataloging-in-Publication Data

Heitlinger, Alena.
Reproduction, medicine, and the socialist state.

Includes bibliographies.
1. Birth control—Czechoslovakia. 2. Youth—
Czechoslovakia—Sexual behavior. 3. Population policy—
Czechoslovakia. 4. Socialism and society. I. Title.
[DNLM: 1. Family Planning—Czechoslovakia. 2. Repro-
duction. 3. Socialism—Czechoslovakia. 4. Socioeconomic
Factors. 5. Women. WQ 205 H473r]
HQ766.5.C9H45   1987   363.9'6'09437   85–26112
ISBN 0–312–67403–1

For David, Daniel and Michael

Contents

Contents

List of Tables

Preface

This study is concerned with the social and individual management of reproduction in the state socialist societies[1] in Eastern Europe, especially Czechoslovakia. Its origin dates back to the summer of 1980, when Sharon Wolchik and Alfred Meyer had invited me, shortly after the birth of my first child, to present a paper on a topic of my choice at the Conference on Changes in the Status of Women in Eastern Europe, which they were organising at George Washington University for December 1981. Since I was at that time very interested in the, by then, growing Western feminist literature on the medical management of childbirth, I decided to extend the Western-based research to the one socialist society with which I am most familiar – Czechoslovakia, and thus provide a much needed cross-national comparison.

What had particularly intrigued me about the prospect of doing research on childbirth management in Czechoslovakia was my total ignorance about the subject, despite the fact that in 1979 I had published a book on the position of women in the Soviet Union and Czechoslovakia, entitled *Women and State Socialism*. That book is largely general in focus, covering such diverse issues as the Marxist theory of reproduction of labour power, actual domestic work under the conditions of state socialism, various aspects of women's labour force participation, socialist women's movements, contraception, abortion, socialist provisions for child care and socialist pro-natalist population policies. However, the management of full-term pregnancy and childbirth was not discussed. The reason for what retrospectively seems a rather strange omission can be easily located in my personal biography as well as in the intellectual climate in the early 1970s, during which *Women and State Socialism* was initially written as a 'feminist' PhD thesis in sociology for the University of Leicester, UK. The dominant feminist concern at that time was the *freeing* of women from their child-bearing and child-rearing roles. As Oakley (1979b, p. 630–1) argues, in the 1960s and early 1970s feminism did not yet conceptualise reproduction as a female resource,[2] but rather

xii

saw it as a handicap, as a source or cause of social inferiority of women. Thus the demands of the British women's liberation movement in the early 1970s focused on equal pay, free and better contraception, free abortion on demand, women's right to define their own sexuality and the free state provision of child care. Apart from the theoretical Marxist interpretation of the function of reproduction in the capitalist family, childbirth as a feminist issue was barely mentioned. Thus, with the exception of attending staff and women having babies (and I belonged to neither of these categories), childbirth in the 1960s and early 1970s was largely 'invisible', unlike today, when the medical management of childbirth is a topic of widespread interest, and the subject of a mounting critique from feminists, organised consumer movements, individual women (and men) and numerous members of the medical and nursing professions. In this sense, *Women and State Socialism*, with its broad yet at the same time also limited focus, is very much a product of its time, and the present study is in many ways a logical extension of this earlier work.

The Trent University Research Committee generously supported my project by awarding me a grant for a research trip to Prague in the summer of 1981. While my mother took full care of my one-year-old son, whom I had taken to Prague with me (without her assistance I would have been unable to do *any* research in Prague), I spent my days at the Charles University Library, reading professional literature in obstetrics/gynaecology, neonatology, demography, psychology, sociology and so on. The official obstetrical/gynaecological journal, *Československá gynekologie*, published ten times a year, proved to be an extremely useful source of information, as did current newspapers, magazines and personal 'expert' advice books on women's private lives as sex partners, child-bearers, mothers and spouses. I soon became convinced that the topic of medical management of childbirth is too limited and that it would be more fruitful to broaden my focus to the whole reproductive sequence, from coitus to post-partum. In turn, the broadening of focus enabled me to consider in some detail various forms of state intervention in reproduction.

My research in the summer of 1981 resulted in a 56-pages-long paper which was well received at the Washington Conference in December of that year. In fact, several participants at the Conference, above all Bogdan Mieckowski, encouraged me to carry the research forward to a book-length manuscript on the subject. Trent's Research Committee generously agreed to sponsor another research trip to Prague (in the summer of 1982), which included several informal unstructured interviews with medical professionals. This time I went to Prague alone, but three months' pregnant with my second child, which turned out to be a real asset for the kind of research I was doing. For example, my, by then visible, pregnancy enabled me to visit a prenatal clinic (with a friend who was also pregnant at that time) without anybody raising any questions about what I was doing there. However, all of the interviews with professionals – two paediatricians, two clinical psychologists, a child psychologist and the chief of obstetrics/gynaecology in a large Prague hospital – were initiated on the basis of my professional status as a sociologist, rather than on the grounds of my pregnancy.

While I agree with Ann Oakley (1979a, 1980) that structured eliciting of women's (and men's) accounts of reproduction and the integration of these accounts into interpretative feminist theories should constitute the chief goals of any current feminist research on the subject, it is not always possible to do this in practice. Apart from short letters published in the press, first-hand accounts of 'reproducers' themselves simply do not exist in Czechoslovakia. I could not conduct any formal interviews with a scientifically selected sample of women (and men) and was therefore unable to generate such data myself. Hence most of the data contained in this book are quite 'conventional', supplied as they are by professionally 'biased' Czechoslovak physicians, demographers, health care administrators, statisticians, psychologists, journalists and sociologists in their official publications. However, whenever possible, they are supplemented by 'anecdotal' observations and information.

I would like to thank the following colleagues and friends for their comments on earlier drafts of bits and pieces of the book as they emerged as chapters and/or articles published elsewhere:[3] Meg Luxton, Heather Jon Maroney, Alfred Meyer, Maxine Molyneux, Maria Victor-Paez and Sharon Wolchik. I also want to thank Marg Tully, Marisa Haensel and Margaret Pearce for typing various chapters of the manuscript. Finally, thanks are due to my husband, David Morrison, who, as usual, and despite his busy schedule, has provided me with invaluable editorial assistance throughout the writing of this book, not to mention the undertaking of more than his share of child care responsibilities. It therefore gives me a great pleasure to dedicate a book on reproduction to my family of procreation, the source of tremendous affection as well as intellectual stimulation.

NOTES

1. The definition of the term socialism (or state socialism) is by no means clear. As Molyneux (1981, p. 169) points out, 'there is a large and contentious literature on how to define socialism and how far any one definition can be applied to existing post-revolutionary societies'. In my usage, the term simply refers to self-declared socialist countries (in their official names as well as constitutions) in Central and Eastern Europe. The term is also applicable to an increasing number of Third World societies, but their concerns are beyond the scope of this study.

2. Rich (1976) in particular has argued that far from rejecting their child-bearing function, women should celebrate it. From a different perspective, Janssen-Jurreit (1982, p. 256–77) has argued that if in the foreseeable future reproduction is detached from the female body, women will have even less chance of controlling society than they have now. In her view, artificial reproduction will lead to the total loss of female power and the complete unimportance of female existence. It may even result in the dream of all totalitarian states coming true: the direct, immediate domination and control of the individual human being from the fusion of the sex cells unto death. For a similar analysis of the potential negative implications of artificial reproduction, see Corea (1984) and Murphy (1984); for a review of current feminist accounts of how biology shapes women's lives, see Sayers (1982).

3. The paper which led to this book, 'Passage to Motherhood: Personal and Social Management of Reproduction in Czechoslovakia in the 1980s' appears in a revised form in a book edited by Sharon Wolchik and Alfred Meyer entitled *Women, State and Party in Eastern Europe* (Duke University Press, 1985). The book is based on selected papers from the Washington Conference. Another article, entitled 'Maternity leaves, protective legislation and sex equality: Eastern European and Canadian perspectives', is to appear in a book edited by Heather Jon Maroney and Meg Luxton entitled *Women in Canada: Political Economy and Political Struggles*.

1 Introduction

Reproduction is a complex and ill-defined term. It has been variously described as an aspect of sexuality, motherhood, health, population, the family, work, and the restoration of labour power. This variety of definitions indicates a lack of precision and clarity. Reproduction has come to mean widely different things in demography, economics, medicine, psychology, anthropology, sociology, not to mention Marxism and feminism. Academic writings on the subject are simultaneously overlapping and fragmented along disciplinary lines, and there is also a problem in the way they are simplified for popular consumptiom. Thus there is no single agreed 'reproductive paradigm', although there is an emerging consensus among feminist academics on how not to do research on reproduction.[1] The fancy academic terminology also tends to ignore the simple fact that, in the minds of most people, reproduction refers to procreation and having children.

The process of reproduction examined in this study is defined in terms of *transition to motherhood*. It is events-oriented and refers to a reproductive sequence from coitus through birth control and conception to ante-partum, intra-partum and post-partum, as graphically outlined in Figure 1.1. This perspective clearly recognises that reproduction is simultaneously individual and social in all societies. It is individuals who make (or drift into) reproductive decisions, but such decisions are subject to considerable social manipulation and control.

Childbirth is the culmination of three events: copulation, conception and birth. In turn, personal strategies pursuing prevention of birth are directed towards eliminating any one of these events. In other words, birth can be prevented either by lack of copulation (this can be achieved by the means of a permanent celibacy or delayed marriage, i.e. by what demographers refer to as 'nuptiality control'); or by the prevention of conception (by means of natural fertility control, contraception or sterilisation); or by failing to carry pregnancy to term (by means of miscarriage, abortion or stillbirth). There is also a fourth possibility of fertility (rather than birth) control, namely

1

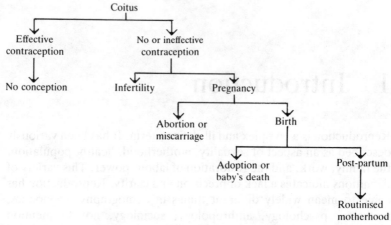

FIGURE 1.1   Transition to motherhood

infanticide, but this particular strategy is so rare in modern industrial societies that there is no need to discuss it in this study. On the other side of the reproductive continuum, there are increasing possibilities of technological forms of conception, such as artificial insemination or *in vitro* fertilisation (IVF). These options are of particular interest to sterile and infertile couples as well as to homosexuals.[2]

The progression (or lack thereof) through the continuum of reproductive decision-making (by women, men, or couples) is influenced by structural, cultural and individual elements. At the most general level of analysis, the major structural influences concern the attained level of economic development, food intake and health. For example, Tilly and Scott (1978, p. 27) and Wertz and Wertz (1979, p. 3) have demonstrated how low standards of nutrition and health in early modern Europe and the colonies inhibited sexual desire, conception, the ability to carry pregnancy to term, as well as the adequacy of mothers' milk supply. Similar evidence concerning the effect of meagre diets on low bodyweight, endemic diseases and resulting high rates of 'pregnancy wastage' in Central Asia is presented by Coale *et al.* (1979, p. 108).

With respect to the initiation of menstruation (menarche) and the maintenance of menstrual cycles, Coale *et al.* (1979, p. 107) quote an hypothesis formulated by Rose Frish and her colleagues at Harvard, who link menarche to the attainment and maintenance of some threshold value of proportionate fat content in the body. Moreover, the attainment of regular menses occurs some years after menarche, when the proportion of fat has increased still further. Hence the onset and maintenance of menstruation is directly related to sufficient food intake. The economic impact on the very 'biology' of menstruation is also evident in advanced industrial societies. According to Delaney, Lupton and Toth (1977, pp. 42–3):

> Those who eat well mature earlier. Today, the average American girl first menstruates when she is $12\frac{1}{2}$ years old. Figures from Norway, where the oldest such records are kept, show that in 1850 the average girl had her first period at 17; by 1950, at $13\frac{1}{2}$. For each generation since 1850, then, a girl's period has come about a year earlier than her mother's.

Consequently, personal decisions concerning fertility regulation now have to be taken earlier and for longer periods of time than in the past.

Bodies are clearly not independent of their economic and social surroundings. A high rate of pregnancy wastage in poor societies is not 'natural' any more than are incidences of sterility, miscarriage and birth defects, caused by the hazardous environment of advanced industrial societies. Like their poor predecessors, 'modern' women often have no control over their own and their unborn baby's health if they live or are working in an environment which may expose them and their child to harmful substances. Reproductive hazards will be discussed in more detail in Chapter 4 in the context of evaluating socialist protective legislation. For now, it is sufficient to say that a distinction between natural and controlled fertility is inadequate, because it ignores the socio-economic context in which the 'natural' form of birth control operates. 'Voluntary' versus 'involuntary' birth control seems a better dichotomy.

The major structural influences upon reproduction examined in this study are demographic and economic variables (namely age, income and marital status), the relationship between work life and home life, population policies and the medical management of reproduction. Culturally, the major influences examined are the pronatalist ideologies of motherhood and the specific norms pre- and proscribing sexual behaviour, methods of birth control, breastfeeding and the 'medicalised' outlook on life. On the individual level, past and present experiences with sexual activities, contraception, abortion, pregnancy, childbirth and motherhood influence the various stages of reproductive decision-making.

EAST–WEST COMPARISONS

How do we compare and evaluate these influences? It is not intended here to draw a sharp dichotomy between a 'socialist' and a 'capitalist' transition to motherhood, because such a rigid distinction would obscure variations among socialist and capitalist societies, as well as similarities between them. While the United States and the Soviet Union are often seen as 'representatives' of their respective socio-political systems, they are at the same time also 'the *least typical* cases of each generic type of society' (Giddens, 1980, p. 21). For most purposes, 'capitalism' and 'socialism' are useful shorthands, but sometimes they can be quite misleading. As Stacey (1982, p. 16) puts it:

> The nature of capitalist society varies from one part of the world to another and one historical period to another depending on how the arrangements which capitalists (not capitalism) introduce, affect and are affected by other previously existing social arrangements and by social, economic and political activities in other places which have a bearing on the developments.

Western European scholars tend to be much more aware of the uniqueness of the American form of capitalism than are their North American counterparts. This is particularly evident in medical sociology. For example, Riska (1982, p. 43), of the Research Institute for Social Security of the Social Insurance Institution of Finland, pointed out that the recent emphasis on self-care and health education 'not only expresses but also re-confirms a long-standing emphasis on individualism, privatism and self-reliance in American society', while in Scandinavia health education is integrated into a publicly supported primary-care system. Moreover, Scandinavian health education is provided by nurses largely within the context of the work-place rather than the family whose therapeutic value tends to be glorified in the US. In this respect, the organisation of health education in Czechoslovakia comes closer to the Scandinavian rather than to the American pattern.

Strong (1979, p. 199) of the MRC Medical Sociology Unit in Aberdeen, Scotland, has argued in his critical examination of the thesis of medical imperialism that the clearest and most systematic articulation of distrust of doctors 'has been largely an American product. The libertarianism of American social thought when coupled with the anti-intellectual tradition noted by Hofstader (to which it is of course related) has led some American sociologists into a sustained attack upon the power and privileges of experts.' An awareness of the differences between the United States and Western European capitalist countries is also evident in political and professional circles in Czechoslovakia. For example, in private conversations several influential Czech doctors revealed that recommendations based on research conducted in Western Europe, especially France and the Nordic countries, have a much better chance of being accepted and implemented in Eastern Europe than suggestions arising out of US-based research. Anything connected to the United States is generally seen as more 'individualistic', 'capitalist' and 'imperialist'.

Analogous differences exist among the socialist countries themselves, as we shall see throughout this book. While a great deal of lip service is paid to the 'superiority' of Soviet obstetrics, very little evidence of this is apparent in practice. True, the liberalised abortion legislation and the introduction of the psychoprophylactic method of 'prepared birth' followed Soviet leads, but that was in the 1950s. More recent changes, such as sex education or the 'rooming-in' system of newborn hospital care, are based entirely on successful Western European rather than Soviet experiences. Foetal monitors and incubators are also generally imported from the West rather than from the Soviet Union. In this light, it is interesting to quote Connor (1979, p. 325), who asserted that 'from several standpoints, the character and structure of social hierarchy in Eastern Europe is better understood as *European* rather than *socialist*'.

Thus broad comparisons and evaluations of 'socialist' and 'capitalist' management of reproduction seem premature without more careful and informed case studies than are currently available. The present book is intended as a contribution to this end.

UNITS AND LEVELS OF ANALYSIS

The distinction between 'personal' and 'social' management of reproduction implies two levels of analysis – the individual and the social. Each level has its own dynamics and, in order to avoid the 'fallacy of the wrong level', we cannot make direct inferences from one to the other (Galtung, 1967, pp. 37–48). The units of analysis at the social level are relatively straightforward, including institutional arrangements and policies as well as aggregate demographic variables such as birth, death and infant mortality rates, net rates of reproduction, rates and ratios of legal and illegal abortions and levels of family allowance and birth payments.

The individual level is more problematic, because the unit of analysis can refer to 'individual' women, men or couples. Clearly, these categories are not the same, yet they tend to be used quite interchangeably. Moreover, exclusive use of only one of these units raises definitional problems as well as issues of empirical accuracy. Firstly, there is a problem in defining a 'couple'. For example, Zollinger (1980, p. 121) notes the difficulties involved in obtaining reliable information of young unmarried men and women living together. The only source of statistics on this phenomenon comes from national census data that are generally based on self-reporting. Since common-law living is not yet fully socially acceptable and in some cases might have undesirable tax consequences (in countries where income tax is based on a couple's joint income rather than on separate individual incomes), one can assume considerable under-reporting of this particular form of a 'couple'. Other data on unmarried couples living together come largely from speculative clues. For example, Swiss registrars have drawn attention to the fact that the same address is given for the bride and groom for a *majority* of couples. Zollinger also notes a recent decline in marriages in a number of Western countries, which in his opinion is mirrored by an increase in common-law marriages. However, this latter phenomenon is extremely rare in Eastern Europe, given the compulsory registration of one's residence as well as the prevalent housing shortage. Most young *married* couples cannot live together in a separate household, at least in the early years of their marriage, and it is hard to see how *unmarried* couples could have found a way of doing so.

However, reproductive behaviour is not predicated on common residence. Decisions whether and when to enter a heterosexual relationship, whether and what kind of fertility regulation to use and so on can obviously be made quite spontaneously by couples who have just met or who are going 'steady' but who live in separate residences. David and McIntyre (1981, p. 70) argue that reproductive behaviour should be understood within a 'psychosocial model of fertility behaviour which emphasizes the subjective assessment of the environment by the individual and the importance of the two partners in a couple influencing each other's perceptions and choices of behavior'. However, a few pages later, the authors report findings which considerably lessen the applicability of their own model.

> One of the interesting features of the 1969 Soviet National Sample Survey was that when women were asked their husband's opinion on desirable family size, they usually responded that they thought their husbands wanted more children (except in the high fertility republics, where opinions were more likely to converge). Many women, however, dismissed their husband's view as irrelevant and having little influence on their childbearing decisions. These comments tend to confirm that women have been the prime decision-makers in reducing fertility. (David and McIntyre, 1981, p. 107)

Data gathered by Greenglass (1981) would also support the view that 'women' is an analytically more significant category than 'couples' in the study of at least some aspects of reproductive decision-making. Her study of psychological adjustment after abortion, based on a sample of 188 women living in Toronto and surrounding areas in 1972–3 who were interviewed approximately 36 weeks after their abortion, presented some interesting results: 48 per cent of the respondents claimed that they had made the abortion decision by themselves; 45 per cent said that they had made the decision with one or two people close to them (e.g. their male partner, a family member or a friend); and approximately 6 per cent said they were pressured into it but they themselves were against it.

However, a similar study conducted by Shusterman (1979) in Chicago came up with different results, asserting the importance of 'couples' rather than 'women'. Her findings, based on a sample of 393 women randomly selected from patients using two abortion clinics in downtown Chicago, revealed that the majority of respondents were involved in a positive relationship with their male partner. Eighty-seven per cent of male partners of the respondents knew that the woman suspected a pregnancy and 81 per cent knew that she was aborting – a decision which they overwhelmingly supported. Similarly, two-thirds of a sample of Hungarian married couples apparently made the decision to terminate an unwanted pregnancy jointly (David and McIntyre, 1981, p. 271).

A different, if related point is made by Woodhouse (1982) in her study of white British young single women who were having abortions at clinics run by charitable agencies in London and in the

Midlands. They found a notable lack of discussion about contraception prior to the relationship becoming sexual and this is explained as follows:

> Many young women may feel unable to broach the subject before embarking on a sexual relationship with their boyfriends, fearing that he might view them as sexually promiscuous and perhaps unfeminine. As Simone de Beauvoir has observed, femininity is equated with passivity, thus a direct and straightforward approach to contraception may be perceived as an indicator of cold-bloodedness and calculation, characteristics which are at odds with femininity. Despite conventional expectations of the man being the dominant and responsible partner, some of the men expected the woman to deal with contraception on the basis of pregnancy being her problem; a situation which is compounded by definition of sex as spontaneous and unpremeditated. . . .Not surprisingly then, young women tend to seek contraceptive advice after they have become sexually involved and not before. For sexual activity to be rendered acceptable on the individual level it must occur within a particular context of romantic love and personal commitment; and even if the relationship is shortlived the perception of the situation is that it is *other* girls who sleep around. The awareness, which sometimes extends to guilt, of engaging in an activity which does not meet with full social approval is neutralized by rationalizations: it is all right if you are in love, committed and thinking of marriage or at least going steady; it is not all right to act as a male and indulge in sex as a whim, purely for fun. One way to neutralize social proscription is not think about contraception, to define sex as spontaneous and uncontrollable, as an activity which is not amenable to rational planning and regulation. This, of course, fits neatly with male abrogation of responsibility for contraception and the definition of pregnancy as a woman's problem. (Woodhouse, 1982, pp. 9, 14)

Similar findings have been reported by Morokvasić (1981), Gordon (1976) and Luker (1975), who all draw our attention to an inherent ambivalence in women's sexual relationships with their partners. In this context, the interlinking of social and individual perceptions of acceptable feminine behaviour and the influence of the man in the relationship *are* significant and support David's and McIntyre's assertion of 'the importance of the two partners in a couple influencing each other's perceptions and choices of behaviour.' However, these perceptions have to be placed in the socio-cultural context of dominant sexual-scripts to have any analytical validity.

At this stage, there will not be a detailed examination of the complex set of relationships between contraception and abortion, between sexuality and procreation and between an unplanned conception, unwanted pregnancy and unwanted child, since these substantive issues will be examined in subsequent chapters. At this point, we look at methodological considerations only. It is clear that the methodological problem of what constitutes an analytically more significant unit of analysis, 'women' or 'couples', cannot be resolved on the basis of empirical evidence alone. It seems that, as one moves from sexuality and contraception to abortion, men's role in reproductive decision-making declines. However, it should be noted that all of the studies quoted above have, in fact, relied entirely on women as their informants. Men have remained rather sketchy figures. Moreover, their perception of and approaches to sexuality, contraception, abortion and a desired family size, were not examined directly, but were filtered through their female partners' evaluations. What is now needed is more comparative research on male decision-making in the reproductive system. We have to learn directly from men how they perceive and interpret their experiences of heterosexuality, contraception, abortion, as well as pregnancy and childbirth. This can be done by including men or actual couples (rather than aggregated individuals) in the research design.

Such research practices are rare, but they appear to be on the increase. For example, Fein (1978) and Romalis (1981), in their respective studies of fathers' roles in pregnancy and childbirth, obtained their data directly from men by interviewing them as well as by participant observation in prenatal classes. Most of the Czech public opinion surveys on population issues have drawn their respondents not only from the population of married women (though these have predominated) but also from the general population over the age of 15, aggregated married couples, as well as specific regions and age groups. To the best of my knowledge, there has been no study focusing exclusively on the reproductive experiences of Czechoslovak males.

Given this paucity of data, as well as the centrality of the reproductive experience to women's lives, I have chosen 'women' as the more significant category. However, this does not mean that this study ignores men or couples. In fact, the contrary is the case. While traditional 'sexist' social science has tended to define women *only* in the context of their relationship to men (and possibly also to children), feminists tend to analyse women in the context of multiple social relations and arrangements. For women's relationships to children are different from their relationships to men or to other women.

Furthermore, concepts of 'men' and 'women' can be further differentiated by a combination of various residential, kin and class categories. It is clearly not the same to have a husband as to have an occasional lover. Moreover, motherhood is not the only means of obtaining self-identity for women – there are other meaningful interactions with co-workers, friends, neighbours, various relatives, the patterns of which tend to vary according to class as well as life-cycle differences. It is therefore necessary to examine 'women' and 'men' as statistical categories not only within the family, but also within the broader economic, cultural and political context. In other words, the concepts of 'women' and 'men' have to be much more flexible, to enable us to focus on particular aspects of their reproductive lives. As we shall see in subsequent chapters, in Eastern Europe, abortion, pregnancy and childbirth are events which hardly touch men at all, though this admittedly applies to men as sexual partners and not to men as doctors. Men also tend to play a minimal part in the determination of family size, though again more evidence on this question is needed directly from men.

An additional reason for choosing 'women' rather than 'couples' is related to the current predominant measurement of biological reproduction – fertility – which refers to the actual child-bearing behaviour of a woman or an aggregated group of women. Two types of fertility measurement exist: period and cohort. Period measures assess the frequency of a given event, at one particular point in time, while cohort measures assess the frequency of a given event (such as birth or an abortion) occurring to a group of people (a cohort) over a period of time. In other words, period measures are cross-sectional whereas cohort measures are temporal and longitudinal. Cohort and period rates therefore measure fertility from very different perspectives.

The best known cross-sectional fertility measures are the crude birth rate (a number of births that occur in any one year in relationship to the total population), the general fertility rate (which restricts the population to women of reproductive ages, usually defined as 15–49 years), and age-specific birth rates (obtained by dividing the number of births to mothers of a certain age by the number of women of that age in the population). By convention, the latter are calculated for women in five-year age groups starting at age 15 and ending at age 49. Thus seven separate rates are computed: women aged 15–19, aged 20–24, and so on. Each rate may be viewed as a general fertility rate for a particular age group. Abortion rates are compiled in exactly the same manner.

With cohort fertility analysis, different groups of women are compared in terms of the number of children that they have borne up to a given point in time and the timing of child-bearing. Demographers generally consider cohort measurements a more accurate representation of the actual reproductive behaviour of couples. For example, Hansluwka (1980, p. 302) sees in longitudinal analysis a powerful tool to separate changes in the timing of births from changes in the eventual number of children born to a cohort of women. Ryder (1974, p. 132) also argues that the size of a cohort bears a significant influence on the level and time of fertility. On the other hand, cross-sectional fertility rates, especially crude birth rates, are useful indicators of population growth and short-term social demand for various health and social services – an issue discussed in the next chapter.

NOTES

1. For examples of recent feminist analyses of reproduction in the biological sense, see Gordon (1976), Bland *et al.* (1978), Chodorow (1978), Oakley (1979a and 1980), Moen (1979), Petchesky Pollack (1980), O'Brien (1981), Morokvasić (1981) and Woodhouse (1982).
2. In recent years, artificial reproduction (e.g. the freeze-storing of ova, sperm and embryo, artificial insemination, *in vitro* fertilisation and embryo transfer), has become a widely discussed, controversial topic and the subject of considerable feminist criticism. For a critical feminist literature on the issue, see Rose and Hanmer (1976), Hanmer and Allen (1980), Hanmer (1981), Holmes *et al.* (1981), Rothman (1982, pp. 113–30), Arditti *et al.* (1984) and Greer (1984); for a conventional sociological treatment of the subject, see Snowden and Mitchell (1981) and Snowden, Mitchell and Snowden (1983). Manipulative reproductive technologies are gradually finding their way also into Eastern Europe. Artificial insemination by donor has been used in Czechoslovakia for some time and there is interest in the more recent techniques as well. According to Závadská (1983), there are 500–600 requests for artificial insemination by donor (AID) or by husband (AIH) annually. In 1983, a new law regulating AID was passed, thus ending several years of what

Štěpán (1984, p. 175) calls 'legal insecurity on the issue'. The state research plan on human reproduction has also given full support to the clinical usage of *in vitro* fertilisation (IVF), to the extent that Czechoslovakia became the first COMECON (Council of Mutual Economic Cooperation) country where an IVF baby had been born (on 4 November 1982). Three subsequent IVF births occurred in 1984 (Křestan, 1985). However, there seems to be considerable opposition to embryo transfer and to surrogate motherhood in general on the grounds of both the uncertain legal status of the foetus and the potential danger of 'mercenary pay' for babies.

Part I
Reproductive Policies

2 Pro-Natalist Population Policies

'Control over our bodies' is more than a feminist slogan; it is a revolutionary concept. In order to be assured of control over reproduction, women, at a minimum, must have economic independence, they must have the freedom to bear or not to bear children regardless of their marital status, and they must be in control of much of society. And having gained control over reproduction, women will possess enormous political and economic power. This is a central dilemma of the feminist movement. On the one hand, the control of fertility by women as *individuals* is necessary for full and equal opportunity in society. On the other hand, the *aggregate* level of fertility is so important that no society can allow the individual full freedom of choice regarding reproduction. A woman's shackles are also her strength, and this is what makes the 'woman problem' so intractable. The major questions emerge from this dilemma. First, can birth control be separated from population control? And second, if not, how can women achieve maximum individual reproductive freedom? (Moen, 1979, p. 136)

All societies intervene in procreation. The processes of giving birth and raising children are too important for societies to leave uncontrolled, though controls do not always work. Aggregate fertility ultimately determines the survival of a given population (which, statistically speaking, depends upon excess of births over deaths), the growth and structure of the economy, the structure of the family or kin group (especially dependency ratios), and national economic, political and military power. All these in turn are critical factors in most international and sub-national, especially ethnic, relationships (Moen, 1979; Breindel and Eberstad, 1980; Besemeres, 1980).

Prolonged fertility decline also introduces some significant changes in the frequency and structure of diseases, which can alter aggregate

15

demand for particular health and social services (Tekse, 1980; Schwarz, 1980). For example, fertility of 1-3 children per woman, concentrated in her early adult reproductive years, decreases obstetrical and neonatal risk. As well, an overall decline in births tends to reduce employment opportunities for paediatricians and obstetricians and corresponding nursing specialties, while an ageing population tends to increase social demand for geriatric care, because the elderly tend to suffer from the 'more expensive' chronic diseases much more frequently, and in greater proportions, than children. However, the existence of a demographic need does not in itself guarantee that it will be socially met. Public expenditures on particular social services are related to political pressures that tend to determine the proportion of the gross national product (GNP) that can be distributed by the central government for social purposes. These processes also tend to determine the social standards of care and quality as well as the provision of trained personnel, all of which can vary over time as well as cross-culturally (Eversley, 1980).

Thus it is important not to fall into the trap of 'demographic determinism'. Economic activity is influenced by other factors, apart from labour. Moreover, dependency ratios also depend on levels of unemployment and age of retirement, not simply on age proportions. The relative post-war shrinkage of younger age groups (especially in the 15–19 range, but also in the 20–25 range) in the labour force of some of the developed countries can be accounted for by increased participation rates in post-secondary education, which have offset the impact of the 'baby-boom' bulge. In turn, the number of persons in higher and further education may decline during the next decade more as a result of public expenditure cuts and reduced job expectations of potential entrants than as a consequence of the end of the 'baby-boom' bulge. Hence, demographic issues have to be always placed in broader political and socio-economic contexts before one can properly evaluate their probable social impact.

Moreover, many decades have to pass before more changes in age distribution will lead to really drastic imbalances. Demographers tell us that exact population replacement occurs when the total fertility rate (TFR) is 2.1 children per woman, i.e., when an imaginary, abstracted cohort of 1000 women end their reproductive lives having given birth to 2.1 children. A replacement level TFR is higher than exactly one child for each parent because not all children born will survive to their reproductive years. In Third World countries with high infant and child mortality rates, a TFR of 2.1 would be therefore insufficient to ensure population replacement in the long run.

However, a stationary population may not be achieved for two or three generations after a TFR of 2.1 has been reached, because of the effects of the age structure of populations. High levels of fertility in the past will have resulted in a large number of women still reaching their fertile years, and these women will continue to bear children well beyond the point at which a TFR of 2.1 is achieved. In other words, even if parents today have only small families, there are still more children being born than there are people dying. In the United States, replacement-level fertility was reached in 1972, but the overall size of the population has continued to grow since then, even after discounting international migration. Why? Although the proportion of old people in the developed countries is growing, it is still not large enough to 'supply' sufficient deaths to compensate for the births. Thus the current age structure of the population, a consequence of past demographic trends, distorts the impact of current crude death rates and birth rates, with the result that crude rates of natural increase are positive and are expected to remain so in most developed countries for the remainder of this century (Frejka, 1974, p. 5 and Wulf, 1982, p. 64).

In the meantime, societies can adjust relatively easily to gradual declines in fertility rates. Macura (1980, p. 107), a noted Yugoslav demographer, suggests that:

> a hypothetical absolute shrinkage of the working-age group might be compensated in Western societies by greater involvement of women, which might call for some adjustment of social institutions. In the socialist societies the compensation could be sought in the growth of productivity, perhaps requiring adjustment in economic policy measures.

Policies attempting to stimulate higher fertility can of course run concurrently with these broader 'social adjustment' policies.

In a market economy, the social procedures of controlling the procreation of children will normally take the form of financial incentives or disincentives (which may cancel each other out), although ideological, emotional, psychological, nationalistic or eugenic factors might also have some importance. This extensive social intervention in procreation arises from what has been called a 'contradiction between the private nature and collective consequences of biological reproduction'. In other words, children are both private and public 'goods' – agents such as the state along with their parents, have an interest in them (Heitlinger, 1979, pp. 29–31).

DEFINING POPULATION POLICIES

State intervention in procreation is generally discussed under the vague and ill-defined rubric of 'population policy'. For example, agencies of the United Nations define population policy extremely broadly, equating it with 'economic and social measures which influence population trends' (*Determinants and Consequences*, 1973, p. 632), while Western political scientists and demographers tend to use the term more narrowly. For example, Stetson (1973, p. 248) defines population policy as an 'action by governmental structures and leaders appearing to be directed toward affecting the environment for reproductive behaviour of individuals: the conception and delivery of offspring'. Others have drawn a distinction between 'policies with population effects and the population policies that explicitly intend to influence population problems' (Hansluwka, 1980, pp. 306–7; Besemeres, 1980, p. 104). In other words, many population measures are simultaneously components of social welfare policies. Moreover, some policy measures which were originally developed to encourage fertility – for example in the Scandinavian countries during the 1930s – have gradually become part of general social policy with their demographic policy attributes presently unclear. Conversely, with the arrival of explicit socialist pro-natalism in the late 1960s, many facilities and measures adopted earlier (i.e. in the 1950s) on social and humanitarian grounds were amplified and expanded to meet explicitly demographic objectives (Macura, 1981, pp. 44–5).

Another conceptual dichotomy refers to 'population-influencing policies' as opposed to 'population-responsive policies' (quoted in Schiff, 1978, p. 173). Macura (1981, pp. 37–42) makes a similar point by separating *ex ante* policies, formulated during the process of planning, from *ex post* policies, which were developed in response to both fertility declines and to earlier measures which came to be seen as ineffective. Yet another distinction is introduced by Besemeres (1980), who separates the political impact of demographic trends from the demographic impact of political decisions (e.g. abortion legislation) in the context of making a case for a politics-oriented rather than policy-oriented approach to the study of population policies in Eastern Europe.

Finally, and for our purposes most importantly, there is a marked difference between socialist and non-socialist countries in their responses to their common 'population problem' – current low fertility at or below replacement levels. For example, McIntosh (1981, p. 182) notes that 'not a single Western European nation has implemented a similarly comprehensive pronatalist policy, despite lower levels of fertility and of population growth than those that prompted Eastern European governments to attempt to raise the birth rate'. This is explained as follows:

> the most significant reason for the lack of decisive action is the political pluralism that characterizes the liberal democracies and finds expression in the policy making procedures of democratic societies. Because of this pluralism, Western European governments are unlikely to emulate their counterparts in the Eastern bloc and adopt vigorous pronatalist policies; it is much more probable that governments in Western Europe will maintain their low key response, introducing incremental changes at the margins of existing policy as and when opportunities present themselves.

Wulf (1982, p. 64) makes a similar point while adding another dimension to this argument:

> The broad difference between the governments of Western and Eastern Europe lies in the fact that the socialist countries believe that fertility levels are susceptible to influence and are the proper concern of public policy measures. In Western Europe, despite some anxiety about the possible ramifications of population decline, reproductive decisions and behavior are generally considered to be private matters between couples and, as such, beyond the purview of public policy consideration.

This is put even more strongly by McIntosh (1981, p. 196) herself:

> . . . comprehensive pronatalist policies have been implemented only by centralized and authoritarian city-states of Greece and Rome, the emerging national states of Western Europe, the Fascist states of the 1930s, and the socialist states of Eastern Europe today. By contrast, more pluralistic states, which have practised

limited government, have been much less prone to intervene in what they considered to be the private affairs of individual citizens.

McIntosh's conclusions are based on her 1978 study of governmental responses to low fertility in France, Sweden, and West Germany, i.e. countries with long histories of low fertility and traditions of pro-natalist policies, adopted for the most part in the 1930s and 1940s. In her comparative assessment of future trends, McIntosh (1981, p. 200) asserts that:

> impediments to the adoption of pronatalist policy are less severe in France than in either Sweden or West Germany. . . . At the other end of the scale, obstacles to population policy formulation appear to carry most weight in West Germany [largely due to the legacy of Nazism]. . . . In the case of Sweden, factors adverse and conducive to population policy formulation are now delicately balanced and difficult to assess.

Hence, as we noted earlier, broad generalisations about East–West policy differences are difficult to make, because of the variations among socialist and capitalist countries, as well as similarities between them. For example, Hungary and Romania shared similar demographic circumstances during the late 1950s and early 1960s (i.e. low fertility and high abortion rates in the context of perceived labour shortage), but:

> similar circumstances elicited nearly opposite policy responses in terms of the measures employed to attempt to reconcile 'social' needs for higher fertility with the negative implication of realization of these goals for the work life and career outcomes of women. . . . The measures selected for use in Hungary were almost exclusively facilitative, in the sense of being generally non-coercive and utilizing what I have called elsewhere 'positive incentives'. Romanian fertility policy was made famous by the extremity of its resolution of the same policy dilemma, which took the form of the nearly complete elimination of legal abortion (at that time the principal means of birth avoidance in Romania) and divorce, and decreased availability of modern contraceptives. (McIntyre, 1981, pp. 10–11)

This does not, of course, mean that no generalisations about capitalist and socialist population policies are possible. The distinction between capitalist 'limited government, reluctant to interfere in private lives of citizens' and a 'strong socialist state, committed to centralised planning which includes the planning of population' is a useful one, acknowledged by some authors in the socialist countries themselves. For example, Koubek (1974), in his doctoral dissertation (in Czech) on the evolution of Eastern European population policies, characterises the relationship between social policy and population as one of 'planned interference in the population process'. Besemeres (1980, p. 146) maintains that socialist policy-makers insist on the state's ultimate right to make all the macro-decisions and to decide what the birth rate should be after careful research and due consultation with experts.

However, it is possible that this line of argument constitutes only a partial explanation for the broad differences in the responses of socialist and capitalist governments to similar fertility situations. What has been missing in these discussions is the recognition of the importance of international migration. Western governments, all of their liberalism notwithstanding, can *afford* to be less concerned about declining fertility because the possibility of importing labour from other countries is usually open to them. However, Schiff (1978, pp. 174–5) has argued that the immigration process:

> is inextricably interwined with political, legal, economic and other factors affecting the potential immigrants in their places of origin, conditions over which the state has no control. For example the ebb and flow of Soviet immigration to Israel is more attributable to restrictive Soviet emigration policies and internal politics, to the Soviet Union's relationship with the United States at any given time, and to the self-perception of Soviet Jews and their desire to emigrate – to Israel or increasingly elsewhere – rather than to Israeli policy. The opposite example, the failure of any but a handful of American Jews to emigrate to Israel, in the absence of any legal, political or even severe economic restrictions, and despite the large sums expended to encourage them, plus the re-emigration of many of those who do, is indicative of the rather volatile nature of immigration as a long-term source of population growth for Israel.

Nonetheless, there are many Western leaders who strongly believe in the curative powers of immigration. For example, the former Canadian Employment and Immigration Minister, Lloyd Axworthy, adamant that a short-term recession should not deflect the country from its long-term immigration goals, was quite explicit on this point in a recent interview:

> Immigration provides a very useful component in maintaining a level of growth, because as the birth rates decline and as the age of the population becomes older, immigration is one way of continually providing new people.(Quoted in Hay, 1982, p. 56)

In contrast, large-scale migration from non-socialist countries has never been a viable option for socialist countries in Eastern Europe, largely for ideological and political reasons. In the absence of external migration,[1] fertility is the only dynamic variable of population growth. It is suggested that this factor be considered another 'significant reason' for the adoption of 'vigorous' pro-natalist policies in Eastern European countries, especially those with a perceived chronic shortage of labour. As I have argued elsewhere (Heitlinger, 1979, p. 29), socialist strategies for economic growth:

> have required population policies that have clearly conflicted with reproductive behaviour among individuals. By and large, these strategies have been aimed at a rapid growth of capital stocks, rather than on immediate improvement in labour productivity. This pattern of growth, based as it has been on a quantitative rather than qualitative improvement in the labour force, has required a substantial increase in the employment of women – the reserve army of labour. This in turn has led, among other outcomes, to the exhaustion of labour supply and a rapid decline in fertility. As the possibility of importing labour from non-socialist countries is limited for ideological and political reasons, further extensive growth depends upon increased levels of natural replacement in the labour force.

Having briefly reviewed several classifications of population policies in the West, we can now examine how population policy is regarded in the socialist countries themselves. It is generally defined in broad social and economic terms, with varying degrees of specificity, emphasis on pro-natalism and a combination of 'positive incentives' as opposed to legal–administrative 'repressive' measures. Defenders of women's rights and of individual reproductive freedom tend to define socialist population policy more generally, at the level of socialist normative 'metaprinciples', while 'pragmatists' tend to rely on more conventional policy definitions. Poradovský (1977b, pp. 60–1), prominent Slovak obstetrician, clearly represents the first tendency:

It is true that population policy in a socialist society follows from the overall societal interest, which is the harmonious development of society in accordance with the development of the means of production, but the policy also aims to develop other social values, such as individual freedom to decide on the extent of one's own reproduction, which in turn is connected with the unfolding of socio-cultural development of society. According to the accepted and implemented principle of sex equality, socialist society has to respect the basic right of women in their freedom to decide how many children to give birth to and when to have them. *Thus incentives encouraging population development must have a preventive stimulative* and not a repressive character (such as the prohibition of contraception, induced abortion, etc.). Such measures are not only relatively ineffective, but they also contradict basic principles of social policy of a socialist state. (Italics in original)

What does this particular definition reveal? The emphasis placed on sex equality and reproductive freedom demonstrates the continued political significance of Marxist egalitarian ideology in Eastern European societies. While it is true that Marxist ideology essentially performs a legitimising function for those in power (although in many circumstances with diminishing returns), it is also true that the strong egalitarian strand in Marxism is available for those who want to defend women's rights not only in procreation but also in other areas. For example, during the public debates and polemics on the questions of the effectiveness of women's employment in Czechoslovakia during the late 1960s, several protagonists effectively utilised the Marxist model of sex equality which, of course, emphasises the importance of the productive employment of women for women's public social role and economic independence.

The condemnation of restrictive state control of reproduction is implicitly aimed at the Romanian population policy. This criticism is echoed quite explicitly in the doctoral thesis by Koubek (1974, pp. 72–3), who notes that the 1966 Romanian delegalisation of abortion and restriction of availability of contraception led not only to a sharp increase in the birth rate (as well as to its subsequent gradual decline), but also to significant increases in miscarriages, criminal abortions and maternal and perinatal mortality.[2] In Koubek's view, reproductive coercion does not work very well, a conclusion which he supports with the fact that the Romanian crude birth rate in the mid-1970s was not very much higher than that evident in 1960 (19.7 in 1975 compared to 19.1 in 1960). However, Bernard Berelson (1979), a prominent US population expert, argues that the Romanian coercive pro-natalist policy was successful at the aggregate level, since it dramatically prevented a further decline in the ultimate average family size and the number of children born.[3]

As we shall see in Chapter 8, various restrictive guidelines for granting abortion on non-medical grounds were also adopted during the last decade in Czechoslovakia, Hungary and Bulgaria, but few women who persist in their request are denied termination of an unwanted pregnancy in these countries. The population policies pursued have generally relied much more extensively on a comprehensive set of 'positive' pro-natalist incentives, including ideological propaganda, financial inducements, a variety of associated taxation and employment benefits, paid and unpaid maternity leaves, child care services, credit and housing programmes. This policy orientation is naturally also reflected in the prevailing definitions of socialist population policy.

Pavlík and Wynnyczuk (1974, p. 320), two leading Czech demographers, belong to this more 'pragmatic' and, one must add, also more influential, group of socialist population experts:

> Population policy includes not only a wide range of economic and social measures but also parenthood education and attention to the qualitative aspects of population development. From this point of view, population policy is regarded as an integral part of Czechoslovak state policy as a whole.

The authors also claim that the various specific policy measures (e.g. tax credit, maternity benefits, family allowances) 'form a comprehensive system of mutually interconnected and interacting moral-political and economic measures'. At the recent International Population Conference, held in Manila in December 1981, Wynnyczuk asserted that population policies in socialist countries:

aim at enhancing the value of children, discouraging materialism, creating favourable housing conditions and making the role of mother more compatible with that of wage-earner.(Quoted in Wulf, 1982, p. 66)

Thus the major policy instruments at the disposal of the state, regardless of its capitalist or socialist form, can be divided into two broad categories: legal–administrative and fiscal. The former type is often, in my view mistakenly, equated with repression, while the latter is usually seen as 'positive', based upon incentives. In reality, the contrast between these two major policy instruments is not as great as the terminology implies. There is often considerable overlap and few, if any, policies rely exclusively on one measure only. Most administrative and legal measures have to be funded and, conversely, 'facilitative' fiscal measures (be they cash grants, leaves or 'free' social services) are generally introduced and implemented with the aid of legal–administrative measures. In most cases (though there are obviously exceptions), legal–administrative measures regulate rather than outrightly repress, while fiscal measures tend to be gradually accepted by the public as social welfare measures rather than as 'pronatalist incentives'.

There are therefore many similarities as well as differences among the capitalist and socialist population policies. As Moen (1979, p. 138) puts it:

every country has a population policy. It may be explicit with highly coercive implementation, it may be a hidden agenda that can be achieved through existing trends, or it may be the sum of implicit and often conflicting policies such as the previously mentioned case of minority opposition to federally funded birth control clinics. Consequently, the availability of birth control in the form of contraceptives, abortion and sterilization, does not necessarily mean that women have reproductive freedom. Furthermore, since the availability of birth control technology and the encouragement or discouragement of its use always reflects some kind of population policy, birth control is not conceptually distinct from population control . . . like all other freedoms there are limits to which freedom to reproduce, or not to reproduce, may be exercised. And these limits will be enforced because birth control is population control and the birth rate has political and economic consequences for every sector of society. It is especially tragic for some women when one part of society believes a certain level of reproduction to be beneficial while another part of society believes it is harmful. It would be to all women's advantage if implicit policies and hidden agendas regarding fertility were made public because women's freedom is to be found more in their participation in decisions about aggregate reproductive goals than in access to birth control.

In this context, the socialist countries present something of a paradox for Moen's argument. For the most part, there are no 'hidden agendas regarding fertility' because to the extent that they have become coercing, population goals and policies have been made quite explicit. Breindel and Eberstadt (1980, p. 47) claim that the state pressure on women in East Germany 'to marry and fulfill their national responsibility by bearing children is intense – propaganda to this effect confronts young women in every facet of their lives'. A similar situation prevails in Czechoslovakia, regarded by Besemeres (1980, p. 263) as the most single-mindedly pro-natalist country among all the East European societies, 'maintaining the most elaborate, all-pervasive and obtrusive media campaign on behalf of increased fecundity'. Moreover, with the exception of Yugoslavia, women as a group have not played a significant part in 'decisions about aggregate reproductive goals', but this has not meant that they have been unable to exercise their reproductive rights individually.

FORMULATING SOCIALIST POPULATION POLICIES

We know almost nothing about *how* socialist policies affecting women have been made, since commentators from the socialist countries themselves generally avoid direct discussion of policies. For example, we have no clear idea of the moves that led to the legalisation of abortion in the Soviet Union in 1920. We do know that it was the Ministries of Health and Justice that were immediately responsible for drafting the abortion bill and we also know that the Ministry of Health spent a year before the legislation was enacted soliciting the views of medical and legal circles and the opinions of women's organisations. But, with the gaps in our knowledge of the social history of the early Soviet period, it is difficult to assess whether the whole initiative for the legislation rested with these two ministries. Did they do the work and then receive support from above, or were they initially encouraged from above? Were there any pressures from other sources? What part, if any, had the women's organisations in acting as a spur or pressure group? According to Kollontai, one of the leaders of the women's movement, the women's section of the party took the initiative in pressing for some changes in the law, but we do not know if there was any grass-roots demand from women themselves.

In contrast to this, we do know that legal and medical circles were professionally interested in the abortion question both before and after the revolution. The Pirogov Society of Russian Physicians argued at their congress in 1913 that repealing the repressive abortion legislation would cut the mortality rate among women considerably, would ease the hospital situation (hospitals in big cities were over-whelmed with women who had undergone some form of illegal abortion and who, as a consequence, required serious medical atten-tion), and would allow abortions to be combated more effectively. However, the questionnaires sent out to provincial doctors by the Ministry of Health in 1919 revealed that many physicians were opposed to the legislation of abortion.

The abortion issue was also raised at the 1914 Congress of the Russian group of the International Union of Criminologists; a motion was passed accepting abortion as a non-criminal act and recommend-ing that the law be repealed. The matter was the source of lively debate for several months until the outbreak of the war closed the discussion for the time being (unpublished papers by Knight and Higgins, quoted in Heitlinger, 1979, p. 122–4).

However, we do know that the Bolsheviks did not legalise abortion until 1920 and this timing separates it from the 1917 decree on marriage and divorce, the 1918 laws on civil registration of deaths, births and marriages, and the codification of these measures in 1922. It was not until 1936 that legislation *prohibiting* abortion grouped it with other aspects of family policy. The moves leading to the 1936 law have also been subjected to a variety of oversimplified, speculat-ive interpretations. For example, Heer (1968) argues that it was a measure intended to check the fall in the birth rate due to the rise in the abortion rate, while Geiger (1968) sees the 1936 legislation as an attempt to 'strengthen' the family as a social unit (in contrast to earlier policy, which had aimed at 'weakening' it), although factors such as the party's concern over the birth rate, problems of labour shortage and the rise of Hitlerism are also suggested as relevant. In Knight's view, both the content and the timing of the law must be considered in the context of wider policy aims (such as maximisation of economic growth, social stability and nationalism) and a trade-off between these when they conflicted.

Abortion was re-legalised in 1955, ostensibly on the grounds of the prevalence of criminal abortions taking place outside hospitals and the recognition of the futility of prohibiting them. However, Heer (1968) sees the legislation essentially as a popular gesture of the post-Stalin leadership to the urban population, living in crowded housing conditions and having no desire to have lárge families.

Not much is known about the genesis of abortion policies in the other socialist countries, although the timing of abortion liberalisation in the East European countries (late 1950s) indicates the importance of Soviet influence.[4] While interviewing doctors in Prague, I was told that the initiative had come from above. Legalisation of abortion was seen by the party leadership as a progressive socialist measure, and, to this end, only 'progressive' doctors were canvassed. The Churches and other interested groups were apparently also invited to express their opinions, but any resulting opposition was ignored. Scott (1974, pp. 145–6) claims that 'the law was introduced without prior consultation with the appropriate experts and on the basis of assumptions for which there was no evidence'. She also quotes from an interview with A. Kotásek, Chairman of the Czech Obstetrical/Gynaecological Society, published in the health workers' weekly, *Zdravotnické noviny*, 19 June 1969, in which he said the following: 'We had certain objections and proposals when the law was drawn up, but the vice-premier at that time, who was responsible for presenting the matter to the government, refused to receive us.'

Opposition from demographers was also ignored. While in the 1950s demographers in Czechoslovakia 'began to acquire both the legitimacy and the tools to enter policy debates concerning the population problems, their opportunities to use these tools to influence policy during this period appear to have been quite limited' (Wolchik, 1983, p. 119). As an example of this limited influence, Wolchik (1983, p. 131) quotes the enactment of the liberalised abortion law, 'which appears to have been adopted over the objections of numerous demographers, who were concerned about the potentially negative effects this law would have on the birth rate'.

According to Besemeres (1980, pp. 124, 137), the liberalised abortion legislation in Poland was passed in the political context of reorientation towards Malthusian anti-natalism in the late 1950s, which was generally supported by the economic planners worried about negative implications of then high birth rates. Moreover, the issue has also to be seen as part of the broader tactical considerations of the state in its struggle with the powerful Roman Catholic Church. Since the Church was strongly pro-natalist, the state converted to anti-natalism, a move that was quite popular among women. During the Gomulka regime, there was a party ban on discussing abortion issues, but, after his removal, this was lifted. David (1982, p. 30) reports that, during 1981, the Polish state through its agent, the Ministry of Health, was backing two bodies, Gradium Vita and the Association for the Protection of the Unborn Child, together with their aggressive campaign aimed at eliminating all mechanical methods of contraception as well as reversing the liberal abortion laws. It is not quite clear what specific political considerations were being pursued at this time, but it is not unreasonable to assume that the state was attempting to appease the Church and detach it from supporting the Solidarity movement. However, this is only a speculation. The 'politics' of socialist population policies is still a relatively unknown area, though Besemeres' excellent book on the subject represents a promising start for this sort of research orientation.

In the West, the issue of politics essentially boils down to 'inside' politics within political parties and the civil service versus 'outside' pressure from feminist, trade union, and consumer movements. However, no opposition political movements are allowed in the socialist countries, where the ruling communist parties retain a monopoly of power and doctrine. The trade unions, women's and youth organisations only rarely involve themselves in autonomous politics, and then only at times of significant erosion of party power (e.g. during 1968 in Czechoslovakia, 1980–1 in Poland). Their primary concern is with day-to-day implementation of official welfare policies. In general, these organisations do not encourage radical thinking or action; at best they might act as mild pressure groups without much power.

With the exception of the 'Prague Spring' in 1968, initiatives for change in Czechoslovak state policies on women's issues have tended to come from specialists – demographers, physicians, economists and the like – rather than women's organisations. It was only during 1968 that the Czechoslovak Union of Women essentially functioned as an interest group. Allied with certain elements of the reform leadership, leaders of the women's organisation bargained with the party and government leadership and defended women's interests. They also attempted to involve large groups of women in proposing solutions to women's problems and worked to increase the power and legitimacy of the organisation.

The process of redefinition and advocacy of women's issues was by no means radical by Western standards. Reacting to the previous emphasis on women's roles as workers, leaders of the women's organisation advocated renewed attention to women's maternal roles and called for measures to ease the conflict between women's roles (Wolchik, 1979, p. 601). This shift in emphasis to women's reproductive roles has now been incorporated in Czechoslovak pro-natalist ideologies and policies, but largely in response to falling birth rates in the 1960s and expert advice rather than feminist pressure.

What then has been the process of arriving at and implementing fertility policy decisions among the experts? Furthermore, what has been the balance of forces among the various professional groups, policy administrators and various political factions? How homogeneous are the various groups and what are their relative powers and influences? Are there any jurisdictional and inter-professional conflicts? As McIntosh (1981, p. 198) pointed out, 'in any society, the creation of a coherent policy presents difficulties in areas that, like population policy, touch on the responsibilities and jurisdictions of multiple departments and agencies. The difficulties are compounded in pluralistic societies that lack highly centralized policy making systems and well developed mechanisms for coordinating policy.' One way to examine these issues in the socialist context is to briefly review the research of various population bodies, especially the activities of the Czechoslovak Population Commission, which, in comparison with population commissions elsewhere, is especially powerful.

THE POPULATION COMMISSION IN CZECHOSLOVAKIA

Research in reproductive behaviour has been reported from numerous bodies: the Statistical Office, the Ministry of Health, the Research Institute of Labour and Social Affairs as well as other specialised research institutes and university centres. A 1956 research project on parenting, sponsored by the State Statistical Office in cooperation with the Ministry of Health, was apparently the first such research in a socialist country. It utilised a sample of 10 645 married women, aged 20–39 and it was explicitly related to the preparation of legislation legalising induced abortion at that time.

Bartošová (1976) also claims that all the national samples of married women sponsored by various bodies during the 1956–75 period had one common goal: to investigate the situation of mothers and families with dependent children to find out how best to develop a population policy.

Since its establishment in 1957, most of the research on population issues and policy has been sponsored by the State (later Government) Population Commission. The Commission was established as an advisory body to the government. Its main task was to monitor the abortion law, passed at the same time (December 1957), to investigate various aspects of the family, to develop educational and political propaganda on questions of parenthood, to review population development, especially the decline in the birth rate, and to recommend policies that might reverse the trend. The Commission consisted of 34 members, who were all experts in their various fields, and who were nominated by ministries, universities, social science research institutes and medical institutions. The chair rotated between the heads of the Statistical Office, the Social Security Office and, since its creation in 1968, the Ministry of Labour and Social Affairs. According to Pavlík and Wynnyzcuk (1974, p. 227), the creation of the State Population Commission represented 'the first link between research and theoretical workers and top-level political authorities, who finally decide definite population and social measures in favor of families'.

Throughout the 1960s, the State Population Commission conducted a number of surveys among married women, and to some extent also couples, on the average planned number of children, the knowledge and use of contraception, and the practical problems experienced by employed mothers with small children. The research findings were made available to government and academic bodies and served as a basis for the preparation of policy programmes for the 12th and 13th Party Congresses in 1962 and 1966 (Bartošová, 1976, p. 12). The leading women's organ at the time, the Central Committee of Czechoslovak Women, was neither informed nor consulted about any of these projects, though it must be admitted that at that time its role was mainly symbolic, representing women at international gatherings rather than playing any role in the domestic political process. A firmer organisational basis was created only in 1967, with the establishment of a new party-controlled 'mass' women's organisation, the Czechoslovak Union of Women (Heitlinger, 1979, pp. 68–70).

Despite this exclusion of women as a group from the decision-making process, the State Population Commission made some useful and popular recommendations on their behalf, which were incorporated into state policies, thus giving us one set of criteria by which we can judge the substantial professional power and influence of the Commission. Paid maternity leave was, over the years, extended from 18 to 22 to 26 weeks (35 weeks for single mothers and mothers giving multiple births). A new measure, unpaid maternity leave up to the child's first (and eventually third) birthday, was also introduced as a result of the Commission's recommendation. Emulating what was deemed to be a successful Hungarian experience, the Commission was also instrumental in introducing the so-called maternity allowance (called a child care allowance in Hungary).

In 1971, the State Population Commission was upgraded to a higher-level Government Population Commission, consisting of 28 members drawn from the leading officials of the trade unions, the Czechoslovak Women's Council (a successor to the short-lived Czechoslovak Union of Women), the Socialist Youth Association, the media and relevant ministries, university departments and research institutes. It is therefore formally more broadly representative than its predecessor, though the balance of forces between the various specialists and political tendencies is difficult to determine on the basis of available data. No Czech commentator has ever written anything on the process of internal and external politics associated with the Commission.

However, Sharon Wolchik, a political scientist from the Institute for Sino-Soviet Studies at the George Washington University, has argued (in a letter to the author) that the group has contained basically the same experts since the late 1960s, and that personal ties are one important factor in explaining the individuals chosen to take part. Her forthcoming work on demographic policy in Czechoslovakia since 1970 describes the coalition of specialists from different areas of expertise and different institutions that have been primarily responsible for shaping population policy during the past decade. Her project should make an important contribution to our understanding of the role of specialists and professionals in socialist policy-making.[5]

More is known about the various interest groups involved in population debates in Poland and it would be useful to reproduce this evidence here. Ziolkowski (1974, pp. 471–3) and Besemeres (1980, pp. 147–9) identify the following principal 'actors' in Polish population policy debates in the 1960s: the Church and Catholic laity, opposed to abortion and artificial contraception (this group is much less powerful in all the other socialist countries); demographers, divided into 'pessimists' favouring an immediate pro-natalist policy, and 'optimists' who expected an 'automatic' new mini-baby-boom as the large numbers of women born right after the war were entering reproductive age, thus eliminating the need for strong policy intervention. The physicians were divided among many more factions than were the demographers. Besemeres (1980, p. 117) draws a distinction between loyal communists, administrators irritated by the strain that legal abortions were placing on scarce health care resources, doctors opposed to abortion on moral and/or professional grounds (i.e. those who believed in the medical harmfulness of abortions, especially repeated ones), and physicians who supported abortion and defended individual procreative rights.

Economists were worried about the negative employment impact of the baby-boom generation entering the labour market in large numbers (an additional 3.5 million persons), while fewer people (only 1.5 million) were leaving it (due to retirement, death and so forth). Thus, they tended to advocate anti-natalist policies. Sociologists and social psychologists were apparently unhappy that population policy came to be seen as a purely demographic problem. They drew attention to their own expertise, on the basis of which they claimed that demographic processes 'are far too complex, too much a part of the intimate and emotional sphere of life, of the internal dynamics and circumstances of each individual family' (Ziolkowski, 1974, p. 473). On these grounds, they opposed the very principle of central planning and control of demographic processes, especially fertility. This conclusion was echoed by social policy specialists, who regarded views about a non-growing or diminishing nation as alarmist and ill-founded. In their view, the quantitative dimension of pro-natalist policy should be replaced with a qualitative focus, which would be more in tune with socialist welfare policies and, of course, their own expertise.

In Besemeres' assessment, the 'qualitative' social scientists (whom he calls social politicians) have been more influential than their more quantitative and pro-natalist oriented colleagues. Polish state policies have been generally aimed at the relief of hardship and redistribution of wealth rather than pro-natalist objectives *per se*. The opposite seems to be the case in Czechoslovakia, which may mean that demographers are considered to be the specialists with the most relevant expertise.

In this context, it is important to point out that 'socialist' demography differs in important respects from the demography as we know it in the West. In the planned socialist societies, the study of demography tends to be much broader in scope, since it includes not only formal demography but also related aspects of economics, geography, sociology and planning. Moreover, demography is generally subordinated to the exigencies of national economic planning, which in turn places a priority on predictive, as opposed to retrospective studies. In other words, socialist demography tends to focus to a larger extent on policy-oriented and prescriptive studies than its sister science in Western mixed economies. According to Demko and Fuchs (1977, p. 52):

the task of the demographic sciences in Northeastern Europe extends beyond descriptive studies and includes a heavy emphasis on predictive capabilities to meet planning needs. There is a further task, which may be described as the formation of *normative* goals. The demographic sciences are called upon to identify desirable or optimal future population and settlement distribution patterns (which then become spatial population goals), to identify problems created by the discrepancies between current realities and desired goals, and to help form policy instruments or mechanisms to aid in achieving the goals.

In this light, the professional power and political influence of demographers and of 'their' Government Population Commission, are hardly surprising. The Czechoslovak Population Commission has a very broad mandate indeed, since it:

will itself formulate population policy, organize the study of individual problems, field studies, and enquiries, and upon their basis will propose further action to the government. According to its statute, it intends also to coordinate the activities of various institutions, give consultations, organize expert opinion on various problems, work with the research institutions, information media, and cultural establishments.(Quoted in Pavlík and Wynnyczuk, 1974, p. 353)

We do not know how many of its recommendations have been turned down, but we do know that a substantial number of them have been accepted and incorporated into current social programmes, despite their high budgetary cost. By the late 1970s, the Czechoslovak government was spending almost 4 per cent of its annual budget on direct cash benefits awarded to families and mothers (e.g. family allowances, birth grants, paid maternity leaves and allowances) and an additional 7 per cent on services and subsidies in kind (e.g. cheap day care and kindergartens, school meals and prices of children's goods, tax and rent deductions according to the number of children in the family, etc.) (Havelka, 1978). According to Frejka (1980, p. 70) these levels exceed comparable expenditures in any other developed country. In Frejka's view, the aggregate demographic objectives of the government are being realised, but this conclusion is disputed by Pavlík (1978) who notes that the major fertility influence has been on the timing and not on the ultimate number of births. Pavlík further observes that popular attitudes about desired family size have not changed, and that the realised fertility increase in the 1970s is due to first and second births rather than higher-order births, although he admits that the pro-natalist policy has served important social welfare goals. These opposing views will be reviewed in more detail in Chapter 12.

NOTES

1. International migration of workers from socialist countries is limited to temporary migration of workers within the socialist countries that are members of the Council of Mutual Economic Cooperation (COMECON). In the 1960s some six nations concluded bilateral agreements concerning temporary migrations of workers. Bulgaria, Poland and Hungary were the sending countries, while the USSR, Czechoslovakia and the GDR were the receiving ones. In recent years, Cuba and Vietnam (both members of COMECON) have been added to the list of sending socialist countries. However, the extent of these migrations is too limited to have any demographic impact.
2. Perinatal mortality refers to deaths per thousand in a given population occurring in the second half of pregnancy through birth to one week after birth. It includes antenatal mortality (before birth), intranatal mortality (during birth) and postnatal mortality (within a week after birth). Because of ambiguities in drawing a consistent line between stillbirths and deaths immediately after birth, various neonatal rates are often combined and labelled as perinatal mortality. The concept is discussed in more detail in Chapter 10.

3. Romanian officials have themselves admitted that their population policy has, on the whole, failed to achieve its demographic objectives. For example, in his 1984 International Women's Day speech, the Romanian president Nicolae Ceauşescu noted that out of 743 000 pregnancies in Romania in 1983 only 40 per cent had resulted in births. He then went on to say that it is every healthy Romanian woman's patriotic duty to have four children. More importantly, in that speech, Ceauşescu announced new 'stern measures' to combat the high abortion rate. While abortions are basically illegal, they have remained very much a part of Romanian life, thanks to the black market. According to Masterman (1984, p. 12), 'poverty-stricken Romanians often pay for them by barter – notably with food and with Kent cigarettes, which people widely regard as a form of currency, throughout the country . . . an abortion can be had for a 200-cigarette carton.' If Ceauşescu has his way, this is about to change. According to Masterman (1984, p. 12), 'married women in the state's massive industrial complexes will have to undergo tests once a month to determine if they are pregnant. Until recently, the state required that they submit to such a test only every three months. Women will have to account for persistent nonpregnancy. They will also have to explain pregnancies present one month and absent the next. If a woman claims to have suffered a miscarriage, she will have to produce a written confirmation from her doctor. If the police find that she has lied, both she and her doctor could face prison terms – as long as one year for the woman and from two to five years for a doctor found guilty of performing an abortion. Women who fail to fulfill their child quotas without convincing medical reasons are unlikely to receive promotions, and they may even lose their jobs.' It remains to be seen whether the outcome of this latest form of state reproductive oppression (comparable to that of Nazi Germany) will exhibit similar patterns as the earlier Romanian anti-abortion legislation: dramatic increase in the birth rate, followed by gradual decline as women find ways around the legislation.

4. For a review of the chronology of socialist abortion legislation see David and McIntyre (1981, pp. 53–7).

5. The proposal for the project, submitted jointly with Jane L. Curry to the US National Science Foundation in February 1980, is entitled 'Specialists and Professionals in Policy-making in Czechoslovakia and Poland'. For the one chapter of this study which has already been published as an article, see Wolchik (1983).

3 Reproductive Ideologies: Education for Parenthood

Each one of us can be substituted in our job by someone else. However, to a child, there is no substitute for a mother. Giving birth and bringing up children will therefore always remain the main mission of a woman. (Šipr, 1981, pp. 39–40)

Education for parenthood is certainly not a one-time action; it is not a mere instruction about the sex life of a man and a woman, and it is not interchangeable with sex education. It is, above all, an essential and inseparable part of the whole education of an all-round developed person, a truly harmonious personality. . . . Education for parenthood which is truly creative is above all a moral matter. It represents an attitude towards the world and life, which does not place my own 'I' in the first place. (Fišer, 1981, pp. 116–17)

We noted in the previous chapter that 'education for parenthood' is regarded in Czechoslovakia as an integral part of the pro-natalist population policy. For this reason, the system of 'education for parenthood' is much broader in scope, more specialised, more self-conscious and much more systematic than any comparable programme in a Western capitalist country. A variety of pro-natalist ideologies, making child-bearing seem 'natural' and thus obligatory, also exists in the West (see Busfield, 1974; Macintyre, 1976; and Veevers, 1980), but they tend to be much less explicit and systematic than in Eastern Europe. Unlike women in the GDR, women in the West today are not continuously urged 'to marry and fulfil their national responsibility by bearing children'. In the past, of course, this sort of exhortation has emerged elsewhere in the context of ideologies of eugenism and 'race suicide'.[1] Moreover, given their political pluralism, Western liberal democracies are characterised by the coexistence of contradictory ideologies. Notions such as 'children

37

make life meaningful' or 'motherhood constitutes the fulfilment of womanhood' exist concurrently with ideologies exposing the advantages of a 'child-free lifestyle'. Such diversity is not tolerated in Eastern Europe, though this is not to argue that there is uniformity of opinion among specialists as to the importance of parenthood for one's mental health.

For some Czech obstetricians and gynaecologists voluntary childlessness represents a form of psychosomatic illness, which has to be treated:

> Motherhood or an acceptance of motherhood belong to the fulfilment of a woman's life. If a woman renounces this fulfilment of her life, consciously or unconsciously, it becomes a matter of psychosomatic illness, which has to be treated (Uhlíř *et al.*, 1974).

Dr Barták (1977, p. 235), a sex therapist, sees voluntary childlessness as detrimental to a happy marriage, while Dr Mrkvička (1977, pp. 73–4), a marital psychologist, claims that childless spouses can lead a rich and meaningful life together and that their marriage suffers only if it is centered around an unfulfilled wish for a child. Dr Vodák (1968, p. 22), an adoption lawyer, has even argued that 'there is no need for each childless family to have a child'.

Thus the degree of expert endorsement of pro-natalism seems to vary according to specialisms – professionals who encounter unhappy couples who can neither conceive nor adopt are generally less supportive of strong pro-natalism than specialists who are not faced with this or similarly negative evidence (e.g. battered babies).

DEFINING SOCIALIST EDUCATION FOR PARENTHOOD

Czechoslovak experts go to great lengths to emphasise the subordination of sex education to parenthood education. Pavlík and Wynnyczuk (1974, p. 349) the influential Czech demographers, quote from government decree no. 71/1966 on the goals of 'education for parenthood' as follows:

(1) Parenthood education is wider than sex education, which forms a part thereof. The term 'parenthood education' includes a whole set of rules and knowledge concerning the relations between man

and woman; this also includes intimate relations and instruction on the use of contraceptives.

(2) Education for parenthood should begin in the kindergarten in such a way as to explain the subject matter to the children earlier than they encounter it in life; in the schools, this education should not form a separate subject but should permeate such subjects as biology, literature, the arts, and so forth.

(3) Before such education becomes obligatory in all schools, teachers should prepare for it not only during their university training but also in refresher and postgraduate courses.

(4) Concurrently with information in the schools, where the main agent for imparting parenthood education is the teacher, information also should be given to parents, in order to balance their degree of knowledge with that of the young persons.

(5) Educational welfare for children and juveniles concentrates wherever children concentrate, that is, in schools of all levels, including universities where information on education for parenthood is given in seminars and meetings with experts; a separate problem in this field, therefore, is created by young people who enter industry or trade immediately upon completion of their basic school training or even leave school from a lower form making it difficult to reach them.

(6) The last opportunity for approaching young men in concentrated numbers is during their military service, and therefore, parenthood education is gradually becoming part of educational activities in the army.

(7) In the case of women, such an opportunity is afforded at the time when a woman expects a child and visits an antenatal clinic, where information is given concurrently with gynaecological and paediatric care.

As concerns the adult population, the Government Population Committee requested that the press, radio and television devote greater attention to parenthood education; during its sessions in 1972, it discussed plans for activity in this sphere.

This description reveals not only the broad mandate of education for parenthood (it includes sex education, contraceptive knowledge, marital counselling as well as pro-natalist propaganda about the importance and desirability of children), but also the multiple overlap of occupational boundaries and institutional jurisdictions.

Education for parenthood is seen as involving the educational system, the family, the mass media, obstetrics and paediatrics, the Population Commission and even the army. However, it is clear (and hardly surprising) that the major role in this process has been assigned to the educational system. As we shall see below, parenthood education has been introduced into the school system only gradually, 'as teachers' knowledge and qualifications in this sphere increase' (Pavlík and Wynnyczuk, 1974, p. 349). To this end, the Ministry of Education and the Institute of Health Education have published two teachers' manuals on parenthood education.

Svobodová and Vodrážka (1977, p. 7), authors of the handbook published under the auspices of the Ministry of Education, further elaborate on the relationship between sex education and education for parenthood:

> Education for parenthood in the broader sense includes sex education and the whole problematic of preparing for a parental role – father and mother. *Sex education* proper is to be understood not only as education for correct sexual behaviour, but also as education for valuable and self-satisfying sexual experiences, perceptions, imagination, appraisal and so on. . . . The link between sex education and *education for parenthood* is the teaching about healthy motherhood and also fatherhood. It includes the preconditions of healthy foetal development, of which genetic factors and consequences of abortion are especially emphasised. A set of complex questions dealing with the care and education of the child at various stages of its development then belong fully to parenthood education.

The same authors (on p. 20) place education for parenthood in the context of overall school curriculum:

> Education for parenthood does not constitute a special instructional subject, but forms a part of a whole educational complex. It cannot be reduced to one-time instruction of children and youth, to one or several talks, to only one instructional subject, but must become an inseparable part of the whole educational process.

These definitions have now found their way into popular advice books – witness, for instance, the quotation from Fišer (1981) at the beginning of this chapter. We should also note that the most recent writings on the subject have enlarged the subject, discussing it in terms of 'education for marriage and parenthood'.

THE DEVELOPMENT OF EDUCATION FOR PARENTHOOD

A limited version of parenthood, or rather sex education, consisting of a single lecture to 14-year-olds in the eighth grade, given by the school doctor to boys and girls separately, was introduced into the school system in 1959. It has been subsequently criticised as inadequate and inappropriate:

> Sometimes the dominant feature of such education consisted only of instruction in anatomy, physiology and hygiene. Moreover, this one-shot lecture did not form a part of an integrated system. There was also a general shortage of suitable literature and educational aids on the subject. (Svobodová and Vodrážka, 1977, p. 9)

These sentiments were echoed by Dr Dráč (1972, p. 490), in an article published in a special issue of *Československá gynekologie*, devoted to planned parenthood:

> Basic nine-year schools, high schools and secondary specialised schools have had since 1959 in their curricula also the so-called education for parenthood, which is usually 'compressed' to two lessons towards the end of the school year. During such a short period of time it is impossible to give biological information let alone 'educate'.

Upon the initiative of the State Population Commission, Government Decree No. 71/1966 charged the Ministry of Education, the Ministry of Health, and the State Population Commission with drafting a new programme of general training for parenthood. However, both ministries were rather slow to respond and new initiatives were undertaken only in the mid-1970s. The Ministry of Education announced in 1972 that it was preparing a new curriculum on education for parenthood, but it was in fact only introduced in 1979–81, and then only in the secondary schools. A unified system of parenthood education, involving both elementary and secondary schools, was initiated on an experimental basis at selected elementary schools during 1980–1 and selected secondary schools as recently as 1981–2. Education for marriage and parenthood was also introduced into post-secondary education (in 1978–9) and into apprenticeship education (gradually between 1978 and 1981). During 1977–8, questions of education for marriage and parenthood were discussed with teachers at special seminars and teachers were also given new pedagogical manuals on the subject.

Involvement of the mass media got off the ground more quickly, and with more direct participation of the Population Commission. In 1963, the State Population Commission helped with the preparation of a serial entitled 'Family and Society' which was broadcast by Czechoslovak television during the spring and summer of 1963. A radio series entitled 'Intimate Conversations', broadcast during the same period, also followed the specific directives of the Communist Party and the Population Commission to educate the public, especially young people, in the 'correct' approach to the questions of parenthood. In 1972, the upgraded Government Population Commission, in its journal *Populační zprávy*, called upon the mass media to influence public attitudes towards children in order to bring about the desired increase in the birth rate. Young people, in particular, were to be converted from consumerism, and to this end the media were asked to stress:

(1) the irreplaceable value of children in making life fuller and richer;
(2) the deep and firm moral and emotional relationships, mutual love and respect between young men and women and between spouses;
(3) the disadvantages suffered by only children;
(4) the notion that the ideal family was one with three children, a size sufficient for the children to interact, thus favouring their intellectual development;
(5) health education for women and the dangers of abortion;
(6) the need for real equality between the sexes, e.g. equal division of labour in housework;
(7) the need for an improvement of living standards by:

   (a) expansion of social services for the care of children;
   (b) improved supplies of children's goods;
   (c) limitation of food preparation in the home, e.g. expansion of canteens and greater use of pre-cooked foods;
   (d) increased output of labour-saving domestic appliances;

(e) improvement of working conditions for women, e.g. part-time work, shorter hours, etc.;

(8) the proposition that conditions of life for families with children would steadily improve; and

(9) the contention that unfavourable demographic developments would hamper economic development and thus have serious effects on living standards.

Indeed, as Besemeres (1980, p. 263) wrote, an 'elaborate, all-pervasive and obtrusive media campaign on behalf of increased fecundity'!

At present, the task of coordinating all specialists and institutions involved in education for parenthood has been assigned to the Ministry of Work and Social Affairs. Its review of developments in this field up to 1977 and plans for the future mentions no fewer than fourteen institutions directly or indirectly involved in the process: Ministries of Education, Health (especially the Institute of Health Education), Work and Social Affairs, Justice and Interior, the trade unions, the Socialist Academy (responsible for adult education), the Red Cross and the unions of youth, farmers', producers' and consumers' cooperatives. Among these, the ministries clearly play the more significant role, since the voluntary organisations of the specific social groups only follow, rather than initiate, bureaucratic instructions.

The Ministry of Justice oversees the courts, which in turn cooperate with marital and pre-marital guidance centres. The latter were introduced by Government Decree No. 137/1972 as an integral part of the system of education for marriage and parenthood. They fall under the jurisdiction of three ministries – the already mentioned Ministry of Justice, the Ministry of Social Work and Social Affairs (which prepares manuals for officials of these bureaux) and the Interior Ministry, which is responsible for marriage licences and the encouragement of engaged couples to attend the lectures offered by the pre-marital advice bureaux. Speakers for these events are trained by the Ministry of Culture, which also supplies speakers for similar events in youth clubs.

However, these pre-marital advice lectures are not very popular. Hepner (1980) found that most of the respondents in his sample had been invited to attend these lectures, but that an overwhelming majority (97 per cent) chose not to do so, stating 'lack of time' as the reason. Informants in another sample asserted that they would attend these lectures only if they had to, i.e. if it were a legal requirement, as is the case in Hungary. (Since 1973, all Hungarian citizens under the age of 35 must participate in marriage counselling before a marriage licence can be issued.) However, when asked about officially organised compulsory forms of preparation for marriage and parenthood, the majority of the Czech respondents expressed a negative opinion. The researcher found this attitude surprising, though he admitted that it reflects the current passive mentality of Czech youth, who tend to 'fulfil their duties rather than seek new ways of gaining further information'. (Kučera, 1981).

The Czech Ministry of Culture (Slovakia has its own equivalent institutions) also oversees the publication of marital and child care advice books in a series entitled 'The Family Circle'. The Ministry cooperates as well with various professional artistic associations, which have been urged to emphasise the importance of harmonious living for the healthy development of youth. In 1978, the Ministry even initiated a competition for composers of popular songs on this theme. In addition, the Government Population Commission annually evaluates the participation of mass media in the educational process, and particularly active journalists and workers in radio, television and film, receive honourable notices (Wynnyczuk, 1981, p. 72). Finally, the Ministry of Health is responsible for various aspects of health and birth control education, including special after-work seminars on these issues with school teachers (*Hlavní směry . . .*, 1977).

While Fišer (1977) and Koubek (1981) express general satisfaction with the current system of education for parenthood, others are more sceptical, especially with respect to contraceptive education. Dissemination of information advocating contraception is now incorporated into the grade eight curriculum, but the subject is discussed in only three lessons. Furthermore, many health clinics have set up special contraceptive advice bureaux, but these institutions often suffer from shortages of printed materials to give their clients ('Koordinační porada . . .', 1978). Hence, the advice remains less than adequate.

'JURISDICTIONAL' CONFLICTS OVER PARENTHOOD EDUCATION

There are two basic types of 'jurisdictional' conflicts related to overlapping occupational boundaries – a desire of one or more occupational groups to expand their activities and jurisdictional control on the one hand, and an attempt to leave particular unpopular tasks to others, on the other. The inter- as well as intra-professional conflicts, as to who is the best (or the worst) qualified person to instruct young people on parenthood in general, and sexual matters in particular, clearly belong to the second category. Since 'education for parenthood' has been introduced as a concept, teachers and doctors have tried to 'pass the buck' from one to the other.

However, there is a general agreement among the specialists, as well as young people themselves, that parents are generally poorly prepared to discuss sexuality with their children in a systematic way. The majority of respondents in a survey sample of young people aged 15–30, interviewed in the summer of 1979, regarded parents as the most important model and source of knowledge on parenthood, *with the exception* of questions relating to sex (Kučera, 1981).

Mareš and Brtníková (1976, p. 3), authors of a manual for women's health care workers (both doctors and nurses), have a poor opinion of both young people and their parents in terms of their level of knowledge on sexual and parenting questions:

> We are finding daily that young people tend to be informed on questions of growing up as well as parenthood from older friends or from co-workers in an unsuitable, often vulgar manner. This state of affairs is unsuitable especially for those young people who are missing suitable education and information from the home or the school.
>
> On the other hand, we are also meeting people who would like to intervene in the educational process, but who have practically no experience and knowledge in this field and who often need some enlightenment themselves. Unfortunately these people are very frequently the parents themselves. This situation can be changed only by close cooperation among all who have most to do with parenthood education – parents, teachers and physicians, especially paediatricians, youth doctors and gynaecologists.

However, Pávek *et al.* (1979, p. 131), marital counsellors, disagree about the wisdom of trying to teach parents to become their children's educators on sexual matters, for fear of increasing family tensions:

> Parents are constantly advised to enlighten their children about sex, but are embarrassed about doing so. One way or other,

tensions between parents and children are often aggravated. Few parents grasp the right moment to discuss sex life with their children. When these discussions do take place, they usually come at a time when the children know almost as much as their parents; the children's curiosity is satisfied and parental advice is seen as humiliating and almost immoral.

Similar kinds of tension were found to exist in the USA. Parsons (1983, pp. 44–5) reports that:

> parents just aren't providing adequate sex education. . . . The problem is compounded further by the fact that much information provided by parents is either incorrect or prohibitive in nature. Parents are much more likely to tell children what not to do than what to do. Many parents and grandparents still react with concern when their children masturbate or exhibit cross-gender behaviours. They mislabel parts of the body or fail to label them at all. Few parents provide children with a full picture of the functions of their genitals. . . . Perhaps most importantly, Gagnon and Roberts . . . found that sexual discussions between parents and children typically result from the child's initiative. Very few parents take it on themselves to provide any systematic program of education.

In any case, in Czechoslovakia as in the United States, planners and educators cannot *formally* rely on parents. If one wants to ensure that all children have some basic information about sexuality, one has to look to paid experts – teachers and/or doctors. Mareš and Brtníková (1976) claim that obstetricians and gynaecologists are in a particularly good position to influence women at various stages of their life-cycles, both directly in offices and during talks at schools, or indirectly through the mothers of adolescent girls. However, several influential doctors have disputed this assertion, for a variety of reasons. Dr Hynie (1977), a leading Czech sex therapist, argues that, unlike parents and teachers, doctors come into contact with their clients only sporadically, and this makes them less suitable for *systematic* sex and parenthood education. Dr Trča (1965, p. 5), the current director of the Institute of Health Education and the author of numerous health publications for women, rejects doctors' participation in school sex education on the grounds of lack of pedagogical skills and, implicitly, male gender:

These talks with pupils should not be undertaken by doctors but by teachers themselves. As far as female students are concerned, instruction should be given exclusively by women teachers. Not every doctor is an experienced teacher. However, since teachers so far do not have specialised knowledge about the sexual problematic, it will be necessary for doctors to transmit this knowledge to teachers, for example in the form of special seminars.

Dr Dráč (1972, p. 490) agrees with Trča about doctors' apparent lack of pedagogical skills and adds excessive workload as another reason why doctors' participation in sex education at schools should be minimal:

> Education for parenthood has to be understood as an integral part of the whole educational process, leading to a responsible approach by a growing person towards all questions relating to the preparation for life. . . . It is a matter for the whole teaching staff of the school. A gynaecologist can participate only as a special adviser for the instruction of teachers about contemporary views on adolescent sexuality, questions of fertility and reproduction and also about the current state of contraception. Such knowledge should help teachers to change incorrect ideas and tendencies of young people, with special sensitivity and individualised approaches, according to need. If a gynaecologist is included in this 'educational' process, he tends to biologise and his activity does not always have an educational character. Furthermore, in these cases the doctor would be required to devote half his work time to the educational work at the school. There are no objections to a gynaecologist being asked to give a professional exposition for special groups of adolescent youth which are prepared for such a lecture (high school graduates, youth clubs, etc.).

Something that Dráč does not mention but which acts as a powerful disincentive for physicians to engage in educational work is the low pay accrued for what is essentially overtime work.

The best summary of the current state of intra- as well as interprofessional dilemmas with respect to sex education is provided by Poliaková (1977):

> Despite the fact that today an overwhelming majority of teachers, psychologists and physicians recognise the necessity for sex

education in schools, one still encounters the problem of being bashful in talking about such questions; some are excessively concerned about telling too little or too much, whether their explanations are of an adequate standard, and others cannot find the best form of pedagogy or do not know how to empathise with the thinking and understanding of pupils. Thus disputes arise as to who should instruct pupils on these questions: teachers of biology or the main class teacher, or an invited physician or psychologist.

Poliaková offers one possible solution to this dilemma – the elimination of the instructor altogether and his/her substitution by a desk computer. A computerised textbook, based on a similar textbook used in the UK, was introduced on an experimental basis in several Slovak schools in 1975–6. It is called *Keď dospievaš* (*When You're Growing Up*) and it consists of six chapters dealing with biological development, anatomy and physiology of sex organs, conception and foetal development, venereal disease, contraception and body hygiene. In Poliaková's view, the use of computerised sex education eliminates the need to separate boys and girls, it encourages them to look for their own answers and, above all, it makes the job that much easier for blushing teachers and unwilling doctors. An intriguing – and expensive – bureaucratic solution!

Similarly formalistic solutions – attempting to avoid the subject altogether or relying exclusively on impersonal audio-visual material – have been sometimes adopted in the USA. As well, Parsons (1983, p. 45) recalls her high school biology teacher, who 'had the responsibility of teaching us the reproductive facts, which were covered in the last two chapters of our textbook. His pace slowed as we approached those chapters, culminating in a three-week session on tuberculosis (the chapter immediately preceeding reproduction). Then we spent two days on reproduction; films were shown on both of those days.'

PUBLIC KNOWLEDGE ABOUT SEXUALITY

Our information about public knowledge concerning sexual behaviour is drawn largely from Czechoslovak surveys. These surveys, in addition to the usual problems attendant to this form of social data, have suffered especially from a lack of clarity in the way questions have been put to respondents. For example, the context does not always make it clear whether 'sex education' refers broadly to gender relations, specifically to physical interaction or even more specifically to knowledge about contraception. Similarly, the precise meaning of the term 'sexual experience' is also often unclear – does it refer only to coitus or does it also include non-genital sexuality and/or homosexual intercourse? Nonetheless, bearing these deficiencies in mind, one can still glean considerable information of interest from the extensive survey material that is now available.

The first nationwide survey research on sexuality was conducted by the State Population Commission in the late 1950s and early 1960s. Focused upon the sex lives of young married couples, the research findings revealed that more than a quarter of the men and half of the women in the sample considered that their sex education had been insufficient or non-existent. Knowledge about contraception was generally absent, the majority of women depended on the responsibility and skill of their partners, both before and after marriage (see Heitlinger, 1979, p. 185).

Subsequent surveys on sources and extent of knowledge on sexuality, conducted among Czech high school students and apprentices of both sexes in 1966, 1972, 1978 and 1979, revealed that school, youth organisations, TV and radio give little or no information on sexual matters. Books and friends consistently emerge as the major sources of knowledge for both sexes, while mothers are significant for females. Lectures by specialists (usually medical doctors) who answer anonymous questions constituted the most preferred source of information among respondents from the 1978 sample, but only 5 per cent of males and females in an earlier sample claimed that they had actually learned anything significant from these sporadic lectures (Kadlecová, 1974; Kadlecová and Brtníková, 1977; Poradovský, 1979). These findings were confirmed by surveys among adolescent girls (Chovanová, 1974) and married women (Trča and Rejmanová, 1974), conducted in early 1970s. Girls in Chovanová's sample claimed to have gained most of their sexual information between the ages 11 and 13, mainly from friends. However, Kučera (1981) found peer influence to be less significant than indicated by earlier samples. The majority of the respondents in his 1979 sample relied on printed literature; only 13 per cent obtained their sexual knowledge from friends and 10 per cent preferred to rely on personal experience.

American youth also acquire most of their knowledge about appropriate sexual codes and contraceptive practices from their friends or from books and the mass media. Parents, the classroom and personal experience all played lesser roles (in order of mention) in providing information (Parsons, 1983, p. 44; Zellman and Goodchilds, 1983, p. 54). Rothenberg (1980) found that only 26 per cent of mothers had talked to their children about birth control by the time the children were 10 to 14 years of age. Only 34 per cent had explained intercourse, and most of the children reported that they had learned about birth control from a teacher at school. Thus teenage peers also teach sexuality to each other in the USA. However, adolescents recognise peers to be poor sex education teachers. Zellman and Goodchilds (1983, p. 54) found that only one-third of those who reported learning about sex from same gender peers thought this course 'most useful'; personal experience and discussion with teachers were seen as more valuable.

Czech adolescents seem to agree with their American counterparts about the poor ability of peers to offer adequate information about sexuality. The breakdown of preferred (as opposed to actually consulted) source of knowledge in Table 3.1 indicates that doctors are the preferred authorities on sex education (most of the books on sex education are also written by physicians), with parents and teachers running significantly behind. (Interestingly, doctors are virtually invisible in the comparable US data.) Yet, as we saw above, physicians are generally reluctant to participate in sex education, preferring to leave this activity to teachers and parents, who are far less popular among young people as instructors on the subject.

Moreover, there is also some reluctance on the part of the targeted audience to receive more 'official' information on sexual matters. Only 12 per cent of the respondents in a recent Czech sample of young people aged 15–30 admitted lack of sexual knowledge. When asked about subjects about which they would like to receive additional information, sexuality figured least frequently, while child care, family law and marital harmony emerged at the top of the list (Kučera, 1981). It would have been useful to know whether Kučera and his respondents were referring to 'factual knowledge' (e.g. types of contraceptives and methods of use) or to 'relationship knowledge'. While many studies indicate that large numbers of children and teenagers in the USA are ignorant about basic reproductive physiology, it is generally agreed that knowledge about the more emotional aspects of sexuality is even less prevalent (Zellman and Goodchilds, 1983, p. 54). In contrast, Swedish children in grade *one* provide quite accurate descriptions of reproduction, and draw rather straightforward and accurate representations of the entire process (Koch, quoted in Parsons, 1983).

TABLE 3.1   *Public opinion on suitability of sex education sources (%)*

	Very suitable	Suitable	Little suitable	Quite unsuitable	Don't know
Parents	50	35	10	2	3
Teachers	28	48	17	3	4
Special lectures by doctors	81	17	0.7	0.2	0.9
Book	43	41	10	2	5
Friends	3	13	39	38	7
'Forbidden' sources (e.g. films for over 18-year-olds)	2	8	29	52	9

Results of an opinion survey of 1056 persons, aged 15–60, in equal proportions of males and females. Small inconsistencies in the figures are reproduced from the original.

SOURCE   Hepner, 1980, p. 52.

PUBLIC KNOWLEDGE ABOUT PARENTING

Child care knowledge among new mothers is generally obtained from books, and verbal information from a paediatric nurse, doctor, relatives and friends – in that order (Urbanová, 1977). However, Cahová (1977) found that only 24 per cent of new mothers in her sample read child care books (28 per cent in urban and 18 per cent in rural areas), and that these were, not surprisingly, women with secondary and higher education. When asked about preferred (as opposed to actually consulted) sources of information, the mothers in Urbanová's sample put doctor's specialised knowledge at the top of the list, followed closely by television, which came first among rural mothers. Books were placed in the fourth and third place respectively. Paediatric nurses came third among urban mothers and only sixth among rural mothers. Peter Kliment *et al.* (1977) ask themselves whether this order of preference reflects the inability of mothers to obtain information directly from nurses or the attractiveness and potency of television as a mass medium. In any case, their conclusion supports the view that the influence of mass media, especially television, is increasingly important in the actual dissemination of health knowledge, while the significance of face-to-face interaction between mothers and health care personnel is declining.

There are gender and age differences with respect to reading and learning from literature in general, and health educational literature in particular. Girls aged 15–19 read newspapers and magazines more frequently than boys, but this is dramatically reversed among those aged 20–30. The declining tendency of women to read in their 'prime' reproductive years corresponds, of course, to the vastly increased domestic responsibilities during those years, which leaves little time for leisure. Older children allow for more leisure of their parents, so that both sexes tend to read more between the ages of 30 and 50, but women never catch up with men. Women's reading of health educational literature is roughly the same as reading in general, while men show very low interest until they begin to experience the problem of ageing in their 50s. Radio and TV programmes about health issues are also followed more closely by women than by men.

Furthermore, women tend to regard the *nature* of the health information as more important than its *source*, while men tend to insist on an 'authoritative' backing of the educational message. Women also talk about health more often than men with their friends and co-workers, thus informally helping to disseminate knowledge among themselves. Moreover, those few men who are interested in health issues tend to be concerned largely about their own health (e.g. how to lengthen their lives, avoid rheumatism, heart disease), while women's chief interest lies in the health of their children. In Kliment's view, these findings confirm the widely held public opinion that the health care of family members is 'women's work'.

This brings us to the point that education for 'parenthood' is an ambiguous concept. On the one hand, it represents an important ideological shift from an exclusively maternal definition to an androgynous conception. For example, the 1981, 'propaganda' booklet, entitled the *Socialist Family*, which was published in English for consumption abroad, does recognise fathers. There are two pictures of them along with their children and they also appear in seven photographs of whole families, both nuclear and extended. On the other hand, mothers appear alone with their children in eight photographs, grandfathers in two and grandmothers (rather surprisingly) in only one. While a gender-based selection of photographs is a rather arbitrary measure, it nonetheless represents a real tendency to evaluate fatherhood and motherhood differently. Fathers are now generally considered more important to their children's upbringing than was the case three decades ago, but mothers are regarded as irreplaceable! Despite the extensive participation of women in paid employment, socialist motherhood has remained what Russo (1979), in her analysis of Western sex roles and motherhood, calls a social 'mandate' rather than an option.

Thus, it comes as no surprise to discover that Czech expert advice books written for parents are, in fact, addressed largely to mothers. Fathers are either given a few afterthoughts in special brief chapters (as is the case in Trča's popular prenatal advice book, entitled 'We're going to Have a Baby') or they are only addressed and then ignored. A preface to a highly esteemed infant care book, written by the internationally-known J. Koch and neutrally titled 'The Upbringing of a Child in a Family', is fairly typical of this particular form of tokenism:

Dear mummy and daddy. . . . our government undertook a whole range of measures within the framework of population policy which enables a mother to stay at home with her small child and to devote herself intensively to his/her upbringing. These measures stem from new scientific findings; it has been shown that to create a solid basis for a child's physical and psychological development, an infant requires the greatest possible amount of individual care. Under normal circumstances such care is best given by you, his/her mother. The bio-psychological arguments can be augmented by economic reasons: the greater chance of illness for an infant in a creche has a negative influence in the child's physical and psychological development and it simultaneously creates frequent absenteeism of employed mothers and thereby creating numerous difficulties in the workplace. (Koch, 1977, p. 5)

Both parents are addressed at first, but most of the remarks are, in fact, directed towards the mother. This tendency is consistent with several recent pro-natalist policy measures, especially extended maternity leaves, which have increased rather than diminished the current differences between parental roles.

NOTES

1. For an historical review of eugenism and 'race suicide' theories, see Gordon (1976).

4 Reproduction, Sex Equality and Protective Legislation

> Despite the positive changes in the nature of women's work brought about by scientific and technological progress, we do not believe that protective legislation has outlived its usefulness. Women clearly have their own distinctive physiological characteristics. (Biryukova, 1980, p. 53)

Protective reproductive legislation can be separated into three distinct categories: (1) protective labour laws, whose primary goal is the reduction of health hazards (including reproductive risks) to employees, (2) social security measures providing job guarantees and financial compensation during maternity leave, thus enabling women to combine their productive and reproductive roles, and (3) family legislation, upholding equality within marriage.

Protective labour laws are seldom discussed as an aspect of population policy, largely because the quantitative demographic impact of labour laws is close to zero. However, in the context of a review of qualitative aspects of population, protective labour legislation assumes new significance. Given the high rates of labour force participation by women in Eastern Europe, the official socialist commitment to sex equality and our uneven state of knowledge concerning the prevalence of occupational and environmental hazards and their impact on child-bearing, it is indeed pertinent to include protective reproductive legislation under 'policies with population effects'.

PROTECTIVE LEGISLATION AND SEX EQUALITY

Socialist protective legislation has been based on the ideological principle of equality based on sex differences. For example, a Czech

54

trade union pamphlet, *Working Women in Czechoslovakia*, published in 1975 as a contribution to the International Women's Year, defines sex equality in the following terms:

> Equality, i.e. generally equal position for women, requires taking into account certain differences in comparison with men. Woman's psychological and physical peculiarities and the demanding situations resulting from the many roles she fulfills at certain times, call for a special adjustment of her working and living conditions. The socialist society does not consider them as advantages or even benevolences but as measures required for the development of the entire society. (*Working Women in Czechoslovakia*, 1975, pp. 9–10)

This fairly typical socialist definition of sex equality goes only part way towards solving a major feminist dilemma: how to take into account women's biology without falling into the trap of defining women *primarily* in terms of their biology. As we shall see below, socialist theory and practice have a tendency to overemphasise the extent as well as the importance of the 'natural' differences between men and women, thus stressing women's reproductive roles at the expense of their productive roles. In other words, the dominant model is that of wife/mother with a job rather than a woman in a responsible position with a family. Moreover, arguments about 'woman's psychological and physical pecularities' tend to imply that male biology is the norm while female biology is in some sense 'deviant'.

The 1960 Constitution of the Czechoslovak Socialist Republic (Article 27), defines the basic principles and means necessary for the realisation of female equality as follows:

> The equal status of women in the family, at work and in public life shall be secured by special adjustment of working conditions and special health care during pregnancy and maternity, as well as by the development of facilities and services which will enable women to fully participate in the life of society.

These general constitutional provisions, which exist in all the East European countries, have been supplemented by a succession of more specific family and labour laws. From a feminist viewpoint, family legislation is the least problematic aspect of socialist legislation because it is based on an androgynous conception of sex equality. In

Czechoslovakia, the legal position of women in marriage is in no way different from that of men. Each marriage partner is obliged to maintain the other to ensure that each has the same living standard; property acquired during marriage is common property of the married couple. 'Division of the common property, which usually occurs on termination of the marriage, is based on the principle of equal shares. . . . Due account is paid to care of the children as well as to the extent to which each of the partners shared the responsibilities of running the common household' (*Working Women in Czechoslovakia*, 1975, p. 12). The duty of mutual maintenance expires after divorce, but 'if one of the divorced partners is unable to secure means for his or her maintenance, the other partner is obliged to contribute to his (her) maintenance, though only to the limited extent for maintenance and not longer than for a period of five years after the divorce'. We should realise in this context that the divorced person is unlikely to find herself or himself unsupported for very long, since the socialist countries guarantee everyone a right to a job.

With respect to custody of children, 'in practically 90 per cent of the cases, the children are placed in the custody of their mother. The partner who is not granted custody of the child is obliged to participate in the education and to pay for the maintenance of children under age after divorce' (p. 16). The authors of *Working Women in Czechoslovakia* neither question the courts' obvious preference for maternal as opposed to paternal care nor consider its implications for sex equality.

As far as employment is concerned, the labour code 'prohibits women to be given work which is physically unsuited to them or which is detrimental to their organism, especially work endangering their mission as mothers' (p. 35). A Bulgarian author, Fina Kaloyanova (1976, p. 32), writing for *World Health*, a World Health Organisation monthly publication, spells out the socialist rationale for the protection of women from the hazards of the work environment as follows:

> Protection of the health of all employees is considered extremely important in our country. Particular attention is paid to women workers, taking into account three basic considerations. The first of these is the anatomic and physiological particularity of the female body (in comparison to men, women are on average smaller and shorter and their normal lung capacity and blood haemoglobin content are lower; overall, it has been estimated that they have 15–20 per cent less physical strength, in terms of physical effort,

than men); the second is the reproductive function (a woman menstruates, she becomes pregnant, she gives birth and she breast-feeds her children, and in the course of these processes many regulatory mechanisms in the body are altered); and the third is the woman's social status (that is, her role in bringing up and educating children and caring for the family).

A. P. Biryukova (1980, p. 56), a secretary of the USSR All Union Central Council of Trade Unions, adds 'the fact that with the increase in its production potential society can afford to do more to safeguard the health of working women' as an additional reason for the socialist commitment to protective legislation for women.

The ideological content is clearly evident: women are to be protected both on account of their 'scientifically' alleged 'nature' as well as 'place' in the family and society as a whole. However, among these considerations, safeguarding women's 'special function of reproduction' is clearly the most important one.

PROTECTING WOMEN AS POTENTIAL MOTHERS

In all the socialist countries, there is an extensive list of jobs forbidden to pregnant and nursing mothers, which is much longer than the list of jobs forbidden to women in general, though the specification of job categories which are closed to women varies from country to country. For example, Romania, but not the USSR, forbids women to drive tractors on the grounds 'that it has been scientifically proven that the vibrations of the tractor seriously shake up a woman's uterus and thereby raise the risk of damaging her ability to bear children' (Jancar, 1978, p. 138).

Czechoslovakia does not explicitly prohibit women from driving tractors, though in practice the situation is not that much different from the Romanian one because of sexist interpretations of the meaning of the legislative term 'perilous to woman's health'. Male authorities in agriculture have tended to define all tasks connected with higher paid mechanised work as 'perilous' (vibration of tractors was used as the main ideological justification), thus excluding women, while unskilled backbreaking manual work, often more tiring, more arduous and always worse paid, was deemed suitable.[1] McAuley (1981, p. 123), quoting a Soviet woman economist, Nina Shishkan, argues that there is a tendency in the USSR 'to regard

manual work (that is *ruchnoi trud*, work done by hand) as synonymous with women's work – both in industry and agriculture. When
particular processes are mechanised, too often, apparently, the female
labour force is replaced by men. This results in the continued concentration of women in low-paid, frequently physically demanding jobs,
despite increases in mechanisation.' And, one might add, protective
legislation which prohibits women from operating heavy machinery
such as tractors or cranes.

Once protective laws determine what types of jobs women (but not
men) may or may not do they inevitably discriminate against women.
While protective legislation may protect women's health (and that of
their future children), this is by no means certain, given our uneven
state of knowledge about what causes reproductive damage and of
what kind. What is certain, however, is that protective legislation has
contributed to the feminisation of certain job categories and the
persistence of wage differentials between the sexes. In other words,
'reproductive' ideologies have certain material effects in legitimising
the social division of labour. In socialist countries, equal pay is given
only for equal work, and in a sexually segregated labour market,
women rarely perform similar work to men. Feminisation of certain
sectors of the economy also virtually ensures that protective legislation is often not observed in practice, because there are no male
workers around who could perform a particular 'forbidden' task. For
example, the Czech protective labour code forbids all women from
manually lifting weights greater than 15 kg, but this restriction is
widely ignored, especially in the feminised labour-intensive retail
trade, nursing and some branches of consumer industry (Kříšťová,
1977, p. 6; Hrabětová *et al.*, p. 17).

The issue of prohibition of night work is even more contradictory,
because the legislation itself makes numerous exceptions for a relatively large category of women workers. For example, women who
are over 18 and who are neither pregnant nor recent mothers (defined as women with children under one year of age) can and often do
work night shifts in health, social and cultural facilities, public
catering, telecommunications and the postal service, animal production, railways and other forms of public transportation, or 'responsible and leading' positions.

A special paradox with night shifts is experienced by nurses. Many
pregnant nurses would like to work during the night on the grounds
that the work is generally less arduous than during the day, when

patients are awake and make many demands, but they are unable to do so because of protective legislation. The remaining nurses, all women, are then forced to work more night shifts than they would really like to undertake. Dr Gronský (1972, p. 657) also claims that nurses experience frequent pregnancy complications and even miscarriages. Some trade unionists claimed at the 19th national meeting of women trade union officials that many more women workers than currently permitted would like to undertake night work, both because of the higher pay and of more available time with their children, values considered more important than the 'protection' of their health (*Celostátní aktiv* . . ., 1977, p. 47).

Similar preferences were found among women night cleaners in New Zealand. Apart from making more money, nightwork allowed women with schoolchildren to be at home before and after school, for the evening meal, during the school holidays or in case of child's sickness. Domestic tasks, e.g. shopping, banking, washing of clothes and dishes, were also easier to accomplish. Nightwork also meant less supervision, more autonomy, a quieter work place and a feeling of comradeship with fellow workers. On the negative side, the respondents in the sample complained of lack of sleep caused not by daylight but by the unending demands of husbands and children. The researchers from the Government Steering Committee on Nightwork Research found that virtually no household reorganisation took place to accommodate the nightworker's own needs. They concluded that nightwork appears to facilitate an adherence to traditional family roles, which prescribe total responsibility for child care and domestic work to the woman, regardless of the nature of her work outside the home (*Social and Labour Bulletin*, 1982, pp. 213–14).

Similar conclusions were reached by Charles and Brown (1981) in their study of women shift workers in seven different industries and occupations (e.g. packing, bakeries, assembly line work in the electronics industry). In their view (p. 702):

> the division of labour within the family determines to a significant extent the shifts that women are able to work, and because hours of work are only adapted to women's needs in specifically 'women's' industries, the organization of hours of work contributes to the reproduction of the sexual division of labour within the work force and within the family . . . protective legislation assumes a minor role in the light of this overall perspective.

RIGHTS OF CHILD-BEARING WOMEN WORKERS

In contrast, the right to be transferred to easier work during pregnancy has to be seen as an important social achievement, even if this legislative provision is not always implemented in practice and does not extend to night work for nurses. It is important to realise that the cost of transferring women to lighter work during pregnancy is usually not borne by the enterprise, but by the socialist system of social security. However, the enterprise often incurs an indirect, short-term cost in the disruption of its productivity – especially if too many women become pregnant at the same time, not an infrequent occurrence in heavily feminised sectors of the economy. In Czechoslovakia, the difference between the pay accrued to the permanent and the temporary job is made up from health insurance funds. If no suitable work can be found, the employing institution is required to lay the woman off and still pay her regular wage or salary (Hrdá, 1977).[2]

A Slovak woman sociologist, Schvarcová (1978, pp. 93, 97) claims that almost 10 per cent of pregnant women workers perform 'forbidden' work during pregnancy and within nine months of giving birth. This non-observance of the law occurs most frequently in agriculture (in 22 per cent of cases), engineering (11 per cent of cases) and education, culture and health care (22 per cent of cases). Nine per cent of employers (out of a sample of 152 enterprises) claim that the forbidden work was requested by the women themselves. Dr Pokorný (1972, pp. 20–1) found negative attitudes to pregnancy transfers on the part of both employers and women workers in his study of the huge shoe factory *Svit* in Gottwaldov (originally founded by Bata). In 1971, there were 1120 new pregnancies among the 12 975 women employees of *Svit* (so that almost 9 per cent of all the women workers were pregnant at the same time), but only 332 women had their work changed. Schvarcová (1978, p. 97) summarises the situation as follows:

> The employment of women in forbidden jobs is an objective reality in our country, on which there is an agreement between the employing organisation as well as women themselves. The extent of this work is not great, but it is also not negligible.

On the other side of the spectrum, Dr Michlíček (1978), a plant gynaecologist, claims that pregnant women often abuse their rights under the protective labour code. Many expectant mothers who are relocated to easier work, or to what Michlíček calls 'pseudowork', work so poorly that management prefers them not to be around. Many leading factory officials then often put pressure on company physicians to declare 'lazy' child-bearing women as 'disabled for work', thus forcing physicians into 'conflict with the law, not to mention medical ethics'.

However, this is a relatively minor problem when compared with the prevailing situation of pregnant women workers in Canada or the United States. For example, a recent case before the Ontario Labour Relations Board involved a pregnant video display terminal (VDT) operator who requested a job transfer and was refused. Murray Hardie, an executive director of a federal task force on microtechnology, said in an interview that some employers have already implemented policies which allow pregnant women to move to alternative jobs, but this is not the case for most companies. The report of the task force recommends that pregnant women who use VDTs should have the right to be reassigned to alternative work without the loss of benefits or seniority (*The Globe and Mail*, 26 October 1982).

The situation in the USA is much worse. According to Felker (1982, p. 3):

> beginning in the mid-1970's certain American industrial firms, including General Motors, Exxon, St. Joe Minerals and Allied Chemical, began to transfer or fire women employees who were of childbearing age. When transferred, these women often lost seniority and were forced to accept lower paying jobs, such as janitorial work, in order to remain employed. Management explained that these steps were taken to protect them from job exposure to chemicals deemed harmful to their reproductive systems. Many were also told their jobs could be retained upon proof of their inability to become pregnant. Needing their jobs more than their fertility, many of these employees were sterilized and many complained subsequently to their unions.

Felker (1982, p. 11) also reminds us that 'there is considerable confusion about the actual reproductive risk to employees' and that:

> there have been *no* instances reported of male employees given a 'choice' of job loss vs. sterilization, though it is known that some chemicals men work with mutate sperm. Instead, when it was

discovered that the pesticide DBCP *caused* male sterility, an uproar ensued brought on by male workers themselves, not by company physicians, ending with a recommendation by the Environmental Protection Agency that the product be banned.

Kaloyanova (1976, p. 34) implies that such sexist double standards do not exist in the socialist countries and that 'if a substance has definitive teratogenic properties, of course, we prohibit its use in industry or agriculture completely'. However, a highly placed Bulgarian woman doctor told Jancar (1978, pp. 184–5) that, while it was dangerous for everyone to work with polyvinyl chloride, someone had to work with it. 'It was worse that women should be the victims, because they were the bearers of the future generations, so the lot fell to men.' Interestingly in this light, Kaloyanova's coverage of Bulgarian research and legislation pertaining to reproductive hazards concentrates entirely on women. We are told that research on the higher incidence of miscarriages and disturbances in the menstrual cycle of workers engaged in plant-growing in greenhouses found that these problems were related to the effect of different pesticides at high temperatures but we are not told anything about male workers.

The same applies to much of Czech research. For example, an investigation of the relatively high incidence of pathological pregnancies among airline stewardesses, even 2–7 years after such work, deals exclusively with women. Among 42 Czech airline stewardesses who gave birth to 53 children, 68 per cent had complicated deliveries and 19 per cent gave birth prematurely. In addition, 31 per cent of previous pregnancies ended in a miscarriage, among some women repeatedly (Hinšt and Bruchác̆, 1981). Yet the work of flight attendants (as well as such high-risk categories as nurses or laundry workers) is not included on the long list of jobs from which women are protected. Moreover, no information is given about male flight attendants or pilots who might be exposed to similar reproductive hazards during the course of their work.

However, there are some indications that this exclusive emphasis on women might be shifting in the context of the emergence of genetic toxicology, a new discipline that combines methods of genetic analysis and traditional toxicological approaches. During the last few years, the Institute of Hygiene and Epidemiology in Prague has investigated in some detail the effects of occupational, environmental, physical, biological and chemical factors on both parents and their offspring. Data including 47 cases concerning the mother and the child and 28 pertaining to the father were obtained from maternity ward records and by interviews with the mother, geneticists and factory physicians. The same method, including basic medical data about the work place, drinking and smoking habits, health status, contact with infectious diseases of both parents (as reported by the woman and the doctors) were also used for analysing miscarriages in Northern Bohemia, which has the highest concentration of chemical industries in the country (Šram, 1978).

Thus, one set of dilemmas with respect to protective legislation stems from the fact that its scope is not sufficiently broad – men as well as a whole range of potentially hazardous jobs are excluded. Indeed, the recent negative experiences in Canada with the impact of video display terminals indicate that rapid technological development makes existing catalogues of 'unsuitable' jobs for women quickly obsolete and irrelevant.

Feminists also face an opposite dilemma, namely the criticism that protective legislation is too broad and too detailed, resulting in unnecessary exclusion of women from areas where they would like to work. Critics exposing these views also exist in the socialist countries. In reviewing some of the critical responses to the revision and extension of Czech protective legislation in 1965, which was fully implemented by 1967, Scott (1974, p. 21) quotes at some length a particularly angry comment from a woman crane operator, voiced at a protest meeting at the Klement Gottwald Iron and Steel Works:

> All of a sudden there's talk about the Geneva Convention . . . but it's nothing new. Why wasn't it observed ten or fifteen years ago? . . . I went to work then, the children on my neck, the youngest only a few months old, and no one asked me whether I minded being in a steel mill or whether I could work at night. . . . It's an injustice, a great injustice. As long as you needed us, we were good enough for you. And health conditions were much worse then than they are now, when the cranes have air-conditioned cabins. . . . Now you offer us employment in a quiet surroundings, when our hands are used to rough work and our eyes have lost their keenness.

Similar sentiments were also voiced elsewhere. When complaining about the effect of transferring women to lighter work at lower pay in the Třinec Iron Works, a woman trade union official pointed out that the reassignment was happening over women's objections and at a time when mechanisation and air-conditioning were being installed, making the work actually easier, but only for the men (Scott, 1974, p. 22).

Thus, all the benefits notwithstanding, protective legislation tends to have a strong controlling and coercive effect on the people whom it is supposed to benefit – women workers. The contradictory impact of policies designed to benefit women is also evident when we consider pregnancy and maternity leave.

SHORT-TERM AND LONG-TERM PREGNANCY AND MATERNITY LEAVES

The 'generosity' of maternity leave provisions varies from country to country, both in Eastern Europe and in the West. Among the socialist countries, Czechoslovakia provides the best benefits, while Romanian and Soviet provisions are very similar to those existing in the UK or Canada. Every employed woman in the USSR receives 16 weeks of paid maternity leave on full pay, half of it before the child is born, though, if there are birth complications, the postnatal leave can be extended to 70 days. Romanian paid maternity leave is 112 days, with 52 days before expected childbrith and 60 days after. New mothers receive 85 per cent of their regular daily earnings during their leave and 94 per cent if the new baby is the third or subsequent child in the family. However, leaves of absence for pregnancy, maternity or for caring for a sick child under the age of two are counted against the yearly vacation (Muresan and Copil, 1974, p. 370), a restriction which does not exist in the other socialist countries.

All child-bearing women in Czechoslovakia are guaranteed 26 weeks of paid maternity leave (35 weeks for single mothers and women giving multiple births), eight of which can, and four of which must, be taken prior to the expected date of delivery. Post-partum leave cannot exceed 22 weeks with the exception of premature births for which mothers are not penalised by the loss of four weeks of maternity leave, as they can be in Canada.[3] Many of the strongly pro-natalist socialist countries also provide lump sum childbirth (or 'layette') grants, though in the case of Romania, the entitlement begins only with the third child.

Among the Western countries, only Scandinavia (especially Sweden) provides better benefits. Swedish paid maternity leave, which used to cover mothers staying at home with their newborns for six months, has been extended to fathers who wish to do this instead. Admittedly, so far only a small, though rising,[4] proportion of fathers have taken advantage of this provision, and then mostly in the case of baby boys (Drude Dahlerup, personal communication).

Pregnancy Leave

The major criticism of short-term paid maternity leave concerns the inflexibility of leave regulations. While many women would prefer to work until the birth to be able to spend more time with their newborn before returning to work, doctors tend to favour extension of pregnancy leaves. For example, Dr Gronský (1972), claiming that 60–80 per cent of all neonatal deaths are caused by premature births, would like to see pregnancy leave extended to at least eight weeks prior to the expected date of birth. He is also a strong advocate of tying maternity payments to early (by 16 weeks) and regular medical prenatal visits (6–8 times) as is apparently done in the GDR. Dr Štembera *et al.* (1979a, p. 26), author of a Czech textbook on risk pregnancies, sensibly argues that:

> the care for premature newborns (annually 2800, one per cent of all newborns) weighing less than 1500 g in special intensive care units costs 15 000–20 000 Czech crowns. If all women with 'risk pregnancies' (approximately 6 per cent of all pregnant women) were to go on sick leave from work for two months, the money loss would be similar. Five per cent of these women will take the leave unnecessarily, so that economically the situation is even, but healthwise far superior.

In this context, the issue of pregnancy leave overlaps with that of protective legislation, since 'risk pregnancies' seem to be correlated with specific jobs and to some extent also with previous miscarriages and abortions – an issue discussed in more detail in Chapter 8. Baran (1980) found a high correlation between employment in sales and the risk of premature delivery, as did the authors of the previously quoted study on airline stewardesses, but this risk appears to be minimal among housewives. Neither author seems to advocate the granting of pregnancy leave during the first trimester, when the experience of fatigue and nausea tends to be particularly severe and when some work flexibility might be particularly welcome for pregnant women. Moreover, no socialist country offers menstrual leaves, a provision that is available in Japan.

Postnatal leaves

Unlike many of their Western counterparts, women in socialist countries have a *statutory* right to unpaid maternity leave, ranging from one to three years, without losing their jobs or seniority. This is especially important for safeguarding length-of-service bonuses, pension qualifications, and the like. However, there are also some definite disadvantages to these provisions, especially if they last longer than one year.

The most obvious disadvantage of any unpaid leave is the economic hardship involved. To maintain what is considered an adequate standard of living nowadays, two incomes in a family are essential – this is one of the major reasons why so many women have entered paid employment in the first place. Childbirth grants, family allowances and the so-called maternity allowances (more on these below) do not constitute an adequate material compensation for the loss of income of one spouse, invariably the wife. While the Czech government was spending, by the early 1970s, 10 per cent of its annual budget on direct cash payments and subsidies in kind (e.g. creches, kindergartens, school meals, rent deductions), personal observations of couples with young children indicate that they find it hard to make ends meet. Indeed, many would find it difficult to survive without some form of aid from their own parents. Legal guarantees of jobs tend to ignore the simple facts that these provisions do not bring in any money in the short-run and that where the woman is on unpaid maternity leave, couples are forced to make significant financial sacrifices. Single mothers face even worse financial difficulties, as we shall see in Chapter 11.

Another problem with maternity leaves, both paid and unpaid, concerns the exclusive way in which they are currently conceived. New mothers are virtually left to their own devices to cope with the feelings of exhaustion, anxiety, depression and insecurity which so often accompany the post-partum experience. Mothers of newborns tend to work under conditions of fatigue, inexperience, uncertainty and isolation, and employers do not particularly seem to care.

Schvarcová (1978, p. 85), the Slovak sociologist cited earlier, reports that, among a nationwide sample of 2621 married women with dependent children, only 10 per cent were satisfied with their employer's understanding of, and support for, motherhood. A Czech trade union official went even further and accused enterprises of sexist double standards:

> When we compare the care of women on maternity leave with that of men currently performing military service [lasting up to two years], the approaches are radically different, though in both cases we're talking about the fulfilment of important social missions. A male worker without completed military service is hired without too many difficulties, and after his return, his job is given back to him. During his leave of absence, the enterprise is in continuous contact with him, sending him regularly the company magazine. However, pregnant women are hired only reluctantly and, when the woman worker begins her maternity leave, she virtually ceases to exist for the employer. And yet, there is nothing easier to arrange than to inform her regularly about what is happening at her place of work, or to invite her for the occasional work meeting (she would easily find somebody who would take care of her child for the two or three hours). It is then hardly surprising that women often do not return to their former employment after the expiry of maternity leave, because during their leave they lost all the connections to their place of work, not to mention that their qualifications have also suffered, a fact which employers almost enjoy pointing out. (*Celostátní aktiv*, 1977, p. 70)

Thus, another major disadvantage of maternity leaves, as currently conceived, is the removal of women from institutional power and politics. The longer the maternity leave, the greater is the loss for the woman. Emphasis on formal guarantees of job security and various accrued benefits tend to ignore the extent to which promotion is due to informal institutional politics. However, it is also important to point out that men on military leave, which can be as long or even longer than maternity leave, do not seem to be affected by their absence from the workplace as much as women. As another speaker at the national meeting of women trade union officials pointed out:

> the majority of our [i.e. trade union] functionaries and leading economic officials continue to see in the care of working women

only 'extra' tasks, which are best left to be sorted out only by women themselves. (*Celostátní aktiv*, 1977, p. 73)

Compare this practice to the official ideology which considers the 'special adjustment of women's working and living conditions' not 'as advantages or even benevolences but as measures required for the development of the entire society'!

Other negative consequences of long-term paid and unpaid maternity leaves, probably unintended but nonetheless real, are revealed by the Hungarian experience. In order to enhance fertility, Hungary introduced in 1967 the so-called maternity (or child care) allowance, paying mothers a flat rate (amounting to substantially less than their average monthly income) to stay at home with any child until it reached age 3. Czechoslovakia introduced a similar measure in 1970, with eligibility starting with the second or subsequent child. Bulgaria followed suit in 1973, but its provision is less 'generous'. Maternity allowance is set at the official minimum wage and the period for which it is paid varies depending on the birth order of the child. It is six months for the first child, seven months for the second and eight months for the third. As well as her paid maternity leave and maternity allowance a mother has the option to take unpaid maternity leave up to three years from the child's birth (Heitlinger, 1975).

After more than a decade of experience with maternity allowances, several Hungarian sociologists have noted a 'backlash' in the forms of less aid given by husbands in the home, reluctance on the part of employers to hire women because they will eventually not return to work, subjective feelings of isolation and frustration, and a shift among younger women from the 'emancipation' model of the family (generally accepted by their mothers) towards goals based on consumerism (quoted by Scott, 1978, p. 194). The East German provision, which gives women, but not men, one day's paid holiday per month to catch up on household chores, must have a similarly inegalitarian effect.

However, these provisions are increasingly popular among *all* women, not just those with lower education. In early 1970, 73 per cent of women with an elementary education applied for maternity allowance, compared to 61 per cent of mothers with secondary education and only 30 per cent with higher education (Heer, 1981, p. 134). However, in Czechoslovakia in the late 1970s, 77 per cent of eligible mothers with university education applied for maternity allowance for the full two years, compared to 88 per cent of those with elementary education – a difference of only 11 per cent, and the percentages were rather high to start with. Furthermore, the most frequently stated reason for utilising maternity allowance, given by 78 per cent of respondents in a nationwide sample survey, was preference for full-time motherhood as opposed to employment. Lack of available day care (only 22 per cent of children aged 0–3 can be accommodated in Czech day care centres) came as the second most frequently stated reason, but only 29 per cent of respondents answered in this way (Schvarcová, 1978, pp. 79–81). Hence, the strong ideology of motherhood, projected in socialist personal advice books, as well as current pro-natalist population policies, is also evident among women themselves.[5]

Among the socialist countries, only Hungary has extended (in May 1982) some of the maternity benefits to fathers. The new provision entitles the father – instead of the mother – to opt for the child care leave and allowance, after the child has reached one year of age. Another new provision enables the parent who is drawing a child care allowance to enter part-time employment, defined as four hours a day counted on a monthly average, after the child has reached the age of 18 months, without losing entitlement to the child care allowance. (*Social and Labour Bulletin*, 1982, p. 357). Among the Western countries, various versions of parental leaves were in recent years introduced in Finland, Norway, Italy, Spain, France and Portugal (see Paoli, 1982, pp. 12–13, for more details).

In contrast, provision for paternity leaves has remained a marginal issue in Czechoslovakia. While Wynnyczuk and Faktorová (1980, p. 3) make a favourable comment on the subject in their comparative cross-national review of population policies in Western Europe, they do not put forward any specific proposals that such androgynous policy be adopted in Czechoslovakia. Child care allowances, extended maternity leaves (up to five years) and part-time work are the subjects of an ongoing debate also in the USSR, but none of these provisions is being considered for fathers. Moreover, it remains to be seen whether any of these proposals will be translated into practice. As argued elsewhere (Heitlinger, 1979, pp. 120–1), Soviet law has for several years allowed enterprises to take on women part-time, but as such labour is comparatively more expensive (holiday and pension rights are retained in full), managers of larger enterprises have been reluctant to introduce part-time work for women. Thus the interests of managers, central planners and women often do not coincide. Moreover, various surveys conducted in the late 1960s and 1970s have indicated that while a majority of women think it is right to stay at home for the first three years or so after the birth of a child, they personally do not want to sacrifice those years.[6]

Thus maternity leaves and child care allowances are closely related to economic issues. As we noted earlier, extended maternity leaves entail substantial financial sacrifice, have a negative impact on women's careers, and tend to reinforce the traditional sexual division of labour within the home. While parental leave legislation is an important step forward towards sex equality, its full implementation can be expected only with the equalisation of male and female wages. As long as child care allowance is set at a flat rate, at or lower than the minimum wage, fathers are unlikely to take advantage of parental leaves, because the financial costs of withdrawing from the labour force are so much greater for them (and their families) than is the case for mothers. Thus for the foreseeable future, it will be mothers who will remain solely responsible for the care of young children.

NOTES

1. This practice was criticised by the Central Committee of the Czechoslovak Union of Women in an open letter to the government, which was published in the mass circulation women's magazine *Vlasta* on 24 April 1968, during the 'Prague Spring'. See also Scott (1974, p. 22) who quotes a study of women in agriculture published in a Czech farmers' daily in 1969.

2. In Canada only Quebec among all the provinces provides similar guarantees. An occupational health and safety act, passed in 1979, gives pregnant women the right to request re-assignment to work she can reasonably perform. If this request is not complied with immediately, the employee may stop working until she is re-assigned or, if this is not possible, until the date of delivery. An employee exercising the rights to job re-assignment shall retain the rights and benefits of her regular employment. After leave, the employee must be returned to her regular job with the same benefits. Under this act, an employee may also request re-assignment if a medical certificate is presented stating danger to the child the employee is breastfeeding. If this re-assignment is delayed she may stop working until she receives such re-assignment or until the child is weaned. The compensation, based on 90 per cent of the woman's net earnings is to be paid by La Commission de la santé et de la sécurité du travail (*Canadian Women and Job Related Laws*, 1981, p. 33; Chenier, 1982, p. 70).

3. If early delivery means that the woman has not fulfilled the qualification period for leave, she may not be eligible for leave, let alone pay, and may even be in danger of losing her job. Only British Columbia does not have

a qualification period in its labour legislation. See *Maternity and Child Care Leave in Canada*, 1983, p. 17.

4. According to Paoli (1982), the proportion of eligible Swedish fathers taking paternity leave has increased from 2 per cent in 1974 to 11 per cent in 1977.

5. There seems to be a stronger relationship between an adherence to a strong ideology of motherhood and poor job prospects in the USSR. Hansson and Lidén (1983), in their book of interviews with thirteen Moscow women, have some interesting quotes on this issue. Results from a survey of Ukrainian women, quoted in Heitlinger (1979, p. 121) showed that women's attitudes towards extended maternity leaves and part-time work do depend upon the jobs they hold and the qualifications they possess: there was a higher instance of negative responses to the suggested benefits among women with higher qualifications and hence more satisfying jobs.

6. A. G. Kharchev, the head of the main Soviet Institute of Sociology, believes that in the past women's work roles were over-valorised at the expense of their maternal roles and what is now needed is a campaign to change women's attitudes. I am grateful to Maxine Molyneux for conveying to me the results of her interview with Kharchev during her visit to the USSR in 1982.

Part II:
Reproductive Services

5 Socialist Medicine and Reproduction

> One might think that 'socialized medicine' potentially could trans-
> fer power over medical services from the doctors to the laymen –
> especially the laymen in strategic government posts. But in practice
> abroad, national health insurance and national health services
> are dominated by doctors . . . A fundamental reason for domina-
> tion by the doctors, of course, is lay deference to professional
> expertise. (Glaser, 1971, p. 43)

The definition of 'free' health care as both an individual civil right
and collective (i.e. state) responsibility is a long-standing feature of
socialism in Czechoslovakia. The organisational conception of socialist health care was worked out during the Second World War by a
group of progressive doctors and published on 21 May 1945, less than
two weeks after the liberation of the capital, Prague, by the Soviet
army. It was enshrined as the so-called Nedvěd's Plan, Dr Nedvěd
himself having perished in 1943 in the Nazi concentration camp
Osvetim. The plan, proposing a system of unified, state directed and
financed care, free at the point of consumption, was, however,
implemented only after the Communist take-over in February 1948.
The National Insurance Act of (15 April) 1948 unified and expanded
existing separate sickness/maternity and old age pension insurance
schemes into a comprehensive social insurance system. At the same
time, the new socialist state nationalised all hospitals, sanatoria and
health spas. However, full nationalisation of the pharmaceutical
industry was delayed until 1955.

The move towards the unification of the whole health care system
was initiated by a government decision to that effect on 3 July 1951.
A conference of health care workers (presumably consisting of spe-
cially selected 'progressive' delegates), which met in the Moravian
capital Brno the following day, fully approved the government decision and suggested that the responsibility for the provision of health

care services be assigned, under the direction of the Ministry of Health, to district and regional national committees on the one hand, and productive enterprises on the other (*Zdravotnictví a populace*, 1971, pp. 8–9). Act No. 103/1951 'On the Unified Therapeutic and Preventive Care' then established a supposedly integrated hierarchical system of district and regional territorial as well as industrial therapeutic and preventive health service establishments.[1] 'Thus a continual, permanent and free health care was secured, so much missed by the people of previous bourgeois formations' (Makovický *et al.*, (1981, p. 286). However, the principle of free universal accessibility to health care (including dental care) was fully implemented only in 1966, when the act 'On the Health Care of People' transferred entitlement from an insurance basis to entitlement based on citizenship, thus including previously uninsured self-employed persons and non-workers. Similar legislation was passed in the USSR in 1969, Bulgaria in 1971, and Hungary in 1975 (Kaser, 1976, p. 115; Szalai, 1981, p. 152).

It is generally acknowledged, with considerable official pride, that the reorganisation of the Czechoslovak health care system was based 'on the principles, experiences and achievement of the Soviet health care system' (Makovický *et al.*, 1981, p. 285). Other features modelled on the Soviet system[2] include:

(1) the separation of medicine into sub-disciplines based on bodily functions and population group to be served;
(2) a clear division of responsibilities between primary ambulatory care and the more specialised secondary out-patient and tertiary in-hospital care;
(3) a restriction on the right of patients to choose their own physician;
(4) a system of special high-quality party and military clinics, restricted to high party officials and their families;
(5) a system of priorities in the provision of medical services, based on the officially-perceived need of industrial development and population replacement.

The highest priority is assigned to workers in certain hazardous high-priority industrial occupations in heavy industry (e.g. mining and steel work), followed by expectant mothers and children. As Pudlák (1978, p. 2), the Chairman of the Scientific Council of the Czech Ministry of Health, and the editor of the English-language journal *Czechoslovak Medicine* put it, 'the Czechoslovak health services are focused in particular on preserving and stimulating mental and physical work capacity and prolongation of life span. The second trend is the participation in efforts to ensure overall mental, physical and social development of the young generations.'

Thus within the health care system, reproductive care has a high priority. In line with other socialist countries, obstetrics/gynaecology belongs to primary care medicine in Czechoslovakia, since women are one of the designated groups with special needs for care. Other such designated groups are workers, children and adults. As Millard (1982, p. 510) points out, this three-fold division of specialisation at the point of first contact, based on age (in the case of paediatrics), sex (in the case of obstetrics/gynaecology) and occupation (in the case of industrial health) has eliminated the concept of family medicine. Industrial doctors only treat workers, paediatricians only treat children and so on, with no or little contact with their families. Physicians tend to have little knowledge of their patient's living conditions, a shortcoming which is magnified by poor or non-existent liaison between district and enterprise doctors. This is particularly unfortunate for women whose health care is split between general practitioners who deal with adult diseases and obstetricians/gynaecologists who focus only on the reproductive system.

Women requiring reproductive care cannot freely choose their own physician but must see one in their place of residence or work. Patients can switch doctors only if they can prove that they have received inadequate care from the physician in their district, and then only after a lengthy bureaucratic complaints procedure. Physicians working in the district or industrial clinic generally do not work in the hospital and vice versa. One consequence of this rigid division of labour is a pronounced hierarchy of medical status and prestige, with primary clinical care at the bottom of the scale. Millard (1981, p. 60) reports that, at least in Poland, 'local doctors, particularly in urban areas, are often described primarily as clerks directing their patients to specialist consultation, having little job satisfaction and itching for a hospital post with its attendant prestige, greater facilities, and interesting cases'. A similar state of affairs has also been reported from the Soviet Union, where many primary care physicians resent being considered 'mere qualified dispatchers' by the secondary and tertiary care specialists (Navarro, 1977, p. 60). As we shall see below, such a pronounced hierarchy of status and prestige is also evident within obstetrics/gynaecology in Czechoslovakia.[3]

OBSTETRICS/GYNAECOLOGY IN CZECHOSLOVAKIA: CHANGES IN ORGANISATION AND CONTENT

An unconditional women's entitlement to special care during pregnancy and motherhood was established by the (9 May) 1948 Constitution, thus making obstetrics a medical specialty 'most advanced in its basic socialist principles', (*Zdravotnictví a populace*, 1971, p. 9). The above mentioned Act. No. 103/1951 both affirmed the principle of free maternity care and initiated the transformation of obstetrics/gynaecology along the previously cited Soviet socialist principles for the health care system as a whole. The medical/organisational goals specific to reproductive care were outlined as follows:[4]

(1) The development of a broad network of obstetrical facilities to enable every woman to give birth in a hospital and be attended by a medical specialist.
(2) The education of sufficient numbers of qualified personnel.
(3) The creation of newborn wards, separate from maternity wards, under the responsibility of paediatricians.
(4) The establishment of a network of antenatal clinics accessible to every pregnant woman. An increase in the number of consultations per pregnant woman, starting at the early stages of pregnancy.
(5) Preferred care for working women.
(6) Campaign for early diagnosis of women's malignant tumours.
(7) Improvement in the quality of work in antenatal clinics, maternity wards and newborn wards.
(8) The development of psychological and sociological criteria in women's health care.
(9) Continued sub-specialisation and the introduction of new techniques and methods of care.
(10) Careful analysis of maternal and perinatal mortality at district, regional and national levels.

Most of these goals were accomplished quickly (see Table 5.1).

Nearly every woman now sees a medical specialist nine times during her pregnancy and not later than 16 weeks after conception. The proportion of hospital deliveries among all deliveries increased dramatically from 41 per cent in 1948 to 86 per cent in 1957 and 99 per cent in 1967. While in 1948 there were only 326 practising obstetricians in all of Czechoslovakia, by 1967 their numbers had

TABLE 5.1   *Developments in maternal and infant health care in Czechoslovakia, 1948–78 (population 13 million)*

	1948	1957	1967	1976	1978
Resources					
Prenatal clinics	434	1 625	1 812	1 840	1 840
Obstetrical/gynaeco- logical beds	6 531	12 624	14 856	15 932	15 935
Specialised obstetricians	326	1 030	1 865	2 341	2 407
Midwives	2 643	4 648	5 570	6 387	6 510
Activities					
Deliveries in maternity homes (%)	41	86	99.2	99.8	99.8
Average number of controls in prenatal clinics per woman	0.6	3.9	7.1	9.2	9.4
Registration of pregnancies up to the third month in the prenatal clinic (%)		49.3	88.0	95.9	97.3
Post-mortem exam- inations of foetuses and newborns (%)		31.5	90.8	97.8	
Outcome					
Maternal mortality rate per 100 000 deliveries	137	63	28	15	13
Cases of eclampsia per 100 000 deliveries		122	68	35	34
Perinatal mortality rate per 1000 live births	51	26.3	20.9	20.3	18.5
Stillbirth rate per 1000 live births	19	11.6	7.1	6.8	6.0
Early neonatal mortality rate per 1000 live births	32	14.7	13.8	13.5	12.5

Source   Štembera, 1981, p. 517

TABLE 5.2   *Obstetricians/gynaecologists in Czechoslovakia, 1960–80*

Year	Total	Women	% of women	% of women in Czech lands	% of women in Slovakia
1960	1387	292	21.1	23.6	14.5
1965	1564	379	24.2	25.2	21.9
1970	1753	470	26.8	27.8	24.6
1975	2179	671	30.8	31.4	29.6
1980	2544	784	30.8	31.8	29.1

SOURCE   *Statistická ročenka ČSSR 1981*, p. 604

increased by more than five times to 1865. Between 1960 and 1980, the number of obstetricians doubled. Women increased their share among them by 10 per cent (15 per cent in Slovakia), from 21.5 per cent to almost 31 per cent (see Table 5.2).[5]

However, the rapid increase in the number of physicians was barely sufficient to meet the greatly expanded workload, caused by an 'increase in the average number of antenatal consultations per pregnant woman, an increasing number of births, introduction of new procedures – contraception, abortion etc., which were not always accompanied by corresponding expansion in manpower' (Štembera, 1977, p. 401). Vojta (1971, p. 76) makes a similar argument:

> Can we cope with it all? The answer is difficult. So far, tasks were always added, without ensuring that they could be adequately met. To basic treatment were initially added preventive consultations, then oncological consultations, abortions, dissemination of contraception, dispensation of pre-cancerous treatment, diagnosis of risks, a check for venereal disease[6], and so on. Nonetheless, it seems that there is a realistic prospect of organising work in polyclinics and hospitals in such a way that its quality will continue to increase with the full utilisation of existing possibilities.

> Poutuch *et al.* (1972, p. 608) also note that 'the work of a gynaecologist is connected with a whole range of bureaucratic regulations, orders and warnings', but add that these 'do not exceed what is required of other medical specialties. With an improvement of the organisation of work, central documentation, introduction of computers and the utilisation of statistical methods we will be able to simplify this unpopular activity [of documentation], which of necessity increases with the more preventive orientation of medicine.'

The pursuit of 'the improvement of the organisation of work' has coincided with the goal of 'continued sub-specialisation', both of which are evident in the 1976 reorganisation of reproductive care. Since 1977, primary care district and enterprise women's doctors are no longer responsible for the treatment of benign tumours, sterility and infertility, and pathological and risk pregnancies. When diagnosed, all these cases are referred to out-patient departments of hospitals of II type. Dr Židovský (1981, p. 81) comments favourably on this particular change in the medical division of labour:

> The narrowing of the concentration of interest and effort of a great number of gynaecologists and obstetricians is, above all, the means towards the optimalisation of patient care. It is evident that it has also made a positive impact on the reputation of our discipline in the eyes of physicians of other specialties, and, from a long-term perspective, in the minds of medical students, thus increasing the attractiveness of this specialty.

The implicit concern about the prestige of obstetrics/gynaecology *vis-à-vis* other medical specialties is interesting. While Jancar (1978, p. 34) argues that surgery and gynaecology are considered the most prestigious medical branches in Hungary, where they are accorded higher entrance quotas, this is apparently not so in Czechoslovakia, at least not with respect to obstetrics/gynaecology. Surely Dr Židovský would express no concern about the 'reputation' of obstetrics/gynaecology if the specialty had an unquestionable high status and prestige among all doctors. Personal anecdotal conversations with several paediatricians revealed that at least within paediatrics, obstetrics/gynaecology does not enjoy a great deal of prestige. 'After all', went the typical comment, 'obstetrics deals with essentially healthy people, doesn't it?' However, there was also a general sense of envy and resentment among paediatricians about the widespread practice of 'tipping' (or 'bribing') of obstetricians and surgeons, which is apparently not so common in paediatrics. This issue is discussed in more detail below. The predicted impact of sub-specialisation on the 'optimalisation of patient care' is also questionable. If Millard's (1981, pp. 60–1) observation of the Polish health care system is anything to go by, rather the opposite appears to be the case.

> The distrust by hospital specialists of their primary care colleagues makes itself felt in widespread, unnecessary duplication of diagnostic

tests. Lack of communication and fragmentation of documentation also means that a primary care physician rarely has a full picture of a patient's hospital diagnosis and therapy, often necessary for proper after-care. Even specialists generally possess only information concerning a patient's treatment in their own specialty: any patient who is referred to more than one specialist may also experience duplication of diagnostic tests or the prescription of duplicate or even incompatible drugs. The upshot is not only a waste of resources but the treatment of patients as mere bundles of symptoms catalogued in 'scientific' compartments.

As we noted above, duplication of expensive tests and disruption of the continuity of medical care have also characterised the Israeli health care system.

Excessive sub-specialisation has also definite undesirable consequences for the under-utilisation and work satisfaction of primary care physicians. Since 1977, the work of primary care district obstetricians/gynaecologists has been rather monotonous and routine, limited as it has been to giving contraceptive advice, writing a prescription for the pill, inserting an IUD, performing routine antenatal care, filling in forms for an abortion and, when required, referring women patients to other specialists and facilities. While Židovský (1982) ignores this dimension of sub-specialisation, Kvíz (1982) notes that 'the knowledge of community gynaecologists, fully separated from hospital beds, exceeds by far the tasks required of them in their restricted community practice'. However, Gazárek and Křikal (1972) disagree and suggest that the work in an antenatal clinic requires more rather than less skill. In their view, antenatal care is undeservedly underestimated and wrongly given only to the youngest and least experienced doctors, who often fail to spot, early enough, cases of potential birth complications. In the authors' view, one consequence of this common failure to correctly separate normal from 'risk' pregnancies has been a relatively high, stagnating perinatal mortality (20 per thousand at the time of writing of the article), while in many Western countries perinatal mortality had dropped to 10–15 per thousand or even below 10, (see Chapter 10 for more details). The authors recommend that antenatal care at early stages of pregnancy be assigned to the most experienced doctors, but admit that these physicians prefer the more prestigious and better-paid work in the maternity hospital.

Another problematic issue is the use of psychological and sociological criteria in medical theory and practice. While all physicians tend to pay lip service to the importance of social perspectives, medicine in Czechoslovakia, as in other countries, is basically physiological in its orientation. As Pavlusová (1980, p. 244) puts it:

socio-medical questions are either debarred from medicine altogether, or they are understood in both research and practice in such a way that their solution is sought only in the course of application in the context of daily social practice. Of course we won't discover these tendencies in general proclamations, which always profess loyalty to socio-medical perspectives, if only because these perspectives are generally identified with political and ideological perspectives. But the tendency to biologise is quite evident when we analyse the nature of the solution of some medical tasks.

As an example of the dominant biological orientation of medicine, the author cites the national research programme on cardiovascular diseases, which focuses on the biological body at the expense of its surroundings. Citing another Czech researcher, Pavlusová (1980, p. 245) argues as follows:

In theory we acknowledge that the decisive factor in determining the quality of health is the environment. However, in practice we act in the opposite way, by looking for the essence of health problems in molecular biology and immunology, at the level of biophysical and biochemical factors, that is, only at the level of the micro-world. Perhaps we think that it would not be very 'scientific' to designate polluted environment, disturbed interpersonal relations, lack of physical activity, disorder in one's workplace, smoking, alcoholism, and so on, as the causes of health problems.

The tension between medical and social criteria is even more acute in women's medicine. As Vojta (1971, p. 194) argues:

gynaecologists cannot be satisfied only with the fulfilment of tasks connected with the prevention and cure of damaged health of women. They are engaged to much greater extent than physicians of other specialties in the social problems of their women patients. Thus another requirement for gynaecologists is to clarify and study what has changed in this field and how it contributes to the results of their work and mission as helpers of women.

However, many gynaecologists resent having to deal with the 'social problems of their women patients'. This is particularly evident in cases involving abortions on social grounds – 80 per cent of all authorised abortions. As Kotásek (1970, p. 328) put it, 'we watch with certain bitterness the fact that we, executors of the law, deal with 80 per cent of cases which are outside the medical sphere'. What the doctors particularly resent is being put in the position of having to make what are essentially social policy decisions. Are unmarried status, inadequate housing, three or more children – the most frequently stated reasons in requesting an abortion – sufficient and justifiable reasons for performing it? These dilemmas may be heightened (or minimised, as the case may be,) by the existing division of labour between primary care and tertiary care physicians. For ambulatory doctors and doctors who sit on abortion commissions deal only with requests, while the actual operation is performed by the tertiary care physicians in the hospital, who only execute decisions made by somebody else.

Another manifestation of the tension between the sociopsychological and medical criteria is evident in the reluctance of obstetricians to promote psycho-prophylaxis, which is discussed in more detail in Chapter 9. According to Brucháč and Sochor (1972, p. 562), psycho-prophylaxis 'goes against the physiological conception of Czechoslovak obstetrics'. One way in which this tension has been 'resolved', at least at the level of theory, is by 'ghettoising' social perspectives within the confines of a separate sub-discipline, called social gynaecology, which in turn is a sub-specialty of social medicine. Müller *et al.* (1972, p. 568) present the following general blueprint of what social gynaecology is all about:

(1) Social gynaecology forms part of the social care of the mother (family) by providing expert opinion so that society can decide what is to its benefit.
(2) Questions of health and diseases of women are addressed in relation to society as a whole; a woman is understood not only as a biological individual, but also as a part of social structure.
(3) The state of health of an adult woman is seen not as a stable phenomenon frozen in time, but as the result of a whole chain of various processes taking place in the preceeding phases of her life, especially in childhood. On the other hand, the woman as a mother is seen as having significant influence on the mental and physical development of her child. For these reasons it is neces-

sary to consider mother and child as one unit. That is why many goals of social gynaecology are identical with the goals striven for by social paediatrics (i.e. population policy, the lowering of perinatal mortality, the struggle against abortions, premature births, social pathologies and so on).

At the more concrete level, Müller, *et al.* (1972) and Kotásek (1975, p. 27) recommend the following content of this specialty:

(1) The study of social influences on reproduction (e.g. analysis of concrete causes of unfavourable population development).
(2) The study of the etiopathogenesis of gynaecological diseases and pathological pregnancies in the context of the psychological and social situation of women, their life-styles (e.g. family and work problems), and the general quality of their external environment.
(3) The deepening of the understanding of the impact of women's work (e.g. the overburdening of women, especially pregnant women).
(4) The study of doctor–patient relations.
(5) The study of health problems and needs of the female population for the scientific planning of health care.
(6) The improvement and modernisation of documentation and collection of information, so that gynaecologists/obstetricians can give more time to patients and less to documents.

Müller and his colleagues admit that, in order to be effective, such a broadly conceived specialty will have to cooperate with a whole range of non-medical disciplines, namely medical sociology, psychology, demography, statistics, economics and law. However, all these disciplines are in their infancy in Czechoslovakia. There are only a handful of medical sociologists in the country and there is no uniform agreement on the content of their work.[7] Even more important is the question of the fruitfulness of such cooperation. Who is likely to benefit most – medicine, the applied social sciences or the patients?

The Czech medical psychologist Říčan (1980, pp. 372–3) has argued that the 'cooperation' between medicine and the social sciences has more often than not led to 'medical imperialism':

Medical psychology and sociology attempt to correct the natural scientific one-sidedness of medicine, unfortunately not always successfully. For both disciplines often only 'prolong' the natural scientific perspective on the patient: apart from a whole range of organs which can become ill and be treated, it is now also the psychic apparatus, with its reflexes, functions and energies. This apparatus is then entrusted to the care of another specialist (a physician or a clinical psychologist), with the same anatomised knowledge, perhaps even treatment, as are the other organs which are entrusted to the care of other specialists.

However, this assessment is disputed by the British medical sociologist Strong (1979, pp. 209–10), who has argued as follows:

> Once again there are certainly worrying developments here, but there are good grounds for arguing that this threat is not all it might be and there are some signs of movement in the opposite direction also.

While Strong acknowledges that psychiatrists 'share the same preference for the strictly biological that is typical of their colleagues', he has also noted that 'the massive and growing emphasis on social factors during the last two decades has led to major reforms of psychiatric institutions and to strong attempts at *demedicalisation* by some psychiatrists' (Strong's italics). In his view, 'in a situation where professionals of very low status [i.e. social workers, clinical psychologists and social psychiatrists] are presented with vast numbers of patients with whom they can do little, demedicalisation, not imperialism, is the strategy which serves their interests best — and also, perhaps, those of their patients'. Thus another dimension of the issue is the low status of applied social sciences and social medicine compared to the organic medical sciences. As Dr Málek (1982, p. 579), a prominent physician who is also a member of the prestigious Czechoslovak Academy of Science acknowledges, there exists a problem:

> of differentiation and integration of science . . . There is a related need to accept new ideas about the relationship of medical disciplines to other 'non-medical' disciplines, without which the development of modern medicine is impossible. It is still necessary to struggle against the anachronistic view of the social sciences as 'helping' or 'servicing' disciplines, and treat them instead as equal partners.

However, if the social model of health and illness is fully accepted, some of the consequences may be quite undesirable, especially from the perspective of patients' rights. If Strong (1979, p. 212) is correct:

a fully social model of health, if implemented in any of the current forms of society, would require the involvement of social health experts in the whole range of industrial, housing, energy and even foreign policy decisions, as well as a much closer supervision of people's nutrition, leisure activities and so on. This strategy would dramatically lower the status of the currently prestigious branches of medicine such as surgery, but would entail even more dramatic rise in the standing of disciplines such as epidemiology, public health, and health education who would now receive far greater political power than is at present available to any branch of medicine. Moreover, there is no good reason to think that the shift to such a social model of health would avoid the detailed medical intervention at the level of the individual citizen which is the subject of so much criticism of the old 'medical model'. Indeed one may expect that a social model would call for intervention on a far more massive scale than anything required by organic medicine, for changing people's behaviour often requires detailed monitoring and supervision . . . A fully social model, because it reintroduces human agency into health and illness, can serve, in a context where the state has still to wither away, as a means for an even more systematic oppression than is offered by organic medicine.

THE BALANCE OF STATE, MEDICAL, AND ORGANISED CONSUMER POWER

Medicine under socialism constitutes what Fielding and Portwood (1980) call a 'bureaucratic profession', an occupation which has achieved a formal working relationship with the welfare state. Professional medicine depends on the socialist state for the provision of the workplace, medical supplies and technology, clientele and the licence to practice, but the determination of clinical practice has been left largely in the hands of the professionals themselves. In other words, the socialist party-state decrees the organisational framework of health services, who shall get it and in what order of priority, but individual doctors have substantial choice in how to handle their clients and how to practice their particular medical specialty. The greatest degree of state intervention occurs in the clinical practice of occupational medicine.

As noted earlier, the most important division within primary health care is between local health centres and the separate industrial centres. In 1974, there were more than 2300 such centres in Czecho-slovakia, compared to 15 industrial health centres in existence prior to the Second World War (Černý *et al.*, 1977, p. 7). The main role of industrial physicians, be they located in the West or in Eastern Europe, is to (1) assess a worker's fitness for a given job and (2) evaluate occupational safety and health hazards in the working environment. These are areas with consequences going well beyond the sphere of organic medicine. As Parmeggiani (1982, p. 282) noted, 'the plant physician, on account of the psycho-social implications and discretionary nature of his professional activities, often finds himself involved in a number of complex and contradictory obligations'. The external non-medical interference in his/her work can come from workers, management or the state.[8] On the one hand, there is frequent pressure from workers to be declared as 'unfit for work', since the physician's certificate is the best and only sure method of escaping work without a major loss of pay.[9] Field (1957, p. 162) summarises the dilemma of the individual doctor in the Soviet Union faced with this type of pressure as follows:

> It is difficult for the physician to sift the worthy from the unworthy cases. Torn by the claims of those who are genuinely in need of medical attention, those who do not need this attention but deserve an excuse, and those who do not, the doctor may oscillate between attitudes of indifference and compassion and acquire, in the long run, a deep sense of frustration.

On the other hand, there is also frequent pressure from higher authorities, interested in uninterrupted production, to reduce the number of medical certificates given, especially if the workers are suspected of malingering. Absenteeism from work due to illness is rather high in Czechoslovakia (approximately 17 days a year per worker)[10] and it is generally acknowledged that this 'reflects less the standard of health than the disutility of work' (Kaser, 1976, p. 119).

Women workers tend to have higher rates of absenteeism than their male colleagues, due to abortions, antenatal consultations, illnesses of children and the socially assigned responsibility for family consumption. For example, the latter may necessitate shopping errands or waiting at home for a repairman during working hours. Under the current medical conditions (discussed in more detail in Chapters 8 and 9), an abortion requires an absence of 12 days from work, while attending antenatal consultations normally leads to the loss of 9 half workdays per pregnancy. When a child falls ill, the working mother has a right to 3 workdays of paid leave. If the sickness lasts for a longer period, this leave may be extended on the strength of a decision taken by the National Health Insurance Committee for another 3 days, and in cases of single mothers up to 9 days. The benefit is paid at the equivalent rate of sickness benefit — 70 per cent of one's earnings for the first 3 days and 90 per cent thereafter (Průcha, 1981, p. 26). The specified leave period of 3–9 days is often insufficient for the convalescence of children returning to creches and has been singled out as an important factor contributing to recurrent illnesses of small children attending collective facilities (Heitlinger, 1979, p. 171). However, a leave which is too short is better than no leave at all. The majority of women workers in Canada have no statutory entitlement to paid, or even unpaid, leave from work when their children are ill, which means that women workers often must lie and 'fake' their own illnesses if they do not want to leave their sick children alone.

Thus, the procedure for obtaining a sick-leave certificate entitling workers to draw benefit from the social security system is clearly spelled out in Czechoslovakia (as well as in other East European countries). However, its manifest emphasis on productivity and the minimisation of absenteeism clearly limits the primary care physician's professional autonomy in granting certification for illness longer than the officially specified number of days. Pancurák (1973) claims that 9 per cent of all lost workdays are due to gynaecological/ obstetrical reasons, but Kliment (1973) points out that these statistics on reproductive work disability are often inflated. For example, if a pregnant woman suffers from a 'normal' disease such as flu, her work disability will still be classified under the heading of 'complications during pregnancy'.

Enterprise gynaecologists, who are responsible for issuing medical certificates for absence from work due to reproductive illness, are also expected to ensure adequate health conditions in the workplace. As Sittková (1979, p. 637), a woman plant gynaecologist argues:

in the course of enlisting women for economic activity, the state ensures that suitable working conditions are in place. Our state declares that women be assigned only to such workplaces which do not threaten their health and their mission as mothers. The certificate activity of an enterprise gynaecologist ensures that this is observed in practice. It is also still necessary to secure required social and hygienic facilities not only in the large but also in the smaller enterprises. A gynaecological examination is therefore an integral part of general medical examination of women entering work. During the examination the gynaecologist has to give some thought to the possibility of harmful effect of the work environment on the woman. The most important task for us enterprise gynaecologists – arising out of the conclusions of the XV Party Congress – is the prevention of both obstetrical and gynaecological illnesses of employed women. The struggle against tumour diseases is also in the forefront of our attention.

However, as noted in the preceeding chapter, both employers and women workers often exhibit negative attitudes towards obstetrical prevention, such as transfers to easier work during pregnancy. Twenty-two per cent of women workers in agriculture, culture and health care, and 10 per cent of women workers over-all, engage in work forbidden by the protective labour code during pregnancy and within nine months of giving birth. Moreover, in 9 per cent of the cases, the non-transfer to easier work is requested by the women themselves. We also noted an opposite problem, involving an abuse of the protective legislation. Some pregnant women who are relocated to easier work during their pregnancy work so poorly that employers (although in some cases it could easily be the women themselves) put pressure on plant gynaecologists to declare the women as 'disabled for work' altogether.

The professional autonomy of practising physicians is also circumscribed by their position in the occupational hierarchy and by professional segmentation. Primary care physicians typically have less autonomy than ward or hospital chiefs, who in turn have less autonomy than medical administrators (themselves physicians) who tend to initiate the previously cited 'range of bureaucratic regulations, orders, and warnings'. Modelled again 'on the principles, experiences and achievement of the Soviet health care system', the administration of the health care system in Czechoslovakia is set up as a bureaucratic pyramid with a series of administrative levels serving as transmission belts for orders, directives and policies from the top down, and transmission of reports, questions and requests from the bottom up (Field, 1957, p. 31). With few exceptions, the entire health service is centralised under the federal and the two national ministries of health.[11] The top–down approach is clearly evident if we examine the role of the department of care for mother and child within the then single national Ministry of Health (Jerrie *et al.*, 1961, p. 11):

> The department lays out the main norms for the national committee's plan and controls its fulfilment by territorial check-ups as well as by the analysis of qualitative indicators and statistical data. It gives expert opinion about the standard of care, the suitability of medical and other supplies, e.g. machines, instruments and drugs used in women's care. It disposes of complaints.

The department of care for mother and child was abolished in 1971 and its responsibilities were transferred to a newly-created department (in existence to this date) of care for the new generation. In turn, this new department was incorporated into the department of medical–preventive care, despite the objections of several members of the advisory committee to the 'chief specialist' (obstetrics/gynaecology) of the Slovak Ministry of Health. The objections were for the most part not against the re-naming of the department, but against the seeming downgrading of maternity care within the health care system as a whole (Sochor, 1971).

The so-called 'chief specialist' is a full-time administrative official of the national Ministry of Health, who is 'responsible for the expert direction and the improvement of standards of individual medical branches' (*Zdravotnictví ČSR, 1945–1980*, 1980, p. 18). Not every medical specialty has its chief specialist within the ministry, but obstetrics/gynaecology has one.[12] His/her role is defined as follows (Jerrie, 1961, p. 11):

> He/she is involved in the planning of the development of the care of women, based on existing principles of its organisation, and influences the orientation of research in the discipline. As an ex-officio member of the Scientific Collegium of the Ministry of Health [composed of all chief specialists], he/she also cooperates with the gynaecological-obstetrical section of J. E. Purkyně Association [the official medical association in Czechoslovakia, established in 1952], as well as with research institutes. He/she is helped in the fulfilment of his/her tasks by an advisory body of practising physicians.

The chief specialist also cooperates with officially designated district or regional specialists. Their role is much more circumscribed than that of their boss, as is evident in the following outline of their responsibilities (Poradovský, 1977a, p. 191):

> Regional and district specialists must be exemplary in the fulfil-ment of new tasks and in the introduction of new diagnostic procedures. They have to be enthusiastic pioneers of better work results and strict critics of ascertained inadequacies. They take up the problems of obstetrical prevention in district or regional semi-nars and in their analysis of perinatal and neonatal mortality. They draw appropriate conclusions and implement in practice agreed-upon measures. By the means of systematic expert controls of appropriate departments in institutions and ambulatory facilities they regulate their activities and depending on established defects, rectify them.

Party membership is normally a requirement for these positions of authority and responsibility in the administration of health services, though this is usually not necessary for the more directly medical work (as opposed to administrative 'paper work') of chiefs of hospital departments.

In theory, the officially designated specialists, especially those at the regional and national levels, play a considerable role in the centralised planning of health care. However, in practice, their influence is limited by the central economic plan, which not only specifies the over-all budget for health care services but also provides detailed spending norms within that budget. As Millard (1981, p. 64) has argued for Poland (an argument that applies to Eastern Europe as a whole):

> this encourages a kind of medical departmentalism, with each specialty vying for scarce resources. The linchpin of the advisory committee should be the province's specialist in health organisa-tion, but in practice s/he can be easily by-passed, either by direct appeal to the Provincial Physician or by appeal to the Regional or National Specialist in the particular sphere. The same kind of lobbying for access to decision-making by highly compartmental-ized specialists appears to operate at the national level, where the Committee of National Specialists is buttressed by the prestigious National Institutes which exist for some specialties. Thus the complex advisory system reflects the highly specialised orientation of the health service as a whole . . . As it stands, the position

appears to be (roughly speaking) that the specialists and the provincial departments lobby the ministry on their own behalf for their existing resources plus whatever more they can get, while the ministry lobbies the Planning Commission of the Council of Ministers on the same basis.

Given this strong in-built tendency towards medical segmentation, the objections of some of the members of the advisory committee to the Slovak chief specialist of obstetrics/gynaecology to the reorganisation and seeming downgrading of maternity care are therefore easy to understand. Given the scarcity of resources, the incorporation of a previously autonomous department with its own budget into a larger department with broader responsibilities naturally indicates potential loss of power and influence of obstetrics/gynaecology *vis-à-vis* other specialties. This fear was recognised even by the Slovak Ministry of Health officials, who went out of their way to publicly assure obstetricians (in an article published in their professional journal) that the department of care for the new generation would remain an influential department within the ministry and that the initial experiences with the reorganisation were very positive (Brucháč and Sochor, 1972). Similarly, Dr Štipal (1972, p. 556), the Czech Deputy Minister of Health, emphasised (in the course of his evaluation of the 1971–5 Five-Year Plan) that the care of women in socialist Czechoslovakia remains a 'preferred' sphere of health care. As evidence, he cited the Plan's 30 per cent budgetary increase for women's health care, compared to a 'mere' 17 per cent increase for general medicine.

However, one should add that in all the East European countries, the Ministry of Health lacks any real bargaining power *vis-à-vis* other, more 'productive' ministries, reflecting the low priority assigned to the service sector, of which health care forms an integral part. The prevailing strategy for industrialisation in Eastern Europe has placed a heavy emphasis on increasing stocks of capital goods, with the result that the 'preferred' industrial occupations (e.g. mining and steel), largely dominated by men, have been allocated more resources for investment and wages than the 'non-preferred' service sector. Compared to the Western capitalist countries, the proportion of GNP allocated for health care in Eastern Europe has been rather low, although there are significant variations among the individual capitalist and socialist countries. While, in the mid-1950s, advanced capitalist countries tended to spend 4 per cent of their national resources on health care, some of the poorer Eastern European countries did not reach these levels even twenty years later. In 1968–73, Bulgaria, Romania and also the Soviet Union spent only 2.4–2.8 per cent of their GNPs on health care. In contrast, the GDR, Czechoslovakia, Hungary and Poland spent 4.8–5.7 per cent of their GNPs on health care, a proportion which is comparable to that of Great Britain. In the meantime, total expenditures on health care (measured as a percentage of GDP[13]) in 1975 in Australia, Italy, Canada and Switzerland had risen to 7–7.3 per cent and in the Netherlands, France, Sweden and the United States to 8.1–8.7 per cent. West Germany even spent 9.4 per cent of its GDP on health care. Moreover, only two years later, in 1977, Sweden, West Germany and the United States were spending 9–10 per cent of their GNP on health care, while other Western countries spent typically between 6.4 and 8.2 per cent. Only Great Britain was substantially below these levels, at 5.2 per cent, which is again comparable to the levels of some of the wealthier East European countries. In 1982, Canada was spending 8.4 per cent and the United States 10.5 per cent of its GNP on health care (Kaser, 1976, p. 33, Maxwell, 1981, pp. 30, 41, *National Health Care Expenditures in Canada, 1970–1982*, pp. 31, 41).

While spending on health care was a subject that attracted little international interest twenty years ago, the sharp, continuing rise in health care expenditures in Western capitalist countries throughout the 1970s has led to a new interest in the subject. In 1979, no fewer than six international conferences and seminars were organised to discuss the topic, with further international discussions having taken place since (Abel-Smith, 1981, p. xi). The continued rapid growth of health care spending in the West is generally attributed to the following six main causes: (1) demographic changes, especially ageing population; (2) related shift of diseases towards chronic illnesses, coupled with an increased awareness and concern about psychiatric illness; (3) advances in (typically expensive) medical technology and drugs; (4) rising public and professional expectations of medical treatment, coupled with increased reliance on formal health services (as opposed to informal coping mechanisms in the family and the community); (5) higher wages and salaries of health care personnel; and (6) a transfer of financing from direct payment by individuals to insurance schemes and/or government, resulting (for most part) in the removal of the barrier to access for those who could not previously afford to pay (Maxwell, 1981, pp. 38–45).

While some of these factors also operate in Eastern Europe, others have been less significant, accounting for the lower levels of total expenditure for health care (5 per cent of GNP or less). For example, expenditures for sophisticated medical technology and drugs are relatively low, as are individual salaries of doctors and nurses. While in the United States, the average doctor makes 3–4 times more than the average wage earner, in Eastern Europe *official* salaries of physicians have been below or similar to skilled industrial workers. (Unofficial salaries are considerably higher, as we shall see below.) However, as Knaus (1981, pp 333–4) points out, 'this low earning scale for physicians in the USSR compared to that of the United States is one factor making a comparison of exact budgets between countries extremely difficult. Referred to as the index number problem, it recognizes that countries like the Soviet Union tend to use more of those resources that are relatively cheap – in this case physician services – rather than those that are expensive, like drugs and medical technology.' Knaus (1981, p. 337) also notes the significant financial implications of the current socialist system of singling out industrial workers as a 'preferred' group in the provision of health care:

> Fortunately young workers [including expectant mothers] are, on average, the least expensive portion of the population to keep healthy. In the United States we spend only $286 each year on medical care for each person under age nineteen and $764 for a person between the ages of nineteen and sixty-four, compared to $2,026 for each person over sixty-five . . . The fact that the United States has made the commitment to provide full services to the elderly is a major reason our medical costs have increased. In just two years, 1976 to 1978, Medicare's total costs went from $16 to $22 billion. Much of that increase (70 per cent) went for hospital treatment where open-heart surgery, kidney dialysis, and other high-cost technologies were provided, services unavailable to most Soviet patients.[14]

Moreover, as a general rule, in Eastern Europe certain complicated surgeries are simply not performed once a person reaches retirement age (of course, with the exception of special party clinics), demonstrating again the priority assigned to maintaining the health of 'productive' workers, children and expectant mothers. An internal comparison of demographic and medical expenditures is even more revealing in this respect. While the total costs of the health care system in Czechoslovakia in 1971 amounted to 13.2 billion crowns, the total cost of population measures (including related social welfare measures) was 20.4 billion crowns. There is an overlap of about 0.5 billion crowns in costs of creches, but this fact does not distort the basic comparison (Frejka, 1980, pp. 70–1, 92). In the absence of available data on the subject, one can only leave to speculation whether or not this indicates that the collective power of demographers to influence policy is greater than that of physicians. All one can say is that while the decline in mortality (infant and otherwise) is seen as contributing in one way or another to a desired population growth pattern, this decline is not perceived to be as important as the optimisation of births. In turn, this official perception might be reflected in the allocation of resources at the central level.[15]

To sum up, the state, through central planning, influences both the definition of medical needs (e.g. reproduction of labour power, including generational reproduction) and the organisational framework of services to meet them. The state exercises tight budgetary control over official medical facilities, technologies, drugs and salaries and a high degree of administrative power over health norms and standards. However, the latter is typically planned by a handful of 'powerful' doctors, the so-called chief specialists. Thus while the sum total of the (financial) resources available to the health services is determined outside the medical sphere by politicians and central planners, the allocation of these resources within the health services is controlled by physicians themselves. 'Moreover', as De Kadt (1982, p. 746) notes, 'the phenomenon exists in non-capitalist countries as much as in capitalist ones.'

Apart from strongly influencing the nature of clinical practice, doctors have also played a prominent role in medical education, which in turn constitutes the basis of their professional credentials and licence to practice. Until 1977, professors at individual medical faculties were able both to design their curriculum and to publish their own cyclostyled textbooks (called student scripts). However, this particular form of control over their work conditions, which incidentally characterised all the other academic disciplines as well, has now been lost. Following the adoption of the 11 March 1977 Party Document entitled 'The Tasks Confronting Universities after the 15th Congress of the CP', which initiated a 'major conceptual overhaul' of higher education (Jeník, 1980, p. 47–8), the Ministry of Education introduced a mandatory nationwide unified curriculum for all academic disciplines. All textbooks are now produced centrally, by a Ministry of Education designated group of prominent university scholars in the discipline. Uniform medical textbooks were available for some specialties in 1980, and after 1985 all subjects of medical study will be required to use the same centrally-produced texts (Jarolímek, 1980, 1982). However, this recent loss of work autonomy of individual professors of medicine is probably more a reflection of the tightening of state control over education (of which medical training is a part), than of increasing state control over medicine. Generally speaking, when compared to professional educators, practitioners of medicine have a much greater degree of work autonomy.

Moreover, the 'medicalisation' of public discourse on matters relating to birth control, pregnancy and childbirth, has proceeded further in Eastern Europe than in the West. While in the politically pluralistic West the dominant medical perspective is never absolutely dominant, because alternatives can be, and often are, presented (witness the efforts of the women's health movement), such freedom to publish criticism simply does not exist in Eastern Europe, where the Communist Party maintains monopoly of power and doctrine. As De Kadt (1982, p. 747) has argued, 'unanticipated or undisclosed costs of supposedly beneficial policies do not get highlighted as long as these policies retain official sanction. Only after the party leadership has changed the party line, can such negative effects be recognised, in retrospect, as "errors".' Thus the political climate in Eastern Europe favours the medical (as opposed to feminist) structuring of reproductive discourse and/or individual reproductive experience. For example, some negative features of modern birthing technologies (e.g. loss of bodily control for labouring women who are attached to foetal monitors) do not get properly highlighted, because (1) the medical profession considers these features as relatively unimportant and (2) consumers are in no position to raise and debate the issue.

As we shall see in Chapters 8–11, new policies, (e.g. the menstrual regulation technique of abortion, psycho-prophylaxis, rooming-in), are normally introduced as a result of professional rather than consumer initiative. Thus in this respect the medical profession in Eastern Europe appears to be more powerful than its counterpart in the West; its ideology and practice cannot be easily challenged by organised consumer groups. In the West, peer self-help groups have become an alternative source of information, social support and therapeutic resources, providing ideas and strategies for coping that can be integrated into the member's everyday living (Suller, 1984, p. 29). These mutual help or support groups are based on the premise that a person can best be helped by another who has been through or is currently experiencing a similar situation. The self-help groups are typically non-hierarchical and involve face-to-face interaction of all members of the group who meet regularly in order to provide mutual aid. Lipson (1981, p. 27) makes a useful distinction between 'groups organised to help their members cope with a long-term problem, such as a chronic health condition or a noxious habit, and those organised to support their members during a life or role transition.' Groups such as Alcoholics Anonymous, Weight Watchers, and for the blind, people with hypertension and so on, are of the first type, while the home-birth movement, Caesarean support groups and La Leche League are of the second type.

Another important distinction is between peer self-help groups that challenge medicine's assumptions and those that do not. Riessman (1983, p. 13) notes that many self-help groups share medicine's disease orientation towards particular human problems, such as weight. Since Weight Watchers or Overeaters Anonymous consider being fat as primarily a medical problem, they do not demedicalise human problems but rather medicalise them under lay auspices. In contrast, La Leche League 'presented an alternative model of infant care and parenting, one that emphasized "mother-wisdom" at the same time that it pointed out flaws in medical knowledge. These ideas became an important part of the ideology of the home-birth movement.' Rothman (1982, pp. 107–8) also points out that unlike prepared childbirth groups:

> La Leche League has not been co-opted by the medical establishment. They have not accepted the medical model, nor have they found places for themselves in the medical establishment. League leaders are all volunteers, unlike ASPO[16] teachers who are paid for their time. . .
>
> Baby care is potentially more resistant to medicalization than is childbirth, for a number of reasons. Infant feeding is not a 'crisis' situation, and it is difficult to invoke the 'life or death' drama one can call up for childbirth. Weight is gained or not gained over time; disagreeing with the doctor does not threaten a mother with the imminent loss of her baby's life. In childbirth, a medical procedure can be phrased as being for the life/health of the baby, and whether or not that has basis in fact, the mother is in no position to determine.

'Lay' peer self-help groups which directly challenge the dominant medical ideology and practice are extremely rare in Eastern Europe, but they do exist. For example, the Czech Association for the Blind, which belongs to the official Union of Invalids, apparently disregards the common practice of doctors to keep secret from patients going blind the full extent of their diagnosis.[17] Members of the Association, who are themselves blind, regularly go during visiting hours to appropriate hospitals to seek out patients with a relevant ophthalmological condition, disclose to them the full diagnosis, and offer the help of the Association to deal with the condition. More common are self-help groups coopted by the medical establishment. Robinson (1981, p. 188) describes the operation of one such organisation, the club for hypertensives in Zagreb, Yugoslavia, as follows:

> Doctors encourage their hypertensive patients to join clubs in their neighbourhood. At fortnightly club meetings, which last for about an hour, all the members have their blood pressure measured by one of their number who has been trained to do this. A nurse is the main day-to-day adviser to the club and is always present at the meetings; she teaches members to read blood pressure, makes occasional checks on those who are doing the measuring, and answers general queries about problems or procedures. After all the measurements have been made, the last half of the meeting is devoted to a lecture on some aspect of hypertension by one of the general practitioners from the local health centre, to a discussion of some member's particular problem, or to a visit from an outsider who talks about some issue connected with hypertension, such as nutrition and diet, exercise, smoking, or relaxation techniques.

Robinson (1981, p. 188) also points out that 'there is more to dealing with most health problems than disseminating information and handling practicalities. For some people a major difficulty is not the particular problem, but the fact that they are the people with the problem. An important function of many self-help groups, therefore, is to disperse the social discreditability of the shared problem.' The Czech voluntary Association for the Aid for the Mentally Handicapped, which counts among its members both affected persons and volunteer helpers (including several doctors), performs such a function. The Association, which receives neither the backing nor any funds from the National Front (an umbrella organisation of political parties, trade unions and various voluntary associations), nonetheless meets regularly and has organised various leisure activities, such as dances, swimming, theatre visits and two-week holidays in an enterprise holiday facility in the mountains of Northern Bohemia. While bringing people in the same situation together may succeed in changing their negative self-perceptions, there is no evidence that the group has made any impact on the cause of the stigma attached to the mentally handicapped – the prejudiced attitudes of outsiders. Moreover, there is no association for single parent families in Czechoslovakia, despite the high divorce rate (approximately 20 per 100 marriages) and the demonstrated ubiquity and significant therapeutical potential of such groups elsewhere. According to the Director of the British National Council for One Parent Families, the organisation has 'a double value to lone parents and their children in providing the mutual support that is so helpful to them and also helping the children to have a real social identity by realizing that there are many lone parents and the children are, therefore, not in any way unusual' (quoted in Robinson, 1981, p. 188). Peer self-help groups providing short-term emotional and information support to basically healthy women who anticipate or who have experienced various reproductive problems also do not exist. In other words, there are no Czech equivalents to the Boston Women's Health Collective (the authors of the now famous feminist health publication *Our Bodies, Ourselves*), the Canadian feminist health quarterly magazine *Healthsharing*, the de-centralised Caesarean support groups in the USA or the previously cited La Leche League. As we shall see in more detail in Chapters 7–11, personal 'troubles' and 'public issues' arising out of difficult experiences with birth control, pregnancy, childbirth and breastfeeding are under undisputed medical monopoly in Czechoslovakia.

INDIVIDUAL PATIENTS AND DOCTORS: THE ISSUE OF TIPPING

The hierarchy of status between doctors, nurses and patients (in that order) is rather pronounced in Eastern Europe. As Millard (1981, p. 61) argues (on the basis on Polish data):

> if the nursing staff are by and large viewed as servants of the physicians, the patients themselves are in a far worse position as the hapless objects of medical attention. Of course this attitude is no monopoly of Polish doctors; but it does seem particularly

pronounced. . .Certainly at present there is virtually no concept of a doctor – patient partnership (with the exception of a few isolated voices, mainly those of medical sociologists). Patients are cases to be dealt with; they are the passive recipients of the treatment and organization manipulated by the experts. Indeed, when a patient does ask about a drug or method of treatment s/he may have read or heard about, the request is regarded as inappropriate or even mischievous. A similar viewpoint is manifested in the attitude of hospitals to patients' families kept out on the grounds that they are disruptive or even dirty. Visiting hours are non-existent on some wards and very limited on most. Families are not always informed about the true condition of the patient. Doctors not only do not always explain, but they sometimes tell deliberate lies to patients and their families in cases which they regard as incurable or doubtful.

A similar situation also exists in the other socialist countries in Eastern Europe. Deacon (1983, p. 86) writes as follows about Hungary:

Although the status of doctors is lower than in the West in terms of their collective power to influence policy, their status *vis-à-vis* their patients is not that different. There is no deprofessionalization in that sense, and patients still acknowledge their traditional 'respect' for members of the profession by payment for services rendered in the same way as in Russia. Two thousands forints, half the average women's monthly salary, is the going rate for delivery.

Tipping of medical and nursing personnel is also widespread in Czechoslovakia, despite official disapproval of the practice. Kops (1981, p. 514), a Slovak sociologist, is critical of the official response to the phenomenon:

A great deal of systematic attention is paid to the struggle with bribery in health care, both in ideological–educational work and from the administrative–legal viewpoint.[18] So far this work has been based only on traditional assumptions and individual cases (e.g. an individual complaint); a deeper analysis of underlying conditions has so far not been attempted. While researching this problem is a delicate issue, we are nonetheless convinced that in the context of a broader framework, for example in the context of research of satisfaction with the provision of health care services, this problem can be studied as objectively as any other question from the area of public opinion.

Interestingly enough, Prokopec (1975, p. 178), the current Czech Minister of Health, demonstrates a good grasp of some of the variables accounting for medical bribery:

> Society gives a physician exceptional rights, because a doctor many a time literally decides about life and death. The public wants to be assured that the physician will always act *lege artis*, without personal, let alone profitable elements entering his/her decision. The modern system of health care does not allow citizens to choose their own attending physician or health facility. Instead the socialist state guarantees that everyone will always and everywhere receive care at the highest possible standard, that he/she will be treated according to the current knowledge of medical science, and that health care services will be equally accessible to everyone everywhere. This is also the main and fully justified reason, why society categorically condemns any kind of effort to obtain real or imaginary advantages in curative or preventive care, although it is willing to consider almost as a matter of course for somebody who wants to obtain goods in short supply or various services, especially repair services, a resort to bribes.

Lay deference to professional expertise in matters of life and death, a patient's inability to choose his/her physician, the uneven provision and lack of quality of the given service, and the institutionalisation of the parallel (or shadow) economy into the socialist economic system, have also been identified as explanatory variables elsewhere. For example, Ferge (1979, p. 292), the renowned Hungarian sociologist, argues as follows:

> Free choice [of doctors] is not accepted because, given the socially unequal distribution of knowledge and information on the one hand, of medical services on the other, there cannot be genuine free choice,[19] and also because it might lead to bottlenecks. The lack of free choice leads, however, to various other problems. The patient may lack confidence in a doctor whom he did not choose. He will try, therefore, to establish a more personal relationship, and obtain more careful services by offering gifts, giving tips to the

doctor, or by looking for private paying consultations. These solutions are in blatant contradiction of the principle of a free health service.

Szalai (1981, p. 152–3), another Hungarian sociologist, explains tipping of medical staff primarily in terms of the 'extraordinary and lasting over-use of the system, that does not permit any improvement in standards':

> The main current problem is a double one: the quality of the services offered is deteriorating, while indices show an intensive and continuous growth of use; on the other hand the basic goal of the health services, equal treatment for all, is in danger. . . One of the typical arguments is that people have become lazy and indolent since the state guarantees them everything. They do not feel the burdens of operating the system and therefore do not value it properly. People go and see the doctor with minor troubles because it does not cost anything, etc. . . . Others look for scapegoats as reasons for disfunctions. Those who tip doctors, it is said, damage the moral integrity of the system. In order to re-establish morality and equal treatment for everybody, those who tip and those doctors who accept tips, ought to be punished. (In this argument a structural problem is handled in a purely moralistic way, proposing prosecution as a panacea.)

For Kemény (1982), a Hungarian economist living in exile in Paris, tipping is an integral part of the whole economic system, which he sees as being characterised by three parallel markets. In the 'official market', production and labour are converted into commodities with their price being centrally fixed; in the 'shadow market' the customer is not paying for extra activity or added investment, but instead he/she is paying an extra unofficial charge for activities carried out within the sphere of distribution; and in the 'real market', independent of the central planning, prices in the redistribution system are determined by bargaining. Tips to taxi drivers, waiters, mechanics, delivery men, 'sealed envelope gratuities' offered to nurses and doctors are part of the 'shadow market', where such gratuities are socially condoned and regarded as an 'inbuilt' part of the average salary. Thus unlike Prokopec, Kemény sees little difference in bribing a doctor or a repair man. In his view, the 'shadow market' serves to adjust the low salaries imposed by the central authorities. The extra income earned this way is normally used for buying consumer goods, such as a cottage, car, boat, and so on, irrespective of whether the recipient is a professional or a tradesman.[20]

In their analysis of the patient–doctor relationship, Parmelee *et al.* (1982, p. 1392) also interpret 'the giving of money or gifts to clinicians as "bribes", as something given by a patient to persuade or induce the clinician to do something the patient desires or simply as means to get around the "system" more easily'. However, the authors argue that, based on their observations in Yugoslavia, tips:

> can also serve the function of a gratuity; that is, something given without claim or demand on the part of the patient. Thus, despite the fact that their care was covered by health insurance, it was not uncommon for patients to give something to physicians or other workers out of gratitude for services provided. Whether this reflects some sort of underlying principle of reciprocity or merely another way to insure against future health needs is something which requires further study.

Millard (1981, p. 62) offers a somewhat similar argument, although her analysis of 'reciprocity' is more structural, since it is based on politico-economic variables:

> Individual corruption is easier to identify than social corruption. Bribery for personal gain appears quite widespread. There are, however, grey areas blurring these two categories. The dividing line between a 'tip' and a 'bribe' is not always easy to determine. More significant, the KOR report mentions and I have also observed the use of cognac as a medium of exchange: the cognac provided by grateful patients is stored not only for personal consumption but also to be used as a bribe for the local warehouse manager in times of acute shortages of essential materials. . . Thus the wards (or whatever) which have (say) cognac will be in an advantageous position *vis-à-vis* those which have little or none, even though their objective need (if such could be assessed) might in fact be less. Thus social corruption may result in a less optimum allocation of resources. In addition, social corruption both depends upon and fosters individual corruption, in this case that of the warehouse staff.

The distinction which Millard (1981, p. 61) draws between individual and social corruption is an important one, since 'not all "corrupt" behaviour can be regarded as dysfunctional or anti-social. To some extent it keeps the ramshackle health service functioning despite the chronic shortages and inadequacies. . . . Both types of behaviour are illegal, but the motivation behind social corruption is to ensure the continued performance of one's professional functions. Individual corruption, on the other hand, is motivated by personal gain or advantage.' Thus in the final analysis, Millard (1981, p. 61) is not all that critical of the medical profession:

> Perhaps, however, the medical profession provides too easy a target. It is important to note that they too are victims of the system and that their behaviour and attitudes are rooted deep in the social structure. The health service is an elitist and hierarchical element of an elitist and hierarchical society. It is not an island of high moral principles; it is a part of Polish society as a whole with its strengths and resilience as well as its weaknesses.

A similar view can also be found in some professional circles in Czechoslovakia. For example, a clinical psychologist who was interviewed characterised the doctor–patient relationship as a 'totalitarian' one, reflecting a 'totalitarian' society.[21] As in Poland, Czech patients are also generally regarded as 'hapless objects of medical attention' and 'there is virtually no concept of a doctor–patient partnership (with the exception of a few isolated voices)'. On the other hand, this does not mean that patients are unable to exercise any of their basic 'bourgeois freedoms'. Although Strong's argument (1979, pp. 210–11) is about Western capitalist societies, he could be easily writing about Eastern Europe:

> The state may have granted doctors a monopoly of practice in certain respects but it has given them almost no legal powers to constrain their patients' behaviour. It may be up to the doctor to decide whether or not patients should receive treatment, but the latter typically reserve the right to decide whether to seek it in the first place and, if offered it, whether or not to accept. Moreover, the belief in patients' rights in these matters is as central to many doctors as it is to patients themselves. . . The right to reject or never to seek it in the first place means that patients can exercise their scepticism, and although some undoubtedly do not, it is clear, as I have argued, that most patients' use of medicine is still too moderate to be called an addiction.

As far as 'bourgeois freedoms' within the medicalised reproductive care system are concerned, there are in evidence several contradictory features. On the one hand, state policies of providing free prenatal care tend to have a strong controlling effect on pregnant women, since expectant mothers do not have a real option of refusing medical antenatal care (unless they are individually willing to be labelled as deviant 'potential risks' and subjected to close monitoring by social workers). On the other hand, there is ample evidence to suggest that expectant mothers exercise their 'medical scepticism' rather frequently by refusing to follow medical 'expert' advice, even if such advice is of proven benefit to them. As we shall see in more detail in Chapter 9, actual sexual behaviour, nutrition and physical exercise during pregnancy diverge significantly from expert advice in these areas. Moreover, data on abortion presented in Chapter 8 suggest that only half of all women requesting a therapeutic abortion see their attending physician as an adviser on the issue; the other half tends to ignore the doctor's view, preferring to rely on advice from relatives, friends or co-workers. Such findings demonstrate definite limits to professional medical power over individual patients, especially if they are basically healthy, as reproducers generally are.

NOTES

1. A medical district is an administrative unit with 150 000–200 000 residents, who are served by polyclinics and hospitals of II type. A region has 1–1.5 million inhabitants, who are served by polyclinics and hospitals of III type, which offer highly specialised care. Clinics and hospitals of I type are generally found only in rural areas. In 1975, hospitals of I type accounted for 29 per cent of all hospital beds, (including maternity beds), but no expansion of these facilities with a limited number of medical specialties (4–13), including obstetrics, is planned for the future (Prokopec, 1975, pp. 58–9). While commentators from the socialist countries tend to emphasise the integration of the system, Western critics have highlighted its organisational fragmentation. Moreover, Millard (1981, p. 60) points out that the rationality of the division between community and industrial health centres is rarely questioned in Eastern Europe. In her view, this is so 'probably because of the ideological aura surrounding the provision of separate treatment of industrial workers and the somewhat suspect notion that prophylactic measures are more effective when undertaken by doctors familiar with particular work conditions'.
2. For books on the Soviet health care system, see Field (1957, 1967), Hyde (1974), Navarro (1977), Ryan (1978) and Knaus (1981). Kaser (1976,

pp. 36–92), George and Manning (1980, pp. 104–28) and Deacon (1983, pp. 70–80) each have a chapter on the subject.
3. It is worth pointing out that this kind of structuring of health care delivery is not confined to Eastern Europe. For example, the health care system in Israel is also characterised by an organisational separation between the clinic and the hospital services. As Shuval (1983, p. 128) argues, 'staff members of one generally have no role in the other. Although some changes have been introduced in the structure to eliminate this sharp differentiation, it continues to prevail in most of the medical care delivery system. This separation is problematic and results in duplication of expensive tests and disrupts continuity of medical care. No less important is the fact that it has resulted in a differentiation of status between professionals in the two settings and in a corresponding differentiation in quality of care: physicians practising in hospitals enjoy higher professional status and are generally thought to deliver higher quality care than their colleagues providing primary care in community clinics'.
4. This blueprint is compiled from Vojta (1971), Kotásek (1975) and K. Poradovsky (1977a).An evaluation of some of these goals is undertaken in Chapters 9–11.
5. This is a slightly lower proportion than that in medicine as a whole, where women comprise 40 per cent of the total (compared to 70 per cent in the USSR). As argued elsewhere (Heitlinger, 1979, pp. 149, 161), women doctors face a lot of problems not encountered by their male colleagues. Although the theoretical standards achieved by female medical students are often higher than those of their male counterparts, when it comes to clinical practice, it is the male doctor who is considered to be the more talented and skilful one. Patients tend to prefer and trust male doctors more than female ones. The latter are not so much appreciated for their expertise as for their 'human' (presumably 'maternal') approach to patients. Women doctors are further handicapped by their family duties, which prevent them from acquiring further qualifications and the more prestigeous and better paid hospital jobs. Slovak women doctors spend only two hours daily on further study, while their male colleagues can afford between three and ten hours a day. Thirty-one per cent of Slovak male doctors but only 10 per cent of female doctors acquire a specialist postgraduate qualification (the so-called first and second degree *atestace*) at the expected age of 34. The first degree *atestace* in obstetrics/gynaecology is obtained after a minimum of three years practice in the discipline, part-time attendance of a postgraduate course and passing of a relevant written examination. The second degree specialty is obtained after three subsequent years of clinical practice, study and another exam. For more information on the Czechoslovak system of postgraduate medical education, see Rödling (1980).
6. A large-scale preventive campaign against VD, especially syphillis, was launched in the early 1950s. Every person over the age of 14 was required by law to undertake a blood test to make sure that he/she was not affected by the disease. A failure to produce the relevant medical

certificate resulted in one's inability to obtain ration tickets. This proved
to be a strong enough incentive for most people to undergo the test,
which led to the treatment of many people who did not know that they
had the disease. The incidence of VD subsequently declined, though in
the 1960s, VD made a comeback. The incidence of VD tripled between
1960 and 1968 from 37.7 to 109.6 per 100 000 population, mainly on
account of gonorrhoea, which increased from 28.8 in 1966 to 104.1 in
1968 per 100 000 population. However, by 1974, the incidence of VD
levelled off to 101.9 per 100 000 population. The increase in the incidence of VD is officially blamed on sexual promiscuity and the lessening
of fear of the disease, which in turn is a result of its successful treatment
by antibiotics (Chalupský, 1984; Kaser, 1976, p. 121).

7. Medical sociology is much more developed in Poland, thanks largely to
the efforts of the prominent Polish woman sociologist, Magdalena Soko-
lowska. The Polish Academy of Sciences has a Department of Medical
Sociology and affiliated departments in several research institutes and
universities. In 1977, the British Medical Research Council (MRC) and
the Polish Academy of Sciences signed a five-year agreement to promote
and facilitate scientific cooperation in medical sociology. The agreement
was mainly concerned with exchange of staff, but it also provided for
alternate joint meetings in Warsaw and Aberdeen. For an account of the
first of these symposia, held at the Jablona Palace near Warsaw, 13–20
May 1978, see Taylor (1979). The symposium was attended by nine
sociologists from the MRC Medical Sociology Unit in Aberdeen and a
similar number of Polish medical sociologists.

8. According to Parmeggiani (1982, p. 279), industrial medicine in Western
Europe is characterised by frequent external hampering or interference
from the management or the state. However, Shuval (1983, pp. 60, 58)
argues that 'conflicted loyalty between the welfare of the state and the
individual's health is hardly sensed by the Israeli physician whose professional orientation is entirely focused on the latter'. In her view, primary
care physicians in Israel are guided by their own professional judgments
and their dominant concern is the individual patient's health and welfare. With the possible exception of army physicians, there is
little institutionalised societal pressure to counter these criteria of decision-
making. The predominant concern of physicians in Israel is not to be
'exploited' or thought gullible by patients seeking such certification.
Their responsibility is therefore to their own professional standards and
to the patient's welfare.

9. As is evident from Table 12.10 in Chapter 12, sickness benefits and
various other forms of social security constitute an important component
of households' income in Czechoslovakia, currently comprising 22 per
cent of total per capita income.

10. In the Soviet Union, estimates of days lost due to illness range from 6 to
15 days per year; in Israel, the range is similar – from 10 to 15 days per
year (Shuval, 1983, p. 58).

11. Following the Soviet model, the health care services of the army and the
railways are outside the jurisdiction of the ministry of health, as are
medical and pharmaceutical faculties, enterprises producing medical

supplies and technology, and the review activity in social security (e.g. absenteeism from work). These activities and facilities are under the jurisdiction of corresponding ministries of defence, transport, industry and social security. Prior to 1969, when Czechoslovakia became a federal republic, there was only one national ministry of health.

12. Millard (1981, p. 64) claims that in Poland there are no officially-designated specialists in general medicine, 'yet this is the specialty, along with pediatrics and industrial medicine, of the primary care system'.

13. Gross Domestic Product (GDP) differs from Gross National Product (GNP) by the exclusion of net income from abroad. Total health care expenditures as a percentage of the two indicators in 1975 was the same in Australia, West Germay, Italy, Netherlands, Sweden and the UK; for the other four Western countries, total health care expenditures as a proportion of GNP was 0.1–0.3 higher than as a percentage of GDP.

14. However, what may be true of the United States may not apply elsewhere. As Strong (1979, p. 206) notes, 'capitalism comes in many guises and, although there is an important sense in which one can talk of a general style of Welfare State capitalism, the extent of working-class power and thus the extent to which control is exercised over medicine, does vary significantly. In the United States the vague attempts to produce Welfare State medicine have merely served the financial interests of private medicine.' Strong (1979, p.208) also notes that while 'the American introduction of federal programs for the poor and the elderly has undoubtedly led to an exploitation of such resources by some doctors, the very fact of government intervention, however inept, has itself politicised medicine and led to demands for more systematic financial control'. Since the capitalist 'purse is not bottomless', Strong (1979, pp. 208–9) argues,' there is a growing emphasis on cost-effectiveness . . . This principle is already clearly at work in some of the areas which are supposed, by some, to be under threat of medicalisation and is in fact one of the principal barriers to any major expansion there . . . Review of British government policy statements concerning the elderly indicates that financial economy and the burden to the taxpayer which care for the elderly represents have been the predominant, if not the only, themes . . . There is little that can be done to prevent aging. Money spent in these areas has a relatively small return. Health administrators are only too well aware of the fact that there are millions of potential "patients" out there and this of course acts as a major deterrent to their medicalisation'. Moreover, as we noted in Chapter 2, the existence of a demographic need does not in itself guarantee that it will be socially met since public expenditures on particular social services are also related to political pressures.

15. Wolchik (1983, pp. 122–3) has argued that disciplinary training and occupational affiliation are often not as important as informal, *ad hoc* coalitions of various experts and members of the political elite in the formulation of particular socialist policy perspectives. In her study of demographic debates in Czechoslovakia from the 1950s on, Wolchik found that experts with the same specialty often held opposing views on particular issues. For example, demographers were sharply divided on

the issue of how to best deal with the care of small children. Moreover, certain demographers opposed the employment of women with small children, thus coming close to a position shared by the majority of economists. However, Wolchik also points out that most demographers were in agreement on the use of positive incentives to encourage child-bearing and opposed restricting the grounds for abortion. In contrast, medical opinion on access to abortion was extremely divided, as we shall see in more detail in Chapter 8.

16. ASPO stands for the American Society for Psycho-prophylaxis in Ob-stetrics. As Rothman (1983, pp. 91–2) argues, 'from its inception, ASPO has been geared to the American hospital and the American way of birth. The only challenge ASPO offered to the American birth con-cerned the use of anesthesia. ASPO substituted psychological for phar-macological control of pain . . . This certainly poses no threat to the control of birth by obstetricians . . . Even more basically, ASPO ac-cepted the medical model's separation of childbirth from the rest of the maternity experience, stating in this first manual that rooming-in (mother and baby not being separated) and breast feeding are "entirely separate questions from the Lamaze method." ASPO thus managed to meet on the one hand the demand of women for a "natural" childbirth and, on the other, the demand of obstetricians for "good medical management".'

17. The widespread medical practice to withhold from patients and their families the full knowledge of their medical condition(s), especially in cases which doctors regard as incurable, is based on the paternalistic ideology of not 'unnecessarily' disturbing or upsetting the patient, who is deemed to be emotionally incapable of dealing with the knowledge of the full extent of his/her disease.

18. Some ward chiefs have pursued the 'struggle against bribery' rather vigorously, while others have reacted only formally, by posting notices that doctors in socialist society serve the people, are paid by the state and do not accept tips. However, I was told of one labour and delivery ward where physicians are not allowed to attend any individual woman in labour for more than four hours, on the grounds that a patient is less likely to tip if there is more than one doctor involved in managing her labour and delivery. Some doctors have apparently found a way around this administrative restriction by inducing labours, which are then much faster (though much more painful) than labours which are allowed to proceed spontaneously for up to 12 hours or even longer. In either case, the outcome is detrimental to patient care. Women and doctors who neither expect nor receive any tips suffer from lack of continuity of care, while women whose labour was induced often experience greater pain and more health hazards (discussed in more detail in Chapter 10).

19. Strong (1979, p. 211) argues along similar, though greatly expanded lines: 'Whereas the British system minimizes choice of doctor for those who decide to seek treatment, the American system allows patients a very wide selection (though in practice this applies only to the rich) . . . However, not only may such choice be delusory . . . but the provision of choice, whatever its other advantages, is a clear incentive to medical imperialism . . . Although patients may have some general distrust of

doctors, they normally lack the knowledge to pass correct technical judgements on the wisdom of any one doctor. Nevertheless, they still make such judgements for what else can they do? . . . The private practice style is one in which the doctor subtly indicates his own individual merit, flatters patients by treating them as particularly promising medical students and congratulates them on having chosen so well . . . In such a pleasant ambience, it is only too easy for patients to be persuaded that they cannot be healthy unless they have regular checkups, nor sane unless they see a psychiatrist once a week. One can even come to believe that only payment demonstrates a proper commitment to analysis . . . Competitive private practice thus enforces product differentiation and creates disease where none existed before.'

20. A similar kind of 'convergence' between the professions and occupations related to 'servicing' of socially valued consumer durables (traditionally unrelated to the 'professions' as such) is also noted by Johnson (1972, pp. 89–90) in his pioneering sociological analysis of various forms of occupational control. Johnson argues that the key sociological questions in this area are the power resources available to occupational groups as well as other social groupings who may attempt to supervise the application of knowledge and skills to further their own or others' interests. Furthermore, Johnson speculates that the importance of consumer durables in a mass-consumption economy may encourage stronger consumer movements and the emergence of 'communalism' as a form of 'client' control over 'servicing' occupational practices. Since state-socialist economies are 'consumer-weak' and since independent consumer movements (i.e. separate from party-state control) are not allowed, 'client control' typically takes the form of individual 'tipping' of all practitioners providing services or goods which are socially desired and/or in short supply.

21. The analysis of state socialist societies as 'totalitarian' has been developed by Western political scientists who have studied the Soviet Union in association with a significantly different political system, namely Nazi Germany. In the context of the Cold War, the concept of totalitarianism acquired a strong, for some an ineradicable, bias against the Communist system, thus making it a useless analytical tool in scholarly discussions. As Brown (1984, pp. 55–6) points out, in the 1960s the concept was sometimes discarded for the wrong reasons. Brown claims that 'the term "totalitarianism" is increasingly used by Soviet and East European scholars in official publications (though not with reference to the Soviet Union and Eastern Europe). It was also used by Trotsky in exile about Stalin's Russia, and it has been used to describe the contemporary Soviet Union and Eastern Europe by many former prominent East European Communists now living in the West. The concept is not, in other words, the exclusive property of any one section of the political spectrum.'

6 Socialist Nursing

In Jablonna village I had a brief conversation (through a Polish colleague) with a middle-aged woman who was busy weeding cucumbers. She had been a nurse but had left nursing for market gardening where she was now earning four times as much as she did as a nurse, and three times more than my highly qualified, but poorly paid Polish colleague. (Taylor, 1979, p. 293)

The women's nurse (who has replaced the midwife) is usually the first worker in the Czechoslovak health care system with whom a pregnant woman seeking prenatal consultation comes into contact. What qualifications is the nurse likely to have? What is the organisational blueprint of *her* work (she is invariably a woman) and how does it compare to the reality of her work situation? What are the differences between the work environments of the clinic and the hospital? As mentioned in the previous chapter, there is a clear distinction between ambulatory and hospital maternity care in the socialist countries and women's nurses, like obstetricians, rarely work simultaneously in both settings.

OCCUPATIONAL JURISDICTION

Nurses (general, paediatric and women's) belong to the category of 'middle-level' health care workers, which also includes physiotherapists, hygienic assistants, opticians as well as X-ray, pharmaceutical and dental laboratory technicians. The term 'middle-level' reflects an occupational requirement for specialised 'middle-level' education, which is acquired at specialised four-year high schools. General, paediatric and women's nurses do not have to work solely in their specialties, though a district women's nurse or labour and delivery nurse has to be formally qualified as a women's nurse. Similarly, nurses employed at neonatal intensive care units have to be specialised paediatric nurses, as do day care or nursery school teachers, who

112

are responsible for the care of children aged 0–3. All general or women's nurses who work as paediatric nurses are required to complete a special course in child psychology and pedagogy. While nursery schools are also under the jurisdiction of the Ministry of Health, kindergartens, caring for children aged 3–6, are run by the Ministry of Education, which in turn is also responsible for the training of kindergarten teachers as well as doctors.

A recent compendium of Czechoslovak social medicine and organisation of health services describes the job content of women's nurses as follows:

A women's nurse works in hospital and ambulatory women's departments. Her work content is basically similar to the activity of a general nurse. However, in addition she performs numerous tasks arising out of the specialty of obstetrics and gynaecology.

A women's nurse leads gymnastics for pregnant and post-partum women as well as for women after gynaecological operations. She gives first aid during home births and if necessary accompanies the labouring woman to the women's department of a hospital with a polyclinic.

Unassisted she examines women with normal pregnancies. She prepares child-bearing women for birth and attends to them during all stages of labour and delivery as well as in post-partum. She performs deliveries under the direction of a physician, provides first care to the newborn and assists with obstetrical interventions.

A women's nurse prepares women for abortions and other gynaecological interventions and examinations. She assists during gynaecological intervention and insertion of various contraceptives. She nurses women after an operation.

A women's nurse is also obliged to undertake home visits to pregnant and post-partum women as well as women suffering from gynaecological illnesses. She follows their health status and gives advice about nutrition, preparation for childbirth and care of newborns. According to her qualification, she also gives contraceptive advice and helps to solve socio-health questions.

In connection with the prevention of gynaecological cancer, she organises preventive medical consultations. She also conducts health education, with special emphasis on nutrition during pregnancy, psycho-prophylaxis of birth, questions of sex education and education for parenthood. (Makovický *et al.*, 1981, pp. 661–2)

Nurses are also encouraged to read specialist literature, which provides information about new developments in their fields and suggests ideal norms for their work. For example, a Slovak woman psychologist, writing in a recent issue of the national nursing journal, *Zdravotnická pracovnice* ('A Woman Health Worker'), informs the reader that the work of a women's nurse:

> requires solid knowledge about good functioning of the family, about the ethics of partners' relations, about the great importance of good mutual emotional relationship, about the upbringing of children as well as about harmonious sex life of spouses in marriage. (Horáková, 1982, p. 46)

Are nurses in Czechoslovakia sufficiently qualified to provide that kind of information? Furthermore, and more importantly, does their work situation allow them to offer such professional advice? In other words, to what extent do the existing legal and professional ideologies of nursing correspond to actual practice? Published research on this topic is rather minimal, but the information that is available is not very encouraging. As we shall see below, much of nurses' work is related to basic nursing care rather than to the more psychologically-oriented ideal.

Compared to the pre-socialist period, nursing in Czechoslovakia has been expanded, specialised and upgraded, but this development is characteristic for most developed as well as Third World societies. The current nurse/patient ratio in Czechoslovakia is 1:127, which compares very favourably with Western ratios, as does the ratio of nurses to doctors, which in 1968 was 1:27, compared to 1:64 in 1949 (Kaser, 1976, p. 128; *Zdravotnictví ČSR, 1945–1980*, 1980, p. 46). However, this favourable development has been somewhat offset by a significant decline in the number of nursing assistants. Their numbers decreased from 19 107 in 1960 to a low point of 7166 in 1970, followed by an increase to 11 343 in 1979, reflecting largely better (or at least fluctuating) employment opportunities elsewhere. Makovický (1981, p. 222) also mentions increasing mechanisation, a proposition that we shall see is somewhat debatable. The nursing assistants who enter this employment are often of Romany (Gypsy) origin and apparently work quite irregularly and unreliably (Holubová, 1981). What this means is that nurses have to perform considerable menial work, for which they are over-qualified. This situation is unlikely to change in the foreseeable future. Only 1.6 per cent of all nurses take the two-year course for nursing assistants. Eighty per cent graduate from the four-year secondary specialised nursing schools and the remainder obtain their nursing licence in special two-year nursing courses for high school graduates (Tenčl, 1980).

HOSPITAL NURSES

The difficult situation of hospital nurses was critically commented upon at the 1977 national meeting of women trade union officials as follows:

> A general shortage of health assistant personnel necessarily leads to a situation in which nurses have to add to their duties menial work. Minimal cleanliness around the patient has to be kept under any circumstances. The situation is even more complicated in very old buildings, where even available assisting personnel connot take advantage of mechanisation, thus being forced to still rely only on a bucket and a rag while performing janitorial work. Similarly, the system of moving food to patients is very primitive in our facilities. A modern supply of meals, when meals are divided according to individual patients already in the kitchen, as well as central washing of dishes, would certainly greatly ease the work of women health care workers, even if the investment involved is costly. (*Celostátní aktiv*, 1977, p. 55)

This 'insider' view is supported by the research findings of 'external' observers, who all confirm that too much time is spent on 'basic nursing care', which is generally performed by nursing assistants in the West, and too little on specialised nursing. Two separate participant observation studies of the work structure of women's nurses in two district hospitals revealed that 35–38 per cent of worktime is devoted to 'basic nursing care', 10–20 per cent to documentation and only 36–42 per cent to 'specialised nursing care' (Kutěj and Hejná, 1972; Jersáková, 1972).

A better designed, more sophisticated research project by Prokopová (1974) conducted in fourteen randomly selected hospitals (which represented 8 per cent of all Czech hospitals), corroborated these findings. Moreover, this research also revealed that women's nurses and paediatric nurses tend to be worse off with respect to 'basic nursing care' than their colleagues in surgical and internal wards (see Table 6.1).

TABLE 6.1　Structure of worktime according to nursing specialties (%)

	Total	Internal medicine wards	Women's wards	Surgery	Paediatrics
Basic care	56	53	57	53	67
Specialist care	22	24	19	25	15
Documentation and organisation	17	17	18	19	15
Other activities	5	6	6	4	4

SOURCE　Prokopová, 1974, p. 545

A detailed observation of nurses' activities in the selected hospitals revealed that women's nurses spend twice as much time on basic hygiene and a third to a quarter less time on specialised tasks (e.g. giving drugs, using medical and nursing instruments) than nurses in the other wards. Slightly more time, comparatively speaking, was devoted to the watching of the physical and psychological state of patients and to health education, but over-all, the time devoted to these more professional activities is minimal among all nurses (see Table 6.2 for the detailed breakdown of typical nursing activities).[1]

What is particularly startling is how little time is devoted to talking to patients. The researchers found that nurses spent 7–12 minutes talking to individual patients in the morning and only 5–10 minutes in the afternoon, when the requirements for 'basic care' (i.e. making beds, helping with personal hygiene and so on) are generally fewer than in the morning. Moreover, women's nurses talk less (by a third!) to their patients than to other people with whom they come into contact during the course of their work (e.g. doctors, lab technicians, cleaners, cooks, patients' relatives). Prokopová concludes her article with the observation that hospital women's nurses are generally not interested in spontaneous contacts with women patients and thus do not actively seek them.[2] She also argues that much of the 'basic' nursing care could be performed by less qualified personnel, namely by nursing assistants. The question of where this less qualified personnel is going to come from, given the nearly universal employment of women, is not raised.

WOMEN'S NURSES IN CLINICS

Ideally, the work of a clinical women's nurse should be divided between home visits and seeing patients in the clinic (individually and

TABLE 6.2 *Direct and indirect patient care*

Activity	Internal surgical and obst/gyn wards combined		Obst/gyn ward only	
	Direct care (%)	Indirect care (%)	Direct care (%)	Indirect care (%)
I Basic health activities	17	37	22	35.5
Personal hygiene	7		10	
Basic tasks	4		4	
Nutrition care				
giving food	4		4.5	
Accompanying patients	2		4	
Other		37	4	35.5
II Specialised health				
activities	18	4.5	15.5	3.5
Assisting doctor	1.5		2	
Rounds	4		3	
Healing tasks	8		6	
Watching psychic & physical states of patients	1		1.5	
Taking urine samples	0.7		0.5	
Talking to patients unrelated to tasks	1.5		1.5	
Health education	0.5		1	
Other		4.5		4.5
III Documentation and organisation		18		17.6
IV Other		5		6
Total	35	65	37.5	62.5

SOURCE Prokopová, 1974, p. 546

in prenatal classes) (Bártová, 1972). However, in practice, work at the clinic takes preference, so that many pregnant women are not visited by women's nurses at all. There has been a decline in the number of home visits by women's nurses during the last two decades (*Statistiká ročenka ČSSR 1981*, p. 603).

This declining tendency of women's nurses to undertake home visits might be nonetheless welcomed by pregnant women. For example, many women of a sample of 300 women pregnant for the first time in

1977, who lived in Prague or surrounding rural areas, were critical of the home visit by a women's nurse, which they saw as useless and a waste of their own valuable time, let alone the nurse's (Trča, 1978). Bártová (1972), a sociologist, also questions the usefulness of home visits, though she is also critical of the nature of nurses' work at the clinic. So much of the nurse's time at the clinic is taken up by the filing of various forms (referred to in technical jargon as 'documentation'), that a meaningful instruction about pregnancy, birth, nutrition and hygiene, is next to impossible, with the result that pregnant women are generally poorly informed about their health, and, as we have seen in Chapter 3, prefer television to nurses as a source of information about reproduction.

Kliment *et al.* (1972b) discovered another dimension to the underutilisation of women's nurses in their investigation of the training of prenatal teachers. Among the 116 Bratislava women's nurses who took a special instructor's course in psycho-prophylaxis during 1967–72, only 17 (15 per cent) were able to use their new knowledge in their work. Doctors Augustín (1972), Šebek (1977), Kliment (1977) and others have argued that psycho-prophylaxis is generally neglected in the theory and practice of both medicine and nursing. Augustín (1972) also claims that each doctor has a different understanding of the meaning of the term. The advice offered is then so diverse that the whole concept of psycho-prophylaxis is discredited.

However, there has been renewed interest in prenatal education in recent years. In 1979, the Institute for Further Education of Middle-level Health Care Workers in Brno published a textbook for prenatal teachers. In the authors' view, somatic preparation for birth should be conducted by physiotherapists, while the more psychological birth preparation should be under the jurisdiction of women's nurses, though it is acknowledged that this division of occupational responsibilities is rarely observed in practice (Suchá and Chlubnová, 1979, p. 28).

In fact, health education is almost entirely the responsibility of nurses, because doctors have generally neither the time nor desire to engage in such work. In contrast, a recent survey of 182 public health nurses (including one man) revealed that most of these nurses liked their work, which they saw as creative, varied, autonomous and interesting. Table 6.3 shows the breakdown of their work activities according to corresponding proportions of time they took to complete.

TABLE 6.3 *Structure of worktime of public health nurses (%)*

Research and analysis, planning	10
Basic organisational and coordinating work	42
Work with film catalogues	7
Work with district health services	11
One's own further education	5

SOURCE Hodanová, 1977, p. 56

According to Hodanová, research, analysis and planning ought to be undertaken by doctors, but they are generally too busy to be bothered. Other nurses apparently also do not appreciate health education as desirable work – out of ten nursing work roles, health education came lowest together with social work nursing and 'clerical' nursing in central documentation. It would appear that health education is more attractive to older nurses – 80 per cent of the nurses in Hodanová's sample were married, 50 per cent were older than 40 and 75 per cent worked in health care for more than 15 years.

Another divisive jurisdictional issue concerns women's nurses' responsibility for the antenatal care of women with 'normal' pregnancies. This upgrading of women's nurses' responsibilities was introduced in the early 1970s, primarily to take some load off overworked obstetricians. A woman diagnosed by a physician as having a 'normal' pregnancy, can be transferred to a woman's nurse, who then performs 'doctor's work': rectal examination, checks on weight, uterine growth, swellings, blood pressure, etc. at each prenatal visit. Some pregnant women then see a physician only once during their entire pregnancy. Dr Gazárek *et al.* (1982a, p. 25) in retrospect see this practice as a 'step backward in the preventive care of pregnant women in Czechoslovakia', while Dr Beer (1972), reports good results from Prague's fourth district. The prenatal visit appointments were set during the doctor's absence, which helped women's nurses to gain more self-confidence in performing more responsible and independent work. The women patients, having no choice as to whom to see, were apparently quite content to see 'only a nurse', though their general preference was for an examination by a physician rather than a nurse.

Health officials in Bílina, a Slovak agricultural district with many scattered villages, also found the system of antenatal clinics run by nurses rather than doctors quite satisfactory. Moreover, they also found it more efficient, since they were able to abolish time-consuming home visits by nurses. The nurse's time was now freed, since it was women patients who had to come to the clinic rather than the nurse who had to visit several scattered homes (Lédr, 1972). The author does not comment on the implications of more travel on the pregnant women's health. However, Dr Gronský (1972) writing in the same issue of *Československá gynekologie* (devoted specifically to obstetric nursing), considers excessive travelling as a 'risk' factor to normal pregnancies. He is particularly critical of required travel to and from work, which is often confined to unhygienic, overcrowded public transportation as well as passengers who give no special consideration to pregnant women. However, given the bumpy state of Czechoslovak rural roads, the off-peak travel experience to a clinic cannot be all that much better for the woman's health.

Another efficiency measure related to women's nurses' home visits concerns the elimination of duplication of services. Mothers in many Moravian districts are often visited at their homes twice – once by a women's nurse and then again by a paediatric nurse. To avoid this duplication, health officials in the Moravian capital Brno have introduced a system whereby women's nurses are responsible for the home care of both the mother and her baby. A paediatric nurse is contacted only after the baby's sixth week, when it is formally transferred to medical and nursing paediatric care at the clinic in its locality. This is a rare example of moving away from the trend of providing centralised, highly specialised rather than a decentralised, home-based system of comprehensive reproductive care. In general, all the East European countries are characterised by the separation rather than integration of obstetrical and paediatric care, though both systems of care share the emphasis on medical nursing care in a clinical setting.

However, the East European example has not been followed in some of the Third World socialist countries. For example, between 1974 and 1976, Cuba reorganised its primary health care system into what is called *medicina en la communidad*, or community medicine, by assigning health workers to neighbourhoods where they are responsible for all the basic health needs. Because much health care is provided in the home, neighbourhood schools or other non-clinical settings, close social relations with the community are necessary. 'Lay' participation is also encouraged by the new system of representative government, local administration and public input, called *poder popular* or popular power, which was introduced during the same period. The participation of mass organisations in advisory councils has been replaced by membership on health commissions which, as part of *poder popular*, have decision-making powers concerning the development and utilisation of health resources. The Cuban Federation of Women has an important role to play in this system. Not only does it participate in health commissions, but it also has a yearly plan for health work which it draws up jointly with the Ministry of Health. The implementation of this plan relies on 60 000 lay volunteers in the neighbourhoods who carry out basic maternal–child health and sanitation tasks (Garfield, 1981, pp. 70–1).

Primary 'expert' care is genuinely interdisciplinary in character. An extensive coordination and interchange occurs between the doctor–nurse team, auxilliary staff (which is in much greater abundance than in Eastern Europe – about half of the nursing personnel in Cuba today are auxilliary nurses), social services, other specialists (psychologists and psychiatrists), administration, the Cuban Federation of Women, the *poder popular* representative and others. 'Since coordinating patient care is an area of traditional nursing expertise the nurse often becomes the team leader in the new model' (Garfield, 1981, p.71). This is quite unlike the situation in Eastern Europe, where health consumers are generally quite passive, concepts of health and disease continue to be based on the traditional medical model and the organisation of nursing in relation to medicine has remained hierarchical and subordinate.

It would appear that nursing in Eastern Europe does not enjoy a great deal of professional autonomy and prestige. Nor does it enjoy a 'professional' income. In line with other 'service' workers, nurses' official salaries are relatively low. Unofficial payments received from patients (to ensure better hospital care) typically take the form of gifts (e.g. box of chocolates, bottle of wine, pound of coffee), rather than the cash payments given to doctors. Holubová (1981), writing in a recently published article in *Zdravotnická pracovnice*, a Czech nursing journal, claims that doctors (their gender is not specified) tend to regard nurses as subordinates implementing their will rather than as co-workers and that communication between doctors and nurses is generally poor. This is in apparent sharp contrast to the situation in Cuba, where nurses seem to enjoy considerable work autonomy and prestige. Garfield (1981, p. 71) argues that the Cuban nurse 'used to be a co-worker; now she is becoming an associate and leader'.[3]

The work situation of Czech nurses is made worse by inefficient organisation of work, the already mentioned lack of nursing assistants, persistent shortages of supplies and modern technology (e.g. linen, food, irregular supply of electricity, unavailability of disposable syringes, needles, etc.) and by the total feminisation of nursing. In addition, the frequency of vacations, maternity leaves, children's or nurses' own sickness, means that there are fewer nurses actually working than indicated by official statistics. As a result, the nurses who do report for work are forced to intensify their labour and often work overtime, to the detriment of patients as well as their own physical and mental health (and that of their families). Holubová recommends the employment on short-term contract of retired nurses or nurses currently not employed during particularly critical periods of staff shortages, but she offers no solution to the other problems. This is not surprising. There *are* no easy solutions to these problems. As one speaker at the 1977 national meeting of women trade union officials pointed out, women workers in the socialist health care system epitomise two serious social problems – that of women and that of the health care system itself.

NOTES

1. Countries differ in the way that they define nursing care activities, so cross-national comparisons may be misleading. For example, a time-budget study of 'direct' and 'indirect' nursing care at University Hospital in London, Ontario, found that registered nurses spent 34 per cent of their worktime on 'direct' nursing, which appears to be highly comparable to the 35 per cent figures in Table 6.2. However, a closer examination of the Canadian data reveals that 'direct' and 'indirect' care are defined quite differently: the former is defined as performing 'activities for the patient in the presence of the patient', while the latter refers to 'nursing activities away from the patient but on behalf of the patient' (Thompson and Wilson, 1981). Moreover, much of what the Czech researchers defined as 'basic health activities' is in Canada performed by nursing assistants, not by registered nurses.
2. Part of the reason for preferring to talk to relatives rather than patients is the fact that it is relatives rather than patients who 'tip' (or bring 'presents' to nurses) in the form of cognac, boxes of chocolates and so on. In turn, nurses' reluctance to talk to patients goes a long way towards explaining the widespread lack of enthusiasm on the part of nurses for the 'rooming-in' system of newborn care, which is discussed in more detail in Chapter 11.
3. Deacon (1983, p. 122) claims that since the replenishing of the physicians who emigrated, Cuba has invested heavily in nurses and related auxiliary

medical personnel. Quoting from another author, Deacon argues that 'nurses, nurse assistants and auxiliary personnel seem to have more clinical responsibility in Cuba than do their counterparts in capitalist countries'.

Part III
Transition to Motherhood

7 Sexuality, Procreation and Contraception

Have you noticed how many different books or pamphlets about proper table manners have been published in our country? There are whole stacks of advice, recommendations and suggestions centred around one single need. Nobody is surprised. Why should sexuality be any different? Why should we be horrified at its cultivation?(Mrkvička, 1977, pp.52–3)

While sex is not the only bond between spouses, it is the most important one. One cannot expect a satisfied marriage without the harmony in intimate life. And vice versa: satisfactory sex contributes to an easier overcoming of difficulties entailed in married life.(Šipr, 1981, p. 41)

During the last decade, our women at fertile age have been subjected to a disproportionate number of demands, the consequences of which are likely to manifest themselves more and more in the health state of the female population. Apart from generational duties, frequently connected with serious risky situations and pathological complications, maternal responsibilities, work loads in the household as well as in employment, and economic problems, the current period brought a substantial proportion of women also the necessity of bearing the risk of possible complications of contraception.(Kadrnková, 1981, pp. 473-4)

Cultural norms pertaining to sexuality have certainly changed so that sex is now socially recognised as playing a central role in society. Unlike the situation in the 1950s and early 1960s, the issue is now discussed relatively openly in Czechoslovakia, both in expert advice books and in scholarly publications.

128   *Reproduction, Medicine and the Socialist State*

EXPERT ADVICE BOOKS

While more open than before, if one compares Czechoslovakia with the West the terms of reference for discussion of sexuality have remained somewhat limited and traditional. For example, 'clinical' book information about the anatomy and physiology of male and female sexual organs, processes of coitus and conception, causes of sterility and infertility or the various birth control methods are given much more freely and in greater abundance than information about homosexuality or masturbation. The former is hardly mentioned, an omission that probably reflects a strong norm of compulsive heterosexuality and parenthood.

Dr Barták (1977, p. 144), a sex therapist and author of a detailed chapter on sexuality in the marital reader *A School for Engaged and Newly Married Couples*, does mention the existence of homosexuality, but only in one sentence. Vaněk, a sociologist who published a book on the 'crisis' of the modern family in 1971, discusses homosexuality at greater length, but the subject is treated as something exotic which 'occurs' only to eccentric artists or in 'decadent' societies (e.g. ancient Rome).

Masturbation is discussed by one expert in a sample of seven current 'expert' personal advice books, but then only in the context of male sexuality. Dr Barták (1977, p. 307) sees masturbation as a 'normal' aspect of adolescent male sexuality as well as an acceptable substitute for sexual intercourse during periods of absence from female sex partners. He also assures his readers that masturbation affects neither health or subsequent heterosexual sex life (concerns that are apparently still very common among the general public), but he advices men who generally prefer masturbation to coitus to consult a specialist to find the cause of this 'abnormality'. Since women do not apparently masturbate at all, and in addition are not involved in lesbian relationships, their sexual pleasure is seen as being entirely dependent on men.

Menstruation is generally described as a barrier to rather than as an integral part of female sexuality. While Dr Barták (1977, p. 173, 203) simply mentions the cultural norm of sexual abstinence during menstruation in two examples from his clinical practice, without further comment, Dr Trča (1980, p. 59) states that 'during menstruation, neither sex nor swimming is allowed', on the grounds of possible infection. The fear of infection extends to the prohibition of tampons (which in any case are not generally available in stores) and to intercourse during the last five weeks of pregnancy and first six weeks of post-partum. We do not know how Czech women themselves relate to menstruation, but, reflecting the general cultural norm, Dr Trča sees it largely in clinical terms, as something which should be concealed from other people as well as oneself. He advises frequent washing 'to remove an unpleasant sense of uncleanliness' and 'to prevent the rise of an unpleasant smell' (Trča, 1980, p. 19). Many Western physicians would regard menstruation in a similar fashion, endorsing general cultural norms with regard to menstruation as 'unclean and polluting'.[1]

Moving from the more 'clinical' features to the more social aspects of sexuality, the picture becomes much more complicated. Most of the authors under examination acknowledge and critically comment on the coexistence of both 'old-fashioned' and 'modern' sexual standards, corresponding largely but not entirely to the generation gap.

> Certainly more than half of our women have openly or unconsciously accepted prudish views not so much of their mothers but rather of their grandmothers and great grandmothers. Yet their daughters are for a change revolting, thus dangerously reaching another extreme in so far as they are reducing the sex life between men and women to mere 'sleeping' with a man. (Pávek *et al.*, 1979, p. 129)

As far as people married for more than five years are concerned, the stereotype that emerges (based largely on clinical practice) is that of sexually active and demanding husbands on the one hand, and passive, uninterested wives looking for various excuses not to have sex on the other. In addition, Barták (1977, p. 149) is particularly critical of the indirect way in which Czech wives tend to thwart rather than outrightly refuse the sexual advances of their husbands, thus reinforcing traditional sexual scripts that a female means 'yes' even if she says 'no'. Dr Barták recommends either unconditional acceptance and participation or a refusal in no uncertain terms. Barták does not attempt to account for female disinterest in sex, but Pávek *et al.* (1979, p. 141) offer the following explanation:

> The causes of female disinterest in sex have to be looked for not in sex itself, but in the incorrect attitudes towards marriage, the woman's role in the family and often also poor self-evaluation.

Dr Trča (1980, p. 84), while basically accepting this analysis, goes a step further and offers the following suggestion on how to 'improve' marital sex life:

> Earlier sex manuals used to recommend that foreplay begin with a kiss. Today our opinion is somewhat different. For we know that a husband will get further with his wife if he helps her in the household. If he washes the dishes, vacuums the apartment, goes shopping, etc. It is important to realise that a husband often finds his wife tired or ill-humoured in the evening after a long day's work. It would be of little use to follow advice from a special publication on sex technique when the greatest wish of the wife is to sleep in peace after rushing all day long.

It is somewhat ironic that this sensible advice appears in a book written exclusively for women, not for couples. Furthermore, not all physicians and psychologists would agree that 'help' with housework, especially with the dishes (neither complete male takeover nor truly egalitarian distribution of household tasks is advocated), would maintain or even improve marital harmony. For example, a psychologist writing in the *Encyklopedie mladé ženy (Encyclopaedia of a Young Woman)* (1978, pp. 222–3), offers the following advice on 'help' with housework:

> There are men who can wash dishes as well and as carefully as women, but these men are an exception rather than a 'mass' phenomenon. A woman is by nature more patient when performing little, unimportant tasks, such as washing the dishes. Furthermore, these tasks also require certain gentleness. A man is capable of performing certain rougher, more athletic, work, which is not so minute. He can do heavier shopping, beat the carpet, hang the curtains, help with washing and wringing of heavier pieces of laundry. This kind of activity gives him a feeling of biological superiority, strength and protectiveness. He is thinking to himself: 'Without me, she would be incapable of keeping the house tidy, or, no, this task requires masculine skills.' This is exactly the opposite with washing dishes, which he finds boring. He may grudgingly accept this work if he likes to eat well and you are an exceptionally good cook. If you prepare his favourite meal for him, then it is quite in order to ask him to wash the dishes which you used. However, if you want to get him involved in the unpopular dish-

washing in some other way, he can read to you or talk to you, so that the work is easier to do.

If your husband persistently refuses to take any part in washing the dishes, do not be angry with him. And under no circumstances be envious if he is reading something, lying on the couch smoking a cigarette or watching a hockey game on TV. For envy is another destructive feeling which in time will destroy you: it will make you feel like a victim.

So, rather than arguing who is going to wash the dishes, it is better to do them yourself and then take some time to rest and have a pleasant talk with your husband. You will both benefit by this rather than by an argument, especially if it occurs in evening hours.

His advice could easily have come out of the 'total woman' concept: adapt to his needs, accept his superiority and build up his ego in all areas of life, presumably also including sexuality.

The major problem for young married couples lies elsewhere: in the discrepancy between the demands of 'modern sexual standards' (e.g. frequent intercourse and orgasms) and the very limited material possibilities for their fulfilment, given the widespread housing short-age and the prevalence of three-generation households in which most newly married couples must live. Psychologists and doctors have little to offer to these couples and their parents, except com-monsensical advice on mutual tolerance, empathy and personal sac-rifice. However, all the experts under examination agree that, on balance, separate nuclear families are preferable to three-generation households. Privacy as a cultural goal is seen as greatly outweighing any possible benefits from three-generation living, e.g. saving of money and domestic labour.

Lack of space also affects pre-marital sex, which is generally acknowledged to be quite widespread. While marital sex is seen as preferable, non-marital sex is condoned by the experts if certain conditions are met. These are summarised by Bárdoš (1978, p. 79) as follows:

(1) the relationship is based on deep emotions (preferably 'love');
(2) sex occurs at the culmination rather than the initiation of the relationship;
(3) the partners are aware of possible consequences of such a rela-tionship, namely pregnancy; and

(4) the individuals concerned have reached full physical, mental and emotional maturity and responsibility. [The meaning of this is left somewhat vague.]

This type of advice usually goes hand in hand with information about family planning, which is encouraged, and with some critical comments on new tensions created by the notion of 'sexual liberation'. As Dr Barták (1977, p. 209–10), perceptively puts it:

> the enforcement of freer sexuality among youth easily leads to the fact that sexual relations among young people are not only permitted (by the older generation), but are directly expected and demanded by the younger generation. As was said already, sexual experience is now related to one's success in life. However, this in itself creates unexpected and previously unknown pressures, which feed neurotic responses among numerous individuals for whom the new conventions are unsuitable. They are unsuitable for a variety of reasons – greater personal dependence on the opinions, demands and conventions of the older generation; inner disagreement with the frequent though not necessary consequences of 'young' conventions, the so-called 'cold sex'; rejection of their undemocratic character because without any doubt the new sexual standards give more chances to men than women, to stronger than weaker individuals, to good-looking than ugly people, to inconsiderate than considerate ones. . . . It is questionable whether the negative effect of freer sexuality can be compensated by its undisputed positive aspects: greater directness, putting aside of false shame, and the abolition of hypocritical moralisation.

Many Western feminists would agree with this view, though what are the attitudes of Czechoslovak youth, the potential consumers of this analysis and advice, is hard to assess on the basis of inadequate data.

PRE-MARITAL SEXUAL BEHAVIOUR

Published data on sexual behaviour of adolescents are rather scarce. For example, only one source was found on non-genital 'sexual experience' – a small-scale sample of 79 girls, aged 9–16. Only 6 per cent of the girls aged 13–14 experienced necking, but 70 per cent of the 16-year-olds had an experience of petting (Chovanová, 1974).

Thus, intercourse tends to be incorporated into adolescent sexuality only at the end of the teens. Moreover, the findings of one recent small-scale survey on attitudes towards parenthood among Czech high school students and apprentices revealed that both sexes tend to agree with the prescriptive advice offered by the experts that pre-marital sex should be based on deep emotions ('love'). However, males considered 1–6 months to be a sufficient period of acquaintance to initiate coitus. Females extended this period to 6–12 months. Only 10 per cent of males (4 per cent of females) consider virginity an important prerequisite of marriage.

Questions on courtship revealed that 40 per cent of males in the sample were either not interested in the other sex or were waiting for 'Miss Right' to turn up; 25 per cent were not 'deeply' involved and were changing partners; and only 10 per cent were going steady with the intention of marrying. This pattern was reversed for females – 20 per cent were going steady with marital intentions; 17 per cent had a steady boyfriend, but marriage has not yet been seriously considered; and 21 per cent were changing or not satisfied with their partners. Thirty per cent had no steady boyfriend, though this does not necessarily mean that they were not sexually active. The rest of the sample is unaccounted for on this particular question. Apprentices were apparently considering marriage much more frequently than high school students, but the former also tended to become sexually active earlier.

Both sexes saw late teens (15–18 years) as the ideal age for first experience of coitus for females; there was more variation of opinion for the ideal time to lose male virginity. Males considered 15–18 years to be the best time, but the female respondents would let the men wait until they reached 19–20 years of age. The report does not attempt to account for these differences; neither does it try to explain why they all but disappear when one examines responses on actual sexual behaviour, as opposed to prescriptive norms. Sixty per cent of males and 54 per cent of females claimed that they had no 'sexual experience' (presumably meaning coitus) by the age of 19 – relatively high proportions – and 33 per cent of males and 36 per cent of females claimed that they lost their virginity between the ages of 17 and 18 (Poradovský, 1979).

Research conducted among women has come up with similar findings. In a sample of 800 Slovak women (mostly university students) undergoing an abortion, 60 per cent reported pre-marital sexual experiences between the ages of 19 and 20. A large majority

(76 per cent) wanted such experiences (though it is unclear whether they actually initiated them), 12 per cent had intercourse on the basis of mutual desire and only 12 per cent of the sample claimed to have agreed to sex for fear of losing their partner. However, more than 50 per cent of another sample of 1334 working-class women in the textile industry acted in this way (Kováčová and Kováč, 1974). Thus, class differences are sometimes a better indicator of sexual behaviour than gender differences alone.

No surveys have come up with any evidence on widespread promiscuity. Ninety-six out of 100 patients undergoing an abortion in the Moravian city of Ostrava, interviewed two days after the operation, reported a strong belief in the close link between sex and deep emotions. Sixty-nine of the women regarded sex as enjoyable, only 6 per cent as unpleasant and 25 per cent were indifferent. Extra-marital sex was considered as acceptable by a third of the sample, but only in the context of an unsatisfactory marriage. More than half, 52 per cent, of the women viewed their sex education as 'unfriendly' towards sex and the rest as 'tolerant' (the meaning of these two categories is not quite clear) (Fukalová and Uzel, 1975).

Dunovský and Zelenková (1977) estimate that, of all single women with unwanted pregnancies, a majority (56 per cent) choose an abortion, 38 per cent marry the father of the child and carry to term, and the rest (4–6 per cent) give birth while single, but hope to marry the father of the child sometime in the future. Kadlecová and Brtníková (1977, p. 112) estimate that every fourth woman in the city and every fifth woman in a rural area enters marriage pregnant. Šipr (1981, p. 56) describes the same phenomenon slightly differently, by asserting that a third of all new marriages in Czechoslovakia occur under the pressure of pregnancy. Pavlík (1982), a leading Czech demographer, claimed in a recent interview in the party daily, *Rudé právo* that '60 per cent of first-born children are born within nine months of the date of marriage. Fifty per cent of these are born within seven months.' These statistics are generally frowned upon, because marriages concluded under the pressure of pregnancy often end up in a divorce.

KNOWLEDGE AND USE OF CONTRACEPTION

In comparison with the United States and many other Western countries, modern contraceptive methods are of relatively recent origin and availability in Czechoslovakia. Post-war research and development in this sphere appear to have been slow, despite the explicit provision in the liberal abortion law, passed in December 1957, that much work ought to be done (Šráček, 1977). Czech-produced pills and intrauterine devices (IUDs) became available only in the mid-1960s, and they have been subjected to periodic shortages, like all other consumer goods.

Moreover, there has been some concern expressed about their safety and reliability. The Czechs have called their intrauterine device 'DANA', a female name, but the initials stand for 'Good and Harmless Contraception' (*Dobrá a neškodná antikoncepce*). Kliment *et al.* (1972a) and Meszárová *et al.* (1973) question the appropriateness of this name in view of the relatively high rate of complications (e.g. perforation and pelvic inflammatory disease) and contraceptive failure rate. While comparative evidence on the aggregate frequency of IUD complications is controversial and inconclusive, it is generally agreed that at the individual level the issue is very important because of the potentially serious health consequences for the woman concerned. Kadrnková (1981) makes similar arguments about birth control pills which have more side-effects than Western-produced pills, many of which have also been shown to be hazardous. Kadrnková recommends 'barrier' mechanical forms of contraception over hormonal ones. These considerations shed somewhat different light on the statistics on the low usage of modern contraceptives quoted below.

Presl (1977) claims that while 51 per cent of women were potential consumers of the pill in 1975, only 5 per cent of Czech women and 2 per cent of Slovak women were using oral contraceptives in that year. Compare this to the usage of 37 per cent in the Netherlands, 31 per cent in New Zealand, 18 per cent in West Germany and Australia, 21 per cent in Austria and 19 per cent in the United States in 1973. Mosher's (1981) statistics on contraception among US married couples indicate even higher utilisation of the pill. The percentage of couples using oral contraceptives increased from 15 in 1965 to a high of 25 in 1973, but dropped to 22.5 in 1976. While there appears to be a trend away from the pill and toward sterilisation (which increased dramatically from 8 per cent of all birth control methods in 1965 to 18 per cent in 1976), the pill remained the most popular method in 1976. The pill is also the most common contraceptive method in Hungary. According to the results of the 1977 Hungarian segment of the World Fertility Survey,[2] it is employed by 36 per cent of all married women.

This rate is considerably higher than the 28 per cent reported among married women aged 20–24 in France in 1978, the 26 per cent revealed among married women aged 15–44 in Great Britain in 1975 and the 22.5 per cent among US married women of the same age. Almost 10 per cent of the Hungarian women used IUDs, 4 per cent relied on condoms and 17 per cent employed withdrawal. This last is the second most common contraceptive method in Hungary, with the highest rate (26 per cent) prevailing among older women aged 35–9. The Hungarian report does not include surgical sterilisation as a contraceptive method, but, according to one estimate, 1 per cent of women categorised as sterile had actually undergone sterilisation for contraceptive purposes (Wulf, 1979, p. 168).

What is particularly interesting about the Hungarian findings is the impression that the use of the two most effective reversible methods – the pill and the IUD – varies relatively little by residence, education, socio-economic status or employment status. Moreover, in 1966, before the introduction of the pill and the IUD, only 0.2 per cent of currently married women aged 15–39 were using either of these methods. Thus, within a decade, the Hungarians achieved a dramatic 46 per cent increase in the consumption of modern contraceptives, well above what the Czechs and Slovaks have been able to achieve. At least a partial explanation for the Hungarian success lies in the requirement that marriage licences may be issued to couples under 35 only upon presentation of proof that they have received contraceptive counselling and supplies from a physician (David and McIntyre, 1981, p. 254).

The Czechoslovak authorities could neither introduce nor enforce such a requirement because of erratic supplies. Presl (1977) claims that, if domestic consumption of hormonal contraceptives were to increase to 20 per cent, supplies would have to increase four times in the Czech lands and six times in Slovakia. He admits that given the past experiences and the current state of the economy, the pharmaceutical industry would be hard pressed to meet this increased quota. Pills imported from Yugoslavia in the mid-1970s, where they had been produced under US licence, somewhat alleviated the supply problem, but not for long, because the government found them too expensive and stopped their import.

Complaints of shortages and poor distribution of oral contraceptives often run concurrently with complaints about underdeveloped sex education, which we discussed in Chapter 3. All research findings confirm persisting general ignorance on modern contraception. As previously mentioned, research conducted by the State Population Commission in the 1960s on the sexual life of young married couples showed that more than a quarter of the men and half of the women in the sample considered their sex education insufficient or non-existent. Knowledge of contraception was generally absent; the majority of women depended on the responsibility and skill of their partners, both before and after marriage (Heitlinger, 1979, p. 185). A more recent fertility survey, conducted in 1977 as part of the World Fertility Survey, revealed only slightly improved knowledge. Only one third of respondents in the sample were adequately informed about contraception and just under 17 per cent had 'partial knowledge' prior to marriage. Thirty per cent of women in the cities and 45 per cent of those in rural areas had no knowledge of contraception at all, yet half of the women entering marriage had pre-marital 'sexual experience' (presumably coitus).

Contraceptive knowledge apparently improves with the length of marriage (Srb, 1979a, p. 304). However, theoretical knowledge is not always translated into practical use. While the women in the sample who were 'informed' knew about all the major effective methods of birth control, *coitus interruptus*, one of the least effective techniques, was the one most frequently used. Two fifths of Czech fertile women and half of Slovak women aged 18–44 used it, especially in rural areas. This is a smaller proportion than in 1956, when 68 per cent of women relied on this birth control technique, but it is still very high, considerably higher than in Hungary. The findings of the survey also indicated general unpopularity of male contraception (e.g. condoms).

The popularity of *coitus interruptus* is also confirmed by abortion studies. For example, among the random sample of 100 women undergoing abortion in 1970, only 15 per cent used no contraception. For 2 per cent of the sample, hormonal pills failed to prevent conception, 17 per cent relied on condom, 17 per cent used the rhythm method and the largest proportion, 54 per cent, relied on the least effective method, *coitus interruptus* (Fukalová and Uzel, 1975). In contrast, Mosher (1981) found that among US couples who were using non-surgical methods of contraception, less than 8 per cent relied on withdrawal, douche and other such methods. Fifteen per cent used condoms, 13 per cent relied on IUDs, 7 per cent on the rhythm method, 6 per cent used foam and an additional 6 per cent relied on diaphragms.

Trča (1965, p. 19) confirms the overemphasis on female

contraception at the expense of male contraception among doctors as well as the general public. However, there seems to have been a noticeable shift toward official endorsement of male contraception in recent years. The Institute of Health Education produced a leaflet advocating male contraception entitled *Boys' Contraception (Chlapecká antikoncepce)*. The leaflet is freely distributed (when supplies permit) in health clinics, which are, however, only rarely attended by male adolescents. Health educators wanted to introduce this leaflet into the school system in order to reach a wider audience, but their request was turned down by education officials on the grounds that the leaflet was written too frankly and that it might thus encourage promiscuity rather than a 'responsible' attitude towards parenthood (personal communication from a doctor). Such a philosophy is also promoted by a very vocal minority in the US, which claims that 'sex education in the schools will put ideas into young children's heads and will increase the promiscuity of the youth' (Parsons, 1983, p. 44). In fact, as Parsons (1983, p. 49) notes, 'little evidence exists that supports the conclusion that sex education increases sexual activity'.

The availability and usage of other contraceptive methods are also very limited. Sterilisation is generally discouraged on the grounds that it is 'unnatural', with possible negative consequences on a woman's personality (Bárdoš, 1978, p. 78; and numerous personal communications). It is permitted for women with medical problems and for older women past their prime reproductive years (aged 35 and over). Healthy women under 35 years of age can be legally sterilised only if they have had at least four children. Schmidt and Tarina (1972) are critical of this requirement, pointing out the inconsistency that abortion for women under 35 is allowed if they have had only two children. In the author's view, sterilisation as a method of birth control should be more freely available on request.

On the other hand, the operation is strongly encouraged for women of Romany (Gypsy) origin, although the Czech law requires their consent, as it does of all patients. In order to obtain the required consent, the municipal government of the Slovak town Piešťany went as far as paying Romany mothers who agree to be sterilised up to 2000 crowns ($200) (Kubica *et al.*, 1978; Mohapl and Dobešová, 1978). The reason for this drive to sterilise Romany women – so far without much success (Poradovský, 1977b) – lies in widespread social prejudice, based on racism, and Romany deviance from ideal norms of advanced industrial societies. The Romanys tend to have not only many children, but also many perinatal problems. Štembera *et al.*

TABLE 7.1 *Level of education of couples using sympto-thermal method of fertility regulation*

Education	Women (Number)	(%)	Men (Number)	(%)
Basic	35	41	28	33
Secondary	37	43	30	35
Post-secondary	11	13	19	22
Unknown	3	3	9	10
Total sample	86	100	86	100

SOURCE Šipr, 1975

(1979, p. 120) estimate the rate of Romany premature births to be 17–20 per cent, of perinatal mortality 31–42 per cent and of infant mortality a staggering 70–80 per cent. Romanys constitute 1.5 per cent of the whole country's population, but their concentration is much higher in Slovakia – hence the stronger drive in that part of the country to 'solve' the problem of high infant mortality among Romanys by discouraging them to have many children. When mutually agreed to, sterilisation is often performed during a post-partum hospital stay or while undergoing an abortion, i.e. when the Romany female patient is already physically present on medically controlled territory.

The 'natural', sympto-thermal method of birth control is also not widely used, although it has a strong proponent in Dr Šipr (1975), who has published an advice manual on the subject. He has also studied the social profiles of 86 married couples living in the Moravian town of Přerov who were using this method of birth control. His results are summarised in Table 7.1.

Reliance on this contraceptive method generally requires a higher degree of education and a commitment to family planning than other methods (such as IUD), because temperature charts have to be constructed and evaluated by the couples themselves. Contrary to Šipr's expectations, the sample consisted mainly of couples with lower education. However, contraceptive failure was relatively high – 24 women (27 per cent) conceived. This is attributed by Šipr to difficulties in obtaining solid information about the method and to the failure of some couples to consult a physician. Šipr (1972) suggests that the knowledge of sympto-thermal method of birth control should be increased both among doctors and the general public. He also sees a possibility of job enlargement for women's nurses who could help with 'the instruction about and evaluation of temperature curves'. He does not consider the possibility of a 'lay' dissemination of knowledge, which has been adopted by the Canadian 'Serena'. This organisation encourages 'lay' learning of the sympto-thermal method of birth control from other couples rather than from doctors. As pointed out in Chapter 5, an organised self-help and self-reliance approach to contraception, which would reject technical medical intervention and control, would probably be seen as politically too threatening, even if it might contribute to the official goal – reduction of unwanted pregnancies by means of contraception rather than abortion.

SEXUALITY, CONTRACEPTION AND GENDER RELATIONS

Researchers in Czechoslovakia seem to be resigned to the continued limited impact of contraception on fertility regulation. Dr Havránek (1978 and 1979a,b), from the prestigious Institute for the Care of Mother and Child,[3] argues that it is unrealistic to expect contraception to become the major method of birth control and that research and development should focus on the improvement of techniques of both contraception and abortion. However, little effort has been spent on trying to *explain* the persistence of contraceptive 'conservatism'.

The few existing studies on the topic have been largely empiricist in their orientation, focusing on the commonsensical reasons reported by women for not using modern contraception, both for themselves and in general. Among the 100 randomly selected women in Ostrava, interviewed by Fukalová and Uzel (1975), the second day after their abortion while they were still in the hospital, 32 per cent answered that the majority of women never think about the issue of contraception, 24 per cent thought that people are frivolous and 16 per cent attributed the failure to use contraception to an inherent ambivalence towards child-bearing, which is often preferred to be left to chance. Five per cent thought that people prefer 'risky' sex, as opposed to careful planning, but with conception always remaining a possibility. The remaining 6 per cent were divided equally among those who attributed failure to rely on contraceptives to partner's refusal or to a 'punishment' for sexual activity.

As far as their own reasons for not using effective contraception

(IUD or the pill) were concerned, the respondents' most frequently stated reason was satisfaction with existing contraception until its failure. The second most frequently stated reason was an unsatisfactory interaction with health care personnel. For example, a nurse refused the patient's request for contraception, stating that 'there is no time left today'; a doctor advised neither IUD nor the pill and when politely asked by the female patient about the likelihood of an infection after an insertion of an IUD, he abruptly answered 'let's leave it, then'. Medical contra-indications, negative previous experiences with IUDs or the pill (both personal and by a relative, friend or a neighbour), wish for a child subsequently reversed, partner's wish for a child, an incorrect calculation of the probable time of ovulation and a belief in sexuality and contraception as being essentially male affairs, accounted for the rest of the reasons. Surprisingly, nobody mentioned the hassles involved in actually obtaining contraceptive prescriptions and supplies, which was witnessed first hand in one Prague clinic – long queues to see the doctor (the contraceptive clinic was open only one afternoon a week) and erratic supplies at chemists.

While these findings are interesting as well as instructive in themselves, they nonetheless need to be placed in an interpretative framework. One way to go about this is to draw a distinction between unplanned conception, unwanted pregnancy and an unwanted child. As Morokvasić (1981, p. 134) pointed out in her study of Yugoslav migrant women living in Western Europe:

> women can be quite clear about not wanting a child, but ambivalent or even positive about wanting to get pregnant. . . . This ambivalence is deeply rooted in the significance of procreation and maternity for Yugoslav women and in their perception of women's sexuality, indeed femininity, as being closely related to procreation. Recourse to abortion may thus not be a result of lack of information or education. . . . Abortions, and the pregnancies that precede them, may therefore be indicators of particular gender relations underlying them; so to understand the former we need to investigate the latter.

As mentioned in Chapter 1, similar arguments have been also advanced by Luker (1975), Gordon (1976) and Woodhouse (1982), who all emphasise an inherent, socially determined, ambivalence in women's sexual relationships with their partners, which in turn has obvious consequences for the usage of contraceptives or lack thereof. As we saw above, a significant proportion of Czech women (16 per cent) also commonsensically believe in an inherent ambivalence in heterosexual relations. An alternative, more 'rational' conceptual framework has been utilised by Luker (1975) and by Tyndale (1980). They examine contraceptive decisions from within the perspective of risk-taking, suggesting that all women balance the costs and benefits of sexually free behaviour against the costs and benefits of possible pregnancy and/or its termination. Czechoslovakia, with its high abortion rate, would be an ideal 'test' case for this approach, but the required empirical evidence is not available.

The only Czech study seen which at least alludes to the complex relationship between sexuality, procreation and underlying gender relations, is concerned with infertility rather than with contraception and men rather than women. A survey of 50 married couples requesting artificial insemination in the Moravian capital Brno in the mid-1970s revealed that sterile men found it much harder to reconcile themselves to their condition than women, who were more likely to expect sterility as a possibility prior to discovering that they were unable to conceive. Moreover, 34 per cent (17) of the men from the sample reported that they had been subjected to persistent attacks and sarcastic questions and comments about their childlessness not only in their workplace, but also in their extended families, from their mothers-in-law as well as their own mothers. This strong communal social pressure towards parenthood was especially pronounced in the rural areas, and it led to increased feelings of inferiority and neurotisation among the men. Because of this 'old-fashioned' cultural link between masculinity, sexuality and natural parenthood, adoption was not a real option for these men, since it would have represented a public acknowledgement of their lack of virility and inability to conceive a child. Heterologous insemination thus became the only way out of their predicament. Seven men in the sample even allowed for the possibility of extra-marital conception of their wives, although this was admittedly seen as a rather extreme solution (Sládek *et al.*, 1976).

If we see conception (or lack thereof) in this light, as a public validation and proof of one's masculine virility and/or feminine fecundity, failure to use contraceptives becomes somewhat easier to understand. It is not just an outcome of ignorance, 'irrational' and 'irresponsible' behaviour or, in the East European context, the erratic supplies problem (though it is all these things), but also an aspect of existing gender relations. As Woodhouse (1982, pp. 9, 14) pointed out, many teenage girls feel unable to discuss contraception before embarking on a sexual relationship with their boyfriends, fearing that he might view them as sexually promiscuous and perhaps unfeminine. This difficulty is compounded by the current cultural definition of sex as spontaneous and unpremeditated, with the result that young women tend to seek contraceptive aid after they have become sexually active and not before – a situation also observed in Czechoslovakia.

Dr Trča (1971) has shown (on the basis of clinical evidence rather than feminist insight) that birth control education is most effective right after abortion or birth. Eighty-nine per cent of women in a random sample of 500 women, living in and undergoing abortion in Prague in 1968 and 1969, claimed to have begun to use reliable contraception only after an abortion or previous childbirth, even though many of the women admitted to having had some knowledge of contraception beforehand.

Morokvasić (1981, pp. 139, 141) went a step further by arguing that, once contraceptive 'ignorance is overcome, as is the case with most Yugoslav migrants, behaviour does not necessarily change'. In her view:

> this is because it is also a reflection of the established relationship of dominance within the couple in which the man dominates and takes care of the sexual act. . . Yugoslav women generally manage to have only the number of children they want. This does not, however, mean that their pregnancies are planned or that they have full control over their bodies. Rather they are still in a subordinate position in their relationship to their partner and they accept that they must bear the brunt of his irresponsibility. For women who adopt the idea that they should control their fertility, but for whom at the same time pregnancy is important for asserting their womanhood to themselves, their partners and others in the community, the knowledge that they can get pregnant is important. They are thus not very likely to seek an effective means of preventing conception until changes in their status and their relationship with the partner take place, and they themselves see contraception as the most suitable way to control their fertility.

I would suggest that Czechoslovak experts who are professionally involved in fertility regulation would benefit from adopting the kind of feminist interpretative framework that is utilised by Morokvasić. It might help them better understand the observed high incidence of contraceptive ignorance, failure to translate contraceptive knowledge into practical everyday use, the continued reliance on abortion as the major form of birth control and of children born within the first year of marriage as logical outcomes of existing gender relations rather than as outcomes of ignorance, irrationality or irresponsibility.

NOTES

1. The social construction of menstruation is a controversial topic. See Sayers (1982, pp. 110–24) for an informative review of the diverse biological, psychoanalytic, structural and liberal feminist accounts of the social construction of menstruation as polluting. Some radical feminists have sought to combat the present negative valuation of menstruation simply by reversing this valuation, by giving menstruation a positive social value. Sayers (1982, p. 124) herself argues, 'if this course is to be fully served, however, it is also essential to acknowledge that biology (menstruation in this case) does have real effects on women's lives and that these effects are not to be dismissed as merely the result of the ideas that societies entertain about it'.

2. The World Fertility Survey is an international research programme which was inspired by the World Population Conference in Bucharest in 1974. It is administered by the International Statistical Institute in collaboration with the International Union for the Scientific Study of Population, and its headquarters are in London, UK. Its participants currently include 49 developing Third World countries and 17 developed countries, 6 of which are state socialist – Czechoslovakia, Poland, Hungary, Romania, Bulgaria and Yugoslavia. For more information about the programme, see Vaessen (1978).

3. The Institute for the Care of Mother and Child coordinates all state (federal) research tasks in the field of care of woman, mother and newborn, both in basic research, and in research included in the plan of technical development, not to mention the departmental plan of the Czech Ministry of Health. In addition, the Institute, which has the country's 'highest concentration of highly qualified scientists in the field of gynaecology, obstetrics and neonatology' (Židovský, 1982, p. 84), provides regular clinical care for women and children who reside in its small district (part of Prague 4). The Institute was 'born' on 3 March 1951, as a result of the amalgamation of the former III obstetrical/ gynaecological clinic and a nursing clinic of Prague's Charles University. According to Vojta and Poláček (1961, p. 8), 'its basic mission was the research of the physiology and pathology of pregnancy, birth and post-partum, the development of women's health in relation to their work and environmental conditions, and the physiology and pathology of the child

in the earliest stages of life. The needs of the organisation of health care of women and children created for the Institute many additional tasks, mainly methodical–organisational in character. While employees at the Institute were relieved of basic pedagogical activity, they were instead given the task of the postgraduate training of doctors and other specialists.'

8 Abortion

All over the world – from countries where abortions are legal to those that jail women who get them – the debate rages on. Men, women, church and governments are in a continual confrontation over artificial termination of a pregnancy before full term. They argue over religion, morality and economics – concepts which are open to interpretation. (Lavigne, 1983)

Of all the reproductive events, abortion is easily the most controversial, although the nature of the debate surrounding it varies from country to country. In North America and most Western countries, abortion is seen as an essentially moral issue. It is generally discussed in terms of 'control over women's bodies' (or a woman's right to choose) versus 'protecting (or killing) the unborn child'. The former argument is clearly related to feminism, while the latter has the organisational support of the so-called 'pro-life lobby', which includes many Catholics and advocates of 'traditional family values'.[1]

The Eastern European debate has been couched rather differently, in medical and population terms rather than in moral concepts. Central and Eastern Europe has a long history of socially acceptable illegal and legal abortion and, at the individual level, it is considered neither sinful nor disgraceful to terminate an unwanted pregnancy (David, 1972). Although the socialist countries were among the first in the world to legalise abortion, a woman's right to control her body has not been accepted as state policy, with the exception of Yugoslavia, where individual reproductive rights are guaranteed by the constitution. In the other countries, abortion is officially disapproved and it is regarded as a 'necessary evil', which is detrimental to women's health and their subsequent pregnancies, and involves the high economic costs that are associated with hospital care. The official goal is to reduce the incidence of abortions by greater reliance on contraception and by a combination of incentives for larger family size on the one hand and legal–administrative restrictions of access on the other.

146

ABORTION LEGISLATION IN CZECHOSLOVAKIA

Socialist abortion policies have received considerable attention among Western population experts in recent years. David and McIntyre (1981) discuss the issue extensively in their recent book on Central and Eastern European reproductive behaviour, both in an overview chapter and in individual country chapters. In order to avoid duplication of efforts, the discussion here is focused largely on Czechoslovakia and issues not covered in their study, namely the politics of abortion policies, the health hazards of the procedure and the menstrual regulation method of abortion.

Abortion was fully legalised in Czechoslovakia on 19 December 1957, following the lead of the Soviet Union in 1955. According to Jerrie (1958, p. 1), the passing of the decree was preceded by 'considerable and passionate discussion in political, health, legal and security spheres, as well as in mass organisations, factories, etc.' Tietze (1981, p. 23) also reports that 'legalization of abortion for nonmedical reasons in 1957 was preceded by almost two years of public discussion'. However, as previously mentioned, a prominent doctor has indicated that the 'discussion' was limited to the canvassing of 'progressive' opinion by the party-state authorities among professionals who were known to be in favour of legalising abortion. Opponents were allowed to express their views but their arguments were ignored.

The major reason for passing the law, apart from the Soviet influence, was the recognition of the futility of prohibiting abortions. Jerrie (1958, pp. 4–5) claimed that the previous law making abortion a criminal offence was outdated and unrealistic, since it did not, and could not, prevent illegal abortions, induced either by the pregnant woman herself or by another person. Moreover, Jerrie argued, the criminalisation of abortion leads to unnecessary and unpopular prosecutions as well as exploitation by unscrupulous abortionists. Illegal abortions have also often caused considerable damage to women's health and at times even led to death.

Between 1954 and 1957, i.e. prior to the legalisation of abortion, 40–50 women died annually on account of botched illegal abortions. In 1958, the first year during which abortion was a legal procedure, the number dropped to 25 and in subsequent years to 10–14 annually. However, in 1966, there were still twelve women who died as a result of undergoing an illegal abortion; in 1967 there were six and in 1968 there were three. Between 1958 and 1968, there were 116 illegal abortion-related deaths, considered by Dr Kotásek (1970, p. 328) as a 'sad phenomenon, since we were certainly expecting much more favourable results'. As Tietze (1981, p. 103) argues, 'it would appear that in practice, even very liberal legislation does not necessarily achieve its goal of eradicating illegal abortion or does so with a considerable time-lag as long as substantial numbers of women find the available services inaccessible, unacceptable, or at least unfamiliar'.

What Dr Kotásek, a prominent gynaecologist, does not mention are the administrative restrictions of access to legal interruption which were imposed in 1963, resulting in an increase in recourse to illegal abortion, as well as maternal mortality. The latter declined when restrictions were eased in 1965 (David and McIntyre, 1981, p. 235). The Romanian experience leaves even less doubt on the correlation between legalisation of abortion and a subsequent decline in abortion-associated deaths and, vice versa, criminalisation of abortion and an increase in abortion mortality. For example, it was reported at the IPPF (International Planned Parenthood Federation) European Regional Meeting in 1969 that, in the area served by the Baco Hospital about 15 000 abortions per year were recorded without any fatality during the decade of liberal abortion legislation, whereas, in the two years after the 1965 decree which made abortion illegal, five deaths were reported owing to complications from illegally induced abortions. Similar experience was noted in a Bucharest hospital. Abortion-related deaths reported to the World Health Organisation rose considerably, from 64 in 1965 and 83 in 1966 to 170 in 1967, reaching 370 by 1970 and 432 by 1976. Not more than five deaths in any one year were attributed to abortions induced on legal indications (David and McIntyre, 1981, p. 187).

Similar statistical correlation has been noted between a stricter attitude towards authorising abortions and a recorded increase in spontaneous miscarriages. Šalda (1978) reports that between 1969 and 1976, authorised abortions in Czechoslovakia declined by 18 per cent, but miscarriages increased by 25 per cent. Many of these 'spontaneous' abortions are suspected of being self-inflicted. A considerable increase in spontaneous abortions was also noted in Romania, though it was officially attributed not to illegal abortions but to repeated legally induced abortions. David and McIntyre (1981, p. 188) argue that these findings are difficult to substantiate and that 'other studies suggest that inexperienced operators using dilation and curettage could have increased the risk for subsequent spontaneous abortion'. The relationship between particular abortion techniques and subsequent pregnancy complications will be discussed in more detail later in this chapter.

ABORTION STATISTICS

More statistics are available on abortion than on any other surgical procedure, but difficulties in interpretation persist (David, 1980, p. 68). Abortion data are generally based on official statistics of legal abortions as reported by health authorities, but the completeness and accuracy of the reporting as well as the quantity and quality of tabulation vary widely among and within countries (Tietze, 1981, p. 2). Among the socialist countries, Hungarian and Czechoslovak data on abortion are both extensive and reliable, but this is not the case for Catholic Poland. Many Polish women, wishing to avoid hospitalisation and thereby conceal their pregnancy termination, go to physicians practising privately, who may make 'errors' in registering all their cases (David, 1972, p. 4). However, even careful collection of abortion data at both the district and central level (as is the case in Czechoslovakia) does not mean that some pregnancies and abortions do not escape official notice. As noted below, follow-up studies of women who were denied abortion requests revealed a rather large proportion of women for whom neither abortion nor delivery records could be found.

Another methodological problem indicated by retrospective abortion surveys is generally referred to as selective 'forgetting' or 'under-reporting'. The classic example is the Fertility and Family Planning Study conducted in Hungary in 1966, more than a decade after the legalisation of abortion. In that survey, the numbers of abortions reported by the respondents for the years 1960–5 amounted to only 50–60 per cent of the number actually performed according to hospital statistics for these years. When known abortions reported in the vital health statistics were correlated with respondents' reporting of those same pregnancy terminations in the 1977 World Fertility Survey, it was found that one year after the women in the abortion sample had undergone the procedure, 63 per cent recalled the abortion, and two years after the operation, only 52 per cent recalled it. The investigators estimated that about 18 per cent of all legally induced abortions were deliberately concealed and that the remainder were unintentionally underreported (Wulf, 1979, pp. 168–9; David and McIntyre, 1981, pp. 266–7).

Selective 'forgetting' about previous abortions was also found among Yugoslav women. A well-designed 1972 interview study of 948 women whose first pregnancies had been terminated by induced abortion (222 respondents) or carried to term (726 women) during 1968–9 in Skopje, Macedonia, revealed that a majority of the women who were not married at the time of their abortion failed to recall that abortion when asked for a complete pregnancy history four or five years later. However, this reticence did not extend to abortions performed after marriage. David and McIntyre (1981, p. 167) conclude that women are more likely to 'remember' previous abortions when problems are encountered with the next pregnancy, thus biasing results of retrospective studies of abortion-related complications. Tietze (1981, p. 2) considers abortion data based on surveys of samples of the general population or on interviews conducted in various medical settings so inadequate that he excludes them from the 1981 fourth edition of his world review of induced abortion, although they were included in earlier editions. As we saw in the preceding chapter, such data are included in this study, but the bulk of the data presented in this chapter is drawn from official statistics.

As illustrated in Table 8.1, the passage of the liberalised abortion law in December 1957 was associated with a sharp increase in total registered abortions as well as abortion rates and ratios.[2] The abortion rate increased moderately already in 1956–7, i.e. prior to the liberalisation of the abortion laws, which, according to Tietze (1981, p. 23), 'reflected the changing attitude of the medical profession'. At the end of 1958, the abortion rate was eight times higher than at the end of 1957, and it continued to rise, albeit at a decelerating pace, until 1961. Another decline occurred in the early 1970s (which can be again attributed to restrictions imposed in 1972), but since 1976, legal abortions have been increasing again. Abortion rates and ratios themselves have remained fairly stable throughout the 1970s, reflecting increases in crude birth rates and in the proportion of women at the prime reproductive age.

It is estimated that every third pregnancy is aborted in Czechoslovakia which means that there are roughly two births for every abortion. This ratio is not high by East European standards. For example, in the Soviet Union the annual number of abortions substantially exceeds that of live births, although no figures have been

TABLE 8.1 Statistics on abortions in Czechoslovakia: selected years

	1958*	1959	1960	1961	1965	1969	1971	1975	1979	1980	1982
Total	89 076	105 536	114 602	120 304	105 756	127 232	122 853	111 779	123 240	127 194	134 063
in which:											
on request	61 418	79 131	88 288	94 306	75 591	102 797	97 271	81 671	94 486	100 170	107 638
spontaneous	27 110	26 062	26 070	25 847	26 098	24 410	25 559	30 075	28 730	26 982	26 391
others	548	343	244	151	69	25	23	33	24	42	34
Applications for abortions	69 633	87 327	96 866	105 029	86 589	110 334	104 647	88 665	100 647	105 932	113 528
Abortions per 1000 inhabitants	6.6	7.8	8.4	8.7	7.5	8.8	8.5	7.6	8.1	8.3	8.7
Abortions per 100 completed pregnancies	27.3	32.5	34.3	35.3	31.2	36.2	34.0	27.7	31.0	33.7	36.3
in which:											
on request	19.0	24.5	26.5	31.7	23.5	29.2	26.9	20.3	23.8	26.5	29.1
spontaneous	8.3	6.0	7.8	7.6	7.7	6.9	7.1	7.5	7.2	7.1	7.1
Abortions per 100 live births	37.5	48.1	52.2	54.5	45.3	56.7	51.4	38.4	45.0	50.8	56.9
in which:											
on request	no data	no data	no data	no data	34.1	45.8	40.7	28.1	34.5	40.0	45.7
spontaneous	11.4	11.9	11.9	11.7	11.2	10.9	10.7	10.3	10.5	10.8	11.2
Performed abortions per 100 applications	no data	no data	no data	no data	91.9	93.2	93.0	92.1	93.9	94.6	94.8

*The first year of operation of the liberalised abortion law.

SOURCES *Statistická ročenka ČSSR, 1963 to 1984*; Heitlinger, 1979, p. 188

published officially for almost four decades. Tietze (1981, p. 24) estimates an abortion rate of about 115 per 1000 women aged 15–44. An excess of total number of legal abortions over births was also experienced in Hungary, reaching its highest level between, 1959–73, with the abortion ratio reaching a maximum of 582 per 1000 known pregnancies in 1964. Restrictions enacted in 1973, which took effect on 1 January 1974, resulted in an abrupt drop of about 40 per cent in the number of abortions (and a concurrent increase in the number of abortions on medical grounds from 2.4 per cent to almost 11.8 per cent of the total number of abortions). Since 1975, abortions have been declining, reflecting both legal–administrative restrictions and a concerted effort to promote more effective contraception (Wulf, 1979; Tietze, 1981, p. 23; David and McIntyre, 1981, pp. 3–4, 264).

Among the Western countries, abortion rates and ratios are highest in Japan, the Nordic countries and the United States. While abortion rates and ratios in Japan peaked in the late 1950s, the number of abortions in 1975 still exceeded the number of births by about 350 000 or one-fifth. Following the passage of the Abortion Act of 1967 in England and Wales, the abortion ratio there continued to increase until 1975 and has since remained approximately constant in the vicinity of 150 per 1000 known pregnancies. At present, both rates and ratios are substantially lower in England and Wales than in the United States or in the countries of northern Europe; the comparable figures for Scotland are about one-fourth lower than for England and Wales. The rates and ratios of legal abortions reported for 1970–9 for Canada are also substantially below the corresponding values for the United States. As illustrated in Table 8.2, the incidence of abortion varies substantially among countries, irrespective of their political systems.

TABLE 8.2   *Number of legal abortions, abortion rates and abortion ratios: selected areas, years and characteristics*

Country and years	Number of abortions*	Abortion rate per 1000		Abortion ratio per 1000	
		Total Population	Women 15–44	Live Births**	Known Pregnancies[+]
Bulgaria					
1960	55 600	7.1	31.6	400	286
1965	97 200	11.6	51.3	782	439
1975	123 700	14.2	65.8	854	461

Canada					
1970	11 200	0.5	2.6	30	29
1975††	59 000	2.6	11.4	159	137
1979	65 000	2.7	11.6	—	—
Czechoslovakia					
1960	88 300	6.5	32.5	405	288
1970	99 800	6.9	32.3	427	299
1979	94 300	6.2	29.4	359	264
England and Wales (residents)					
1968	22 300	0.7	3.5	40	39
1979	119 000	2.4	12.0	184	156
German Democratic Republic⊕					
1960	800	0.04	0.22	2.6	2.6
1972	114 000	6.7	33.1	599	374
1977	80 100	4.8	22.5	350	260
Hungary					
1960	162 200	16.2	76.4	1 129	530
1970	192 300	18.6	83.5	1 296	565
1979	80 000	7.5	35.9	525	344
Japan					
1960	3 150 000	33.5	138.1	1 972	663
1970	732 000	7.1	28.0	375	273
1979	613 700	5.3	23.1	372	271
Sweden					
1970	16 100	2.0	10.2	143	125
1979	34 700	4.2	20.9	358	264
United States (Abortions reported to Alan Guttmacher Institute) ⊕⊕					
1973	744 600	3.5	16.6	239	193
1978	1 157 800	5.3	23.1	342	255

*All numbers rounded. Data for most recent periods may be subject to revision.
**Six months later.
†Live births, plus legal abortions.
††Includes residents of Canada obtaining abortions in United States.
⊕Abortion laws were partially liberalised only in 1965 and fully (permitting abortion on request during the first trimester) in 1972.
⊕⊕The Alan Guttmacher Institute (AGI) obtains its data from nationwide surveys of providers of abortion services.

SOURCE   Reprinted with the permission of the Population Council from Christopher Tietze, *Induced Abortion: A World Review, 1981* (New York: The Population Council, 1981) pp. 26–35.

An examination of demographic characteristics (age, marital status and parity) reveals that abortion rates in Eastern Europe peak among married women over age 25 with two children, while in the West the most rapid growth of abortions is among young childless single

TABLE 8.3   *Percentage distribution of legal abortions by age of woman at termination: selected areas, years and characteristics*

Country and years	Age					
	19 or less	20–24	25–29	30–34	35–59	40 or more
Canada						
1978	30.4	31	19.2	11.3	5.7	2.4
Czechoslovakia						
1978	5.6	22.4	29.3	24.5	13.6	4.6
England and Wales						
1978	27.0	24.2	18.0	15.7	10.2	4.9
German Democratic Republic						
1976	13.5	20.5	19.2	19.4	19.9	7.5
Hungary						
1978	10.8	21.9	22.9	20.0	16.6	7.8
Japan						
1978	2.5	15.3	25.9	27.2	19.5	9.6
Sweden						
1978	19.6	21.9	19.8	19.6	12.8	6.3
United States (Estimated by AGI)						
1978	30.8	34.7	18.9	9.5	4.6	1.5

SOURCE   Reprinted with the permission of the Population Council from Christopher Tietze, *Induced Abortion: A World Review, 1981* (New York: The Population Council, 1981) pp. 45–7.

women. In 1978, women aged 18–19 accounted for 16 per cent of all abortions in Canada, 18 per cent in the USA and 13 per cent in England and Wales, but only 4 per cent in Czechoslovakia, 6 per cent in Hungary and 7 per cent in the GDR (Tietze, 1981, p. 53). To return to an earlier finding, these data would appear to confirm the veracity of the relatively large number of Czech high school students and apprentices who reported no 'sexual experience' by the age of 19. Conversely, in 1978, women aged 24–34 accounted for 52 per cent of all abortions in Czechoslovakia, 43 per cent in Hungary and 53 per cent in Japan, but only 31 per cent in Canada, 33 per cent in England and Wales and 29 per cent in the United States. Thus the Japanese pattern is similar to that of Czechoslovakia and Hungary, while the statistics from the GDR show that country to have a relatively even percentage distribution of legal abortions by age of woman.

Since statistics on the percentage distribution of aborted women by age reflect, to some extent, the age distribution of the female population within the reproductive age group, Tables 8.4 and 8.5 present

TABLE 8.4 *Legal abortion rates by age of woman at termination and total abortion rates: selected areas, years and characteristics (rates per 1000 women)*

Country and years	19 or less (per 1000 women 15–19)	20–24	25–29	30–34	35–39	40 or more	Total abortion rate
Canada							
1978	16.3	17.2	11.9	7.8	5.0	2.4	303
Czechoslovakia							
1978	10.0	34.3	43.3	40.1	27.4	10.5	828
England and Wales							
1978	16.1	16.0	11.8	9.9	8.0	4.0	329
German Democratic Republic							
1976	16.9	26.2	31.3	31.3	24.4	11.4	708
Hungary							
1978	27.3	41.8	45.0	45.0	39.0	19.1	1 086
Japan							
1975	10.3	82.2	116.0	129.4	98.2	51.3	2 437
Sweden							
1978	23.9	25.5	21.2	19.0	15.8	9.0	572
United States							
1978	41.9	48.3	29.4	16.8	9.8	3.6	749

SOURCE Reprinted with the permission of the Population Council from Christopher Tietze, *Induced Abortion: A World Review, 1981* (New York: The Population Council, 1981) pp. 48–50.

data on age-specific abortion rates and ratios as more accurate indicators of the true age pattern of the incidence of abortion.

As far as marital status is concerned, 61 per cent of women obtaining a legal abortion in Canada in 1978 were not married (75 per cent in the USA and 51 per cent in England and Wales), compared to only 13 per cent in Czechoslovakia, 21 per cent in Hungary and 37 per cent in the GDR (Tietze, 1981, p. 58). The distribution by parity[3] also reveals major differences among countries. In recent years, women without prior births were a majority among all women obtaining legal abortions in Canada, England and Wales, and the United States, while in Czechoslovakia and Hungary, abortions are most frequent among women with two children (see Table 8.6). In fact, 'sufficient number' of children in a family (two or more) has been consistently the most frequently cited reason for seeking an

TABLE 8.5   *Legal abortion ratios by age of woman at conception:
selected areas, years and characteristics (ratios per 1000 known
pregnancies, i.e. live births plus legal abortions)*

Country and years	Age					
	19 or less	20–24	25–29	30–34	35–39	40 or more
Canada						
1977	254	124	83	109	220	430
Czechoslovakia						
1978	113	149	271	452	635	795
England and Wales						
1977	267	116	87	141	314	513
German Democtratic Republic						
1975	182	183	340	598	763	871
Hungary						
1978	220	214	321	533	747	872
Japan						
1975	402	415	401	697	890	968
Sweden						
1978	425	199	160	247	438	731
United States						
1977	371	283	207	233	368	522

SOURCE   Reprinted with the permission of the Population Council from
Christopher Tietze, *Induced Abortion: A World Review, 1981*
(New York: The Population Council, 1981) pp. 51–2.

abortion in Czechoslovakia, accounting for 18–19 per cent of all
abortions.

These statistical patterns confirm the major differences in sexual
behaviour among teenagers and contraceptive practices among adult
women discussed in the preceding chapter. Two typical profiles of
women obtaining legal abortion emerge from these data. On the one
hand, we have a married woman in her twenties or thirties, who does
not want any additional children – a type more common in Eastern
Europe (with the possible exception of the GDR) and Japan than in
Western Europe and North America. On the other side of the
spectrum, we have a young, single woman, pregnant for the first
time. While demographers, concerned as they are about the contribution of abortions to declining birth rates, would prefer to lower the
total abortion rate and ratio, medical doctors, concerned about
alleged health hazards and the reproductive risks of abortions, are

TABLE 8.6 *Percentage distribution of legal abortions by parity: selected areas and years*

	Previous deliveries/live births					
Country and years	0	1	2	3	4	5 or more
Canada						
1979	63.1	15.8	13.6	5.0	1.6	0.9
Czechoslovakia						
1979	11.4	15.7	46.9	19.3	4.5	2.2
England and Wales						
1978	52.1	13.0	19.1	9.9	3.8	2.1
Hungary						
1979	21.0	20.9	38.5	13.3	3.7	2.6
Sweden						
1979	39.2	18.3	26.3	11.7	3.3	1.2
United States						
1978	56.6	19.2	14.1	5.9	– 4.2 –	

SOURCE Reprinted with the permission of the Population Council from Christopher Tietze, *Induced Abortion: A World Review, 1981* (New York: The Population Council, 1981) pp. 54–6.

particularly worried about young women terminating their first pregnancies.

REPRODUCTIVE HEALTH HAZARDS OF ABORTIONS

When Czechoslovakia introduced legalised abortion legislation, it also introduced a statutory one-year follow-up as a legal requirement. The results were appalling, much worse than expected. While Jerrie *et al.* (1961, p. 78) claimed that only 3–12 per cent of all abortions led to 'early' or 'late' complications, the current figure is between 30 and 40 per cent (Havránek, 1978). Infections, menstrual irregularities and psychic alterations are seen as 'early' complications and chronic infections and the incompetency of the cervix as 'late' complications. Infections often lead to sterility, while the incompetence of the cervix is the most frequent cause of both miscarriage and premature birth. In turn, premature births significantly contribute to perinatal mortality and morbidity, given the low birth weight of most premature babies.

The magnitude of the problem in Czechoslovakia was first publicly discussed by obstetricians/gynaecologists at their December 1969 conference on the after-effects of abortion. Speaker after speaker presented evidence on the high incidence of post-operative complications of abortions – 70 per cent of patients returning to work experienced various temporary difficulties (e.g. overall weakness, bleeding, back pains), 20 per cent had infections, 30 per cent suffered from lowered sexual appetite (although 15 per cent experienced a higher sexual desire!), 17 per cent became sterile, 30–43 per cent miscarried in a subsequent pregnancy, 11 per cent gave birth prematurely and there was a three-fold increase in the likelihood of a subsequent ectopic pregnancy (Kotásek, 1970). Only one speaker found no correlation between previous abortions and subsequent pregnancy complications (See Heczko *et al.*, 1970).

Several of the more recently published studies have also found evidence for abortion-related complications in a subsequent pregnancy. For example, Macků *et al.* (1978) found that miscarriages were two and a half times more frequent among women who had previous miscarriages or abortions. While the majority of women with a first pregnancy abortion in the sample[4] (77 per cent) had a successful full-term pregnancy, 23 per cent did not. A small-scale study by Vorlová and Němec (1976) on correlations between abortion, premature births and perinatal mortality, also found abortion to be a 'risk' factor in subsequent pregnancies. The authors examined the circumstances of all perinatal deaths (365 cases) in Brno in the period 1973–5 and found that 22.5 per cent (91 women) had previous abortions. However, an examination of a control group of 377 randomly selected live children born in the same period revealed that 15 per cent of their mothers had previous abortions.

The precise assessment of the negative impact of abortion on subsequent reproductive events on the basis of Czech data is complicated by the continued reliance on old-fashioned and more hazardous abortion techniques. The most widely used method in Czechoslovakia is that of dilation and curettage (D&C), which requires a greater dilation of the cervix (thus increasing the risk of the incompetency of the cervix) than the more modern techniques of vacuum suction or aspiration (VA). Only one-third of all abortions in Czechoslovakia used the vacuum suction method in 1975 – a bitter irony in view of the fact that this technique was used in Czechoslovakia already in 1963, well before it was introduced to the United States. Moreover, according to Hodgson (1981b, p. 225), one of the first two articles on the subject that appeared in specialised American literature (in the July

1967 issue of the scholarly journal *Obstetrics and Gynecology*) was by the leading Czech obstetrician and gynaecologist, M. Vojta, at that time the editor of *Československá gynekologie*. He reported 350 successful cases of therapeutic abortion by vacuum aspiration. The technique was rapidly introduced into the USA after the 1970 legalisation of abortion by the state of New York and is currently the most widely used abortion technique in North America. Its major advantages over the D&C technique are as follows: less time required for the procedure, smaller dilation necessary, more complete removal of the tissue, less blood loss, fewer major complications and easier adaptability to local anaesthesia (Hodgson, 1981b, p. 229). According to Havránek (1978), the continued reliance on the more hazardous D&C abortion technique in Czechoslovakia in the 1970s was due both to severe shortages of necessary medical technology (e.g. Czech- or Soviet-produced aspirators and vacurettes) and to doctors' unwillingness to use the method.

In recent years, the problem of long-term sequelae (outcomes) of induced abortions has been extensively investigated and discussed also in other countries. In an effort to clarify the issue, the US National Institute of Child Health and Human Development (NICHD) coordinated a workshop on the subject to evaluate studies conducted in 13 cities in the United States, Europe and Singapore. The consensus of the workshop was that problems appear to be small. Some studies have established no correlation between abortion and an adverse outcome of subsequent pregnancy. The studies which did report some adverse reproductive effects of abortions were associated with the classical D&C method, thus confirming the Czech data (see Maine, 1979). Collaborative studies involving nine cities in eight countries,[5] designed by the WHO Task Force on the Sequelae of Induced Abortion, also do not implicate induced abortion as an important factor in the adverse outcome of subsequent pregnancies, as long as the procedure is performed by the vacuum suction method.

In contrast, the D&C abortion technique was found to be a significant factor in accounting for subsequent pregnancy complications. Because of marked differences in abortion techniques and population characteristics, for purposes of analysis the cities were divided into three clusters: those in which most abortions were performed by D&C (Debrecen, Lodz, and Warsaw); those in which most abortions were performed by VA (Copenhagen and Newcastle); and those in which both methods were used (Helsinki, Stockholm and Ljubljana). The East European cluster was the only

group in which an adverse effect of both single and multiple terminations of pregnancy could be shown; in the other groups multiple
terminations of pregnancy did not have strong adverse effect when
compared to the outcome of single terminations or to the experience
of women in control groups. However, this is not to imply that
repeated abortions or the VA technique are entirely safe – they
appear to be safe only to a certain limit. Women who had had two or
more abortions had significantly higher risks than women who had
only one abortion, regardless of the method used (Maine, 1979;
Barron, 1979).

One factor often overlooked in the analysis of the association of
one abortion technique or another with adverse outcome is that even
the same procedure may be practiced quite differently by different
physicians and in different countries. While it is widely recognised
that the amount of dilation for the D&C technique is generally
greater than for vacuum aspiration at any given gestation, it is not
often appreciated that the amount of dilation for any given gestation
for the same abortion technique may vary quite markedly in different
countries. In fact, in WHO studies the skill of the operator accounted
for the greatest variance in the rate of complications: between the
best operator and the worst operator there was a four-fold difference.
Moreover, there has been a growing recognition that women who
seek an induced abortion may vary in important characteristics from
women who have not had an induced abortion. They may differ with
respect to smoking patterns, education, contraceptive history, etc.
Many of these factors are associated with an adverse outcome of
pregnancy, the most notable one being smoking (Belsey, 1979).

Thus the dimension of the risk of abortion to subsequent child-
bearing has not yet been established. Dr Syrovátka (1975), from the
Prague Institute for the Care of Mother and Child, argues that there
is no single most important factor accounting for pregnancy complications (e.g. miscarriage, premature birth or low birth weight). In his
view, these problems must be ultimately attributed to our modern
way of life, characterised by pollution, stress and individual isolation,
rather than simply to previous abortions. However, the WHO study
has demonstrated that method of abortion is a crucial reproductive
health factor, and that the least hazardous abortion technique should
be adopted. At present, this technique is menstrual regulation –
clearly demonstrated as being less hazardous than vacuum aspiration.

THE MENSTRUAL REGULATION TECHNIQUE OF ABORTION

The menstrual regulation method of abortion, also known as endometrial aspiration, pre-emptive abortion, menstrual extraction, menstrual induction, mini-abortion or a micro-abortion, began to gain international popularity in early 1970s (Laufe, 1979). It is a procedure 'which disrupts the intrauterine environment so that embryonic implantation cannot occur or cannot be maintained' (quoted in Morokvasić, 1981, p. 139). As presently used, the method involves vacuum curettage of the uterus which has to be performed within a few weeks after a missed menstrual period. A tiny 4–8 mm flexible plastic cannula is connected to a vacuum source and inserted into the uterus. Once a vacuum is created the cannula is gently rotated for about 30 seconds and the contents of the uterus evacuated. The whole procedure lasts no more than 2–3 minutes, requires virtually no anaesthetic or cervical dilation and can be performed by trained paramedics (Morokvasić, 1981, p. 140). The National Medical Committee of Planned Parenthood Federation of America has recommended that the procedure be performed between the fifth and fourteenth day following day one of the expected but missed period (Soderstrom, 1979), but Laufe (1979) urges that the procedure not be used prior to the seventh day after a missed menstruation. According to the results of one clinical study, 50 per cent of the procedures were found to be unnecessary if used within the first week of a missed period.

There is general agreement in the English sources that endometrial aspiration cannot be used after the fourteenth day beyond the missed period, but Dr Havránek's clinical evidence from an experimental study at the Prague Institute for the Care of Mother and Child, suggests that the procedure can be used on women whose pregnancies are slightly over that limit (see Table 8.7).

The majority of women from the sample (62 per cent) were aborted by the seventh week, and in 7 per cent of the cases, the pregnancy was terminated by the menstrual regulation technique in its ninth week. Havránek suggests 45 days without an expected period as the upper limit for women of zero parity and 60 days as an 'exceptional upper limit for multiparas or for women who had recently given birth'. If 28 days is taken as the 'normal' menstrual cycle (though many women do not conform to this 'norm'), the upper limit for the menstrual

TABLE 8.7   *Gravidity in weeks (from the first day of the last menstruation) of 700 women undergoing mini-abortion*

Days	32–35	36–42	43–69	50–56	57–60
Weeks	5	6	7	8	9
Number	8	102	327	214	49
Percent	1.1	14.6	46.7	30.6	7.0

SOURCE   Havránek, 1981, p. 482.

regulation method of abortion could be extended to 17–32 days, on the basis of Czech evidence.

Thus, menstrual regulation can be performed either on women for whom there is a positive proof of conception or those who only suspect that they are pregnant. The uncertainty about conception makes this method highly attractive to some and highly problematic to others, depending on specific moral and legal, as well as medical, standards. For example, in France, menstrual regulation does not fall under the abortion act (Loi Veil) of 1975, since it is defined as but one instance of an endouterine action. However, in the UK, menstrual regulation falls under the 1967 Abortion Act, because abortion is defined as the *intention* to terminate a pregnancy, regardless of whether or not there is a positive proof that pregnancy had occurred (Morokvasić, 1981, p. 143n).

Edelman and Berger (1981, p. 221) view menstrual regulation as 'particularly useful in countries which have restrictive laws governing abortions', but Butler Jr (1979, p. 82) argues that 'menstrual regulation without a prior pregnancy test violates the basic precept that medical or surgical treatment should not be initiated until a definite diagnosis has been made. . . . Another reservation is that part of the attractiveness of MR for some people may lie in its deceptiveness, as it is utilized in those parts of the world where abortion services are repressed by political or religious systems.'

Havránek (1981, p. 482), the leading proponent of the method in Czechoslovakia, basically shares Butler Jr's concerns. In debating which term best describes the method, he opts for a mini- or micro-abortion or an early interruption rather than menstrual regulation in order 'to prevent moral–legal objections about the possibility of [the method's] abuse'. On the other hand, Fukalová (1981, p. 491) argues in her review of the psychological aspects of menstrual regulation, that 'the very term "menstrual regulation" plays a positive role and from this standpoint is a very suitable one. A woman who does not want to be pregnant need not know with certainty whether or not she is really pregnant. Vacuum aspiration actually only stimulates menstruation, which in any case was likely only delayed, and the whole matter can be safely pushed out of consciousness after the procedure is performed.'

Hodgson (1981a, p. 224) bases her argument on relative risks and on different standards of medical care in different parts of the world. In her view, there are few instances that would justify an evacuation procedure before confirmation of pregnancy in the USA (and by implication, the rest of the developed world), because legal abortion and sensitive pregnancy tests are generally available. However, in the developing countries, characterised by high maternal mortality and morbidity rates and no access to contraception or legal abortion, 'early uterine evacuation by almost any means is always the lesser risk'.

The menstrual regulation technique of abortion was introduced in Czechoslovakia on an experimental basis between 1977 and 1980 at the Institute for the Care of Mother and Child in Prague and in selected hospitals in Ostrava and Mladá Boleslav (Havránek and Šmeral, 1979; Havránek, 1981), although the obstetrical/gynaecological journal, *Československá gynekologie*, had published an informative article on the technique (by Dr Havránek) already in 1975. The experimental research programme on 'mini-abortion' was initiated under the sponsorship of the state technical development research plan 'Health Care of New Generation'. It had the following mandate (Havránek 1981, p. 482):

(1) Verifying [the method's] clinical effectiveness in comparison with existing methods and its acceptance by women patients (since it is a procedure without an anaesthetic, performed on out-patient basis; with no or only short period of work disability).

(2) Determining if it is possible to use this method within the framework of the law no.68/1957 which requires all women to obtain an authorisation for an abortion from an interruption commission.

(3) Securing the technical conditions for its execution, especially the production of plastic aspiration cannulas.

By September 1980, Dr Havránek was ready to report the results of the research programme at an obstetrical/gynaecological conference on the subject. Since vacuums are already used for the vacuum aspiration method of abortion, the only new equipment that was required was the production of plastic cannulas. This was not all that difficult to arrange even in Czechoslovakia. An enterprise called Optimit Odra introduced cannulas into its production plan at the request of the Czech Ministry of Health in 1979. By 1981, the enterprise was expected to produce 10 000 cannulas, and by 1982 cannulas were to be produced on a serial basis (Havránek, 1981; Gold, 1981). This, of course, does not mean that there might not be shortages of the product sometime in the future, but for the time being, lack of necessary technology is not the reason why the introduction of the menstrual regulation technique on a nationwide basis has been held back in Czechoslovakia.

The mini-abortion method has fewer side-effects and complications than the more traditional methods, especially dilation and curretage – 5 per cent compared to 30–40 per cent under Czech conditions (Havránek, 1978 and 1981). So why has the method not been adopted on a nationwide basis? The main stumbling block is the existing abortion legislation, requiring each woman seeking an abortion to first obtain permission from her local abortion commission. The experimental mini-abortions that were performed at the Prague Institute for the Care of Mother and Child, occurred under exceptionally favourable conditions for eliminating bureaucratic red tape and delay. Havránek freely admits that such favourable conditions are not available elsewhere, because the processing of applications by local abortion commissions usually takes two to three weeks. Further delay is caused by late reporting of a missed menstruation. Few women in Czechoslovakia react immediately upon a missed period. In Havránek's clinical experience, women tend to report a missed period after ten to fourteen days rather than the required (if menstrual regulation technique is to be used) four to six days. Thus the majority of abortions in Czechoslovakia are performed between the seventh and tenth week of pregnancy, which is usually too late for the mini-abortion method.

ABORTION (INTERRUPTION) COMMISSIONS

As we have seen, the legalisation of abortion in Czechoslovakia has not meant abortion 'on demand'. The law provided for the so-called abortion commissions, composed of at least three members – always a doctor, usually a social worker, and one or more 'lay' representatives from the trade unions, the Council of Women or the Population Commission – to which each woman seeking an abortion must apply in her locality. Over the years interruption commissions have been subjected to a variety of conflicting criticisms ranging from bureaucratic inflexibility, smug moralism, hypocricy and insensitivity on the one hand, to leniency and a lack of professionalism on the other, both by 'lay' women and by doctors and psychologists. For example, the cultural weekly *Kulturní tvorba*, published on 17 June 1965, the following moving letter: 'The operation itself caused me no specific trouble but every time I think of the commission (and especially one of the woman members) I'm filled with panic and I can't bring myself to sleep with my husband.' Another woman, a mother of five, described her feelings in this way: 'Few members of the commission realise what it means for a sensitive mother with human feelings to sit before them as in a pillory' (Scott, 1974, p. 145; Heitlinger, 1979, p. 186).

From the feminist standpoint, the greatest criticism concerns the almost total lack of men's responsibility for conception and its termination. The woman, not the couple, makes the application; she alone must go before the commission (bringing an escort is optional). There she receives a moralistic lecture about getting herself into 'trouble', and she is subjected to pressures to have the child and, if she is single, to get married. She is the one who pays the fee, ranging from 200 to 800 crowns (approximately $20–$80). The steepness of the fee is decided by the commission on the basis of an assessment of the 'social acceptability' of the reasons for seeking an abortion (i.e. an advanced reproductive age or marital breakdown are more 'acceptable' than single status or a small apartment). These practices are consistent with the general attitude towards contraception, which is also generally seen as a woman's responsibility. Male lack of accountability for reproductive behaviour is in turn reinforced by the existing sexual division of labour, especially around child care.

Fukalová (1981, p. 492), a clinical psychologist, describes the effect of the abortion law and the abortion commissions as follows:

There still predominates a punitive approach towards a woman in our country. Even if interruption is permitted in the majority of cases, the existing required procedure contains for the woman a whole range of stressful and at times even humiliating moments. Psychopathological phenomena are then more frequent and last longer, before they pass, which in turn is reflected in marital harmony, thus contributing to a higher rate of divorce.

However, Květoň and Vojta (1972) claim, on the basis of findings from a small-scale survey of 62 women who underwent an abortion, that a majority of women (13 out of 22 single women and 22 out of 40 married women in the sample) saw abortion commissions as necessary. Professional opinion has been, of course, more influential than that of the lay public. However, experts, especially doctors, have criticised abortion commissions for opposing reasons, making it difficult to come to an agreement. One group has seen them as too permissive, granting too many abortions for social reasons, while others have seen them as too cumbersome, preventing women from taking advantage of less harmful abortion techniques which can be used only during the first few weeks of gravidity. The former have advocated stricter criteria for granting abortions, while the latter want abortion commissions to be abolished. Balák (1972), the current editor of *Československá gynekologie*, puts forward an argument for strengthening the social criteria for granting abortions on the grounds of health hazards, especially for women terminating their first pregnancy. This view is shared by Dr Kotásek (1970, p. 328), who in addition also resents the fact that doctors are put in a position of having to make what are essentially social policy decisions:

> Our energies are, however, limited. We can severely analyse, draw attention to various preventive measures, such as sex education, education for responsible parenthood, improvement of contraception, etc. This we can all do as medics. But we watch with certain bitterness the fact that we, executors of the law, deal with 80 per cent of cases which are outside the medical sphere.

The abortion legislation allows for abortions to be performed on medical as well as other (i.e. social) grounds. The range includes advanced age of the woman, a minimum family size of three children, loss or disablement of a husband, breakdown of the marriage, financial hardship caused by an additional child, unmarried status, inadequate housing, rape and so on. Only 20 per cent of abortions are performed on medical grounds; the rest, 80 per cent, are authorised for social reasons. The most consistently stated and accepted social reasons have been unmarried status, inadequate housing and a large number of children (three or more) in a family. Thus gynaecologists are forced to deal with such issues as the seriousness of the housing problem, whether a marriage which is entered into under the pressure of pregnancy will last, the ideal family size and living standards. These questions are obviously unrelated to the biologically-oriented medical training of a doctor, yet they constitute the bulk of a gynaecologist's work in the clinic as well as in the abortion commission (which usually meets once a week for a whole day).

Some doctors have resolved their social dilemma by adopting a purely formalistic, rubber-stamping approach towards abortion requests. Among the 40 married women studied by Květoň and Vojta (1972) soon after their abortions, 24 claimed that their doctor's approach to the abortion request was largely indifferent and formalistic. On the other hand, 16 out of the 22 single women in the sample claimed that their doctor tried to reverse their decision to interrupt the pregnancy, obviously unsuccessfully. Only half of all the respondents saw in their doctor an adviser on the issue; the other half ignored the doctor's view, preferring to rely on advice from relatives, friends or co-workers. Such attitudes illustrate the limitations of medical professional power over clients and support Strong's (1979) criticism of the thesis of 'medical imperialism'.

A decrease in authorised abortions performed on social grounds is also advocated in a thoughtful article by Dr Birgus (1979). He questions (on p. 75) the validity of the 'traditional assumption in the minds of many psychiatrists and clinical psychologists that an unwanted child during pregnancy will always remain unwanted, and that its eventual and conspicuous difficulties in behaviour are related to the initial negative attitude of the mother towards its existence. On the other hand,' he argues, 'the opposite assumption, trading among the lay public, not excepting many women members of the interruption commissions, that the birth of the child will change everything and that the mother will immediately love it, is also not valid.' In an attempt to find a solution, Birgus (1979, p. 73) advocates a more professional approach to the selection of commission members:

It is necessary to pay particular attention to the selection of women members, because they must be capable of orienting themselves in some unusual situations. They must also display great sensitivity and an individualised approach to each woman applicant and her possible companion. For each woman applicant is more or less psychologically disturbed, requiring both an understanding as well as firm regulation. . . . an additional advantage would be if women members of the commission could obtain some training prior to their assumption of office, and if methodological training continued in district seminars, which should take place at least once a year. For work in the abortion commissions is very responsible, troublesome and predominantly overtime.

Birgus also suggests that mothers of the applicants be invited to the commission's proceedings (with the agreement of the applicant) with the view to convince the woman not to terminate her pregnancy. Another suggestion put forward (if housing difficulties are stated as the reason for seeking an abortion) is that the allocation of an apartment be guaranteed if the request is withdrawn and pregnancy carried to term. In concluding his article, Birgus (1979, p. 75) argues as follows:

The problem of unwanted pregnancies is socially very serious and has to be resolved in a complex way, in all of its dimensions, both from the the perspective of the positive development of the child and from the viewpoint of preserving the health as well as the possibility of motherhood of the woman. It is not possible to expect workers of only one discipline to reach valid conclusions and to find optimal solutions. I think that it would be useful to organise a national conference under the auspices of the Ministry of Health and the Government Population Commission, with broad participation of specialists from related professions – psychologists, psychiatrists, pedagogues, sex therapists, paediatrists and sociologists. . . . The conclusions of this conference could significantly move forward the problem of unwanted pregnancies, and simultaneously diminish the hesitations of interruption commissions as how to proceed in contentious cases.

Birgus' final comment goes against the recommendation from the 1980 Conference in Vsetín on menstrual regulation where Dr Havránek and others argued for the *abolition* of abortion commissions.

Havránek (1981) supports his proposal by the following three arguments:

(1) some other socialist countries, namely the USSR, GDR, Poland and Yugoslavia do not have abortion commissions;[6]
(2) over the years, the complicated, time-consuming bureaucratic

procedures of the commissions have turned down only 2.3 per cent of all requests; moreover, the unsuccessful requests have often led not to childbirth but to a 'spontaneous' abortion;
(3) Czech child psychiatrists have demonstrated the unfavourable development of the so-called unwanted children.

The latter two arguments refer to a longitudinal study of 220 Prague children born to women twice denied abortion (once on initial request and again on appeal) during 1961–3, and of 220 children in a matched control group, i.e. children born to women who did not request an abortion. (Not requesting an abortion does not, of course, guarantee that the child is 'wanted', but, short of extensive interviewing, it is the only relatively easily obtainable measure available). The matching criteria included age and sex of the child (the children were equally divided between boys and girls), school class, mother's age, birth order, and socio-economic status of the family.

The study started with the examination of records on 555 women who requested but were denied an abortion in Prague during 1961–3. By 1977, it had been established that only 316 (57 per cent) of these women had carried their pregnancy to term. In other words, 239 (43 per cent) of the original women managed to avoid giving birth, either by obtaining a legal abortion from another district abortion commission, or by re-applying in the same district but under an assumed name and address (of a sister, mother or friend, whose IDs were relatively easily obtainable), or by aborting 'spontaneously'. Twenty-two per cent, twice the national average for the ratio of miscarriages to completed pregnancies, 'resolved' their unwanted pregnancy in this way, either deliberately or by sheer luck.

However, the research focused primarily on the children rather than on the mothers. Compared to the 'wanted' children in the matched group, the 'unwanted' children exhibited higher incidence of illness and hospitalisation (despite an identical initial biological start in life), slightly poorer school marks and performance (despite the same level of intelligence) and somewhat worse integration in the peer group. While the aggregate differences between the 'wanted' and 'unwanted' children were not dramatic, and not easily detectable in individual cases, they were nonetheless significant, because they were consistent, cumulative, and persisting or actually increasing into adolescence. School, social, and family life was less satisfactory and less stable, especially for the boys and only children. A continuation of the study was planned for 1983–4, to determine whether developmental differences between 'wanted' and 'unwanted' children persist into adulthood.

The results of this study are well known to Western population experts because they have been published in several journals and books in English (see Dytrych *et al.*, 1975 and 1978; Matějček *et al.*, 1978, 1979, 1980; David, 1981; David and Matějček, 1981; David and McIntyre, 1981, pp. 236–8). The study is also well known in Czechoslovakia itself. It was published in a two-volume book of 463 pages under the title 'Unwanted Children'. Although it was issued as an internal, specialist publication, it also received some general publicity. For example, on 19 May 1978, the second Czech TV channel devoted 20 minutes of its programming to a discussion of its content. Birgus (1979, p. 71) even wonders 'whether and to what extent the conclusion of the Prague study . . . . influenced the thinking of district interruption commissions in the sense that they began to refuse fewer applications'.

An additional argument for mini-abortions and the required abolition of the interruption commissions, suggested by Presl *et al.* (1982, p. 91), rests on the economic advantage of the procedure. If 50 000 out of 90 000 annual abortions were performed by this method, Presl *et al.* argue, '500 000 working days would be saved (by reduction in the length of work disability) and 200 000 hospital beds would be also saved (the current average abortion hospitalisation being 4 days)'. Additional cuts in costs could be realised by utilising paramedics rather than doctors for performing the procedure, although this argument is stronger for the capitalist than for the socialist countries, because the gap between the official salaries of doctors and paramedics is much greater in the former than in the latter. However, savings in doctors' time are equally applicable to both systems.

Štěpán (1981a, p. 215), a medical lawyer, provides a good summary of the issues in the current controversy:

(1) Is it appropriate if still today, almost quarter of a century after the passage of the abortion decree, there survives a conception of abortion as an exception from criminal prosecution rather than as a woman's right – enshrined in the legislation and even in the constitutions of several countries – to decide about her motherhood?

(2) Is it correct to make the authorisation of an abortion dependent on exacting administrative licensing preconditions, which

considerably aggravate the woman's situation, and which in broader practice prevent the utilisation of a new method, requiring an early measure, which, to be sure, is less harmful and economically substantially more effective?

(3) From the perspective of the theory of the state and the law, is it appropriate to establish an administrative commission for the granting of permission, which deals with almost 100 000 cases annually, and with few exceptions decides on all of them positively?

In another paper, presented at the Vsetín Conference, Štěpán (1981b, pp. 493–4) goes a step further and makes two concrete suggestions as to how to change existing legislation to accommodate the menstrual regulation technique. The less radical solution would be:

a partial measure, without any changes in the [abortion] law (which requires a permission of a 'commission established for this purpose'), by the issuing of new decrees of the Czech and Slovak governments; there could be stated, in contrast to the current situation, that an abortion request submitted within 8–10 weeks of pregnancy could be decided upon by a short route by an expert health care committee in a health care establishment, while commissions would only deal with requests submitted later. This would at the same time conspicuously motivate early submissions of requests.

As a more radical, 'more basic' solution, Štěpán suggests the issuing of a:

new law on planned parenthood, in which there could be enshrined a basic woman's right to decide about her motherhood, and the whole problematic would be resolved in a more complex way – including education for parenthood, contraception, interception, abortion, sterilisation and castration for social reasons, artifical insemination, together with measures which encourage successful parenthood. Our health legislation, which enjoys a high degree of international recognition, would thus gain a desirable standard also in this field.

This concerted campaign to get the abortion law changed has so far produced no results. A prominent obstetrician in Prague stated in the summer of 1982 (i.e. almost two years after the Vsetín conference and seven years since the appearance of Havránek's first article on mini-abortions) that a new government decree (rather than a new law), along the lines suggested by Štěpán, would be issued by the end of the year. However, at the same time another doctor warned that if a new abortion decree or law was not passed by the end of 1982, it would probably not be passed at all in view of declining birth rates and rising abortion rates – a reversal of the situation prevailing during the mid-1970s. It would appear that opponents of liberal abortion legislation, fearing that it might encourage 'reproductive irresponsibility', have gained enough political support to prevent legislative changes. However, the issue is by no means closed. For example, on 17 December 1983, the popular Saturday edition of *Rudé právo*, the party daily, published a lengthy interview with Dr Šráček, the chief of obstetrics/gynaecology in the largest hospital in the steel city Ostrava (which took part in the experimental research programme on mini-abortion) and a member of the Government Population Commission. In the interview (which dealt with both contraception and abortion), Dr Šráček, explained the numerous advantages of the menstrual regulation technique:

> We have commented that the existence of commissions prevent the use of the method. Recently Dr Rott and I visited the GDR where we studied their practice. There are no abortion commissions in the GDR in the sense in which we have them. A woman alone decides within 12 weeks of her gestation whether or not she will remain pregnant. She does not go to a commission but instead goes directly to her gynaecologist. Thus this new, more modern and, for the health of women, less hazardous technique can be used much more easily.

When asked outright by the reporter Štěpánková (1983) whether he is against abortion commissions, Dr. Šráček's answer was equally forthright, if more diplomatic:

> Since you've put the question in this way, I will answer it. I am not at all against abortion commissions, but I do not consider it right that commissions decide whether or not a woman will keep her child. Commissions which also include a physician and a psychologist should advise her, possibly also solve some of her problems, but they should not make the decision for her. There is one very

nice study, which statistically proves that the most dangerous period for the health and life of a woman is her pregnancy, childbirth and post-partum; less so an abortion. The majority of women want to have children and therefore willingly exchange the health risk for becoming a mother. The duty of health care workers is then to give her the best protection during this period against possible negative consequences. But if the woman does not want to take the risk I believe that nobody has the right to pressure her into it. Again I could recall research which proved that children who were born as unwanted, when women were twice denied abortion, were children who were damaged in various ways.

Thus Dr Šráček, a man of some influence, came out strongly as a defender of women's reproductive rights. The publication of this interview thus indicates that if the abortion legislation is not changed, then it at least will eventually be modified to accommodate the menstrual regulation technique. However, for the time being, women in Czechoslovakia are stuck with what has been acknowledged by numerous Czechoslovak experts as a somewhat anachronistic abortion law as well as abortion techniques that are more harmful than well-known alternatives.

NOTES

1. For historical reviews of the various issues and groups involved at various times in the abortion debates in the USA and the UK, see Luker (1984) and Francome (1984).
2. Statistical analysis of the incidence of abortion generally relies on two distinct indicators: rates and ratios. Measures relating the number of abortions to the number of women (or total population) are referred to as rates, whereas measures relating abortions to births or pregnancies are called ratios. All abortion rates are period measures, not cohort measures, because data permitting computation of the latter are not available. Even if such data were available, they would be of limited interest because they would describe the reproductive experience of a cohort that had most of its pregnancies and abortions some time in the past. Moreover, a computation of the total first abortion rate (the proportion of all women that has experienced or will experience an induced abortion in their lifetime), sometimes referred to as 'prevalence' of abortion, on the basis of current *period* data would also produce very misleading results because the rapid changes in the incidence of legal abortion in recent years may have resulted in age patterns quite different from the patterns ultimately experienced by the cohorts of women now in the early portion of their reproductive years.

Abortion rates and ratios yield different but complementary information and it is important not to confuse them. Since an abortion ratio corresponding to a given abortion rate is higher when the birth rate is low than when the birth rate is high, countries with comparable populations could easily differ on these two indicators (Tietze, 1981, pp. 4–5).

3. As Tietze (1981, p. 42) points out, the term 'parity' is somewhat ambiguous. Some countries report it in terms of the distribution of legal abortions by prior deliveries, others by prior live births, still others by surviving children. However, where infant and later childhood mortality is low, these procedural differences are of little consequence.

4. The study, based on a random sample of 13 144 women experiencing their second pregnancy, 820 of whom had previous abortions, was conducted in the district of Plzeň in 1974–6. The proportion of first pregnancy terminations in the sample is significantly less (almost by half) than the national average of 15–17 per cent for single and childless women, the majority of whom are first pregnancy terminations. The authors of this study do not comment on this discrepancy.

5. These were Copenhagen in Denmark, Debrecen in Hungary, Helsinki in Finland, Ljubljana in Yugoslavia, Newcastle-upon-Tyne in the United Kingdom, Seoul in Korea, Stockholm in Sweden and Warsaw and Lodz in Poland.

6. Yugoslavia abolished abortion commissions in 1969. Apart from Czechoslovakia, they exist only in Hungary and Bulgaria. However, throughout the period of liberal abortion legislation (1956–73), the function of the Hungarian commissions has been purely advisory since applications had to be approved if the woman persisted (Tietze, 1981, p. 12).

9 Pregnancy and Prenatal Care

'There are measurements, analyses, consultations . . . . "Attend for physiotherapy" . . . "Consult an endocrinologist" . . . "When did you last see the dentist?" And I've hardly left the surgery when the phone starts ringing. I know – it's the clinic again!' Vera says she has been ill so seldom that she hadn't any idea that the doctors could be so nagging. 'I'm not really annoyed, though,' she grins. 'I know the doctors have to take care not of me alone, but of both of us.' ('Vera, in our office, is expecting . . .', *Soviet Weekly*, 2 July 1983).

Pregnancy, like other transitional social conditions, is character-ized by ambiguity and hence, is open to contrasting styles of management. (Comaroff, 1977, p. 131)

Pregnancy straddles several boundaries simultaneously. Like other reproductive events, it is at the junction of 'nature' and 'culture', involving a biological process that is accomplished by social beings in particular social settings. It is both an individual and a social process: child-bearing is associated with a 'fixed' biological person,[1] but it is also subject to considerable social manipulation and control. In advanced industrial societies, the major agencies responsible for the social management of child-bearing are the state and the medical profession. As we saw in Chapters 4 and 5, state intervention ranges from protective legislation through maternity leaves to the provision of free antenatal medical care, while medical management is typically experienced as thoroughly pervasive.

Biologically speaking, child-bearing is a normal reproductive proc-ess, but the borderline between health and illness is not very clearly marked during this time. The numerous changes that occur in the mother's body leave the status of child-bearing rather unclear and open to various interpretations. For example, potential complications (e.g. hypertension, toxaemia, miscarriage or premature birth) as well as some normal pregnancy symptoms (such as morning sickness or general fatigue) mark pregnancy as akin to illness, but feelings of general physical and emotional well-being (experienced by many women) place child-bearing firmly in the category of health.

The experience of Vera, the Soviet woman in the quotation above, is quite typical for all women in advanced industrial societies. Drawing on data from two British studies, Graham and Oakley (1981, p. 57) have argued that:

> the most common way in which the 'as if ill' rule is manifested in antenatal care today is through the routine prescriptions of various tests and procedures such as ultrasonic scanning, twenty-four hour urine collection for the measurement of placental function, and frequent internal examination to assess the competence of the cervix. The subject of tests and procedures occupies an important place in the antenatal encounter . . . For some women these sophisticated procedures and forms of treatment are the hallmark of a 'proper' pregnancy. Other women felt less happy about this medicalisation of childbearing, unaware perhaps of the equation between pregnancy and illness until they began their careers as antenatal patients. The first antenatal visit thus comes as a considerable shock, disturbing long-held notions about pregnancy as a natural process.

Another British study found that many women contemplate pregnancy, especially their first, with considerable ambivalence and with an anticipation of personal loss as well as gain. Some women had a clear definition, but others were unsure about the meaning of child-bearing throughout their pregnancy. Moreover, many expectant mothers perceived that others in the community were also not sure whether to treat them as ill or well (Comaroff, 1977, p. 116). Thus ambiguity is a fundamental, rather than a peripheral, feature of child-bearing, and it reinforces differences between, as well as within, lay and medical perspectives on pregnancy. Health care professionals tend to diverge in their opinion about approaches and procedures – about whether a particular pregnancy is normal or pathological, or how many prenatal visits with a physician or a nurse are necessary. The differences between the maternal and the medical perspectives are often more fundamental, revolving around such issues as who is the expert (the expectant mother, the doctor or the midwife), or the already mentioned status of child-bearing as health or illness. The three British researchers also found that antenatal ambiguities (or competing frames of reference[2]) significantly distort and hinder communication between mothers and doctors.

UTILISATION OF MEDICAL ANTENATAL SERVICES

In contrast with North America and many Western European countries, socialist obstetrics belong to primary càre medicine. Moreover, there is a clear distinction between ambulatory and hospital maternity care. Physicians (as well as women's nurses) working in an antenatal clinic for most part do not work in a hospital, and vice versa. Most pregnant women see an obstetrician at the prenatal clinic in their locality and only if there is a diagnosis of complications or risks is the woman referred to the out-patient obstetrical ward of her local hospital. About 30 per cent of expectant mothers in Czechoslovakia are diagnosed annually as having 'risk pregnancies', though only 6 per cent of all pregnant woman actually experience serious complications (Kotzmanová, 1979, Štembera *et al.*, 1979). This is a smaller proportion than in the West where 'the distinction between normal and abnormal pregnancy has become blurred. Some doctors reject the word "normal" as inappropriate, and classify all pregnant women as low risk, medium risk or high risk patients.' (Lumley and Astbury, 1980, p. 74). In a similar vein, Rothman (1982, p. 132) has argued that contemporary medicine:

> has distinguished between 'low risk' and 'high risk' pregnancy, with the emphasis always on risk, and then goes on to define an ever increasing proportion of pregnancies as 'high risk'. That is, normal pregnancy may exist and be only 'low risk', but there are many factors that will make any given pregnancy 'high risk' . . . The tendency is clearly to broaden the 'high risk' category.

Women in Eastern Europe generally cannot freely choose their own physician (or an independent women's nurse performing 'doctor's work' – see Chapter 6 for more details) but must see one in their place of residence or work. All the available popular and professional literature on prenatal care in Czechoslovakia suggests that nearly every woman sees a medical specialist nine times during the course of her pregnancy and not later than 16 weeks after conception, with the exception of Romanys (Gypsies). Fewer than 1 per cent of all Czechoslovak pregnant women do not have any prenatal medical care but 21 per cent of Romany women are estimated to have no such care and an additional 23 per cent register their pregnancies only six months after conception. The Romanys also exhibit a high incidence of premature births (17–20 per cent), perinatal mortality (31–42 per cent) and infant mortality (70–80 per cent), thus 'tarnishing' the favourable international image of Czechoslovak perinatal medicine. As we saw in Chapter 7, Czechoslovak authorities have tried to reduce the high incidence of perinatal problems among the Romanys by encouraging sterilisation, so far without much success.

The quality and accessibility of prenatal and postnatal care in Eastern Europe is generally highly regarded, both by Western commentators (see, for example, Mieczkowski, 1982, pp. 22–3) and in the socialist countries themselves. Prokopec (1975, p. 65), the current Czech Minister of Health, and Petro (1980, p. 120), a prominent Slovak physician, go as far as arguing that the high frequency of prenatal consultations in Czechoslovakia indicates a superiority of the socialist maternity care system compared to the system existing in some Western capitalist countries, notably France and West Germany, where pregnant women see a medical specialist only half as frequently (3–5 times during a pregnancy). However, this sharp dichotomy between maternity care 'under socialism' and 'under capitalism' is largely rhetorical, obscuring an increasing similarity between the two systems of maternity care as well as variations within them. For example, Polish antenatal care is characterised by significant rural–urban disparities in provision and utilisation. Mieczkowski (1982, p. 22) reports that in 1977 pregnant women in Polish villages 'received 9.8 per cent of all consultations to pregnant women. Yet the proportion of women between the ages of 15 and 49 living in villages was at the same time 37.4 per cent.'

In contrast, the 66 carefully selected expectant mothers studied by Ann Oakley (1979a) in London, England, reported making between 7 and 18 visits to the GP, local authority or hospital clinic: the average was 13, which is not that dissimilar from the Czech experience. Even in the United States, characterised by the most 'capitalist' system of health care in the developed world, 'only' 1.4 per cent (approximately 44 000) of pregnant women have no medical care. The majority of pregnant women – 49 per cent – see a medical, specialist during the first or second month of pregnancy; an additional 30 per cent do so by the third month and 11 per cent by the fourth month. This leaves 'only' 12 per cent of pregnant women who begin their prenatal medical care in the second half of their pregnancy (see *Health United States 1980*, p. 155). Lumley and Astbury (1980, p. 74) convincingly argue that:

> as pregnancy has become more a medical and less of a social event, the rules about appropriate behaviour in pregnancy have changed too. The medical rules state that *the* way to have a healthy baby is by attending a doctor for regular antenatal care, preferably at 8, 12, 16, 20, 24, 28, 32, 34, 37, 38, 39, 40, 41 and 42 weeks of pregnancy and by having a number of special tests and investigations . . . The medical rules about antenatal care are a dominant feature of most Western cultures. They are one example of a general tendency found in many cultures to deal with the ambiguous nature of pregnancy by setting up rules which prescribe certain acts for pregnant women.[3]

Moreover, the cultural definition of pregnancy as a 'series of medical encounters' which is characteristic of all advanced industrial societies, is also increasingly penetrating Third World countries to the extent that non-attendance at prenatal clinics has become synonymous with deviance. For example, Erna Brodber (1974, p. 10), in her study of child abandonment in Jamaica, has argued that 'to seek prenatal care from the hospital in which one intends to have one's baby delivered has become so widely accepted a procedure that failure to adopt it may well indicate a negative predisposition towards the child'. Researchers in Czechoslovakia who have studied the problem of high infant mortality among the Romanys have tended to approach the issue from a similar perspective. Seeking medical care during pregnancy has become such a broadly accepted social norm, that a mother's failure to conform is likely to result in her being (1) labelled as a 'potential risk' and (2) referred to a social worker for close observation. Thus state policies of providing free prenatal medical care tend to have a strong controlling effect on pregnant women, since expectant mothers no longer have a real option of refusing it.

Yet are prenatal medical consultations all that beneficial? While the social-work-type concerns about mothers who fail to seek *any* prenatal medical care are generally well founded, the correlation between the frequency of prenatal consultations and pregnancy outcome is much more problematic. As Rothman (1982, p. 157) put it:

we do have any number of studies showing us that more prenatal care is associated with lower infant mortality rates. These studies can, however, be misleading. For one thing, measures of good prenatal care count prenatal visits – the more visits, the lower the infant mortality. But if births are premature – a leading cause of infant mortality – there is less opportunity for prenatal care. This does not show that having fewer visits causes prematurity.

A similar, though methodologically more sophisticated argument is put forward by Harris (1982, p. 15):

> The role of prenatal care has been the subject of serious dispute in the obstetric and public health literature for nearly four decades. This dispute has been fomented in great part by the nonexperimental nature of the evidence. Virtually all studies of prenatal care analyze cross-section data on the uncontrolled experience of thousands of women and their pregnancies. The subjects under study are therefore self-selected. There are no randomized treatments. Possible confounding variables cannot be eliminated. Nor do the data reveal how the subjects actually made use of the medical services.

Although the conventional wisdom (medical as well as political) holds that prenatal medical care contributes to favourable pregnancy outcome, Harris speculates that prenatal care may be serving as a proxy for a more complex set of phenomena. In his view, 'the most feasible approach is to design clinical studies that are more narrowly focussed on certain types of prenatal intervention. They may not resolve the value of millions of routine visits women make to their obstetricians. But we could at least learn something about prenatal diet, weight gain, vitamin supplementation, exercise, ultrasound studies and other aspects of medical care.' (p. 48). As we shall see below, at least one Czech doctor has been engaged in conducting such a study.

Dr J. K., an anonymous physician from the Prague Institute for the Care of Mother and Child, has argued that the current emphasis on regular monthly prenatal consultations is misguided, since in some instances it may even contribute to adverse pregnancy outcomes. A survey of 881 consultation visits in seven prenatal clinics in various parts of Bohemia revealed a whole range of teratogenic potentials which are inherent in the practical arrangements for clinic attendance, such as travel to and from the clinic, time spent waiting at the clinic and the presence of small children of multiparous women.

Women in this nationwide study were prepared (forced?) to spend a considerable amount of time travelling and waiting at the clinic. The majority (66 per cent) of attenders come to the clinic by public transport, mainly relying on the bus. One third of the sample walked and a negligible proportion used a car. Each single journey took on average 60 minutes, with significant regional variation. Waiting to see the doctor at the clinic took an additional 90 minutes, during which the woman registered with the nurse, took her urine sample, stepped on the weight scale and so on, but for the most part, just sat and waited. Dr J. K. also points out that many Czech medical waiting rooms are poorly ventilated and illuminated, thus adding to the discomfort of the waiting mother-to-be. However, the modern pre-natal clinic at the housing estate in Prague's eighth district is quite bright and spacious. There are benches around the wall and posters on the wall, encouraging proper diet, breastfeeding and physical exercises, and discouraging smoking. A notice on the bulletin board informed the women that prenatal classes at a nearby gymnasium were temporarily cancelled 'due to reconstruction' but that women were free to attend them in another district (about an hour's ride on the streetcar). There was no other reading material available and the waiting women passed their time either talking to each other or reading whatever they brought with them. They were called to the office to see the doctor in batches, re-emerging in 10–15 minutes. This anecdotal observation of 'assembly line' prenatal medicine seems to confirm the more general results in J. K.'s study that in 80 per cent of the cases, the doctor–patient consultation did not last longer than 10 minutes. What all of this amounts to is that pregnant women in Czechoslovakia typically spend $3\frac{1}{2}$ hours in travel and waiting every month to see a doctor for 10 minutes!

In contrast, women attending a prenatal clinic in Glasgow, the largest city in Scotland, reported taking 'only' up to half an hour on a single journey to the clinic and an additional 30–60 minutes waiting to see the doctor. Only six mothers in the sample took their children with them to the clinic. Fifteen mothers had all their children at school, while the remaining 35 relied upon support from friends and/or family (Reid and McIlwaine, 1980, p. 365). Eighty-eight children under the age of five accompanied the 881 mothers in the Czech sample – roughly the same proportion as in Glasgow. While the British authors (who are sociologists) make no medical comment on the presence of children, the Czech doctor considers *any* presence of small children in a clinic waiting room as a health hazard, on the grounds that small children constitute a major source of both viral and bacterial infections. The lengthy period of waiting only compounds the problem, especially among women whose gestation is in its early stages (5–8 weeks). Travel to and from the clinic by the means of public transportation is also not free of infectious risks, not to mention the lack of comfort entailed in noisy, bouncy and crowded buses and streetcars.

In addition to these 'practical' objective health hazards, Dr J. K. found that only 7–8 per cent of all the prenatal consultations led to the diagnosis of 'risk pregnancy.' Moreover, the Czech doctor also found no correlation between the duration of medical consultation and a diagnosis of some form of pregnancy pathology. Among the 164 women (19 per cent of the sample) whose prenatal consultation took longer than 10 minutes (i.e. 15, 20 or even 30 minutes), only 28 women (3 per cent of the original sample) were found with some negative indications. This is not a criticism; quite to the contrary. Dr J. K. (1978, p. 666) genuinely admires the 'splendid achievement of a doctor in a clinic, who is able in a relatively short period of time (a norm = 12 consultations per hour) to deal in five minutes with serious, risk states'.

In contrast, Dr Gazárek and his colleague (1972, p. 613) are quite critical of the medical work performance at the prenatal clinic. In their view, the work at the clinic is undeservedly underestimated, thus contributing to its lack of prestige. It tends to be assigned to the youngest and the least experienced doctors and in some cases only to women's nurses (see Chapter 6 for more details). In the authors' view antenatal clinic work ought to be allocated to the most experienced obstetricians, who are better able to differentiate normal from pathological and risk pregnancies in the early stages of gestation. All too frequently, apparently, there is insufficient recording as well as interpreting of individual and family medical history (especially with respect to diabetes and potential toxaemia), neglect of vaginal examination for the incompetency of the cervix, lack of active treatment of discharge and insufficient encouragement of psycho-prophylaxis.

Another criticism concerns excessive paperwork required of doctors and nurses. According to Kvíz (1972), a typical Czech pregnancy must be recorded in eleven to thirteen different places and forms, and if the expectant mother requires an approval for work disability, the number increases to fourteen to sixteen. Pulling all this information

together apparently constitutes an important part of the women's
nurse's work at the clinic, leaving little time for meaningful instruction about various aspects of prenatal self-care. The typical 5–10
minutes doctor–patient interaction also allows no time for meaningful health education, assuming that doctors are interested in such
work in the first place. According to Graham and Oakley (1981, pp.
69–70), in Britain the main aim of medical explanation in a typical
antenatal encounter (lasting an average 3.9 minutes), is to allay
anxiety rather than share information. Thus the 'assembly line'
organisation of antenatal clinics, when one doctor must see a large
number of patients in a short period of time, goes a long way towards
explaining why mothers in Czechoslovakia prefer TV, than health
care professionals, as their source of information on reproduction.

The current organisation of prenatal medical care is therefore
coming under criticism, both from within the medical profession and
from women. Dr J. K. (1978, p. 667), points out that 'the existing
system of prenatal clinics has made no impact for some time now on
the lowering of stillbirth and postnatal mortality'. Dr J. K. favours a
reduction in the number of required antenatal consultations, which in
turn should be based on the specific conditions of the actual pregnancy rather than on some abstract statistical norm. This doctor is
not unique in this view. For example, Hall *et al.* (1980, p. 80), from
the Department of Obstetrics and Gynaecology at Aberdeen Maternity Hospital, Scotland, suggest that normal multigravidae should
have only 5 full medical examinations during the course of pregnancy, at 12 weeks gestation (to arrange booking for care and
confinement and to clarify doubtful dates), around 22 weeks gestation (to detect multiple pregnancy and to establish a baseline weight
for later weight-gain analysis), at 30 weeks gestation (to diagnose
interuterine growth and weight-gain pattern), at 36 weeks gestation
(to detect breech or other malpresentation) and around full term (to
assess whether induction is advisable). The authors also suggest that
much more responsibility for antenatal care be given to midwives, on
the grounds that 'in Sweden, where perinatal mortality is low, doctors see women on only two of their twelve antenatal visits'. Lumley
and Astbury (1980, pp. 80–1) quote remarks made by a senior British
obstetrician during his visit to Australia in 1978, who 'suggested that
it would be sensible to reduce the number of antenatal visits to a
doctor and to spend the money thus saved on extra routine tests such
as two ultrasound examinations and weekly recording of the foetal
heart for the last month of pregnancy'. In a similar vein, Lumley and

Astbury quote an eminent American doctor 'who has written a brief article advocating a shorter hospital stay after birth (in the USA at present it is about three days), so that the $300 so saved could be used to finance "routine intensive obstetric surveillance"'. Lumley and Astbury (1980, pp. 77–87) identify 21 antenatal tests and investigations currently in use, but conclude (p. 81) that 'for many antenatal tests we have no clear information about either cost or reliability, nor do we know the tests' contribution to long-term outcomes for mothers and infants'.

Medicine in Eastern Europe tends to rely on tests less extensively than its counterpart in the West, but this is due more to lack of resources than to professional opinion. Greater professionalisation of medical prenatal care. (advocated by Dr Gazárek and colleagues) implies more tests, as does the proposal for urine self-examination by Dr J. K., with the important difference of placing greater emphasis on self-care. Interestingly, Dr J. K. makes no mention of antenatal home visits, presumably being of the opinion that their usefulness (or rather lack thereof) is similar to that cited in Chapter 6. Many Czech women see no usefulness in prenatal home visit by a women's nurse (Trča, 1978). In any case, during the past two decades, the frequency of home visits by women's nurses has been consistently declining and there is no sign that this tendency is about to reverse itself. It seems that women who are eager to learn more about their pregnancies have to rely on sources other than their attending physicians and nurses.

EXPERT ADVICE AND INDIVIDUAL BEHAVIOUR

Apart from regularly visiting doctors, pregnant women in Czechoslovakia are also expected to read antenatal health educational literature. However, the choice is quite restricted. A search through Prague bookstores and public libraries during the summer of 1981 produced only *two* antenatal guides, although there were four additional books which included pregnancy as one of their topics.[4] Moreover, Šabata and Fišerová (1974) restrict themselves to advice on nutrition and diet during complicated pregnancies so that one is actually left with only one advice book – Trča's immensely popular and comprehensive book entitled *Budeme mít děťátko* (*We Are Going to Have a Baby*) (Trča, 1979). In its 270 pages, the book offers advice on physical exercises, suitable maternity clothing, nutrition (including recipies), foetal development, sex, entitlement to maternity leave, the recognition of signs of labour, hospital birth procedures, post-partum (interestingly I could find no mention of post-partum depression), the elimination of 'bad' habits and infant care.

While the book is ostensibly written for couples, most of the remarks are in fact, addressed to the mother. The expectant father is given a brief chapter – five pages long – in which he is portrayed rather stereotypically, as a 'helpful' and 'caring' partner but also as one who is really quite incompetent, especially when it comes to the birth itself:

Your wife needs to rest more frequently during her pregnancy; she will certainly be grateful to you if you help her with shopping, tidying the apartment, etc. Some husbands even go as far as doing physical exercises with their wives . . . Your sexual relations with your wife during pregnancy have to be suitably adjusted. For we know of cases when a husband out of ignorance damaged the health of his wife and the developing foetus by his incorrect sexual practices. That is why this book devotes a whole chapter to the question of sex life during pregnancy. Read it carefully.

With the approaching due date of birth, help your wife to prepare everything that she needs to take with her to the hospital. When labour begins, don't lose your head. Don't at that time be as incompetent as the husband of one woman writer. We were able to read the contents of her letter which she sent to her woman friend after she gave birth. We are excerpting these few sentences from it: 'When my labour contractions started during the night, my husband was fast asleep. For a long time, I didn't dare to wake him up. But when I felt that the time had come to go to the hospital, I decided to gently wake him up after all. My husband became so agitated that he got a bad headache. I tried to calm him down in vain; I finally gave him a pill against his headache and then a cold compress on his head. During our taxi ride to the hospital I had to soothe him continuously and put him at ease. When we arrived my husband sat down in the waiting room near the obstetrical ward, but he looked so ill at ease that a midwife who saw him there decided to call a doctor because she thought that he was seriously ill.' The birth itself, concludes the woman in her letter, was an insignificant episode in comparison with the worries about her husband's health.

We are quoting this story so that you, the expectant father, are better prepared for the birth than the husband of the above mentioned woman writer. We are convinced that you are going to conduct yourself quite differently. When labour begins, you're not going to lose your head, but instead you'll call the ambulance, take the suitcase and accompany (full of joyful expectation) your wife to the maternity ward.

As Coleman Romalis (1981, p. 92) points out, antenatal literature in the Anglo-Saxon countries has also given relatively short shrift to the father, and where he does appear, it is usually in a semi-comical role, or else inclined toward pathology.

Generally the assumption has been that in contemporary Western culture the man is less interested in childbirth and less well equipped to take a significant role in it. Culturally, of course, this assumption had some basis: men widely accepted the belief that after the important and irreplaceable function of 'planting the seed', their manly duties were completed for a time. They could sit back and watch with pride as their wives swelled and eventually with the assistance of a midwife or a doctor, gave birth. Only then did the father re-enter the picture.

If we accept this line of reasoning, then we could argue that Czech men have remained very much within the mainstream of Western contemporary culture, since their interest in pregnancy has been relatively weak. Alternatively, if we go along with Bittman and Zalk (1978), who make a case for a new cultural emphasis upon an increased male presence in the whole child-bearing process, then Czech men are on the cultural 'periphery'. The typical husband is relatively uninterested in his wife's pregnancy and has no particular desire to be present during his child's birth, an attitude in which he is generally supported both by his wife and the medical profession. As we shall see in the next chapter, current medical regulations exclude the father from the maternity hospital for the entire duration of the mother's stay there (5–8 days). However, there is some evidence that Czech expectant mothers would like their husbands to be better informed about and take more interest in child-bearing (Trča, 1978).

Sexual practice during pregnancy is another area of controversy. We noted that Dr Trča cautions husbands to be 'careful' in this regard but this advice tends to be ignored. For example, 90 per cent of pregnant women from a survey research on sexuality during pregnancy reported to have had intercourse throughout their pregnancy. Moreover 80 per cent of the respondents believed intercourse not to be harmful during pregnancy, though many of them (50 per cent) did not particularly care for it. One-third of them even found it 'bothersome' and 'disagreeable', yet they agreed to it, citing fear of the husband's infidelity as the major reason (Procházka and Černoch, 1970). Interestingly, a wife's fear of her husband's infidelity is not mentioned in the review by Lumley and Astbury (1980, pp. 69–73) of cross-cultural studies investigating the effect of pregnancy on sexual behaviour. Lumley and Astbury report steady and consistent decrease in sexual activity during pregnancy for the majority of respondents (residing in Chicago and Seattle, USA; Melbourne, Australia; Copenhagen, Denmark; and Thailand, presumably Bangkok), with no major discrepancies in experiences between the sexes. Husbands and wives tend to attribute their reduced sexual activity during pregnancy to both physical and emotional reasons: fear of harming the foetus, fear of miscarriage, morning sickness, fatigue and sleep disturbances, physical awkwardness and advice to abstain.

Expert advice has had even more limited impact in the field of nutrition, though this is due both to food shortages and to cultural practices. For example, Šabata and Fišerová (1974) as well as Trča (1979 and 1980) advocate lots of fresh fruit and vegetables in the pregnant women's diet, but it is well known that these are not available in winter and early spring. Moreover, the low consumption of some vitamins (especially vitamin C), calcium and iron has been 'compensated' for by an undesirably sharp increase in the intake of carbohydrates and fats, by as much as 20–30 per cent and in many cases even 50 per cent. Pregnant women also tend to suffer from anaemia due to the lack of iron in their diet. The incidence of anaemia is about twice as high among pregnant women than among women as a whole. As a solution to this problem, Hejda (1979) recommends increased consumption of foodstuffs rich in iron such as liver, spleen and leaf vegetables, but these are both unpopular and unavailable. Moreover, Dr Štembera *et al.* (1979, p. 93) claim that the over-all insufficiency of vitamins and the inadequate preparation of food in canteens have led to excessive weight gain in pregnancy. As evidence they cite the increased proportion of newborns over 4000 g, which rose from 6.5 per cent of all births in 1963 to 9 per cent in 1973, thus apparently contributing to higher perinatal morbidity.

Štembera *et al.* (1979, p. 102) and Brucháč (1977, p. 27) also claim that the majority of pregnant women use too many drugs, drink excessive amounts of coffee and continue to smoke.

Trča (1977) advocates more intensive propaganda against smoking at schools and in the mass media, but, as we know from the research findings on contraception quoted in Chapter 7, abstract knowledge is not always translated into systematic everyday use. In fact, the incidence of smoking seems to be increasing rather than decreasing in Czechoslovakia, especially among schoolchildren. A survey among a representative sample of 25 000 schoolchildren in grades 4, 6 and 8 across the country revealed a large number of initial experiences with cigarette smoking in schoolchildren aged 8 and over. However, girls attempt to smoke one or two years later than boys, and their over-all number has so far also remained smaller, though there is no guarantee that this will not change in the future, as has been the case in other countries. For smoking is one of the few means by which adolescents of both sexes can *publicly* validate their independent, semi-adult status. According to the Czech results, the number of occasional daily smokers increases rapidly after the age of 10 (Svobodová, 1981). Moreover, 60 per cent of children do not stop at the initial experience, but try smoking again. Many become addicted and find it difficult to quit, even during pregnancy.

Women are also 'deviant' with respect to physical exercises. Glos (1978) found that out of a random sample of 500 mothers who gave birth in Northern Bohemia in 1976, only 9 per cent attended special gymnastics classes for pregnant women and less than 4 per cent exercised by themselves with the aid of a guidebook. Thirty-one per cent of the respondents never exercised or took part in sport at all, and 56 per cent exercised or took part in sport *before*, but not *during* pregnancy. More mothers expecting their first child than mothers bearing a subsequent child exercised. All women in the sample were well informed about the importance of sport and fitness during pregnancy, but many were either not interested in putting this ideal into practice, or time pressures connected with work and care of other children at home did not allow them to be physically active. Glos also found that very few of these women attended prenatal classes, but this apparently had no negative impact on the length or the difficulty of their labour. In contrast, V. Kliment (1977, p. 536) discovered that prenatal gymnastics can have a positive impact on the reduction of premature births. Among a group of 300 women who systematically exercised during their pregnancy, only 1 per cent gave birth prematurely, while among a control group of the same size, almost 5 per cent did so.

Thus the positive case for physical education before, during and after pregnancy is quite overwhelming. Moreover, all experts are in agreement on its desirability, yet women of all ages continue to show little interest in it. According to the results of the 1979/80 nationwide time-budget study, women of all social classes devote on average only 1–2 minutes a day to sport, not counting a half-hour weekly walk on a non-working day. Students and apprentices allocate 10–15 minutes daily to sport, but, once they leave school, their engagement in movement activity remains low. If it were not for dancing and jazz gymnastics, most adolescents would probably not be engaged in any movement activity at all.

These data on sexual behaviour, nutrition and physical exercise during pregnancy do not support the current sociological notion of client addiction to expert advice. As Strong (1979, p. 207) has pointed out:

> in solving their daily problems, and this of course is to assume that something is defined as problematic, people rely on all kinds of sources, and medical advice is only one of these. It has value to us, no doubt, and it may on some occasions prove extremely valuable, but it is only one of a variety of possible solutions that we may try.

Fear of husband's infidelity, laziness (about exercise or attending prenatal classes), enjoyment of smoking and/or eating of fats, dislike of eating liver or drinking milk, are all good examples of factors which on particular occasions override medical advice.

PRENATAL EDUCATION

All matters relating to 'easy', 'painless' or 'prepared' birth are discussed under the term psycho-prophylaxis in Czechoslovakia. As in other countries, psycho-prophylaxis is portrayed 'not as a radical alternative, but rather as a practical complement to medical practices during pregnancy and childbirth' (Graham, 1977, p. 24). The method used in Czechoslovakia is that of I. Z. Velvovskii, the Soviet inventor of the technique, rather than the bewildering variety of methods – Lamaze, Dick-Read, Bradley, Kitzinger – which are commonly utilised in the Western countries.

The psycho-prophylactic method of preventing or minimising pain in childbirth was developed in the Soviet Union in the late 1940s. It had two components. First, an educational element, covering a period of several weeks, involved small groups of pregnant women, who were given an explanation of the birth process in order to understand their bodies and the role of medical staff during labour; they were also told that properly handled childbirth need not be painful. The second component involved training in techniques of breathing and massage to be employed by the woman during the various stages of her labour.

The introduction of the method was widely publicised in the popular and medical press and rapidly introduced in China and Eastern Europe. Inside the Soviet Union it was presented as a gift to women from Soviet science and a benevolent government. However, the enthusiasm for the method was short-lived. After Stalin's death in 1953, and as a result of negative clinical experiences (the technique did not produce painless birth), professional interest in psycho-prophylaxis declined, though the method was never openly abandoned or repudiated. In 1960, Velvovskii's *Painless Childbirth through Psycho-prophylaxis* was even published in English, presumably for Western consumption. The technique continues to occupy a prominent place in the Soviet Ministry of Health's directives on obstetrics, but little attention is paid to it in practice. It probably remains 'on the books' only because of its popularity abroad (Bell, 1981). The *Washington Post* correspondent Peter Osnos reported the account of one woman whose entire experience with the method consisted of instructions shouted at her during delivery to 'breathe right, or you will kill the baby'. Other women interviewed indicated that serious programmes of psycho-prophylaxis preparation were not generally available (quoted in Bell, 1981, p. 16).[5]

The method has been utilised more successfully in Czechoslovakia than in the Soviet Union. When it was introduced in early 1950s, it was greeted with great enthusiasm, at least among the more research-oriented physicians. The Prague Institute for the Care of Mother and Child not only set up an experimental clinical research project on the technique's effectiveness, but also developed a new curriculum for prenatal classes which integrated the Soviet method with special physical exercises, referred to as 'gymnastics for pregnant women'. Unlike the Soviet experience, the Czech experimental results were generally positive. The length of labour was shortened (its first stage by as much as $2\frac{3}{4}$ hours) and there was less fatigue as well as lower reliance on analgesia throughout labour. The birthing women who used the psycho-prophylactic technique also recovered more quickly and were more successful with their lactation. However, the doctors and nurses who were trained in the method at the Prague Institute remained for the most part sceptical about its effectiveness (Vojta, 1961a).

However, between 1966 and 1972, *Československá gynekologie*, the obstetical journal, published no original article about psycho-prophylaxis and, until recently, little attention had been paid to the subject in the education of women's nurses (Augustín, 1972). Two instruction manuals for prenatal teachers were published in 1965 (Chalupa and Friedlanderová, 1965; Slunský, 1965), but the next did not appear until 1979 (see Suchá and Chlubnová, 1979). Čepický *et al.* (1984) claim that by the 1970s psycho-prophylaxis became a mere statistical formality. However, there has been some renewed interest in prenatal education among professionals (if not women themselves) which is also evident in the support given to psycho-prophylaxis in recent popular advice books for women and couples. According to Bárdoš (1978, p. 98), the aim of prenatal classes:

is to acquaint the expectant mother with the process of labour and delivery and to obtain her active and conscious cooperation during birth.

This essentially 'medicalised' ideology of prepared childbirth is echoed in all the popular and professional antenatal literature examined. Moreover, there is some indication that this is also how it works in practice. Havlík *et al.* (1978) selected two small groups of women, one of which attended prenatal classes in Hodonín, a town in southern Moravia. The most significant difference between the two groups was not in the ease and painlessness of childbirth, but in the better cooperation with attending obstetricians by the women who were appropriately socialised as 'good' compliant patients in prenatal classes.[6] Lumley and Astbury (1980, p. 45) also conclude that the majority of studies undertaken to evaluate the effects of childbirth preparation 'show that childbirth education has no effect on either the duration of labour or the incidence of obstetrical complications'.

A Czech course in psycho-prophylaxis consists of six lessons in the anatomy and physiology of conception, pregnancy, labour and delivery and it often also includes a visit to a maternity hospital. Ideally, the six classes are attended twice a week during the last month of pregnancy, usually during the day, when the expectant mother is already on her maternity leave from work. However, the required (by Velvovskii) six hours of instruction are sometimes reduced to 2–4 lectures lasting more than two hours each. Moreover, the audience is 100 rather than the recommended ten. Lack of suitable rooms and personnel also contribute to relatively low interest in the method, both among physicians and women (Čepický *et al.*, 1984). The pre-natal classes are not compulsory and attendance fluctuates across the country, ranging from 18 to 55 per cent. The highest participation, with 55 per cent, is in the Slovak capital Bratislava; Prague comes second with the much lower participation rate of 32 per cent. In other regions, attendance varies between 18 and 30 per cent, due to lack of interest as well as availability. 'For those women who are unable to attend classes of special gymnastics because of poor transportation conditions or because of the classes' distance from where the woman lives', Trča (1979, pp. 54–71) offers in his antenatal advice book, descriptions as well as pictures of various exercises. However, as we saw above, pregnant women have so far shown little interest in 'gymnastics for pregnant women', in line with their relative lack of interest in sport as a whole.

Prenatal classes are led by women nurses at local health clinics and they are designed exclusively for women. Trča (1978, p. 39) sees this practice as desirable:

> The fact that pregnant women regularly meet for individual lessons creates something like a cooperative of women, who want to have an easy birth and a healthy baby. They have the same goal and form friendships among themselves.

Since men are excluded from childbirth preparation and participation, this argument makes sense, though it is another example of the persisting reinforcement of the sexual division of labour, assigning all matters relating to small children exclusively to women. Only professional expertise can override female gender in this respect – for almost 70 per cent of all Czech obstetricians are men.

In assessing the value of prenatal education, Lumley and Astbury (1980, pp. 52–3) point out that:

> it seems psychologically dangerous to provide women with a model of childbirth which avoids all mention of pain and, furthermore, sees pain as a form of psychological failure. There is no strong

evidence to suggest that pain in labour can be prevented for most women as long as they attend classes and firmly believe that by doing certain things in pregnancy (such as attending classes and practicing breathing techniques) they are ensuring a particular pain-free kind of labour, only to find that their actual labour deviates from their expectations, then marked feelings of disappointment in oneself and others can result . . . Quite distinct from the model of labour presented in childbirth education classes is how a pregnant woman selects certain pieces of information from an overall view which she believes will be most relevant to her . . . A teacher might tell a class of women that a high percentage of them will have episiotomies and a significant minority will require a forceps delivery. But whether a woman believes she is likely to be one of the significant minority is a matter of individual personality, past obstetric history and how strongly she believes that following certain guidelines in pregnancy will affect her labour.[7]

Another important, and a more fundamental point is raised by Wertz and Wertz (1977, p. 236):

The women who take childbirth education classes approach their deliveries with far more anatomical and technical knowledge but with less actual experience than their uneducated forebearers of the seventeenth, eighteenth, and nineteenth centuries, who had actually witnessed other women's labors and deliveries before their own time came. Studies have shown that women who have had childbirth education have more positive feelings about birth but no less anxiety than women without such education. Only the multipara, the woman having her third or fourth delivery, can draw upon her own experience and relax. Much of our anxiety and the resulting willingness to become passively dependent upon medicine result from the removal of birth from direct human experience.[8] We fear what we do not know. How many children witness birth, even at a distance? Children learn, instead, that birth is a 'sickness' that requires the hospital and the doctor.

In conclusion there seems to be no general dissatisfaction among women in Czechoslovakia with their experience of 'medical management' of pregnancy, although relevant data are extremely hard to come by – only two references were found in the literature. The Institute for Research of Public Opinion (of the Federal Statistical

TABLE 9.1   *Satisfaction with prenatal health care (%)*

	Sample I*	Sample II+
Very good	41	40
Sufficient	55	56
Insufficient	2	3
Don't know	2	1

* Sample I consisted of 1800 men and women older than 18.
+ Sample II comprised women aged 18–34, both single and married, with as
well as without other children.

SOURCE 'Výsledky sociologického . . .', 1978

Office) recently conducted a nationwide research on questions connected with children and the family. The responses shown in Table
9.1 suggest that women were generally satisfied with the health care
which they received during pregnancy. Fifty-nine per cent of female
respondents considered the approach of health workers (obstetricians and nurses) as 'pleasant'.

The other source is the already mentioned small-scale study in 1977
of 300 pregnant women from the Prague area expecting their first
children. All respondents who attended prenatal classes (we are not
told how many actually attended) liked them and preferred them to
all other sources of knowledge. This leads Trča (1978) to believe
attendance in prenatal classes could be increased by better advertis-
ing in prenatal clinics, either by formal notices on bulletin boards or
more directly, by personal invitations by women's nurses. Trča also
suggests that the existing six classes can be compressed into two or
three lessons, which would be particularly suitable for rural women.

Personal anecdotal observations confirm the general satisfaction
with prenatal care. The long wait at the clinic is generally not seen as
particularly troublesome, since standing in line is an East European
way of life. Moreover, many pregnant women prefer waiting in an
antenatal clinic to working at their place of employment.[9] In other
words, the time taken for an antenatal visit is not taken from leisure
but from work, with the exception of the last month, when the
woman is already on maternity leave. However, by that time she has
usually transferred to the out-patient department of the hospital
where she is going to deliver her baby. In any case, patients' satisfaction is not the dominant criterion of evaluation of prenatal care. That
decision is usually left to the discretion of the professional physician,

who generally assesses pregnancy care in terms of its successful
medical outcome – a physically healthy mother and a baby.

NOTES

1. New reproductive technologies, such as extrauterine conception (also
   referred to as *in vitro* fertilisation or IVF) increasingly challenge our
   traditional notions which equate child-bearing with one 'fixed' biological
   person. As Rothman (1982, pp. 117–18) points out, 'it is not yet possible
   for a human female to avoid pregnancy and still "reproduce," but it is
   possible in animals and doubtless will soon be possible for people . . .
   When embryos, or just ova, can be transplanted from one person to
   another, it is debatable whether the "donor" or the "host" will be
   considered the biological mother. The donor, the one who mates and
   conceives, can in one sense be thought of as a biological father; she
   contributes half of the genetic material, and there her biological contribution ends. Women who are "infertile" because they cannot conceive
   would enter biological motherhood at the point after conception, carry-
   ing and birthing transplanted embryos. The mother–host would not be a
   genetic parent, but there would be a biological tie between mother and
   child, and social motherhood would begin normally, with pregnancy.'
2. Graham and Oakley (1981, pp. 51–2) define the concept of a frame of
   reference as follows: ' "Frame of reference" embraces both the notion of
   an ideological perspective – a system of values and attitudes through
   which mothers and doctors view pregnancy – and of a reference group – a
   network of individuals who are significant influences upon these sets of
   attitudes and values.'
3. Holland and McKevitt (1985, p. 163) argue that a significant proportion –
   roughly a third – of Soviet pregnant women see no medical specialist
   during the first trimester of their pregnancy, despite the importance
   which Soviet doctors attach to the initiation of early antenatal medical
   care. Soviet studies also show that pregnant women often fail to keep
   their regular medical appointments and that the most likely group to
   avoid medical supervision during pregnancy are single mothers.
4. For the more general advice books, see *A Woman = Health + Beauty*
   (Bárdoš, 1978), *The Art of Healthy Living – A Book for Women* (Trča,
   1980), *The Encyclopedia of a Young Woman* (*Encyklopedie mladé ženy*,
   1978) and *A School for Engaged and Married Couples* (*Škola pro
   snoubence a novomanžele*, 1977). The latter two are edited books, with
   articles on sexuality, family planning, motherhood and the domestic
   division of labour, which are written by doctors, psychologists, sex
   therapists and lawyers. The former two books were written by two
   doctors, Bárdoš and Trča. Trča also wrote the immensely popular
   antenatal guide *We Are Going to Have a Baby* (Trča, 1979), which is
   discussed in this chapter. He is also the author of the article on pregnancy in *A School for Engaged and Married Couples*, more or less

repeating what he has said in his other writings. In addition, there are also free leaflets, distributed at antenatal clinics (when supplies permit), which cover nutrition, physical exercise and post-partum care, and which are for the most part written by the same authors who wrote these books.

5. These anecdotal, journalistic observations are not supported by the findings of Ispa (1983) who interviewed 30 Soviet women who recently (within the last 3 years) emigrated to the United States. They were all well-educated women of Jewish origin, from large cities, who had chosen to leave the USSR, and in this sense were 'unrepresentative' of Soviet women as such. The women interviewed reported that, at least in the large cities, there are prenatal classes and that they are attended during the eighth or ninth month of pregnancy. The classes focused on lectures on prenatal health, the physiology of birth, post-partum self-care, new-born care and the Communist Party's concern for mothers and children. Exercises and breathing patterns are explained, but group practice sessions do not take place. Separate classes for men are apparently beginning to be available, but few attend.

6. It is worth noting that prenatal education in North America (started by the American Society for Psycho-prophylaxis in Obstetrics in 1959) stemmed from a radically different perspective: to raise women's consciousness of her body and her ability to birth without the use of anaesthesia. It was meant to rock the system, not to comply with it. However, as we noted in Chapter 5, ASPO accepted the medical model's separation of childbirth from the rest of the maternity experience and thus managed 'to meet on the one hand the demand of women for a "natural" childbirth, and, on the other, the demand of obstetricians for "good medical management" ' (Rothman, 1982, p. 92).

7. While Lumley's and Astbury's assessment seems persuasive, it is worth pointing out that they seem to be judging across the board, without indicating variations among countries, types of prenatal education, and findings on the impact of childbirth education on the childbirth experience. As we noted earlier, Glos (1978) found that non-attendance of prenatal classes had no negative impact on the length or the difficulty of the women's labour while Vojta (1961a) found that psycho-prophylactic education resulted in shorter labour (its first stage was shortened by as much as $2\frac{3}{4}$ hours), less fatigue, lower reliance on analgesia throughout labour, faster post-natal recovery and more successful lactation. Oxorn and Foote (1975), authors of a widely used American medical textbook, also maintain that pre-natal education tends to lead to shorter and less traumatic labours, less medical intervention, less blood loss and less lack of oxygen to the baby. Kitzinger (1962) and Elkins (1980), renowned British and Canadian childbirth educators, respectively, are for obvious reasons also strongly in favour of antenatal education. As to 'painless' childbirth, initially (i.e. in the 1950s) Lamaze himself used the term. Currently no antenatal teacher manual, class, workshop or popular advice book mentions the absence of pain. Instruction in classes is geared towards reduction of unnecessary pain due to tension, and the acceptance of unavoidable pain through psychological techniques and breathing exercises (Maria Victor Paez, personal communication, Childbirth

and Parent Education Association of Toronto Teacher's Handbook, 1979.)

8. While Wertz's and Wertz's comments are well taken, it is important not to look too romantically at the past. Bogdan's (1978) and Macintyre's (1977) accounts of childbirth practices in nineteenth-century America and primitive societies of the mythical golden age (in which childbirth was a purely 'natural' affair) suggest that the 'human experience' most people got out of viewing births first-hand was most likely harrowing. As Strong (1979, p. 205) has pointed out, 'the plea of working women fifty years ago was for far more proper medicine to save them from the horrors that childbirth then entailed'. The movement for 'natural' childbirth only arose when medical advances had largely freed women from these fears. It is thus a product of 'medical imperialism and entirely dependent upon it'.

9. In Poland, 'the pregnant woman has a right to a *paid release from work*, if unable to do so after work, in order to go to a free medical examination if connected with said pregnancy. A medical direction to such an examination is the only basis necessary for the release from work.' (Mieczkowsli, 1982, p. 53). While similar provision has been recently enacted in Britain, it appears to have no equivalent in the Soviet Union. Holland and McKevitt (1985, p. 154) speculate that 'the loss of wages that results from attending clinics may well be a disincentive for some women'.

10 Childbirth

> Much of the current obstetrical controversy revolves around the word 'unnecessary'. A growing number of obstetrical personnel genuinely believe that routine medical 'management' of labour is in fact necessary, in order to ensure the best outcome for mother and child. (Elkins, 1983, p. 53)

> The details of obstetric practices may change in response to societal pressures. What shows no sign of changing is a deep consensus, shared by all of us, that, at least for us, the justification for any way of doing birth must include as its most fundamental concern the issue of medical safety for mother and child. In other societies, other considerations may be more important. Even in our own there was a time when the most salient concern was not with life and death, but with the status of the unborn child's soul. (Jordan, 1980, p. 88)

In recent years there has been considerable discussion and criticism of the way in which childbirth is handled in modern Western society. The debate has focused on a broad range of issues connected with the 'medicalisation of childbirth', such as the displacement of midwives by male obstetricians, home and hospital confinements, the increasingly active medical management of birth, the value of mortality statistics, and the relevance of current research on the importance of early bonding. Debates about some of these trends are beginning to take place also in Czechoslovakia.

HOSPITAL BIRTHS

The rapid acceleration towards hospital confinements for births in the 1950s (see Table 10.1), coupled with the relegation of midwives to the role of obstetrical nurses, marked the completion of the trend towards the medical management of childbirth in Czechoslovakia.

198

TABLE 10.1 *Hospital births in Czechoslovakia (per 100 births)*

Year	1937	1946	1950	1955	1960	1965	1970	1975
Percentage of all births	18.5	31.0	44.0	79.4	93.7	97.8	99.0	99.6

SOURCE *Československé zdravotnictví 1979*, p. 56

TABLE 10.2 *Specialised maternity hospitals in Czechoslovakia*

	1954	1960	1970	1979
Czechoslovakia	35	33	11	5
Bohemia and Moravia	14	12	4	–
Slovakia	21	21	7	5

SOURCE Makovický *et al.*, 1981, p. 44

While in 1950 more births took place at home than in the hospital, five years later only 20 per cent of all deliveries remained at home. Ten years later, in 1960, 94 per cent of all births were hospital confinements. The collection of statistics on the place of confinements ceased in 1974 after hospital births exceeded 99 per cent of the total.

Births typically take place in maternity wards of large general hospitals rather than in small specialised maternity hospitals. In Czechoslovakia, maternity hospitals for 'normal' births have been gradually phased out, reflecting the dominant view of birth as a pathological and risky process that requires all that modern medicine and technology have to offer.

The evolution of a uniform system of hospitalised births is seen as an important achievement of socialist maternity care. Prokopec (1975, p. 65) argues as follows:

At the time when the working class in our country took state power, half of all children were still born at home. Since 1960 practically all children have been born in maternity wards, with the exception of sudden births, but even then the mother and child almost always obtain a hospital bed. Yet . . . in England, one third of all women still give birth at home.

A similar argument is offered by Petro (1980, p. 122), who also regards British home births (he quotes a rate of 25 per cent) as another indication of the 'inferiority' of capitalist maternity care. In reality, of course, domiciliary confinements in the UK have become a thing of the past – 'in 1974 the hospital confinement rate was 96 per cent. In 1975, 99 per cent of first babies were born in hospital' (Oakley, 1979a, p. 16).

Significantly, the Czechoslovak authors do not mention the Dutch experience of combining 50 per cent rate of domiciliary confinements with the world's second lowest perinatal mortality rate.[1] (The lowest perinatal mortality rate is in Sweden, characterised by 100 per cent hospital confinement rate.) Thus, nobody in Czechoslovakia currently envisages a return to the previous system of home births attended by midwives. There is such a general agreement among the medical profession, the state officials and the general public that births outside the hospital are dangerous, both to the infant and to the mother, that criticisms of the hospital system have been relatively minor, confined to such 'trivial' issues as occasional overcrowding, lack of comfort, and offers of bribes to attending staff to ensure better care. However, research on patients' satisfaction is extremely limited and what data are available are either anecdotal or deal with hospitals in general, rather than specifically with maternity care.

For example, Kops' (1981) research revealed general satisfaction of patients with their hospital stay – only 2 per cent of respondents were dissatisfied with their attending doctors and 3 per cent did not like their nursing care. However, the latter apparently included a high proportion of obstetrical/gynaecological patients.[2] In contrast, Taufrová (1981, pp. 168–9), writing for the professional nursing journal, does not depict a pleasant view of the patient's hospital experience:

> For the majority of people with an average standard of living, hospitalisation means the worsening of their living conditions. Apart from the complete loss of privacy and the inability of expressing one's personality, there is the worsening of conditions for the maintenance of basic personal hygiene, especially if the patient is bed-ridden and dependent on others for these tasks . . . A basic environmental standard is normally maintained, but it is usually characterised by an austere impersonality and an emotional coldness.

Taufrová also mentions that in most hospitals, it is compassionate patients able to walk, rather than the overworked (or uninterested) nurses, who provide basic nursing care to those who cannot feed, void or turn by themselves. Impersonality and lack of privacy are also experienced by maternity patients. The labouring women who enter the hospital for their confinement are surrounded by complete strangers – hospital nurses as well as other women in labour whose pain and cries are only too evident in the multi-bed labour room. Neither the husband nor any other visitor is allowed in the hospital for the duration of the woman's stay (5–8 days). This rigidly enforced policy is justified on the grounds of 'danger of infections' and 'the need for mothers to rest', reasons which in turn also 'explain' why mothers have been separated from their newborns – an issue explored in the next chapter.

Finally, from the perspective of planning of hospital facilities, there is also the problem of unpredictability of the timing of individual births. According to Vojta (1974), demand for obstetrical beds fluctuates by as much as 25 per cent on various days and months (provided births are not routinely induced!), yet attending staff remains the same throughout the week, with fewer people around at night time. Sudden increases in the birth rate also tend to put a strain on hospital facilities. For example, Vojta (1974, p. 371) claims that the dramatic increase in the Czechoslovak birth rate in the early 1970s (from 14 per thousand in 1968 to 18 per thousand in 1973) required at least 400 additional obstetrical beds, but only 62 were provided, with staffing ratios remaining basically unchanged. As a result, maternity wards experienced overcrowding, shortages of beds and birth attendants, and the subjective birthing experience of mothers left a lot to be desired.

MEDICAL OBSTETRICAL INTERVENTION: INDUCTION OF LABOUR, CAESAREAN SECTION, OBSTETRICAL TECHNOLOGY

While Western feminists have in recent years severely criticised the medical profession for excessive intervention in the birth process, the dominant criticism coming from Eastern Europe concerns *lack of* care and intervention. At least in the Soviet Union, sedatives and anaesthesia are seldom given.[3] Several women interviewed in Prague also considered their delivery an unpleasant experience, best to be suppressed and forgotten, though those with shorter labour had a better time of it than those whose labour was long. Prokopec (1975,

p. 65) claims that more than a third of all births in Czechoslovkia are managed with the aid of analgesia. Moreover, he also admits that the incidence of active management of labour, especially the use of oxytocin in induced labours, is increasing. Kazda *et al.* (1961) claims that active medical management of labour has been accepted as a policy in Czechoslovakia since 1954. This has led, among other outcomes, to the shortening of average labour, to eight hours for women having their first baby and to four hours for mothers giving subsequent births. However, in the early 1960s, artificial breaking of the membranes was still considered a controversial, though generally acceptable procedure.

In recent years professional obstetrical opinion has shifted more towards *elective* intervention (i.e. before anything goes wrong). For example, Štembera *et al.*, (1979, p. 23) the previously cited author of the medical textbook on risk pregnancy, is quite critical of the alleged indecisiveness and conservatism of many Czechoslovak obstetricians who apparently have a tendency to intervene in the birth process only when it is too late. This sentiment is echoed by Gazarek *et al.* (1928b, p. 26), who advocate 'programmed birth' as the best way of lowering 'immediately, and under existing conditions, perinatal mortality and neonatal morbidity'. According to Gazárek *et al.*:

> the term programmed birth implies a controlled initiation of the onset of labour, active stimulation of uterine contractions in an already established completed term of pregnancy, by the means of breaking of membranes and the infusion of glucose and oxytocin during the time when personnel staffing in the maternity ward is adequate, with the explicit goals of the birth of a healthy child and the least possible hazard to the birthing woman, of course with her consent. The advantage of programmed birth is the elimination of the possibility of an accidental onset of labour, which often unexpectedly surprises the birthing woman at work or even at home, and which creates a whole range of difficulties not only for her, but also for her surroundings . . . Another advantage concerns the fact that the birthing woman gives birth when she herself decides to do so, when she is mentally and physically prepared for it, when there are fewer risks involved, because everything is ready for the birth. I believe that when evaluating our professional activity, the indicator of the proportion of operative births must lose its negative character. For out of fear not to have a high percentage of surgical

births, we often delay surgical intervention in a given birth, with the result that the child is damaged or that it sometimes even dies.

While the model of 'programmed birth' (i.e. induced labour) is popular also among many obstetricians in the West, this does not mean that most of the ideas expressed in it are not controversial. As Lumley and Astbury (1980, p. 100) point out, 'there are still many unanswered questions about the benefits and hazards of a high induction rate'. Far from decreasing maternal and perinatal morbidity and mortality, 'programmed birth' may actually lead to their increase. For induced labour has been implicated in causing inadvertent premature birth (the leading cause of perinatal mortality); more intense and more rapid labour contractions, requiring more medication for pain relief; and higher incidence of foetal distress and neonatal jaundice. In turn these complications have been known to have impaired mother–infant bonding (Lumley and Astbury, 1980, pp. 105–6).

Another contentious aspect of the 'programmed birth' model is 'daytime obstetrics', which has been criticised on the grounds that it negates everything that is natural in childbirth, since it reinforces the view of birth as a surgical emergency requiring intensive care. More importantly, the long-term medical impact of induction of labour for the mother's and/or obstetrician's convenience is not yet known, because the complex processes governing the onset and duration of spontaneous labour are still not fully understood, despite intensive research on the subject in many countries. Lumley and Astbury (1980, p. 105) also point out that artificial induction of labour may be associated with other medical interventions, such as foetal heart monitoring, epidural anaesthesia, forceps delivery and Caesarean section.

The latter has been a particularly controversial subject in current obstetrics, reflecting the dramatic rise in North American Caesarean births throughout 1970s. According to the US National Institute of Health statistics (quoted in Elkins, 1983, p. 87), 'the surgical birth rate in the United States trebled in the seventies, from 5.5 per cent in 1970 to 15.2 per cent in 1978, with Canadian statistics close behind. Today's rate has climbed to around 20 per cent, and even higher in some institutions.' In contrast, the Caesarean birth rate in Czechoslovakia has remained much lower, though it is both rising and widely fluctuating among different institutions (from 1 to 10 per cent). For example, Prague's Caesarean birth rate rose from 2 per cent in 1968 to 5 per cent in 1979, but this aggregate figure obscures a much sharper increase in the larger teaching hospitals. For example, the proportion of abdominal deliveries among all births at the Second Obstetrical Clinic of the Charles University Hospital increased from 3 per cent in 1968 to 10 per cent in 1979 (Trnka *et al.*, 1981, p. 724)

Thus, professional opinion is shifting towards more surgical intervention on the grounds that it may reduce perinatal mortality and morbidity. For example, Štembera *et al.* (1979, pp. 23, 174) argues that Caesarean sections are not performed frequently enough in Czechoslovakia, well below the expected 4 per cent for maternity hospitals with 'normal' clientele and 5–8 per cent for hospitals with a large concentration of risk pregnancies. In his view, many of the babies who had died after a C-section (their percentage increased from 7.5 of all postnatal deaths in 1967 to 8.5 in 1974), could have been saved if the operation had been performed earlier in the delivery process.

Caesarean births increased throughout the 1970s not only because the operation had become much safer, but also because of the liberalisation of the range of indicators for performing them. In the United States, the most common indicators for a Caesarean birth are (1) dystocia, a residual category which includes foeto-pelvic disproportion (an insufficient pelvic outlet for the size of the presenting head) as well as 'lack of progress of labour', and (2) repeat Caesareans, accounting for 31 per cent of Caesarean sections each. Breech presentations account for another 12 per cent and foetal distress for 5 per cent; Elkins (1983, pp. 87–8) does not account for the remaining 21 per cent.

In Czechoslovakia, obstetricians tend not to agree with the common North American slogan, 'once a Caesarean, always a Caesarean', and a previous C-section is not considered in itself a sufficient indicator for another one. This policy is reflected in practice – 40–50 per cent of mothers with a previous C-section deliver vaginally in subsequent births (Trnka and Doležal, 1978; Gazárek *et al.*, 1982b). In contrast, fewer than 2 per cent of women in the United States deliver vaginally after a previous Caesarean birth (*Cesarean Childbirth*, 1981, p. 10). In their examination of a sample of 149 women who gave birth by a Caesarean at the Second Obstetrical Clinic of the Charles University Hospital in Prague in 1966–75, Trnka and Doležal (1978) found that 74 mothers, almost 50 per cent, delivered vaginally in subsequent births. There were no incidents of imminent or actual rupture of the uterus (the most frequently cited medical justification for a repeat Caesarean) and no cases of perinatal or maternal mortality. The authors also note that vaginal deliveries occurred also among women whose previous birth complications were diagnosed as disproportion in the mother's pelvic structure. The Czech experience may be soon replicated also in North America. In 1982, the American College of Obstetricians and Gynecologists issued new guidelines for vaginal delivery after a Caesarean childbirth, which cited studies indicating that 50–60 per cent of women can safely birth vaginally after a Caesarean. Elkins (1983, p. 118), who quotes these guidelines, also claims that these statistics are borne out by the women who attend her prenatal and postnatal classes.

The management of breech presentations – approximately 4 per cent of all pregnancies – is another medically contentious issue, largely because breech presentation is associated with higher morbidity and mortality than vertex (i.e. head first) presentation, irrespective of whether delivery is vaginal or Caesarean. There is therefore tremendous cross-national variation in how breech presentations are managed, though again, the trend has been towards more Caesarean deliveries. For example, in Melbourne teaching hospitals about half of all breech infants were born by a C-section in 1978, three times as many as ten years before (Lumley and Astbury, 1980, p. 121). In the United States, 60 per cent of breech presentations were delivered by a Caesarean section in 1978 (11.6 per cent in 1970), while the Czechoslovak rate in the mid-1970s stood at only 6 per cent (*Cesarean Childbirth*, 1981, p. 12; Blašková *et al.*, 1977). Poradovský *et al.* (1981) argue that 20–50 per cent of breech presentations should be delivered by a Caesarean section, which would still make it a smaller proportion than elsewhere. The authors base their suggestion on statistics from a maternity hospital in Košice (a sizeable town in Eastern Slovakia), which associate Caesarean section of breech presentations with a decline of perinatal mortality from 89 per cent to 43 per cent. However, since we are given no detailed information on the type of the breech, the mother's health, and so on, these statistics are not as useful as they could be.

Dr Martin, the principal investigator of a study of all C-sections performed between January 1973 and December 1979 at the Sir Mortimer B. Davis Jewish General Hospital in Montreal argues that as far as breech deliveries are concerned:

you just have to assess each case on its own, and keep in mind your own experience . . . and a lot of time the method of delivery depends on whether you're prepared to use forceps or not. The statistics show that doing a forceps delivery of a breech is much safer than doing a Caesarean . . . I'm very careful with my screening. But as long as it looks like a normal breech, head size not excessively large, adequate pelvis, I prefer to deliver vaginally. I always use forceps when I deliver a breech vaginally. And with good outcomes . . . This assumption that abdominal delivery is a breeze really ought to be corrected – immediately – in the profession, and in the patients' minds, too (quoted in Elkins, 1983, pp. 117–18).

While obstetricians in Czechoslovakia tend not to believe that abdominal delivery of a breech presentation is a 'breeze' – indeed, Blašková *et al.* (1977) see the spontaneous delivery performed by the Bracht's or Covjanov's technique as remaining 'the method of choice in most cases' – their professional opinion is favouring more elective intervention, on the grounds that a higher rate of Caesarean births would lower both perinatal mortality and morbidity. As Gazárek *et al.* (1982b) argue:

> we have to create such conditions in our workplaces that a Caesarean birth becomes a routine, though completely safe operation for the mother and her child, because the completion of pregnancy by a Caesarean section will continue to increase in our workplaces. And this is right, because a timely performance of a Caesarean section will result in fewer asylum children, fewer children in special schools, and also fewer people suffering from epileptic seizures.

Since the main rationale for the worldwide increase in Caesarean section has been the attempt to lower both mortality and morbidity, 'it is particularly unfortunate that there is a dearth of follow-up studies which could show whether the intended better outcome actually happened' (Lumley and Astbury, 1980, p. 124). The scepticism of the benefit of Caesarean births is shared by Uhlíř and Čupr (1982), who disagree with their Czechoslavak colleagues' advocacy of more surgical intervention in childbirth. The Czech authors argue that:

> the current state of Caesarean indicators gives obstetricians broad freedom, which often leads to operative hyperactivity. This is not

right. It is an abuse of such freedom. An obstetrician who is erudite and who has a lot of experience, is even today bound not only by tradition, but above all by the responsibility towards the mother and her child, not to mention the need for the maximum utilisation of all methods of conservative obstetrics.

For Caesarean birth is not without hazards to both the mother and the baby. Abdominal delivery may increase the risk of developing the respiratory distress syndrome, the main life threatening disorder of premature infants. It may also create a number of health problems for the mother. Lumley and Astbury (1980, pp. 123–4) cite the need for blood transfusion (in 10 per cent of cases), fever (in 23 per cent of cases), pain, enforced immobility, subjective depression, guilt and lowered self-esteem as the main hazards, which in turn limit the caretaking the mother can provide, thus creating 'a major health hazard for mother and infant in the first few months after birth'. The noted Canadian childbirth educator, Valmai Howe Elkins (1983, p. 121), who claims to have 'pored over everything I could get my hands on' on the subject of Caesarean births, is also against the Caesarean birth 'except in clear-cut cases, not only because of the proven increase in maternal and infant morbidity and mortality, but also because of the human implications, the emotional complication rate'.

Finally, connected with both induced labour and abdominal delivery, is the question of modern obstetrical technology, which has made the common use of these procedures possible. In Czechoslovakia, the impact of the 'scientific–technical' revolution on obstetrics is seen as positive. Suk (1979) argues that interest in obstetrical technology ought to be encouraged, though he warns physicians to maintain their 'medical common sense and evaluation and not intervene unnecessarily'. Given the current worldwide trends, Kotásek (1975, p. 25) is probably quite right in arguing that:

> currently we cannot do without the modernisation of technical equipment. Stethoscope and the manual control of uterine activity are no longer adequate. We need monitoring which automatically registers uterine activity, the foetal heart beat, and depending on need, we have to evaluate the actual state of the foetus with the aid of microanalysis of its blood. It is without any doubt that the delivery room becomes of necessity a workplace of intensive care, and that if one looks at it in this light, one has to equip it accordingly. Connected with this is, of course, continuous paediatric

care and also resuscitation help. All these measures are introduced not only to further lower perinatal mortality, but also – and this is extremely important in view of further progress – to lower perinatal morbidity.

By the mid-1970s, fully automated monitoring systems were established in most intensive obstetrical care units in the country, and the expectation was that they will be eventually introduced in all types of maternity wards and hospitals (Srp *et al.*, 1978). In a personal interview in 1981 it was indicated that out of 25 000 births in a large maternity hospital in Prague, only 250 labours, i.e. 1 per cent, were electronically monitored, but that other hospitals may have a higher rate. It is interesting to note that the large-scale utilisation of foetal monitors, ultrasound machines and incubators represents a serious drain on foreign currency reserves, because this technology is not produced domestically but must be imported, predominantly from the West. The expenditure of the precious hard currency is justified by the assumed resulting decrease in perinatal mortality and morbidity. For example, Srp *et al.* (1978, p. 756) claim that the uniform monitoring of risk pregnancies at the obstetrical unit of Prague University Hospital lowered the hospital's perinatal mortality from 4 per thousand in 1960 to 1.2 per thousand in 1977. As we are given no additional information about the social and medical history of women giving birth during this period, these statistics cannot be taken at their face value, though clearly modern obstetrical technology has made a positive contribution. However, the authors conclude their article with the warning that:

> today's obstetrician, who has much more information available about the state of the mother and the foetus, is obliged to use the freed time capacity for the support of the mother and her psyche, and thus fulfil the raison d'etre of our specialty, which the most perfect technical equipment and methods cannot replace.

PERINATAL AND MATERNAL MORTALITY AND MORBIDITY STATISTICS

We have seen that the increasingly active medical intervention in the birth process is generally justified by the assumed improvement in perinatal mortality and morbidity statistics. The prevention of death, measured in terms of concrete statistics on the incidence of perinatal and maternal mortality, has in fact become the major *social* yardstick of judgement of a successful reproduction, thus providing us with yet another example of the prevalence of the medical definition of childbirth. As we shall see below, mortality statistics have also become an important political issue, because they involve historical and cross-national comparisons.

For example, Haire (1973, p. 172) a US author, begins her authoritative report on 'The Cultural Warping of Childbirth' as follows:

> While Sweden and the Netherlands compete for the honor of having the lowest incidence of infant deaths per one thousand live births, the United States continues to find itself outranked by fourteen other developed countries.

Haverkamp and Orleans (1983, p. 115) even assert that 'American health care is under societal and professional pressure to improve maternal and infant health outcomes as it becomes widely perceived that infant mortality in the United States is higher than that of other Western nations. This record has, in fact, improved, even though other countries have been more successful.'

The British sociologist, Ann Oakley (1979a, p. 18), while critical of the excessive social importance attached to mortality statistics, nonetheless begins her discussion on the issue by asserting that 'both the United States and the United Kingdom are in the bottom half of the perinatal mortality table, doing impressively worse than countries such as Japan, Czechoslovakia, Finland, France, Malta and Israel'. In turn, Petro (1980, p. 123), the previously cited Slovak health official, smugly asserts that perinatal mortality is very low in Czechoslovakia, lower than in such 'economically developed capitalist states as England, France, West Germany, Belgium and Italy', thanks to the quality of socialist health care. In contrast, Černoch (1980), a Czech obstetrician, complains that the perinatal mortality of 20 per thousand placed Czechoslovakia in the mid-1970s only eighteenth among European countries.

However, valid international comparisons are difficult to make, at least prior to 1970 or so, because of (1) the unreliable collection of statistics on both stillbirths and live births in several countries: (2) cross-national as well as historical variations in the definition of live births as well as perinatal deaths: and (3) the reliance on different indicators of mortality. Cernoch (1980) claims that as late as 1960,

10–15 thousand live births in several southern European countries were not recorded and that the existence of these children was discovered only when they started attending school or when their parents applied for family allowances. The under-reporting of still-births in these countries also weakens the reliability of their mortality statistics. Moreover, prior to 1965, when WHO changed the definition, Czechoslovakia recorded the birth of an infant weighing less than 1000 grams as a live birth only if the infant survived the first 24 hours after delivery. Some countries e.g. Bulgaria, continue this practice to this date. Obviously, such variation makes valid historical or cross-national comparisons of mortality statistics quite difficult.

To add to the confusion, there are at least *seven* different indicators of infant deaths. The most general, infant mortality (utilised above by Haire, 1973), refers to the number of deaths of infants under one year of age, per thousand live births. Neonatal deaths are deaths within 28 days of birth; deaths within seven days are considered early neonatal deaths. Post-neonatal deaths are deaths that occur from 28 days to 365 days after birth. There are also late foetal deaths (foetal deaths of 28 weeks or more gestation) and intranatal deaths (deaths during childbirth). Because it is usually difficult to draw a consistent line between stillbirth and death immediately after birth, late foetal, intranatal and early neonatal deaths are usually combined and la-belled as perinatal mortality. Thus perinatal mortality rate is the number of late foetal deaths plus infant deaths within seven days of birth, per thousand live births. However, the Australian authors Lumley and Astbury (1980, p. 220), include all neonatal deaths (i.e. within 28 days of birth) in their definition of perinatal mortality, though they acknowledge that 'countries differ in the way that they define perinatal death, so comparisons may be misleading'. Foetal deaths of unknown gestation are normally included in the late foetal deaths statistics though there is cross-national variation in this respect as well.

Infant and post-neonatal deaths are generally believed to be less closely related to pregnancy and childbirth than are neonatal deaths. Moreover, early neonatal deaths under one week of life, now account for about 60 per cent of all infant deaths, while at the turn of the century they represented only 20 per cent (Rydell, 1976, p. 165). For these reasons, it is perinatal rather than infant mortality that is normally utilised, by the World Health Organization as well as by national governments, as the best indicator of good prenatal care and delivery procedures. The previously cited Czech physicians, Černoch (1980) and Gazárek *et al.* (1982a) also argue that statistics on the

TABLE 10.3 *Maternal mortality in Czechoslovakia (%)*

Year	1937	1946	1950	1960	1965	1970	1975	1979
Maternal mortality	4.45	1.29	1.7	0.45	0.35	0.22	0.18	0.13

SOURCE *Statistická ročenka ČSSR, 1961 to 1980*

incidence of perinatal mortality are the major criteria for judging the quality of care for mother and child. Hence the political implications of national variations in the incidence of perinatal mortality among countries with different national health care and political systems!

Maternal mortality statistics are much less contentious in this respect[4] because (1) there is no ambiguity as to when death occurs or how it is defined and (2) its incidence is very low. While the fear of death was central to women's perceptions of birthing throughout the nineteenth and early twentieth century, women today 'experience the idea of death in childbirth only as a fleeting image' (Leavitt and Walton, 1981, p. 120). The incidence of dying as a result of pregnancy or childbirth is now so rare that, at least in Czechoslovakia, each actual case is automatically investigated to establish its cause(s). Maternal mortality, while relatively low to start with, has declined consistently since the end of the Second World War (with minor fluctuations), and the risk of birth-related death has been virtually eliminated (see Table 10.3).

This reproductive success is attributed both to improved prenatal health care and to hospital births (Vojta, 1961b) Petro, 1980, p. 122), as well as to favourable changes in maternal age and parity (Štembera *et al.*, 1979, p. 40, Dvořák, 1982a, p. 13). The proportion of women having five and more babies declined from 10.5 per cent of all births to the current 2.9 per cent, thus automatically lowering the over-all number of risk pregnancies and potential maternal and perinatal deaths. Cross-national comparisons of maternal mortality statistics are rarely invoked, because similar decline has taken place in all other advanced industrial countries. Thus Vojta (1961b, p. 47) makes no mention of other countries with an 'inferior' maternity care system, but emphasises that maternal mortality in Czechoslovakia has been reduced to a tenth of the pre-Second World War rate, thanks to the socialist 'organisational measures, especially the widely developed and continuously deepening system of prenatal care and almost 100 per cent hospital confinements'.

However, the interpretation of perinatal mortality statistics is not so straightforward, and unfavourable cross-national comparisons are

TABLE 10.4   *Perinatal mortality in Czechoslovakia (per thousand)*

Year	1937	1948	1950	1955	1960	1965	1970	1975	1980	1982
Perinatal mortality	52.1	36.7	40.7	24.8	20.9	22.8	20.0	19.6	16.3	15.2

SOURCE   Prokopec (1975, p. 188); *Statistická ročenka ČSSR, 1960 to 1984*

often involved. In her comparative review of perinatal statistics, Rychtaříková (1982) divides the various developed countries into three major categories: (1) countries with the lowest perinatal mortality (under 10 per thousand), which include all the Scandinavian countries, the Netherlands, Switzerland and Japan; (2) countries with relatively low perinatal mortality (10–15 per thousand), including the UK, Ireland, East Germany, West Germany, Austria, Canada, the USA, Australia, New Zealand, and to some extent also Belgium and France, whose definitions of perinatal mortality do not fully correspond to that adopted by WHO; and (3) countries with a stagnating perinatal mortality, which includes Czechoslovakia. Rychtaříková also notes, with some concern, that in the 1960s and early 1970s, perinatal mortality in the GDR, Austria and West Germany was higher than in Czechoslovakia but that it is now lower.

As we can see from Table 10.4, perinatal mortality in Czechoslovakia declined substantially after the end of the Second World War and throughout early 1950s, but that during the period from 1960–75, it remained relatively stable, fluctuating between 20 per thousand and 23 per thousand. Over the years, there has been substantial concern about the lack of improvement in perinatal mortality statistics, and a lot of research has been directed towards discovering and analysing the various causes of perinatal deaths. It is generally agreed that the two leading causes of perinatal mortality are prematurity and placental insufficiency, accounting for as much as two-thirds of all the deaths (Štembera *et al.*, 1979, p. 23; Štembera, 1979).[5] In an opening address of a special medical conference on perinatal mortality, which took place in Prague in November 1980, Černoch (1982) also put some blame on the doctors themselves, namely on their inadequate screening and diagnosis. Twins and breech presentations are apparently often diagnosed late or not at all (i.e. the condition becomes apparent only during delivery). Moreover, in 1976, the incompetence of the cervix was diagnosed in advance only in 54 per cent of premature births, and treated in only 3 per cent of the cases. Interestingly, Černoch (1982, p. 14) also notes that the leading cause of premature birth is not abortion (which is listed as third), but previous premature births, stillbirths and miscarriages, which together account for three times as many premature births as abortions.

In contrast, Trnka *et al.* (1981) give a lot of praise to the medical management of childbirth in their discussion of improvements in perinatal mortality in the capital Prague. While Prague's environment is generally unfavourable to good health because of its high level of smog pollution, noise and general stress (in part caused by inadequate public transportation), perinatal mortality has been nonetheless consistently declining since 1968. In 1977, during the peak of the mini 'population explosion' (the authors' own term), Prague had the lowest perinatal mortality in the whole country. This medical reproductive success is attributed by the authors to (1) better availability of modern obstetrical technology, especially foetal monitors and incubators, compared to the rest of the country (largely due to the well equipped Institute for the Care of Mother and Child, which is located in Prague); (2) a slight decrease in premature births, from 6.5 per cent of all births in 1968 to 5.9 per cent in 1979; and (3) an increase in Caesarean sections, from 2 per cent in 1968 to 5 per cent in 1979. As mentioned earlier, the rise in surgical deliveries during this period was much more dramatic in the large teaching hospitals, from 3 per cent in 1968 to 10 per cent in 1979.

The obsession with favourable perinatal statistics has been recently intensified by the initiative of Dr Gazárek and his colleagues, who advocate the lowering of perinatal mortality to less than 10 per thousand:

North Moravian gynaecologists and women's nurses have vowed, in order to mark the XVI Party Congress, to work in such a way that perinatal mortality in the whole county would decrease during the seventh Five Year Plan below 10 per thousand, and simultaneously we would also decrease neonatal morbidity . . . It will not be an easy task, because it will mean the lowering of perinatal mortality in the North Moravian county by more than a third . . . We are urging all other counties to follow us, because we are convinced that this will be the most beautiful and most prized gift that we can give to our mothers and their children, our new generation. (Gazárek *et al.*, 1982a, p. 27)

This initiative was first announced at the November 1980 conference on perinatal mortality, and it was met both with scepticism and guarded optimism. However, in his editorial in the February 1981 issue of *Československá gynekologie*, the national obstetrical/ gynaecological journal, Balák (1981, p. 2) is quite confident that the target can be reached:

> If after the XVI Party Congress we manage to equip obstetrical and neonatal wards with more and better technology, and if we better educate our staff and secure adequate bed capacity, we would have ensured the health of our new generation. Perinatal mortality will substantially decline (below 10 per thousand), as will perinatal morbidity (below 3 per thousand) and neonatal mortality (below 12 per thousand).

However, not all physicians in Czechoslovakia (and that includes some of those working at the Ministry of Health) want to direct all their effort towards lowering perinatal mortality to current Scandinavian or Dutch levels. For example, Michlíček (1976) suggests that perinatal mortality is already so low, that further possible decline is negligible, only in tenths of per cents. Hence, he argues, preventive obstetrics should re-examine whether the priority should continue to be placed on the decrease of perinatal mortality. In his view, the rise of perinatal morbidity, especially mental and neurological disturbances, is a more significant and a more worrisome problem, a view shared by the Ministry of Health and its physician Minister, J. Prokopec.

For example, the Ministry of Health publication, *Zdravotnictví a populace* (1971, p. 23) and Prokopec (1975, p. 69), looking at the issue from an essentially demographic perspective, evaluate the attempts to lower perinatal mortality with some scepticism:

(1) Given the current state of medical science, further lowering of perinatal mortality is possible, but very difficult.
(2) The lowering of perinatal mortality per one mille represents in Czechoslovak conditions 220 saved children, which from the perspective of population problems seems inconsequential.
(3) However, it is necessary to continue to pay systematic attention to perinatal mortality, largely because it is closely related to perinatal morbidity.

In addition to these quantitative demographic arguments, others have advanced more qualitative psychological arguments. Herinková *et al.* (1981, p. 45) put the case rather succinctly:

A continuously growing number of children surviving risk pregnancies and complicated deliveries is forcing obstetricians to
broaden the measures which attempt to ensure the child's survival.
Contemporary medical care enables almost all children to get
through the hurdles of complicated deliveries. However, medical
ethics is not opposed to the view that perinatal death is not the
worst outcome for mother and child, despite the fact that this is still
the main criterion for the management of birth. Obstetricians
remain for most part ignorant of the tragic destinies of children
who have survived severe birth-caused brain damage.

The authors welcome the desire of some obstetricians to cooperate
more closely with neurologists, child psychiatrists and child psychologists. In the view of Herinková *et al.* (1981, p. 49) psychologists
especially 'can give obstetricians precise objective data about the
psychiatric state of children with various types of birth damage and
thus influence preventive obstetrical measures'.

According to the Ministry of Health estimates, there are 4–6
seriously damaged babies requiring permanent institutionalised care
per thousand live births; the estimate for less severely damaged
children is 20–30 per thousand. What this means is an annual addition
of 5 000–10 000 handicapped children, and even if they live only until
the age of 35, they still add up to 300 000 people in the population.

The ministry officials also spell out the economic implications of
these figures:

> The annual increase of severely handicapped children, forced to
> live permanently in institutionalised care, represents the loss of
> 20 000 labour powers. An additional 300 000 individuals have
> lowered or limited work capacity. The affected individuals either
> do not contribute at all, or only to a limited extent, towards the
> creation of national income; severely handicapped children have to
> be cared for by the state and the family for their whole lives. The
> social loss, caused annually by perinatal morbidity, is estimated
> federally to run into milliards of crowns. (*Zdravotnictví a popu-
> lace*, 1971, p. 26; Prokopec, 1975, p. 73)

In the authors' view, perinatal morbidity is therefore another indicator of obstetrical/paediatric care, but 'it is a much less exact
measure, because we still do not have enough information. This is
why data available domestically, or from abroad are very incomplete
and inexact' (*Zdravotnictví a populace*, 1971, p. 23; Prokopec, 1975,

p. 69). The unreliability of morbidity statistics is largely due to the inherent difficulty in establishing a direct causal link between the various stages of reproduction and a particular handicap. Not only is it difficult to establish with any certainty whether a particular defect was caused by a pathology in conception, or during pregnancy or delivery, or immediately after, but the handicap could be related to a variety of factors: genetical make up; infectious disease, taking of drugs or being subjected to X-rays during pregnancy, some other pregnancy complication, or mechanical, anaesthetic or analgesic damage during delivery, and so on. Moreover, certain handicaps (e.g. epilepsy) may manifest themselves only in puberty, when it is particularly difficult to link the disorder fully to perinatal damage.

Thus the over-all evaluation of perinatal mortality and morbidity statistics is complex and controversial. How does one then evaluate these statistics? It is clear that the argument as to whether perinatal mortality can, or indeed should, rest at 10 per thousand related births or go still lower, is largely academic, though, as we have seen, it has political implications. The decline in perinatal mortality *naturally* slows down as lower values are reached, and once the degree of levelling off has been achieved, it is doubtful as to both the feasibility and wisdom of trying to push the average much lower. Moreover, attempts to lower perinatal mortality have led to the often unthinking application of practices that undoubtedly benefit a minority of mothers and babies to the majority who do not need them, with disastrous psychological results. However, as Oakley (1979a, p. 19) argues, physical trauma, discomfort and emotional and social distress are measures that:

are not easy to obtain: they are not like deaths or stillbirths or congenital malformations that can be counted. Perhaps for this reason they have been left out of the medical reckoning. Obstetricians deal with death and illness and acute pain, but they do not deal with discomfort, with failures in emotional health and relationships and with 'social' problems. So it is in the field of social science research that we expect measures of the social and emotional costs of current maternity care to be computed.

As far as perinatal morbidity is concerned, one can argue that qualitative (i.e. social and psychological) variables may, and often do, override the more quantitative medical indicators of birth injury, variously described as anoxia, hypoxia, asphyxia, or shortage of oxygen to the foetal brain. Indeed, Lumley and Astbury (1980, p. 98) claim that *'intervention to prevent all degrees of hypoxia may be based on a false premise'* (author's italics). In refuting the theory of the 'continuum of reproductive causality', the main rationale for elective medical intervention, Lumley and Astbury (1980, p. 98–9) persuasively argue as follows:

> Clearly, some infants do die from hypoxia and some suffer from immediate, severe and permanent brain damage. What is in question is the outcome of less severe instances . . . Apparently the infant brain has a great capacity for recovery in favourable circumstances . . . Environmental factors seem to be highly important in determining whether the abnormal infant behaviour resolves or persists. Interaction between the abnormal infant and a less than good environment may be the crucial thing. The quality of maternal care-taking thus has tremendous significance for the outcome of infants asphyxiated at birth, even more so than for normal infants. This suggests very strongly that interventions in pregnancy and birth which aim to produce a physiologically more perfect infant, one with high levels of oxygen in the brain, but which do so at the expense of maternal self-esteem or satisfaction, will in the long run be self-defeating. Things which affect a mother's capacity to care for the infant and to respond to his/her needs will compromise the long term outcome, especially when the infant is abnormal.

A similar conclusion (as well as a starting point for research on 'bonding'!) is reached by Klaus and Kennel (1976, p. 2):

> An important impetus to studying the mother–infant bond occurred ten to fifteen years ago when the staffs of intensive care nurseries observed that after heroic measures had been used to save prematures, these infants would sometimes return to emergency rooms battered and almost destroyed by their parents, even though the infants had been sent home intact and thriving. Careful studies show an increase in the incidence of battering as well as failure to thrive without organic cause among premature infants and those hospitalized for other reasons during the newborn period when they are compared with infants not separated from their mothers.

So what about the mother herself? As Oakley (1979a, p. 20) points out, 'we must not be deceived into thinking that criticism of maternity care centred on the welfare of babies is necessarily "feminist"; it may be designed to put the baby, and not its mother, at the centre of the stage'. In Czechoslovakia, both supporters and critics of active medical intervention have been for most part interested in practices seen as harmful to the physical and mental health of babies; mothers' own feelings and satisfaction have been of no particular concern. There has been no explicit recognition (as there has been in the West, thanks to the efforts of the feminist and women's health movements) that active, independent, healthy women may wish to 'give birth' rather than 'be delivered'. In Czechoslovakia, as in the rest of Eastern Europe, all matters relating to childbirth are decided and controlled by the medical and nursing professions.

Furthermore, there has been little awareness of the importance of the childbirth experience for the parents, as opposed to the baby, whose 'birth trauma' has occupied several influential Czech psychologists, including the internationally known S. Groff, who currently resides in the United States. Czechoslovakia also lags behind the West in research and policy relating to men's role in the process of transition to parenthood. As we have seen in the previous chapter, Trča's popular prenatal guidebook briefly mentions (in one sentence) that in France husbands are present during childbirth, and adds (in another sentence) that, according to the results of one unspecified survey, male presence during childbirth is not desired by Czech women.[6] One could question this off-hand conclusion. People generally do not respond to new 'radical' suggestions with immediate enthusiasm, because they need some time to consider the various pros and cons of the proposal. If the recorded experiences with 'rooming-in' – examined in some detail in the next chapter – are anything to go by, allowing husbands into labour, delivery and post-partum rooms may be welcomed by many parents in Czechoslovakia. However, given the existing sexual division of labour around birth control and child care, men's initial reaction is more difficult to predict. Much would depend on the encouragement offered by the medical profession. The doctors interviewed for this study had no objection to the father's presence in principle, but they cited many 'practical' difficulties (e.g. shortages of cleaners, lack of adequate facilities, danger of infections, their professional belief that not seeing the baby for a week will do no harm to the father or the baby, father's fainting and so on). As a result, it seems at the present there is still strong medical resistance to the presence of fathers. Currently, fathers can be present during labour and delivery only in very small rural maternity hospitals which have no more than 1–2 births a day, and even then only if hospital policy is broken.

NOTES

1. The Dutch system of maternity care is positively evaluated in the more professional literature – see, for example, Šráček's (1981) report on new international developments in obstetrics, published in *Československá gynekologie*.
2. The survey was conducted in Zvolen, a small town in central Slovakia, in 1979. The sample consisted of 332 men (39 per cent) and 522 women (61 per cent), who filled in an anonymous questionnaire six months after their hospital stay. The sample included maternity patients, but we are not given their share of the total.
3. For first-hand anecdotal accounts of childbirth experiences in the Soviet Union, see Hanson and Lidén (1983, pp. 22, 75, 105–6, 147–8), a collection of thirteen unofficial interviews which were tape-recorded in Moscow in the spring of 1978 by two Swedish women journalists, Carola Hansson and Karin Lidén; and *Women and Russia* (Mamonova and Matilsky, 1984, pp. 101–5), the first feminist *samizdad* (underground) publication almanac. See also Ispa (1983) who has conducted interviews about childbirth experiences with 30 Soviet women, who recently emigrated to the United States. Ispa (1983, p. 3) found that 'horror' stories about inadequate sanitation, poor food, overcrowding, and rudeness and neglect on the part of hospital personnel abound; on the other hand, some of the women interviewed expressed complete satisfaction with their experience. Officially, care is entirely free, but most of the women reported that 'tips' to nurses and doctors were expected and that women who do not offer money or who have not established personal connections received inferior care.
4. However, this was not always the case. In the UK in the early twentieth century, both infant and maternity mortality rates were compared with those of other countries as 'indices of national strength and international supremacy' (Oakley, 1982, p. 672). In fact, the failure of the British maternal mortality rate to fall during 1838–1936 was the main impetus for the development of a national system of antenatal care. See Lewis (1980) and Oakley (1983) for a detailed discussion of the political implications of stagnating and unfavourable (in comparison with other countries) maternal mortality rates in the UK during the first half of this century.
5. However, throughout the 1970s, there has been tremendous improvement in both the survival and long-term outcomes of premature, low birth weight babies. Today, the majority of infants survive at birth

weights between 800 and 1000 grams or 30 weeks gestation, while a decade ago, 80 per cent of those infants would have died (*Cesarean Childbirth*, 1981, p. 37).

6. Similar findings have emerged from the Soviet Union. Hansson and Lidén in *Moscow Women* (1983, p. 115) report that 'sexual prudery follows the woman all the way into the delivery room. To give birth to a child is painful, but above all unaesthetic – or so people think. The most common argument against having the father present at the delivery is that it is too grotesque. At most he is allowed to sit in a room next door. Another reason for his absence is that the woman herself can't always be guaranteed a separate room for delivery. Other women in labor may be present as well!' Ispa (1983, p. 10) also reports that most of the women in her sample were either amused or horrified by the idea of father's presence in the labour and delivery rooms. 'The reasons they gave were telling. Several of the women feared that their husbands would not be able to stand the sight of blood or pain; others commented that they would not want their husbands to see them suffering or less attractive than usual . . . Remarks generally suggested that men are weaker than women and should be spared the shock of witnessing or participating in childbirth.' However, a large teaching maternity hospital in Kiev has recently changed its policy and is now allowing fathers in, on an experimental basis, while only ten years ago, its official claimed that such a policy would never be introduced in the Soviet Union (personal communication from Tova Yedlin and Landon Pearson).

11 After Birth

Few human cultures emphasize immediate postpartum bodily contact and suckling, practices shown to prolong breast feeding and to increase early maternal involvement for individuals in industrial societies. Yet in non-industrial groups, mothers are affectionately involved with their infants, and breastfeed successfully for two or more years . . . Thus the sensitivity of industrialized parents to immediate postpartum contact may reflect disruptive influence of our pattern of infant care and our hospital routines, rather than a brief sensitive period for parenting in the human species. (Lozoff, 1981, pp. 137–144)

Until recently, it was standard practice in all maternity hospitals in Czechoslovakia (as well as the rest of the world) to segregate infants in a nursery immediately after birth. Dr Šráčková (1981, p. 690), a paediatrician from Brno, characterises what used to be typical postpartum hospital experience in Czechoslovakia as follows:

Under the current system of institutional obstetrics, mothers remain separated from their children and are together virtually only during breastfeeding, six times per day, 20–30 minutes, that is 2–3 hours per day. The remainder, 21–22 hours, that is practically 90 per cent of the day, is spent on separate wards under the care of specialised physicians and nurses. Access to the newborn ward is strictly forbidden. A mother who was shown her carefully wrapped baby (after its first bath and treatment) immediately after delivery, is not allowed to unwrap the baby even during breastfeeding, so that she is able to see the whole child only after a week, when she is discharged home. Moreover, during her hospital stay she does not learn how much her baby has drunk each time it nursed; neither is she present during its weighing. She is sometimes (not every day) given some information by the attending paediatrician, or she occasionally succeeds in obtaining some information from the nurse who is thus breaking a hospital regulation.

In the majority of Czech hospitals, the first contact (excluding a brief glimpse immediately after delivery) between the mother and her baby used to be 12 hours after birth when the baby was brought to her for its first feeding (it has now been reduced to 4–8 hours); further interaction was limited to two hours a day during the strict three-hour nursing intervals. Not only was the mother not allowed to see the whole baby, but the baby could not see all of her, since nursing mothers had to wear a face mask. These rigidly enforced policies were justified on the grounds of 'danger of infection' and 'the need for mothers to rest'.

As we noted in the previous chapter, the fear of infection is offered as the reason for keeping fathers (as well as all other visitors) from the maternity hospital. The 'danger of infection' dictum goes to such absurd lengths that Trča (1979, pp. 178–9) advises mothers against kissing their babies:

A baby is an amiable creature; it's no wonder that the mother has a frequent urge to kiss it. But beware. Most people have in their mouth infectious germs, which are not harmful to them but which can cause various illnesses (of the respiratory tract of the digestive tract, and so on) to the newborn. Thus it would be best not to kiss a newborn baby at all. However, if you cannot always resist the desire to kiss the baby, then never kiss it on the lips or on those parts of the body which the child can put in its mouth (i.e. hands). Nobody else apart from the mother should kiss the baby.

As far as 'the need for mothers to rest' is concerned, it is interesting to note that before and immediately after the Second World War, maternity wards in Czechoslovakia kept mothers and babies in the same multi-bed room, but this meant that 'newborns disturbed their mothers' sleep by frequent crying' (*Encyklopedie mladé ženy*, 1978, pp. 345–6).

Dr Švejcar (1980, p. 550), the eminent 'dean' of Czechoslovak paediatricians, who was responsible, among other things, for the post-war introduction of formula milk, has recently become an outspoken critic of these practices:

Newborn wards, which were established in consideration of both the need for post-partum rest and the possibility of infections, took baby care in the wrong direction. A mother cannot have her peace after childbirth and simultaneously not disturb her relationship to the baby. Fear of infections did not take into account the enormous protection against them which the mother provides by her breast-feeding, which is much greater than the protection achieved by the separation from the mother.

Dr Švejcar, along with some other prominent physicians, is now a vocal advocate of introducing 'rooming-in', a term for which the Institute for Czech Language has not yet found a Czech translation (Ouřadová, 1981). In fact, the word rooming-in has been incorporated into Czech in its original English form.

THE POLITICS OF 'ROOMING-IN'

In the rooming-in system of newborn care, the child is placed in the mother's room rather than in a nursery, and this is supposed to facilitate both mother–infant bonding and breastfeeding. As DeVries (1984, p. 91) points out:

> with the exception of a few isolated studies, it was not until the last decade that systematic inquiry into mother–infant interaction and the nature of the mother's bond to her child has begun. Since the early 1970's an overwhelming number of articles dealing with human attachment have appeared, but only the portion of these which deal with bonding are relevant to the present discussion. Work on bonding can be separated from the larger issue of attachment on the basis of its special concern with the immediate post-partum contact between an infant and its parents. Some researchers have suggested that there is a 'sensitive period in the first minutes and hours of life' during which bonding occurs. Because bonding is imputed to occur precisely when mother and infant are under medical supervision, it has been research related to bonding that has had the most influence on medical organizations.

DeVries (1984, p. 96) also argues that:

> evidence from California suggests a link between the publication of Klaus and Kennell's seminal work on bonding and the proliferation of alternative birth centers. In that state there were only three such centres in 1975; by December of 1978, within three years of the

appearance of Klaus and Kennell's book, the number of centers in California had grown to 70. It was also after the Klaus and Kennell volume that evaluations of alternative birth centers and guides to their implementation began to appear in great numbers.

It is interesting to note that contrary to common assumptions, the spread of medical innovation is not solely controlled by a process of professional communication and interaction, but is instead strongly influenced by the action of consumers. In my survey of 25 hospital-based alternative birth centers, I discovered that without exception the primary factor in their creation was consumer demand. These centers were not opened because doctors on staff had read and were impressed by the results of studies of parent–infant attachment. Rather, alternative facilities were the result of the efforts of consumers pressuring hospitals either directly or through the choice to give birth elsewhere.

However, the situation in Czechoslovakia is somewhat different. While the link between the publication of Klaus and Kennell's (1976) book on bonding and the alteration of standard obstetrical practices also holds, this does not apply to consumer demand. In fact, it would appear that the rooming-in system of newborn care in Czechoslovakia can be attributed almost entirely to the fact that doctors 'had read and were impressed by the results of studies of parent–infant attachment'.

Moreover, there is a long tradition of indigenous research on 'birth trauma' and on various aspects of deprivation in children,[1] and there is only a short step to be made from accepting research findings about childhood deprivation to being concerned with deprivation immediately after birth. Thus, when Klaus and Kennell's book reached Czechoslovakia (incidently, only a few years after it was originally published in the United States), it was immediately well received. However, the book, described by DeVries (1984, p. 93) as 'perhaps the most influential work on bonding', was published only in a limited edition aimed at concerned specialists, not at the general public. Thus, unlike California, consumers in Czechoslovakia were in no position to press for any changes in routine obstetrical practices, since they were quite unaware of any new developments in bonding research. The utilisation of bonding research as a basis for challenge to modern obstetrics remained entirely in the hands of other professionals, namely child psychologists, and paediatricians rather than 'lay' consumers.

In fact, some domestic professional criticism of standard hospital management of birth pre-dates the publication in Czechoslovakia of Klaus and Kennell's volume. For example, the psychologist who wrote an article on motherhood for the popular women's advice book, *Encyklopedie mladé ženy* (*Encyclopaedia of a Young Woman*) (1978, p. 634) argues that babies born in the hospital find themselves in superb hygienic conditions, and are cared for by professional nurses, but their environment is artificial and harsh, characterised by hygienic but scourging shower, mass changing of nappies (diapers) and mass feeding at an hour specified by the hospital staff.

> Compared to the womb, the first environment around the baby is enormous, white and the light is on uninterruptedly. These arrangements are certainly justified by a whole range of hygienic and health reasons, but it is arguable whether these advantages exceed the psycho-educational damage. The first experience of existential frustration is quite in order here.

The article, written before the emergence of the current debates about rooming-in, recommends that mothers be allowed in the forbidden newborn ward. The author believes that nurses would both accept and benefit from the mothers' help and mothers themselves, especially new mothers, would learn more from direct observation and changing of babies than from one post-partum home visit by a nurse.

> One week's rest may be pleasant, but the trauma of coming home, being afraid to touch the baby and being overwhelmed by the crying as well as by the escalating hygienic demands (e.g. boiling nappies, bottles, pacifiers) is so much greater.

The author is also critical of the exclusion of fathers from the birth event and of mothers who insist on exclusive child care responsibility and control.

> Our expectant and new father cannot be near his wife during childbirth. Frequently he only takes her to the hospital, learns by phone whether he has a son or daughter, and then waits for the

several days before he will be able to see his offspring. The mother's start is thus increased and father's helplessness intensified.

However, the real impetus for change can be traced to the III Neonatological Congress, on the theme 'mother–child bond', which took place in the Moravian town of Olomouc on 11–12 September 1980. The Congress was attended by 250 specialists, including Dr Michel Odent from the Lamaze Clinic in Paris, France and Dr Rumler, from Halle, GDR. Dr Švejcar, the paediatrician mentioned above, and Dr Damborská, the woman director of one of Czechoslovakia's best homes for orphaned and abandoned children and the esteemed author of many studies of deprivation in children, received standing ovations at the Congress (Švancarová, 1981). The special welcome given to Dr Damborská was in recognition of her highly regarded article entitled 'What is Unphysiological in the Approach towards the Child of the Tenderest Age' which was published in the Slovak professional psychological journal *Psychológia a patapsychológia dieťaťa* (*The Psychology and Patopsychology of the Child*) earlier in that year.

Damborská's article has four critical themes: (1) the management of birth, (2) the separation of mother and baby, (3) the retreat from breastfeeding and (4) insensitive approaches towards child-rearing. Like her colleague who wrote in 1978, Damborská is critical of the harsh hospital environment, characterised by bright lights and noise. She also criticises insensitive obstetrical/paediatric practices, such as slapping of the baby's bottom and the immediate cutting of the umbilical cord. As a solution, Damborská advocates the Leboyer method of childbirth,[2] as well as the presence of the father. In her discussion of infant bonding, based to a large extent on the work of Klaus and Kennell, she is very critical of the standard practice of immediate separation of mothers from their babies. She disagrees with the traditional obstetrical dictum that the 'exhausted mother needs to rest' and instead suggests that a prepared mother need not feel exhausted after delivery. In Damborská's (1980, p. 26) view, 'the separation of the child from its mother after birth and its transfer to the newborn ward is *unphysiological* [her italics]. It is also unphysiological to exclude the father from the newly developing relations.'

As far as breastfeeding is concerned, Damborská (1980, p. 26) is critical of its traditional exclusive medical justification:

It seems that physicians have emphasised for far too long the advantages of breastfeeding only from the nutritional standpoint. It has been necessary for a long time also to use psychological arguments.

Thus Damborská (1980, p. 29) reminds her colleagues that breastfeeding is also important for the mother, since it not only accelerates the postnatal return to normalcy, but also facilitates the development of motherly love. The author strongly recommends rooming-in, along with the earlier initiation of breastfeeding (3–6 hours after birth rather than the standard 12 hours), the respect of the baby's individual feeding rhythm, i.e. feeding on demand (as opposed to the hospital-oriented 3–4 hours routine), no night breaks in breastfeeding and abandoning the practice of giving newborn babies tea. The recent knowledge about the importance of birth without violence (i.e. the Leboyer method of childbirth), early breastfeeding and high quality interaction with the mother are discussed again in a subsequent article (1981) by Damborská, published in the same journal.

The article by Dr Šráčková (1981, p. 690), originally presented as a paper at the Olomouc Congress, adds other specific criticisms of standard postnatal hospital care, and offers additional rationale for change. In her view:

> if mothers see their baby only during breastfeeding, they are preoccupied too much with themselves, and their interest in their child either grows lax or, in the case of overly anxious mothers who were anxiously looking forward to the baby throughout the pregnancy, they are agitated and tearful, worried about their child . . . A mother who sees her child also has greater will to nurse, which in turn influences the creation of her milk supply also from the psychological standpoint.

Šráčková (1981, p. 691) also advocates the abandoning of face masks during breastfeeding[3] as well as the reduction of attending staff:

> It was found that if the mother wears a face mask during the nursing of her child, the child drinks poorly and also sleeps poorly. If newborns are cared for by several people, they are restless, refuse to drink and often cry. If the number of attending staff is reduced, these symptoms are less frequent. Under the current

system of obstetrical and newborn wards, a child will encounter during its hospital stay 5–6 nurses.

The author is a strong supporter of rooming-in, but she admits that 'despite all the listed advantages, we have not been very successful with the introduction of the system of rooming-in under our institutional conditions', due to 'a whole range of negative factors'. These are attributed to (1) the conservatism of the mothers themselves, (2) lack of suitable space and equipment and (3) resistance from attending personnel. In Šráčková's clinical experience, mothers distrust the new system simply because they are used to the old system (in existence for already two generations) of separating mothers and babies.

It is not so easy to immediately reverse this system in the minds of contemporary young women, who place greater demands on their personal comforts, be they first-time mothers who obtained birthing information from their own mothers, who in turn gave birth in the traditional system, or mothers having subsequent births, who have their own personal experiences from their previous births.

Šráčková is even more critical of individual nurses, who tend to dislike rooming-in because:

it implies a change in the routine of her work, and in practice requires additional work, when she has to deal with tact and tenaciousness of purpose with an often nervous and unstable mother, a woman in a childbed, and teach her how to handle the baby, how to care for it – changing it, bathing it and so on. Simultaneously she has to teach lactation, how to express milk, and to some mothers even impart basic rules of hygiene. Compared to the current system of work on the newborn ward, all of this increases the nurse's work load. If the paediatric nurse works independently on the newborn ward, nobody apart from the head nurse and the physician – a neonatologist – interferes with her work. Routine, automatic movements are quite sufficient and her work proceeds very smoothly. However, these automatic and hurried movements as well as the impersonal behaviour are elements which have a negative impact on the newborn baby. It is obvious that nurses in rooming-in must be not only sufficiently qualified, but above all must behave with tact, be patient and at the same time communicative. Women in the immediate post-partum period appreciate these qualities.

In contrast, other doctors have reported more positive experiences. Dr Mendl *et al.* (1982, p. 89), from the modern, recently built (in 1976) hospital in the northern Bohemian town Most, which was the first maternity hospital in the country to introduce rooming-in in November 1980 (with Dr Švejcar, back from his visit to Basel, Switzerland, acting as an advisor), argue that:

> nurses became very soon enthusiastic about rooming-in. They are less burdened with routine work, they have more time for the mothers, whom they not only help but also advise. Relations between mothers and paediatric nurses have improved enormously. We have not received a single complaint about the care of the baby.

The authors admit that what had increased are:

> demands placed on the work of paediatricians. Hospital rounds have become longer both because the assistance of mothers is naturally slower than that of nurses and because a great many questions are raised. However, the time loss is greatly compensated by the positive effect of the physician on the mother.[4]

Mendl *et al.* (1982, p. 89) also report the results from questionnaires sent to 70 rooming-in mothers six months after their deliveries. The responses were generally very positive, and they also revealed some earlier negative experiences:

> I personally did not like it during my first pregnancy when my child was taken away from me immediately after birth. One then feels like a stranger in a relationship with one's own child.

> A fatigue which one feels practically disappears when the child is continuously present.

> It all went much faster in the maternity hospital.

> I didn't feel like a wet nurse, but right from the first day I felt like a mother, and that's a great feeling.

When interviewed in 1981 for *Mladá fronta*, the youth daily, two of the co-authors of the article claimed that:

> it has not happened to us yet that a mother who was well informed about the advantage of rooming-in refused this system of care. More likely we will soon have a problem of how to satisfy all requests. And this is good, because interest and pressure on the part of mothers can do a lot for a faster introduction of this system of care of newborns in our hospitals. (Drs Kysela and Choděrová, quoted in Ouřadová, 1981)

Thus socialist consumers have *some* input into decision-making about policy changes, but their role is much more limited than that of their counterparts in California and elsewhere in the West. It is one of reaction to rather than initiation of change. This becomes quite evident when we review the way in which the issue of rooming-in has been covered in Czech mass media. During the last few years, several articles and interviews, exalting the virtues of rooming-in, have appeared in the mass media.[5] However, when readers of *Mladý svět*, the youth weekly, were invited in early 1983 to respond to one such article (entitled 'The Experiment'), their responses were both negative and positive. Examination of some of these letters is particularly relevant to the present discussion, because: (1) they give us some interesting first-hand accounts of childbirth experiences, which are so hard to come by in Eastern Europe; (2) they touch on the issue of fathers' presence during childbirth; and (3) they include some letters from fathers themselves.

> I belong to the generation who birthed earlier. I had three daughters and I fully support the opinion of Eva Kocembová [whose critical letter sparked off the readers' debate about the pros and cons of rooming-in]. I am fundamentally opposed to this method. A mother should have peace and not be forced to take care of her baby straight away . . . I think we have more than enough of these hurried novelties.

> I didn't come to the maternity ward to rest but to give birth to a healthy baby, to learn how to best care for it and to generally learn as much as possible about the baby. I can compare both the old and the new system of childbirth, it was not my first birth. Previously I only knew the crying and hungry face of my daughter for twenty

minutes every three hours and at home I was afraid to touch her. Now I was learning everything simultaneously with my son and I have at home a healthy, quiet, smiling boy.

Naturally we could not stand the screaming of the children for very long. They also had an admirable ability to take turns in their screaming. I slept on average two hours a day and towards the end I was utterly exhausted. I didn't feel a deeper bond with my child, as you write. On the contrary, I kept getting more and more annoyed with him. I am therefore against putting babies together with mothers . . . The system, which is now being introduced, should exist only on a voluntary basis.

I learned in the maternity hospital how to change, dress, bath the baby and so on. Children were indeed crying during the night, but not one of the five mothers in the room minded. The behaviour of doctors, nurses, even cleaners, was so perfect, that I will never forget the several days which I spent in the maternity hospital.

I don't understand the opinion which disapproves of both father's presence during childbirth and the joint placement of mothers and children . . . On the contrary, my husband and I think that this joint experience could have great influence on the mutual relations of both partners. It may even be reflected in divorce statistics, but this is only speculation.

When I fall asleep in the maternity hospital of 'normal type', I fall asleep with the knowledge that somebody watches over the child the whole night. When I have the baby with me, I am so worried that I cannot fall asleep at all . . . Every paediatrician or obstetrician apparently does not have the same opinion, because before my third birth, my former classmate, currently a woman obstetrician in K., wrote to me as follows: 'I hope that in your place they have not yet introduced the placement of newborns with their mothers; that would be quite an experience for you. I would feel sorry for you in anticipation.' I am sure you won't publish my letter, since it speaks against the so much praised new method.

I have always wished for my husband to be present during childbirth. I think this experience is important for the marital bond.

I gave birth in the Bulovka hospital [in Prague's eighth district] . . . The child is only briefly shown to you and then taken to the newborn ward. Yet precisely during this time, when it is 'all over', one would like to have nearby somebody close, with whom one could share the enormous joy. But visits in this hospital are really a humiliating affair. There are only two little windows two by one metre for the whole ward . . .

I was interested in your article 'Experiment' that the husband's presence during childbirth is being considered. I think it is a good thing.

I am not so concerned whether or not the child should be with its mother. This is a women's problem. But what about us, men? How much happier are those who can come with flowers or some other little consideration . . .

In Uherské Hradiště the sight in front of the maternity hospital is really pitiful. The fathers stand on the pavement outside the hospital while the mothers are inside behind bar windows. How can such a father thank, touch or exchange a few words with his wife, who is shouting from the second floor that she cannot understand him . . . I would understand the prohibition of visits during epidemics, but this way?

Earlier, when children were born at home, the husband was often present. And maybe because of this he had then greater respect for his wife. It could possibly make some impact on the lowering of divorces.

According to the editors, approximately half of the letters received strongly advocated an immediate nationwide introduction of rooming-in. Others wanted to preserve the existing system and some preferred mothers to have a choice as to what system to use. In 1981, only two maternity hospitals in the country had moved fully towards rooming-in; 48 hospitals retained the old system and 41 hospitals now have a combination of both systems of care. The most rapid change occurred in North Bohemia, where in 1982 thirteen out of seventeen maternity wards introduced some form of rooming-in, and others were planning to do so in the future. Prague was lagging behind, with the two hospitals in Prague's fourth district (one of which was the

Institute for the Care of Mother and Child) leading the way. For the rest of Prague's maternity hospitals, rooming-in in the early 1980s remained in the experimental or planning stage. (Ouřadová, 1981; 'Stále s matkou', *Rudé právo*, 6 October and 'U matky je dítěti nejlépe', *Rudé právo*, 6 November 1982).

The relative slowness of change in the capital was due both to consumer resistance[6] and lack of space. However, it is quite obvious from some of the letters quoted above that the former is at least partially related to the latter. Private or semi-private rooms – the preferred form of rooming-in in the West – are quite rare in Czechoslovak hospitals, though they may be more common in special party or military clinics. The more modern hospitals sometimes offer semi-private rooms; indeed when rooming-in was first introduced in Most, it was the six available semi-private rooms (i.e. with two beds) that were used for the purpose. However, since June 1981, rooming-in in that hospital has been also available in four rooms with five beds each (Mendl *et al.*, 1982). The mass media have quite cleverly attempted to justify the need to make virtue out of necessity by offering the following professional/practical criteria:

At first it was assumed that it's best to place two mothers with children in one room. But it seems that 3–4 beds are better; primiparas together with secundiparas. They can offer help to each other; after all one's own practical experience is extremely valuable. Some maternity wards have even 5 mothers in one room. ('U matky je dítěti nejlépe', *Rudé právo*, 6 November 1982)

Thus the role of consumers notwithstanding, the evolution of the medicalised birthing system in Czechoslovakia has followed the Western pattern of interprofessional conflict, with the main challenge to modern obstetrics coming from paediatrics, psychology, and, most recently, also consumers via the mass media. For the most part, critics have been concerned with practices seen as harmful to the physical and mental health of babies (though mothers and fathers occasionally also figure), with paediatricians being most concerned about the 'optimal' environment for breastfeeding and psychologists being more worried about 'optimal' infant and parental bonding. However, as DeVries (1984, p. 100) points out, 'bonding should not be regarded as a mystical process which inevitably draws families together . . . Obviously the birth environment is only one of several factors shaping parental behavior; the focus on early parent–infant contact should not

be allowed to obscure other elements that influence the quality of
relationships between children and their parents.' In any case, new
medical literature is raising serious doubts about the existence of an
early 'sensitive' period when bonding is imputed to be maximised
(Hluchy, 1983). To conclude with another quotation from De Vries
(1984, pp. 100, 101)

> while no one could question the benefits of early parent–infant
> interaction, insistence that all parents participate in 'bonding pro-
> grams' of one type or another appears unwarranted and potentially
> harmful . . . In spite of the fact that much of the research on
> bonding demonstrates that the home is an ideal environment for
> parent–child interaction, medical ideology dictates that the clinical
> advice of bonding studies ignore this true alternative in favor of
> recommendations for in-hospital programs to facilitate attach-
> ment . . . The concern with bonding also serves to convey images of
> proper parental behavior. The measures used to assess attachment –
> smiling, touching, gazing in the eyes – reflect conceptions of good
> parenting held by major consumers of bonding research: the edu-
> cated, middle to upper-middle class heterosexual couple. These
> behaviors are not an essential component of attachment, but as
> bonding programs become more common they could become part
> of a general conception of good parenting applied (coercively) to
> all individuals.

BREASTFEEDING

According to Jellife and Jellife (1978), women throughout the world
have been altering their feeding practices, substituting artificial milk
in place of breastfeeding. Czechoslovakia is no exception. As Damborská (1980, p. 27) puts it, 'statistics show that 15 per cent of women
are unable to breastfeed. However, we are today in a situation where
only 15 per cent of women *do breastfeed*' [her italics]. She is, of course,
referring to long-term breastfeeding – for three months and more –
rather than to lactation as such. In fact, almost 90 per cent of mothers
in Czechoslovakia nurse their babies while still in the hospital,[7] where
breastfeeding is encouraged to the extent that it is the only opportunity a mother has to see (part of) her baby. It is hoped that recent
changes in hospital routines (e.g. rooming-in, feeding on demand,
the shortening of the long delay between birth and the first attempted

feed), will achieve even better results – 95–97 per cent lactation rate. (Šráčková *et al.*, 1975; Švejcar, 1981).

However, within two weeks of childbirth, only 77 per cent of babies are still nursed. After three months, the percentage drops to 30. Only 10–12 per cent of mothers breastfeed for more than five months. In 1966–70, the average length of breastfeeding was six weeks, though by 1974 this had increased to nine weeks and by 1979 to ten weeks (eleven weeks in 1978). Moreover, breastfeeding does not normally imply an exclusive reliance on the mother's milk. More than a quarter of all nursing mothers start adding formula milk during the baby's first month, 38 per cent do so during the second month and 83 per cent by the third month. Fruit juices and various gruels are added to the baby's diet also quite early: 61 per cent of babies are nourished in this way by their sixth week (Bokšajová, 1977; Urbanová, 1977; Houštek, 1978; Horanská, 1982).

Švejcar (1980, p. 551) argues that the 'mother's return home threatens most the nursing of babies', although he also blames nurses and doctors for advising too readily a recourse to bottle feeding 'if the baby does not seem to have enough'. Bokšajová (1977) also sees in the return home an increased danger of early weaning, and suggests a home visit by a women's nurse within 24 hours of discharge from the hospital as one way to safeguard lactation. This opinion is shared by Jones and Belsey (1977, p. 178) who found in their study of breast-feeding in an inner London borough that 'an increase in hospital advice produced no sustained increase in breast feeding after discharge from hospital. These results, together with the finding that many women choose their feeding method even before pregnancy, suggest that programmes confined to antenatal clinics and classes are unlikely to have much effect.'

However, Janovský and Procházková (1981) assume that prenatal care can make a positive impact, since they blame the existing system of care for paying little or no attention to breast care during pregnancy and to lactation in general. Similarly, Horanská (1982) claims that, at least in the Slovak district of Piešťany, intensive health education propaganda in the mass media, antenatal clinics and classes, as well as in doctors' consultations and nurses' home visits, have arrested and to some extent even reversed the decline in breastfeeding. As evidence, she cites the above quoted figures on the lengthening of lactation from six weeks in 1966–70 to eleven weeks in 1978. Horanská (1982) also points out that prior to 1972, the decision to wean was left entirely to the mother, with the result that 53 per cent of mothers stopped nursing on the basis of self-diagnosis of inadequate milk supply. Since 1972, the mother has been expected to consult her physician prior to her decision to wean her baby, but Horanská admits that mothers generally ignore medical advice to lengthen their nursing and quit breastfeeding anyway.

In Horanská's view, shared by Dr Švejcar in a recent interview with the party daily, *Rudé právo*, 15 May 1982, there is a general cultural indifference or even hostility towards prolonged breastfeeding, especially if it takes place in public places. Švejcar (1982) described the situation a mother is likely to face if she attempts to breastfeed in public:

When two young people are publicly embracing each other on the street, nobody is particularly surprised. However, a nursing woman in a park or on a train – a common sight in the past – would now create quite a stir. Instead of being left alone, she is likely to hear inept comments from pubescent male adolescents.

However, this cultural restriction on breastfeeding in public (or prolonged breastfeeding in general) does not apply to Romany women who can and generally do breastfeed in public. A somewhat similar situation exists in an inner borough in London, where several African women 'found it difficult to give a reason for breast feeding, never having considered any alternative'. Jones and Belsey (1977, p. 178) also speculate that 'it is possible that the large number of breast feeders among immigrant mothers in Lambeth, has influenced the British mothers with the result that they too breast feed more than in other areas'. However, the opposite seems to be the case in Czechoslovakia. Personal experience indicates that the fact that Romany women freely (i.e. without any inhibition) nurse their babies, ironically, reinforces the conservatism about breastfeeding among the public, given the general prejudice towards gypsies.

The general lack of interest in breastfeeding on the part of women is also reflected in the findings of a previously cited sample survey (in Chapter 9) on questions connected with children and the family. Table 11.1 shows that only 2–3 per cent of mothers stopped nursing because of inadequate instruction on how to nurse. Only 11 per cent of the respondents did not attempt breastfeeding but more than half (57 per cent of first-time mothers and 53 per cent of mothers with a subsequent child) weaned them after less than three months. The reasons given for early weaning are not very illuminating because

TABLE 11.1 *Reasons given for nursing for less than three months (%)*

	Sample I	Sample II
Health	88	87
Inadequate instruction	3	2
Other (e.g. cosmetic)	9	11

SOURCE 'Výsledky sociologického průzkumu "Rodina a děti"', 1978.

'health' is a very general and vague term. 'Cosmetic' reasons probably refer to the cultural concern about 'sagging breasts' and the misguided conception that lactation may 'ruin the mother's figure' (Matoušek, 1980, p. 31).

The majority of mothers wean their babies well before the expiry of paid maternity leave, despite the fact that maternity legislation enables them to nurse while working. A nursing mother is entitled to two half-hour breaks for breastfeeding a baby younger than six months and to one half-hour break for nursing a baby aged six to nine months. However, only mothers whose babies are cared for at nurseries in their place of work can take practical advantage of these provisions. Most infants and toddlers are cared for in nurseries run by the local authorities in the mother's place of residence, which means that in a big city nursing during work is not feasible. Thus the usefulness of the legislation, so favourably commented upon by the renowned childbirth educator Sheila Kitzinger (1980), is substantially reduced if most mothers do not or cannot nurse their babies.

However, the most important variable mitigating against successful breastfeeding is clearly the availability of a safe, cheap alternative 'for all those with reasonable housing, clean water, cooking facilities, a western style income' (Lumley and Astbury, 1980, p. 201). These requirements were first provided for a majority of the population in the United States, but they now exist in all advanced industrial countries, be they capitalist or socialist. Following the North American pattern, the decline in breastfeeding in Czechoslovakia has also coincided with an increasing reliance on formula milk, the consumption of which is now more than double the 1955 level (see Table 11.2).

However, the decline in breastfeeding has been much more dramatic in the United States. While in the 1930s, 70 per cent of first-born infants were breastfed, by the late 1960s and early 1970s this proportion had declined to less than 30 per cent. The decline in

TABLE 11.2   *Annual consumption of formula milk in Czechoslovakia*

Year	1955	1960	1965	1970	1976	1977
Consumption (per infant in kg)	12.3	18.6	25.4	25.8	27.4	28.1

SOURCE   Sommerová, 1978a, p. 49.

TABLE 11.3   *Percentage of infants breastfed in Victoria, Australia*

Year	3 months old	6 months old
1945–50	50	40
1971	20	9
1977	38	24
1978	41	27
1984–5	52	37

SOURCE   Lumley and Astbury , 1980 p. 207 and Maternal and Child Health, Department of Health, Victoria.

long-term breastfeeding – the proportion of mothers who breastfed their babies for three months or more – has been even more precipitous. Less than 10 per cent of the mothers whose first child was born from 1966 to 1973 breastfed their infant for three months or more, compared to 17 per cent who did so in 1951 and 32 per cent prior to 1950. These figures indicate that more than two-thirds of the women breastfeeding their babies in recent years had stopped by the time the children were three months old (Hirschman, 1979). In Victoria, Australia, social trends in breastfeeding have followed similar patterns (see Table 11.3).

As in Australia, the overall decline in breastfeeding in the United States levelled off in the early 1970s and currently appears to be on the increase, resulting largely from the efforts of lay women's health movement organisations such as La Leche League (and the Nursing Mothers' Association in Australia), formed to promote breastfeeding and to support women making that decision. Moreover, while early in the twentieth century lactation was a largely lower-class practice in the USA, in recent years it has become more common among educated middle-class women. This pattern is replicated on a world scale. As Lumley and Astbury (1980, p. 210) argue, 'the irony is that while high status mothers in the West take up breastfeeding again, the bottlefeeding practices they have discarded are exported [to the

Third World] and advertised as a high status aspect of industrial civilization'.

No lay organisation devoted to the promotion of breastfeeding exists in Czechoslovakia, where the promotion of lactation has been left entirely in the hands of professional health educators. However, it has recently become clear that under current environmental conditions in Czechoslovakia, prolonged breastfeeding is not the panacea it is sometimes thought to be for the physical and mental health of babies and mothers. While it is true that irregular supplies and occasional problems in the quality of formula products mitigate against bottle-feeding, environmental pollution cuts both ways. Quoting Czech sources, Kramer (1983, pp. 207–8) has argued that 'pesticides and chemical fertilizers utilized in agriculture are often washed or blown into nearby streams and have now contaminated almost all surface and underground water in Czechoslovakia. Among the many adverse consequences of this pollution, according to a 1975 study, were "surprising and serious" concentrations of insecticides in mothers' milk, far above the daily margin of safety established by the World Health Organization.' In 1981, the Government Population Commission gave Dr Švejcar a special honour in recognition of his meritorious work in the advocacy of breastfeeding as the best form of nutrition for infants. However, under the conditions of environmental pollution, there is little to choose, nutritionally speaking, between an indirectly contaminated breast milk and a formula milk contaminated directly from the unsafe water supply.[8] Environmental pollution has recently become an issue of public controversy in several Eastern European countries, including Czechoslovakia, and some measures are being taken to alleviate the situation, but it will obviously take some time before the environmental damage is reversed. In the meantime, the argument on the nutritional and immunological advantage of breastfeeding cannot be made all that strongly in Eastern Europe. The emotional advantage of nursing, the sheer pleasure which feeding and physical closeness to the baby can evoke in the mother, of course, stands, but only if the mother is personally convinced this is to be the case.

Breastfeeding also entails some definite disadvantages for the mother; these are summarised by Lumley and Astbury (1980, pp. 208–9) as follows:

> If work is not the reason, what is? One factor is the wish for a completely reliable form of contraception; something which is

240   *Reproduction, Medicine and the Socialist State*

likely to be more important after a second or subsequent birth and which is more problematic with the restricted range of contraception available to breastfeeding women. Another, still rare but possibly increasing, is the wish of both parents to share equally in the care of the child. A third is the restriction which breastfeeding places on the mother's freedom to move freely in society taking the baby with her. The restriction occurs because breastfed babies need to be fed frequently, because two-thirds of them will not accept a substitute bottle, whatever it contains, and because breastfeeding in public places is still relatively unacceptable . . . Work, leisure and study situations can all be difficult to negotiate if the woman wants to combine responsiveness to the infant's needs with respect for other people's sensibilities.

Thus for the time being, 'breast or bottle' is likely to continue to be a matter of personal choice, irrespective of the dominant professional or feminist opinion.

GOING HOME: MARRIED AND SINGLE MOTHERS

Dr Švejcar recently said that babies are born twice, first in the hospital and for the second time when their mothers return home. He is, of course, referring to the sudden and dramatic transition to motherhood from being a helpless patient in the hospital, a transformation which is often accompanied by feelings of exhaustion, anxiety, depression and insecurity. As a paediatrician, Švejcar is particularly concerned about the resulting decline in the supply of breast milk and the will to nurse. In contrast, feminists, social scientists and social workers have tended to emphasise the lack of institutional postpartum support system, i.e. an on-going, day-in, day-out access to a network of helpers, which is quite different from the limited short-term post-partum visit by a women's nurse or female relative. Feminists in particular have drawn public attention to the conditions of fatigue, inexperience, uncertainty and frequent isolation under which new mothers work in advanced industrial societies.[9] However, in contrast to their Western counterparts, young mothers in Eastern Europe tend to get more help from their mothers or mothers-in-law, given the prevalence of three-generation households. For example, only eight respondents, less than a third of the sample of 30 Soviet women interviewed by Ispa (1983), lived alone with their husbands during pregnancy and after birth, while all the respondents in a matched sample of 33 American-born Jewish women did. The majority of the Soviet women lived with their own parents; only two lived with their parents-in-law. However, the prevalence of extended families is the result less of personal choice and more of necessity, caused by the enormous housing shortage in most of Eastern Europe.

In Czechoslovakia, the housing situation for young couples is substantially better than in the Soviet Union, but worse than in the West. In 1980, 57 per cent of childless couples, 71 per cent of young families with one child and 87 per cent of families with two and more children dwelt independently of their parents – a considerable improvement on an earlier situation (Havelka and Ottomanský, 1983, p. 15). However, this still leaves approximately half of all new mothers in three-generation households, a situation which might lead to new kinds of tensions if mothers' and grandmothers' views on child care differ, as is frequently the case. The situation of mothers in Czechoslovakia (and Eastern Europe as a whole) is made more difficult by persistent shortages of consumer goods, smaller apartments (babies are generally kept in the same room with parents) and persistent refusal of husbands to help with the less pleasant and more arduous household tasks.

For example, ready-made solid baby food has only recently begun to appear in stores and on a highly irregular basis. During the summer of 1981, only tins of puréed fruit and powdered gruels were to be found. Meat and vegetable baby foods were not available, although they had apparently been available in the spring. Although blenders are now more commonly available than they used to be, much of baby food is still puréed manually by the mother herself. Neither are disposable diapers on sale, though they are sometimes available in special foreign currency stores called 'Tuzex'. Most people seem to know that they are widely used in the West, and Matoušek (1980, p. 19) comments favourably upon them in his infant care guide book. On the other hand, there were sufficient supplies of cribs, carriages and strollers (buggies), including collapsible strollers – an improvement on an earlier situation. Collapsible strollers could frequently be seen on the streets but rarely in stores which means that they were bought either on the black market or in the 'Tuzex' stores.

In comparison with the West, the lives of parents in Czechoslovakia are made somewhat easier by a less confusing variety of expert advice books on how to parent. As far as infant care is concerned, there is only one general guide book available, Matoušek's (1980)

První rok dítěte (*Child's First Year*), though the quarterly magazine for parents, *Děti a My* (*Children and Us*) often publishes articles about infants. In addition, Trča's (1979) antenatal advice book contains one chapter (30 pages long) devoted to various aspects of infant care. There is also the more specialised book by the child psychologist, Jaroslav Koch (1977), highly regarded beyond the boundaries of Czechoslovakia for his experiments on the acceleration of the physical development of infants through various exercises. His book, the bulk of which has been translated into English,[10] offers advice on how to accelerate the development of a child's gross and fine motor skills, language, cognition, emotions and so on, on the basis of a series (up to 120) exercises. However, the more 'mundane' tasks of feeding, changing and bathing the baby, cutting his/her nails, going out for a walk, taking care of it when it is sick, and so on, are left to the two more general advice books, both written by doctors, and to regular consultations at paediatric clinics.

As in other areas of life, mothers do not always follow what experts say they should be doing. For example, while doctors and nurses recommend a daily bath, only 64 per cent of urban and 53 per cent of rural mothers follow this advice. Experts also recommend (somewhat unrealistically) daily outings lasting 5–6 hours in the summer and 3–4 hours in the winter, but only 45 per cent mothers claim to leave their baby out that long. The majority – 65 per cent – take the baby out for only 1–2 hours, and one-third do so only when it is sunny – an increasingly rare occurrence in some of the highly polluted cities (Urbanová, 1977). Thus, given the current high level of environmental pollution, urban babies might be better off staying at home, where they do not breathe exhaust fumes or some other form of air pollution.

However, mothers tend to be in general agreement with experts on early toilet training. While Matoušek (1980, p. 138) is critical of mothers who initiate toilet training at six months, he nonetheless recommends eight months as the appropriate time to start, a view shared both by Koch (1977, pp. 183–4) and Trča (1979, p. 189). By North American standards this is extremely early, but then mothers in affluent North America do not have to cope, for the most part, with the seemingly endless daily diaper washing, even if it is nowadays done largely in automatic washing machines.[11] The lack of disposable diapers not only provides a powerful incentive for early toilet training, but also explains why one rarely sees parents travelling with infants. At most, some move in one day from the apartment in the polluted city to the cottage in the country, where the air is cleaner and where the mother and baby remain for the summer, while the father visits on weekends. When together with their infants, many fathers are now willing to take the baby out for a walk (seeing father pushing the pram is socially quite acceptable), but this usually only frees the mother to do more housework rather than to have some rest or well-deserved leisure. All surveys indicate that domestic work, including diaper changing, continues to be performed predominately by women.

However, most of the problems connected with the care of infants by married mothers pale into insignificance when we examine the desperate situation of single mothers (5–6 per cent of all new mothers). Single mothers are generally seen as 'socially and mentally unprepared for motherhood'. Bárdoš (1978, p. 68) also claims that:

> unmarried mothers with existential, housing, family and mental problems have more difficulties with their pregnancies and frequently have premature births or give birth to immature babies.

The national statistics largely confirm this view – the incidence of premature birth and stillbirth is more than double among single than that among married mothers, and this is largely due to the stress caused by the 'existential and housing problems'.

Single mothers receive little or no help from the state. Many single mothers have no knowledge of or only a minimal contact with the department of care of family and children, preferring to rely on help from their family of origin or the father of the child (Dunovský and Zelenková, 1977). Single mothers are entitled to 35 weeks of paid maternity leave (as are mothers giving multiple births), which is nine weeks longer than the regular maternity leave, but this leave is meaningless if the mother has nowhere to live. A longitudinal study of mothers of all illegitimate children born in 1970 in Prague (586 women, 81 of whom were gypsies) showed housing and low income to be the greatest specific difficulties experienced by these mothers.

The House for the Unmarried Woman and Child, designed for eleven mothers and babies to stay for up to a year, opened in Ostrava in 1965 and remains, to this date, *the only* such institution in the whole country. Women who have passed through the Ostrava House apparently did not cope too well, and no additional institutions of this type are planned for the near future (Fukalová and Uzel, 1974; Němcová and Langrová, 1977). However, Niederle (1982), the director of family care and youth of the Czech Ministry of Work, argues that such institutions are needed and expects more of them to be built in the not too distant future. Mothers who are unable to stay with their family of origin have to rely on special nursing institutions, many of which accept the mothers for only two months or not at all; the baby can stay for up to a year before being moved to a children's home if the mother still has nowhere to live. One single mother interviewed said that she was forced to agree to a research experiment on her baby son in order to get him and her accepted in the nursing institution and that this was only a temporary solution to her housing problem. The inadequacy of the current set-up is also recognised by professionals. For example, Zeman (1982) argues that at least as far as teenage mothers are concerned, the infants' institute can meet current requirements only partly and with difficulties. He therefore recommends the establishment of a special home with 20–25 places for needy mothers from all over Czechoslovakia, as well as special psychological and pedagogical supervision, since many teenage mothers come from deprived backgrounds and some are even under court probation.

Dunovský and Zelenková estimate that of all the single women with unwanted pregnancies, a majority (56 per cent) choose an abortion, 38 per cent marry the father of the child and the rest (4–6 per cent) give birth while single but hope to marry the father of the child sometime in the future. These expectations often remain unfulfilled – after three years, one-third of the women in their sample were still single and 16.5 per cent were divorced from a spouse other than the father of the child. Half of the mothers married the father or some other man within three years of the birth, and some mothers lived with the father as common-law wife. Fathers were known in 85 per cent of the cases, but generally showed no interest in their unwanted children. The researchers found the mothers to be uniformly 'good' mothers and recommended changes in state policies which would make it easier for single mothers to keep their babies.

How does one evaluate the post-partum experience of new mothers in Eastern Europe? Existing data on both single and married mothers are too limited to draw any general conclusions, but one could agree with Ann Oakley (1979a, p. 24) that:

> first childbirth has a capacity that other births do not have to brand reproduction with a lasting meaning for the mother, to influence all other reproductive experiences. And it is a turning

point, a transition, a life crisis: a first baby turns a woman into a mother and mothers' lives are incurably affected by their motherhood; in one way or another the child will be a theme for ever.

Research on the psychic load of married women with at least one pre-school child, carried out in Prague in 1975, revealed that mothers tended to experience situational anxiety and decrease of self-assurance much more frequently than women generally (Prokopec and Mikšík, 1978). One can safely assume that the situational exhaustion and insecurity is much greater among women who had just become mothers. It is therefore hardly surprising that women in Czechoslovakia do not want to experience motherhood too many times.

NOTES

1. For a review of the nature and political implications of Czechoslovak research on childhood deprivation, see Scott (1974, pp. 175–86).
2. See Leboyer (1975). See also Lumley and Astbury (1980, pp. 134–40) for a critical evaluation of this type of birth.
3. However, Dr Matoušek (1980, p. 54) is a strong supporter of face masks, on the familiar grounds of 'danger of infections'. His infant care guide book advises mothers as follows: 'During the first few weeks, you should wear the mask whenever you're doing anything with the baby. You never know whether you have in your throat or your mouth germs which cause no harm to you, but which could make your child sick. All visitors who come to admire the baby during the first few weeks should also wear a mask.'
4. This last comment seems to support DeVries' (1984, p. 95) thesis that 'the results of bonding research, however, offer a scientific rationale for altering styles of practice, and in fact, justify *further interventions* on the part of medical personnel, to insure proper attachment between parent and infant'.
5. See, for example, Ouřadová's piece in the 13 June 1981 issue of *Mladá fronta*, the youth daily, and two anonymous articles in the party daily, *Rudé právo*, on 10 October 1982 and 6 November 1982, entitled 'Stále s matkou' ('All the time with the mother') and 'U matky je dítěti nejlépe' ('The child is best off with its mother') respectively. See also the interview with Dr Švejcar in the 15 May 1982 issue of *Rudé právo*, which marked the occasion of Dr Švejcar's 85th birthday. The youth weekly, *Mladý svět*, published in 1983 in its 12th issue an article entitled 'Experiment', which discussed not only rooming-in, but also the father's presence during childbirth. Readers were invited to respond and many of their letters were published in subsequent (19th and 25th) issues.

6. In my interviews with several Prague physicians I was told that there were no problems with semi-private rooms, but when mothers were assigned to the more typical rooms with 3–4 beds, they often broke down in tears and begged to be transferred to the traditional segregated system of care. The policy of coercively assigning mothers to rooming-in was itself introduced only after there were few initial volunteers. During the first four months of the new system, there was apparently only one volunteer – a woman psychologist – who requested rooming-in on her own initiative. However, reports from Most and some of the letters published in *Mladý svět* indicate a much greater enthusiasm on the part of mothers for rooming-in, thus demonstrating the limitations of anecdotal evidence.

7. This is a relatively high proportion by Western standards, though cross-national or even regional statistics have shown tremendous variation in the frequency of lactation. For example, only 16 per cent of mothers in Dublin, Ireland, attempt to breastfeed. The frequency is somewhat higher in the UK, ranging from 39 per cent in Newcastle to 62 per cent in an inner London borough. About 80 per cent of women in Australia start breastfeeding but at least a quarter of them change to bottle feeding before they leave the hospital (Jones and Belsey, 1977, p. 178; Lumley and Astbury, 1980, p. 208).

8. In fact, mothers in Czechoslovakia are now advised to mix formula with a mineral water as opposed to tap water, thus adding both to the expense and inconvenience of bottle-feeding. Mineral water has to be bought in stores, often after a lengthy wait, and the bottles in which it is available are usually quite heavy to carry.

9. For a controversial feminist position on this issue see Greer (1984) who has argued that poor women in the Third World are better off than their affluent Western counterparts precisely because motherhood in underdeveloped countries is both communal (as opposed to being socially isolated in nuclear families) and socially highly valued (as opposed to being institutionally discouraged).

10. See Koch (1978), which reproduces the practical, but not the theoretical part of the Czech edition. See also a more recent work by Koch, published in English in Prague in 1982. This is available in the UK, but does not appear in the 1983 List of Books in Print in the United States.

11. This problem is sometimes compounded by an irregular or insufficient supply of diapers. For example, during my visit to Prague in December 1979, there was a widespread shortage of diapers, presumably another unforeseen side-effect of the mini-population boom in previous years. One young mother whom I visited managed to obtain the grand total of 10 diapers for her baby son, which meant that she was constantly worried that she might run out altogether. To avoid this she was washing each diaper almost immediately after she took it off her baby to leave enough time for drying and ironing.

12 Becoming a Mother Again

Throughout the political spectrum, everyone agrees that external measures, financial or other, are needed in order to change the trend of the birth rate. Is it not, on the contrary, more justifiable to think, as Emile Levasseur wrote as early as the end of the nineteenth century, that French couples act in accordance with their intentions, and, if they have a limited number of children, it is because 'they don't want any more'? (Girard and Roussel, 1982, p. 341)

Although the socialist countries of Eastern Europe experienced some of the lowest fertility levels in the world in the 1960s (since surpassed by many Western countries), fertility trends were reversed in the 1970s. Because the reversal of fertility decline occurred in the context of comprehensive pro-natalist measures, the increase in the East European birth rates has received a lot of attention, not only from population planners in Eastern Europe, but also from many population specialists in the West. However, the experts have differed considerably in their assessment of both the long-term significance of the fertility changes and the usefulness of some of the standard fertility indicators, especially family size. This should come as no surprise, given the fact that 'we lack a generally accepted or at least undisputed theory about post-transitional reproduction' (Acsadi and Johnson-Acsadi, 1980, p. 25).[1]

FAMILY SIZE: IDEAL, DESIRED AND REALISED

According to the results of numerous nationwide fertility opinion sample surveys among married women, couples, and young people of both sexes before marriage, an overwhelming majority of Czechoslovak women and couples consider two children to be the desirable

247

TABLE 12.1   *Reproduction research in Czechoslovakia (1981): basic characteristics and survey results*

	CSSR	CSR	SSR
Average age of women (yrs)	25.72	25.74	25.69
Average age of men (yrs)	28.52	28.68	28.40
Duration of marriage (yrs)	4.60	4.69	4.43
Number of living children	1.31	1.29	1.34
Number of children desired by women*	2.20	2.16	2.29
Number of children desired by men*	2.21	2.17	2.31
Ideal number of children	2.23	2.16	2.39
Total desired number of children[+]	2.24	2.17	2.41

* Only those who have planned.
[+] This indicator was calculated from the average number of living children and from the average number of planned children in the future as reported by respondents.

SOURCE Dvořák, 1982c, p. 15. A nationwide sample of 3029 married women aged 18–39 years, 2059 (68 per cent) of whom were residing in the Czech Socialist Republic and 970 (32 per cent) of whom were Slovak residents. The majority, 1218 (41 per cent) were aged 20–24, 954 (31 per cent) were aged 25–29, 456 (15 per cent) were aged 30–34, 214 (7 per cent) were aged 18–19 and 187 (6 per cent) were aged 35–39 years old.

number of children in a family, both in general and for themselves.[2] While over the years there has been some fluctuation in the average numer of children women and couples have desired,[3] recently the expectations about family size have come full circle. Both in 1956 and in 1981, women aged 18–39 desired 'to have 2.2 children on the average when married' (Srb, 1981b, p. 44, Dvořák, 1982c, p. 12).

Table 12.1, which summarises the results from the most recent nationwide fertility survey, carried out in August and September 1981, interestingly reveals an agreement on the number of desired children by wives and husbands (as reported by their wives), an issue discussed in Chapter 1. Another interesting finding is the close correspondence between the number of children couples consider 'ideal' for themselves and in general, a phenomenon which is also revealed in Tables 12.2 and 12.3.

While data on the *average* desired family size are informative, they are not as useful as data presented in Tables 12.2, 12.3 and 12.4,

TABLE 12.2 *Desired number of children in the family in Czechoslovakia (%)*

	Czechoslovakia	Czech lands	Slovakia
No child	3.2	4.5	0.7
One child	13.3	15.7	8.4
Two children	59.0	60.6	55.9
Three children	24.5	19.2	35.0

SOURCE Schvarcová, 1979, p. 36.

TABLE 12.3 *Optimal number of children in a family in Czechoslovakia (%)*

	Czechoslovakia	Czech lands	Slovakia
No child	3.2	4.5	0.7
One child	8.6	8.9	7.9
Two children	69.4	71.3	65.9
Three children	18.8	15.3	25.5

SOURCE Schvarcová, 1979, p. 39. Results of a nationwide sample survey of 2612 women, employed in 274 institutions. Age and marital status were not specified.

which give us more information about modal values and about the narrowness of the distribution. Tables 12.2 and 12.3 in particular reveal the broad popularity of two-children families, while Table 12.4 indicates an increased proportion of women under 30 desiring to be childless or to have only one child.

Moreover, the findings presented in Tables 12.2 and 12.3 indicate significant differences between Czech and Slovak women in their desired fertility. Virtually no Slovak woman desires to be childless and more than a third want to have three children, while the proportion of Czech women desiring only one child is almost double that of Slovak women. Schvarcová, the Slovak sociologist cited earlier (in Chapter 4), comments favourably on the Slovak pattern, which she would like to see extended to the whole country. In her view the 'ideal' family size is three children, which would be sufficient to solve the Czechoslovak 'population problem'.[4] Her model is based on the 1972 'Directives of the Government Population Commission on Education for Parenthood', which claimed that 'the ideal family was one with three children, a size sufficient for the children to interact,

TABLE 12.4   *Number of planned children in a family in Czechoslovakia*

| | Ages of Women | | | |
	19–24	25–29	30–34	Total
Number in sample	335	569	132	1036
Number of planned children:				
none	108	287	88	483
one	143	195	30	368
two	37	24	5	66
more than two	10	7	0	17
don't know	20	31	5	56
don't plan children	17	25	4	46
No additional children wanted because of:				
health	30	82	18	130
age	3	10	22	35
employment	7	19	4	30
financial situation	36	51	10	97
housing conditions	69	89	16	174
domestic duties	8	10	1	19
few children's facilities	20	28	3	51
husband's attitude	13	14	0	27
other reasons	96	170	23	184
don't want to	53	96	35	289

SOURCE   Šteker, 1979, p. 150. A nationwide sample of 1036 women who married after 1 April 1973 and who were then under age 30. One-third were aged 19–24, more than one-half 25–29 and the rest 30–34 at the time of the survey in 1977.

thus favouring, their intellectual development', and that 'unfavourable demographic developments would hamper economic development, and thus have serious effects on living standards' (quoted in Heitlinger, 1979, p. 183).

However, all the developed countries, with the exception of Ireland, have witnessed the progressive disappearance of values higher than two children (Girard and Roussel, 1982, p. 340). Findings from both Western and East European fertility opinion surveys present a rather narrow distribution of families by size, and as such provide no basis for predicting a future increase in the number of larger families (with four or more children) in the foreseeable future, which is deemed necessary for the demographic compensation of people who do not reproduce themselves – childless couples and families with only one child.[5]

Acsadi and Johnson-Acsadi (1980, p. 10) regard 'expected family

size' as a good reproductive indicator, given the 'increased precision
with which couples and individuals are able to realize their reproductive goals'. However, Girard and Roussel (1982, p. 336) view 'ideal
family size' as a rather imprecise indicator, since 'it does not measure
the number of children that each woman will have in a given year,
nor does it measure what the final number of descendants of a certain
generation will be'. In the authors' view,[6] 'ideal family size is a
"collective" model, based on opinion polls, and is no way an objective behavioural fact' (quoted in Wulf, 1982, p. 67). Reality is always
more diversified than the model, and a whole range of unforeseen
circumstances (e.g. divorce, re-marriage, poor health, career success,
contraceptive failure) will force couples or individuals to revise their
initial fertility expectations. Some women will have fewer, some
more children than desired. However, Girard and Roussel (1982,
p. 333) emphasise that all plans tend to indicate the *maximum* rather
than the average number of desired children. For this reason, the
French demographers take issue with the prevailing view in France
(as well as in Eastern Europe) that couples actually wish to have
more children than they do, but are deterred from doing so by
financial constraints. Moreover, the authors argue that the speculation as to whether the gap between actual and ideal fertility would
close with more pro-natalist incentives is idle, because ideal family
size and a total fertility rate (TFR) are such different measures that
they cannot, and should not, be compared. Unlike ideal family size,
TFR reflects actual human experience and allows for 'personal preferences, individual life circumstances, variations in age at marriage,
differing degrees of control over fertility, differentials in physiological
infecundity, and differences in such factors as health and living
standards' (quoted in Wulf, 1982, p. 67).[7]

In the course of their methodological critiques, Girard and Roussel
draw our attention to the apparent discrepancy between the number
of children the French say they want (2.5 per family, on the average)
and the number they actually have (1.8–1.9).[8] Similar discrepancy
has been observed in Czechoslovakia. Data presented in Tables 12.5
and 12.6 indicate that one-child families are much more popular in
theory than in practice, confirming the view that a substantial proportion of women in Czechoslovakia do end up having fewer children
than they consider to be 'optimal'.[9] There seems to be less of a gap
between desired and actual fertility with respect to three or more
children. The proportion of three-children families increased only
very slightly during the last decade, and then largely at the expense of

TABLE 12.5   *Family size in Czechoslovakia (%)*

Year	Number of Children in a family				
	1	2	3	4	5 and more
1976	40.1	43.6	12.1	2.8	1.4
1977	39.2	44.4	12.4	2.7	1.3
1978	38.2	45.3	12.6	2.7	1.2

SOURCE   Víšek, 1979, p. 125. The data in the table are calculated from statistics on family allowances, which are collected annually.

TABLE 12.6   *Structure of households, by number of dependent children in Czechoslovakia*

	1970		1980	
	Number (thousands)	(%)	Number (thousands)	(%)
Total number of households of which households:	4 602	100.0	5 348	100.0
without children	2 356	51.2	2 857	53.4
with 1 child	1 000	21.7	953	17.8
with 2 children	860	18.7	1 133	21.2
with 3 children	268	5.8	319	6.0
with 4 children	73	1.6	61	1.1
with 5 and more children	45	1.0	25	0.5

SOURCE   Rýdl, 1982, p. 21

larger families (with four and more children), which in turn have declined as a percentage of all families. Between 1970 and 1980 there was some decrease in the proportion of one-child families, and a corresponding increase in two-children families, but both types remain popular (see Tables 12.5 and 12.6).

Thus there is a clear trend towards greater homogeneity. This trend is also evident when we examine crude birth rates and fertility rates by parity and age – alternative, and more refined, forms of measurement of actual family size.

DISTRIBUTION OF BIRTHS BY PARITY AND AGE

As we noted in Chapter 1, cohort fertility (statistics on the fertility of successful generations) and cross-sectional fertility measures (data on births relating to specific calendar years) measure fertility from very different perspectives. Cohort measurements are generally considered as a more accurate representation of the actual reproductive behaviour of women and couples, but statistics on cohort fertility are more difficult to come by. For example, no cohort fertility data are available for Slovak women and Lesný (1978) is the only source for such data for Czech women. His longitudinal analysis of the fertility of Czech women born in 1930–54, who entered their reproductive years during the 25 years between 1945 and 1969, provides data for the five-year cohorts of 1930–4, 1935–9, 1940–4, 1945–9 and 1950–4.[10] In contrast, statistics on age-specific and crude birth and fertility rates are rather plentiful, since they are available in every annual statistical year book.

Czechoslovakia experienced relatively high birth rates immediately after the Second World War, (see Table 12.8), but fertility started to decline in the early 1950s; so too did the average age at which women started and completed bearing children. Cross-sectional statistics on fertility by birth order during the 1960s indicate an increase in first-order births, little variation in second-order births, and a large decline of third- and higher-order births. However, cohort fertility measures for the 1960s indicate a decline in the proportion of women of the younger cohorts (i.e. the 1940–4 and 1945–9 birth cohorts) having a second child. Subsequently, during the early 1970s, the frequency of second births increased significantly among practically all cohorts, even those that were already in their 30s. This trend was particularly noticeable among the younger cohorts. For example, 22 per cent of the 1950–4 cohort had had a second birth by age 22, compared with only 16 per cent of the 1945–9 cohort. The younger cohorts also increased their share of third-order births, although to date they still have a much smaller proportion of third children than the preceeding older cohorts (Frejka, 1980, pp. 79, 80).

An increase in the number of births of all ranks in the first half of the 1970s is also evident in cross-sectional data. Between 1970 and 1974, first births increased by 12.2 per cent, second-order births by a staggering 48 per cent, and third and subsequent births by 29.6 per cent. Among all births, the share of first births declined from 46.7 to 41 per cent, a trend that was 'mirrored' almost exactly in the corresponding increase of second-order births, from 33.4 per cent to 38.8 per cent of all births. The share of third and subsequent births increased only slightly, from 19.9 to 20.2 per cent (Srb, 1981b, p. 47). However, percentages compiled in Table 12.7 indicate a more

TABLE 12.7   *Live births by birth order, Czechoslovakia, 1960–76*

Year	Live births (thousands)	Percentage distribution by birth order					
		1st	*2nd*	*3rd*	*4th*	*5th and over*	*3rd and over*
1960	217	39.3	30.6	14.7	6.7	8.7	30.1
1965	232	41.0	31.8	14.1	5.9	7.2	27.2
1970	229	46.7	33.4	11.3	4.1	4.5	19.9
1975	289	40.8	39.3	13.7	3.6	2.6	19.9

SOURCE   Srb and Konečná, 1977

TABLE 12.8   *Crude birth rate in Czechoslovakia in selected years (per thousand)*

1937	16.3	*1968*	14.9	*1975*	19.5	*1981*	15.5
1945	19.5	*1970*	15.9	*1976*	19.2	*1982*	15.3
1948	23.4	*1971*	16.5	*1977*	18.7		
1955	20.3	*1972*	17.3	*1978*	18.4		
1960	15.9	*1973*	18.8	*1979*	17.9		
1965	16.4	*1974*	19.8	*1980*	16.3		

SOURCE   *Statistická ročenka ČSSR, 1960 to 1984*

significant increase in third births, from the low point of 11.2 in 1971 to almost 14 per cent in 1976. However, the share of third-order births in 1976 was still lower than in 1960.

While a simple extrapolation of these trends is not warranted, one can speculate, as Frejka (1980, p. 82) does, 'that by the mid-1970s the higher proportions of second- and third-parity women formed a larger pool of women able to have third- and higher-order births in the late 1970s and early 1980s'. In the absence of data on the nationwide distribution of births by birth order in the 1980s, it is impossible to say whether Frejka's pro-natalist optimism is being realised in practice. Opinion survey findings presented in Table 12.4, as well as the available statistics on crude birth and fertility rates, suggest otherwise. The reversal of the decline in post-war fertility[11] seems to have peaked in 1974 (see Table 12.8).

Between 1975 and 1980, live births in Czechoslovakia declined by 14 per cent. Typically, the decline has been more marked in the Czech lands (where it amounted to 20 per cent) than in Slovakia (where it amounted to only 3 per cent). Moreover, in 1982, the absolute number of live births was the lowest since 1970 and the

TABLE 12.9   *Live births according to birth order and mother's age in Czechoslovakia in 1976 (%)*

| Age of mother | Birth Order | | | | | |
	1	2	3	4	5	6 and more
15–19	85.8	12.7	1.4	0.1	—	—
20–24	52.2	38.7	7.4	1.3	0.3	0.1
25–29	21.5	49.6	21.2	5.0	1.5	1.2
30–34	11.8	37.3	31.5	11.0	4.2	4.2
35–39	9.3	22.0	28.7	16.7	9.3	14.0
40–44	8.8	12.5	17.7	15.2	11.7	34.1
45–49	4.5	14.4	16.2	14.4	15.3	35.2
50+	—	20.0	20.0	20.0	—	40.0
not given	20.8	33.4	8.3	—	—	37.5
Total	41.0	38.3	14.0	3.8	1.4	1.5

SOURCE   *Statistická ročenka ČSSR 1979*, p. 112.

crude birth rate was the lowest since 1968, which in turn was the lowest fertility point in Czechoslovak history. There were 4.4 thousand fewer children born in 1982 than in 1981 and 60 thousand fewer than during the peak years of 1974 (Aleš, 1983, p. 6). However, 'in spite of this essential decline', the author adds, 'natality in Czechoslovakia henceforth exceeds even the European average'.

Lesný's (1978) longitudinal analysis of Czech women's fertility shows that one-third of all women bear their first child before reaching the age of 21, and one-half before reaching the age of 23. Eighty per cent give birth at least once by the age of 26; and, by the age of 30, only 10 per cent of Czech women remain childless. Lesný also claims that second children are typically born before the mother reaches the age of 28. Cross-sectional data presented in Table 12.9 also confirm that most children are born to young women under 20 and under 24, while the birth of second children is most common to the age group 25–29 and then evenly split between the 20–24 and 30–34 cohorts. Subsequent children are obviously born to older women around the age of 30.

How has the increased fertility in the 1970s discussed above manifested itself by age? Srb (1981b, p. 47) claims that the pro-natalist measures 'were to influence the increase of the number of second and third children in the families and were to affect the women above 25 years'. As expected, the largest growth – by 28 per cent – occurred in the age group 25–29, who bore 'children the birth of which has been postponed or where the delivery would not be realised at all'. Women aged 27 in particular had more children – from 1970 to 1979 their fertility had increased by 32 per cent. There were more births also among women past their prime reproductive years. The child-bearing of women aged 30–34 grew by 24 per cent and even women aged 35–39 had 14 per cent more children in 1979 than in 1970. According to Srb (1981b, p. 49) this extension of child-bearing years beyond the age of 30 or even 35 represented a 'qualitative reversal' in fertility patterns. It is too early to say whether this pattern will continue during the 1980s or whether it was only a short-term deviation from the norm, a temporary response to an attractive package of pro-natalist incentives.

THE EFFICACY OF PRO-NATALIST MEASURES

The comprehensive system of pro-natalist incentives in Czechoslovakia, consisting of both direct cash benefits awarded to families and mothers (e.g. lump sum birth grants, paid maternity leaves and allowances, sharply progressive family allowances, low interest loans to young couples), and subsidised goods and services (e.g. tax and rent deductions according to the number of children in a family, subsidised child care services and children's goods) is based on a combination of ideological and demographic beliefs. As we noted in Chapter 2, the arrival of explicit socialist pro-natalism in the 1960s marked the extension and amplification of many measures adopted earlier (i.e. in the 1950s) on social and humanitarian grounds. Moreover, unlike many of its East European counterparts, Czechoslovakia had a relatively developed social security system already at the time of its socialist transformation. Paid maternity leave for 12 weeks was in existence since 1926 and nursing mothers were entitled to additional six weeks at half pay. Since 1924, there was also compulsory old-age, disability, life and sickness insurance for all workers. Even family allowances were in existence, but only civil servants were eligible to receive them (Koubek, 1974, pp. 27–8).

A universal system of family allowances was introduced after the Second World War. As in other welfare states, the universality of family allowances was meant to affirm social justice, egalitarianism and the responsibility of the state for the welfare of children and the family. To safeguard the welfare of the family with a larger number of children, family allowances soon moved from uniformity by parity to initially mild and then substantial 'progressivity', especially for third and second children in a family. Over the years, there were various increases in the cash value of family allowances, but only the more recent raises made a noticeable impact on the levels of family income. While the 'population sums' (to use Schvarcová's term) as a percentage of national income doubled from 1948 to 1970 (from 1.5 per cent in 1948 to 3 per cent in 1970), family allowances for one child in 1970 in fact covered only 15 per cent of average expenses for that child. However, the cost of second and fifth children could then be covered up to 40 per cent by family allowances. Third and fourth children were then almost 'free' to their parents during their first three years of life, but between the ages of 15 to 18, family allowances compensated parents for only 40 per cent of expenses incurred on behalf of these children (Schvarcová, 1973, p. 13).

Throughout the 1950s and 1960s, the cash value of family allowances was eroded by increases in real wages and to some extent also by inflation. Between 1948 and 1970 average earnings increased by 135 per cent, but family allowances as a proportion of net family income increased only by 1 per cent for one child, 9.5 per cent for two children and by 20.5 per cent for three children (Schvarcová, 1973, p. 9). In contrast, between 1967 and 1973, family allowances, especially for second and third children, nearly doubled, but their importance to family income increased by a much smaller margin (see Table 12.10).

While family allowances in Czechoslovakia are relatively high by Western standards, especially for second and third children, they do not really solve the financial problems of families with children. Moreover, from a pro-natalist (as compared to social welfare) viewpoint, they are not as effective as loans to newlyweds. A special loan scheme was introduced in April 1973 to help young married couples under 30 years of age to obtain or furnish an apartment or flat. Its value is up to 30 000 Czech crowns, to be repaid with 1–2 per cent interest within 10 years. For the first child born after the signature of the contract and surviving to its first birthday, 2000 crowns of the loan is written off, and for each subsequent child 4000 crowns is cancelled. As Frejka (1980, p. 90) argues:

the loan is, by definition, borrowed money that has to be repaid (at very low interest), but it is an advance payment that the couple can utilize at the beginning of their married life. By taking a loan, the

TABLE 12.10   *Structure of incomes of the households, by number of dependent children in Czechoslovakia (%)*

	Year	Total house-holds	Households with number of dependent children of:				
			1	2	3	4	5 and more
Net per capita money income		100.0	100.0	100.0	100.0	100.0	100.0
of which income:							
from employment	1970	69.1	79.1	75.8	65.6	58.6	52.0
	1980	67.3	78.3	74.1	61.9	52.5	46.5
from health insurance scheme and social security scheme	1970	22.0	12.9	16.0	23.4	29.1	37.9
	1980	24.4	13.0	17.7	26.2	32.8	39.8
of which: children's allowances	1970	4.7	2.4	7.9	15.3	21.5	29.3
	1980	5.5	3.2	10.0	17.9	24.1	30.9

SOURCE   Rýdl, 1982, p. 22

couple can transfer future earnings to an earlier stage of their life cycle when they have not yet accumulated much property or savings. A desired family environment can be achieved with fewer obstacles and earlier than might otherwise be the case.

Although such measures as family allowances and subsidized nurseries also make a difference in income and thus in living conditions, these benefits are spread out over time and represent supplements to the family budget for 'current' expenses. The loan, by contrast, represents a large sum that can significantly affect crucial life-cycle decisions of young people.

The hypothesized pro-natalist effect of the loan is two-fold. Improvement in the material living conditions at the beginning of the couple's married life may in itself influence childbearing decisions. Subsequently, the reduction in the principal of the loan obtainable by having one or more children may also affect family-building decisions.

Maternity contributions or allowances (also known as child care grants) and extended paid and unpaid maternity leaves (all discussed extensively in Chapter 4) are also regarded by Frejka (1980, p. 90) as having significant pro-natalist effects:

The optional extended maternity leave is more closely linked to fertility behavior, and its possible effect on the couple's living conditions is straightforward. The conflicting demands of work in the household and work outside the household are presumably more acute when the couple has young children than at any other stage of the life cycle. Under the current policy, a woman with a second or higher order child can remain in the home without a significant loss of income up to the second birthday of the youngest child. The demands of dealing with both a job and work at home are postponed to a time when children are older and child care is somewhat less exacting. Since comparable maternity leave for the first child lasts only five to six months, the measure clearly benefits those having higher order births. It holds out the possibility of an appreciable difference in the flow of the family's life cycle if and when an additional child is born.

While there is room for disagreement with Frejka's contention that extended maternity leave involving a maternity allowance entails no 'significant loss of income', his argument about the importance of the measure to women is essentially correct. The popularity of maternity grants among all mothers, not just those with lower income and education, was already noted in Chapter 4. Additional evidence can be obtained from the results of the 1981 fertility opinion survey. Dvořák (1982c, p. 14) asserts that 'the interviewed women most favourably valuated a half-year paid maternity leave and possibility of drawing further unpaid maternity leave. Only afterwards there follow the financial stimuli (i.e. children's allowances, maternity grant, maternity contribution, etc.).'

Thus mothers tend to value time more than money. This reality presents considerable obstacles to population planners, since the preference usually translates into desire to limit child-bearing altogether. As we can see from Table 12.4, the most frequently cited reason for not wanting more children is lack of desire, followed by other reasons (another large category immune to policy intervention), inadequate housing, poor health (which may imply lack of energy) and financial difficulties. Findings from another recent fertility opinion survey revealed that 51 per cent of women with two children would under 'no circumstances' consider having another child. The rest of the sample answered as shown in Table 12.11.

An increase in the husband's income (rather than one's own) is by far the most important financial pro-natalist incentive in Czechoslovakia. This may come as a surprise to Western feminists; however,

TABLE 12.11 *Required conditions for having a third child (%)*

No need to work	13.2
Higher husband's income	32.9
Higher own income	2.8
Higher family allowance	1.0
Better housing	13.4
Help in household	10.8
Other	9.6
Don't know	7.7

SOURCE Srb, 1979b, p. 28

this seems simply to confirm that women in Czechoslovakia are generally well informed about their social conditions. In 1976 husbands' earnings accounted for 44–48 per cent of the average family income, while wives' earnings accounted for only 12–22 per cent, with the rest coming from family allowances, sickness benefits and pensions (Heitlinger, 1979, p. 155). Women's incomes would have to increase substantially more (by more than 22 per cent) than men's to make it financially possible to have another child, a policy which the Czechoslovak government is extremely unlikely to pursue. The substantial increases in the prices of many children's goods in 1979 (by almost 50 per cent) and the official pronouncements on satisfactory population development indicate that no further financial incentives are planned. In fact, given the pressures of recession, the contrary is clearly the case. Nentvichová (1982, p. 4) justifies the removal of state subsidies for children's goods on the following grounds:

> Permanent intensification of society's care of families with children brings also some problems. Low price of children's dresses led, for instance, to their excessive purchase by foreign tourists and a shortage in home trade. Retail prices of children's wear and footwear were, therefore, increased.

This argument should be placed in the context of the large state expenditure on social welfare of families with children. According to Nentvichová (1982, p. 4), between 1971 and 1980, state aid to families grew by 58 per cent. In 1980, almost 60 per cent of it went to direct financial aid, 20 per cent was allocated for aid in kind (e.g. subsidies for child care services) and an additional 20 per cent went for indirect aid, (e.g. tax and rent deductions). The classification of subsidies for children's goods is unfortunately not made clear. These are high expenditures by any standards, and as we noted earlier (in Chapter 2), Frejka (1980, p. 70) regards them as 'exceeding comparable expenditures in any other developed country'. Faced with a difficult economic situation and a satisfactory rate of population increase, it is hardly surprising that the government decided to lower its pro-natalist expenditures.

However, the evidence on past and future fertility trends is quite difficult to evaluate because it is so diverse. While Frejka (1980) and Srb (1981b, p. 44) consider the various pro-natalist measures adopted during the years 1968–73 to have had 'an extraordinarily effective result', Pavlík and Zbořilová (1978, pp. 75–6) note that:

> population provisions affected in particular the minor component of the population climate (spacing of children) but have had practically no effect on its basic component (planned number of children). In recent years, children have been born that were not born earlier, perhaps even those who would have been born later. From this it is obvious that a decline of fertility must be expected in ensuing years. In addition, lower natality will also be motivated by a drop in the age structure of the population.

Srb's (1981) population projections for the next two decades also indicate a slight decline in fertility due to the worsening age composition and continued limitation of family size, neither of which are seen as particularly troublesome. Dvořák (1982b, p. 15) acknowledges the significant decline in both Czech and Slovak (but especially Czech) fertility during the period 1978–81, but his population projection until the year 2000 'does not anticipate that the realised fertility of women should decrease up to the present low fertility level in West European countries. At the beginning of the 1990s the anticipated decline will be stopped and specific fertilities of women will remain on a stabilised level or they will have a slightly growing trend.'

In his assessment of these projections,[12] Frejka (1980, p. 88) notes that they are based on recent fertility experience:

> The 1968 fertility patterns are the basis for the low projection and 1974 fertility patterns the basis for the high projection, while the average of the 1968 and 1974 fertility patterns is the basis for the medium projection and 1977 patterns the basis for a current constant fertility projection. It is interesting to note that the

authors of these projections feel that 'the projection utilising 1977 fertility patterns appears as the most realistic one'.

In Frejka's view, 'if the 1977 fertility pattern were to prevail during the last quarter of the twentieth century, the total population in the year 2000 could be of the order of 17 million rather than the 16 million that would result with 1968 fertility patterns. The difference of one million amounts to about 6 per cent of the total population.' If Frejka is right (which is by no means certain), this represents a significant difference in population size indeed.

Apart from these demographic evaluations, there are also medical assessments, which seem to be more concerned with the *quality* of a new population 'capable of realising the demanding tasks of scientific – technical revolution and the building of developed socialist society'.[13] Dr Židovský (1978, p. 489), the director of the Institute for the Care of Mother and Child, would also like to see a decrease in 'the social burden posed by handicapped and retarded individuals'. Dr Kviz (1978) actually views the pro-natalist policy emphasising quantitative population increase as mistaken, because it ignores the social and individual costs of unwanted children. A related medical concern is the age structure of women having babies, which is imputed to be related to maternal and perinatal mortality and morbidity.

Dvořák (1982a, p. 13) comments favourably on the existing dominant patterns of childbearing:

> Improved infant and post-neonatal mortality during the last few years has been positively influenced not merely by the success of the socialist public health services within the scheme of mother's and child's care but also by a considerable shift of realised fertility of women to younger age groups, i.e. to the period between 20–4 years and 25–9 years.

What this implies is that the extension of child-bearing by age and parity, 'the qualitative reversal' referred to earlier, which was positively commented on by demographers Frejka (1980) and Srb (1981b), might not be viewed in such a favourable light by physicians. As we noted in Chapter 10, the current primary goal of obstetrics in Czechoslovakia is the lowering of perinatal mortality below 10 per thousand, the achievement of which might be made somewhat more difficult by an increase in the number of 'risk' pregnancies of multiparous women in their 30s. However, given the evidence on the ever more typical pattern of young couples (in their 20s) having only two children, this medical concern is likely to prove groundless.

Finally, and from the perspective of this book most importantly, there is also the critical feminist viewpoint. In his comments as a rapporteur on one of the sessions at the 1981 International Population Conference, Charles Westoff, an American demographer, observed the following underlying male bias in much of pro-natalism:

> The image held by many pro-natalists is that what women really want is to marry early and have several children, but that modern economic conditions such as inflation and housing shortages conspire to frustrate the achievement of such goals. Accordingly, the pro-natalists believe, the working woman secretly yearns for the kitchen and the nursery. Therefore, what is required is economic subsidy to relieve this frustration and to enable women to return to the home.

Westoff offers an alternative interpretation, arguing that a different reading of history suggests that 'women are increasingly tasting the freedom and rewards that come with education and income (and which have traditionally been considered the province of men), and that this new independence, coupled with the disappearing economic value of children, combine to reduce the functional importance of the family and to keep fertility low . . . To argue for a reversal of this long-lasting fertility trend is to argue for a reversal of history' (quoted in Wulf, 1982, p. 69).

NOTES

1. Feminists have also neglected the theoretical implications of declining fertility in developed countries. For a recent attempt to develop a general feminist theory of fertility decision-making, see Folbre (1983).
2. The various surveys have differed considerably in size and the social characterstics of respondents, as well as the questions asked. For example, the 1963 and 1964 surveys sampled young people of both sexes under 30 before marriage, while the 1966 and 1967 surveys restricted its population to young women under 21 before marriage. The 1956, 1977 and 1981 nationwide surveys drew their samples from the population of married women aged 18–39, while a more selective survey published in 1979 restricted its sample to women who got married after 1 April 1973 and who were then under the age of 30. Special surveys of young people before or directly at the point of marriage often give more accurate

responses than retrospective surveys. When asked about the number of children desired prior to marriage, women (or couples) who have been married for some time frequently adapt their response to their current situation. A more serious problem is caused by the lack of rules governing the use of a whole range of very different concepts describing an 'ideal', 'optimal', 'desired', 'expected' or 'planned' family size or number of children. For example, Srb (1981b, p. 45) uses terms such as 'the number of desired children' and 'the children the women wished to have' interchangeably, yet 'desired', 'wished' or 'planned' family size or the number of children are not the same things.

3. Between 1956 and 1967, the average number of children desired (or planned) in a family declined from 2.1 to 1.8 (or 2.03), depending on whether we use figures provided by Srb (1981b, p. 45) or those provided by Švarcová (1970, p. 183). In 1972, the desired family size grew to 2.20 children and in 1977 it grew again, to 2.27 children. However, the 1981 retrospective fertility opinion survey revealed that 'the number of children planned by women before marriage' dropped again to the familiar figure of 2.20 (Srb, 1981b, p. 45, Dvořák, 1982c, p. 12).

4. In the context of pro-natalism, the term 'population problem' normally refers to fertility levels well below the levels of population replacement. According to Frejka (1980, p. 69), by 1968 the total fertility rate (the meaning of which is discussed in note 7 below) in the economically more advanced Czech part of the country was almost as low as it had been during the 1930s, and in Slovakia it was at its lowest recorded level. The total fertility rate for the country as a whole was 2.0 (down from 3.0 in 1950), appreciably below population replacement level. An alternative measurement of population replacement – the net reproduction rate – remained below 1 until 1971.

5. However, as Wulf (1982, pp. 68–9) points out, 'population projections are a hazardous undertaking. Most demographic predictions are based upon the assumption that birth and death rates will remain constant, at least within a given time period. Reproductive inclinations, however, are to some degree the product of social fashions and, as such, are highly volatile in nature. . . . Although statistical analyses may show that population replacement cannot be reached unless a given proportion has large families, there are many different distributions of family size that will achieve the same result . . . Moreover, the human reproductive instinct is clearly susceptible to more complex influences than the state of the housing market, current interest rates or pronouncements about the decline or value of the family.'

6. Girard's and Roussel's (1982) article first appeared in French in a 1981 issue of *Population*, the journal of the French Institut National des Études Demographiques. Since I do not read French, I am relying on Wulf's (1982, p. 67) English summary of that article.

7. The total fertility rate refers to the average number of children per woman of reproductive age, defined as 15–45 years. It represents the sum of age-specific fertility rates for a given period, and it is only in this sense that it constitutes an abstraction from reality.

8. These figures are arrived at by averaging opinion survey responses or

actual live births in order to arrive at a single aggregated figure for the ideal or actual number of children per family (or women).

9. However, it is worth reiterating that a precise measurement of the fertility gap is impossible, because of the lack of comparability of the various reproductive indicators. For example, data in Tables 12.5 and 12.6 are cross-sectional data, relating family or household size to specific calendar years, while the information on fertility opinion in Tables 12.2 and 12.3 implies a longer generational perspective. Moreover, figures in Tables 12.2 and 12.3 are based on the opinion of a random sample of married women, while Table 12.5 statistics measure all existing families with dependent children eligible for family allowances. Data in Table 12.6 measure yet another category – households – which includes both childless marriages and families with grown-up, financially independent children.

10. For a detailed exposition and recalculation of these statistics see Frejka (1980).

11. It is estimated that 20–25 per cent of the increase in the crude birth rate between 1968 and 1974 was due to a demographically more favourable age structure, i.e. a larger relative number of women in their prime child-bearing years (Srb, 1981b, p. 47, Frejka, 1980, p. 74). As the latter author points out, 'age structure is an important variable in fertility measurement because the total number of births and the crude birth rate are, among other things, a function of the number of women (couples) in their child-bearing years in general, and in the prime child-bearing years in particular. Because of relatively low fertility in Czechoslovakia in the past, the generations in their prime child-bearing years were relatively small in the 1950s and especially the 1960s, but they increased at the end of the 1960s and into the 1970s. Women aged 20–29 years constituted 28 per cent of all women of reproductive age in 1965 and 34 per cent in 1975.

12. Several articles on the projection of Czechoslovak population until the year 2000 have appeared in Czech demographic and medical journals. Frejka (1980) utilises an article by Srb and Konečná (1977), published in the demographic journal *Demografie*, while I am relying on more recent articles by Srb (1981a) and Dvořák (1982b), published by *Československá pediatrie* and *Demosta* respectively. However, all these articles are based on the same population projection.

13. The current Czechoslovak state plan of basic biochemical research includes Task VII–3, entitled 'Human reproduction and the healthy development of the child population'. Its emphasis is explicitly on the quality of population, on questions connected with select genetical problems, mechanisms of ovulation, fertilisation and implantation, and various aspects of labour and delivery (Houštek and Syrovátka, 1982).

13 Conclusion

The examination of the passage to motherhood from conception to post-partum has revealed many similarities and some differences between socialist and capitalist societies. We noted the similarity in the material and social conditions under which reproductive choices on the timing and number of children are made (e.g. age, marital and financial status, medical management of pregnancy and childbirth). Contrasting experiences were seen in the later initiation of sexual intercourse among Czech teenagers, the reliance on abortion as the major method of birth control, the exclusion of fathers from prenatal classes and the maternity hospital (related for most part to specific socialist conceptions of what constitutes womanhood and, in turn, sex equality), and lesser reliance on bottle-feeding in the first few months after birth. We have also noted the extent to which reproduction has become dominated by professional medicine and state population policies.

REPRODUCTION, WESTERN LIBERAL DEMOCRACIES AND THE SOCIALIST STATE: TOWARDS A COMPARATIVE PERSPECTIVE

We have seen that all states intervene in procreation. The processes of giving (or not giving) birth are too important for societies to leave them totally uncontrolled, although social controls do not always work. The state intervention in procreation arises out of the fact that potential or actual children are public 'goods' – agents such as the state, along with their parents, have an interest in them. Thus, as Moen (1979, p. 138) has argued, 'every country has a population policy. It may be explicit with highly coercive implementation, it may be a hidden agenda that can be achieved through existing trends, or it may be the sum of implicit and often conflicting policies.' Moreover, we have also seen that the state comes in different guises and what may be true of one country might look rather different elsewhere.

While all the developed countries, with the exception of Ireland, have witnessed low fertility, at or below the population replacement level, their responses to these similar circumstances have differed. For example, France has been more open to the adoption of an explicit pro-natalist population policy than most of the other capitalist states, while among the East European societies, the extent to which a woman has a legal right to terminate her pregnancy differs. Only Romania has made abortions (the country's principal means of birth avoidance) illegal, but various restrictive guidelines for granting abortion on medical grounds have been adopted during the last decade in Czechoslovakia, Hungary and Bulgaria. In contrast, the GDR, with one of the world's lowest birth rates adopted in 1972 a particularly liberal abortion law, reversing its previous restrictive stand.

Family allowances schemes in Eastern Europe have been broadly similar (favouring two or four children in a family), but the Soviet scheme seems to be effective only at the top end of the scale (eight or nine children in a family), and has therefore been less geared than those elsewhere to encouraging procreation. The state socialist societies also differ with respect to maternity (child care) allowances, paid monthly to mothers (in Hungary under certain circumstances also to fathers) who stay at home to raise their child during its first 2–3 years. Such benefits are now provided in varying degrees in Hungary, Czechoslovakia, Bulgaria, the GDR, but not in Poland, Romania or the USSR, although the Soviet Union is considering adopting such a scheme in the future. On the other hand, the delivery of reproductive health care is broadly similar throughout Eastern Europe, since the individual health care systems are all based on the Soviet model. The Soviet state also pioneered many current reproductive policies commonly referred to as the social protection of motherhood – namely the protective labour laws for women, pregnancy and maternity leaves, free comprehensive maternity medical care, work breaks for nursing mothers and legalised abortion.

Thus, despite some individual variations, there is nonetheless an important sense in which we can compare the general styles in which welfare state capitalism and state socialism intervene in reproduction. For example, we have noted (in Chapter 3) that in Czechoslovakia 'education for parenthood' is regarded as an integral part of the pro-natalist population policy. For this reason, the scheme is much broader in scope, more specialised, more self-conscious and much more systematic than any comparable programme in a Western capitalist country. A variety of pro-natalist ideologies, making child-bearing seem 'natural' and thus obligatory, also exists in the West, but they tend to be much less explicit and systematic than in Eastern Europe. Moreover, given their political pluralism, Western liberal democracies are characterised by the coexistence of contradictory ideologies. Notions such as 'children make life meaningful' or 'motherhood constitutes the fulfilment of womanhood' exist concurrently with ideologies exposing the advantages of a 'child-free life-style'. Such ideological diversity is not tolerated in Eastern Europe where 'unanimity rather than dissent is characteristic of its civility and is taken to confirm the organic unity of society and state' (Harding, 1984, p. 309).

Apart from political pluralism, the capitalist welfare state also practises 'limited government', reluctant to directly interfere in what are considered to be the private affairs of individual citizens. Rather than adopting vigorous pro-natalist policies, governments in Western Europe have maintained a low-key response, 'introducing incremental changes at the margins of existing policy as and when opportunities present themselves' (McIntosh, 1981, p. 182). The United States has practised a particularly limited form of government, failing to even establish a comprehensive system of maternity care. As Wertz and Wertz (1977, p. 221) point out, 'today the federal government provides larger sums for maternity care than ever before, yet the sums go for temporary, experimental programs that affect only selected populations of women. This care is not visible to most women and it may not include basic care, which many women do not yet receive and which it was the intention of federal involvement, since Sheppard-Towner, to provide.' As a result, the non-selected populations, i.e. the majority, have to rely on various private insurance schemes.

In contrast, the Soviet-type state formation is effectively the sole distributor of social welfare benefits in the realms of health, education, housing, culture and recreation. Moreover, welfare inducements and welfare sanctions provide the socialist state with its most potent and pervasive weapons of social and political control, and their efficient management is the principal guarantee of political stability and legitimacy (Harding, 1984, p. 309). As we noted, the socialist state's intervention in reproduction is particularly extensive, encompassing systematic ideological programmes on the 'education for marriage and parenthood', protective legislation for women, pregnancy and maternity leaves, the provision of free pre-, intra- and post-natal medical care, and a comprehensive system of pro-natalist fiscal incentives consisting of both direct cash benefits awarded to families and mothers, and subsidised children's goods and services. Moreover, while the issues of reproductive rights, protective legislation and sex equality are similar in principle in both the East and the West, they are resolved differently in the two specific socio-economic contexts. In Eastern Europe there is a distinct set of tensions between the following:

(1) the socialist state concern over fertility rates at or below levels of population replacement – hence a desire by the socialist elites to increase birth rates;
(2) a chronic shortage of labour – hence a commitment to maximising employment of married women;
(3) the realities of people's daily lives, especially for women, for whom the current situation (e.g. low wages, lack of adequate socialisation of domestic labour) does not encourage having many children; and
(4) an official ideology which is committed to sex equality.

We have seen that the outcome of these tensions has been a policy that stresses women's reproductive roles at the expense of their productive roles.

Wolchik (1981, pp. 140–1) has argued that in Czechoslovakia, the formerly unitary model of the 'ideal' socialist woman has now:

> been replaced by a variety of approved models, which vary according to a woman's age and stage in the life cycle. While the ideal still embodies the expectation that women will be model workers, active citizens, and good mothers, women are no longer expected to fulfil all roles simultaneously. Rather, the new approach expects women to attach different degrees of importance to each role at different times. Nonetheless, there is still an ideal career and life pattern, and the needs of young women who deviate from this pattern (i.e. by working while raising young children) are not seriously considered . . . The weakness of the new approach to women's multiple roles arises from the fact that the elites have not given serious attention to the impediments which the approved life pattern poses to women's achievements. There has been very little discussion, for example, of the unequal impact parenthood will have on men and women's careers if women remain at home for

three to six years at the start of their working lives. Nor have the elites considered the impact which emphasis of women's maternal and domestic roles will have on their aspirations and opportunities to participate in political leadership. Finally, neither political leaders, nor the leaders of the women's organisation have examined the effect the interruption of women's work lives will have in reinforcing the traditional division of labour within the home. The current approach, in fact, does not challenge this division, but it is based on the presumption that it will continue.

Who has initiated and formulated these policies and approaches? What has been the input of the party leadership, the professional elites, and members of the group most directly affected by the outcome of these policies, i.e. women? The answer to these questions depends on whether we examine periods of political orthodoxy or periods of political reform. The latter typically allow for more open debates as well as more diverse input than the former. As Wolchik (1983, p. 120) has argued, during the 1950s and early 1960s, the input of demographic experts into demographic policy-making in Czechoslovakia was limited to bringing particular problems (e.g. the declining birth rate) to the attention of the political elites. Throughout the 1960s, the role of specialists in both policy planning and policy evaluation expanded, along with the number of groups involved in the discussion of population issues. According to Wolchik (1983, pp. 122–3):

this process went through two fairly distinct phases. During the first, specialist elites used professional meetings, articles in specialised journals, formal and, presumably, informal contacts with the political elites, to raise previously discussed issues and point out possible conflicts which might arise from the adoption of particular policy measures. This phase . . . saw a gradual extension of the limits of debate on many types of social issues, as well as a more open expression on the part of specialists of a desire to take a more active role in the formation of policy. At the same time, however, debate over various policy alternatives remained confined to the elite level.

In the mid to late 1960s, the number of groups involved in discussion of population issues increased. Although the most important actors continued to be political and specialist elites, debate over the consequences and desirability of various policy measures spread beyond the elite level to include certain members of those groups which would be most directly affected by the outcome of the debates. In these conditions, certain specialists came to serve as a conduit for bringing the desires of citizens to the attention of political decision-makers.

The re-establishment of political orthodoxy in the 1970s has created less favourable conditions for both specialist and consumer intervention in policy-making. Many specialists who played a major role in the debates of the 1960s, especially those who were active in the reform movement of the 'Prague Spring', were removed from their formal positions of responsibility. The remaining experts, as well as those who became experts in the 1970s, now have far less opportunity to act as purveyors of mass desires to political elites, at least directly, than their immediate predecessors. However, as Wolchik (1983, p. 125) points out, despite these limitations, specialists continue to take an active part in demographic policy-making and evaluation. While greater care must be taken to frame research questions in acceptable Marxist–Leninist terms, empirical research continues on a broad variety of population and women-related issues. The coordinating body for this research, as well as the focal point for specialists' participation in the making of policy in this area, remains the Population Commission (discussed in some detail in Chapter 2). As we noted in Chapters 10 and 12, much of the current input of physicians and demographers to Czechoslovak population policy is focused on increasing the effectiveness of the medical management of reproduction (to decrease perinatal mortality) as well as on the existing pro-natalist measures (to maintain the existing birth rate). While greater specialist participation does not necessarily lead to more effective policy, it at least ensures that policy choices are based on information and analyses other than those of the top political elite alone (Wolchik, 1983, p. 128).

Thus *all* collective debates in the socialist countries, even debates on such a personal issue as child-bearing, are initiated from the 'top down', by the party and professional elites, rather than from the 'bottom up', by various consumer and interest groups. As Harding (1984, p. 309) argues, citizens' rights in the socialist societies 'are expressly confined in their exercise to those activities that serve to strengthen the social system of production superintended by the state. They may not be exercised to challenge or limit its prerogatives nor to canvass alternative formulations of its proper objectives.' In other words, if the communist party–state insists on the monopoly of power and doctrine, an independent feminist or women's health movement of the current Western type cannot legally emerge to promote a discussion of reproduction as an issue detached from state and professional medical control.[1] A truly radical reassessment of women's reproductive freedom seems to be possible only in the politically pluralistic Western liberal democracies, which are more tolerant of conflicts and dissent, thus offering much wider scope to the efforts of organised social movements.

The socialist emphasis on the unity of society, party and state, and a corresponding disapproval of dissidence and conflict,[2] place medical doctors in a rather powerful position *vis-à-vis* patients. While in the pluralistic West the dominant medical perspective is never absolutely dominant, since alternatives can be, and often are presented, such freedom to publish criticism simply does not exist in Eastern Europe.The professional domination of medicine in general and obstetrics/gynaecology in particular, has in recent years come under considerable criticism from Western social psychiatry, the sociology of medicine and of the professions, the media, and the feminist and consumer health movements, but no such broad critique is possible in Eastern Europe. Thus the state socialist political climate does not favour current Western feminist discourse on reproductive issues, which has encouraged both informed consumer participation and various forms of 'de-medicalisation' of maternity care (e.g. home births, birth attendance by midwives rather than by medical doctors and so on).

As we noted in Chapter 11, consumers in the USA have been able to utilise published research on infant bonding as a basis for challenge to several modern obstetrical practices and to demand the establishment of alternative birthing centres. In contrast, in Czechoslovakia, the 'privilege' to openly challenge some current obstetrical practices (e.g. separating mother and baby after birth) remained in the hands of the professionals themselves. In state socialist societies, changes in particular medical practices are always initiated from within the profession, by a process of professional communication and interaction, which can, and sometimes does occur, across national and political boundaries. For example, we have seen (in Chapter 8) that one of the first two articles on the vacuum suction abortion technique which appeared in specialised American literature (in the July 1967 issue of the scholarly journal *Obstetrics and Gynecology*) was by the leading Czech obstetrician and gynaecologist, M. Vojta, at that time the editor of *Československá gynekologie*. The vacuum suction method of abortion was used on an experimental basis in Czechoslovakia already in 1963, well before it became known in the United States. The technique was rapidly introduced after the 1970 legalisation of abortion by the state of New York and is currently the most widely used abortion technique in North America. In contrast, the majority of Czechoslovak physicians (i.e. all those located outside the prestigious research institutes and hospitals) continued to rely well into the early 1980s on the more hazardous D&C technique, both because of their professional conservatism and because of a severe shortage of the necessary technology (e.g. Czech- or Soviet-produced aspirators and vacurettes). The latter may have, of course, reinforced the former.

The least hazardous abortion technique to date, the menstrual regulation method, also known as mini-abortion, was developed in the West in the early 1970s and has enthusiastic supporters among several prominent obstetricians in Czechoslovakia, but use of the technique has not moved beyond the experimental stage. The major stumbling block appears to be the existing abortion legislation, which requires each individual woman seeking an abortion first to apply to an abortion commission in her locality. This bureaucratic procedure unfortunately prolongs the gestation of the pregnancy past the required two weeks from the missed period, making it impossible to use the early abortion technique. So far, the medical profession has not succeeded in having the abortion commissions abolished, despite strenuous effort and in view of the fact that such commissions exist neither in the USSR nor in the GDR. It seems that the current political climate of vigorous pro-natalism is not favourable to a policy of 'abortion on demand', which the abolition of abortion commissions would undoubtedly imply.

Unlike political pluralism, professional pluralism is evidently permitted in the socialist societies. As pointed out at various points in this study, there are many influential professionals in Czechoslovakia, who have addressed reproductive issues of the medical management of pregnancy and childbirth, post-partum and newborn hospital care, breastfeeding, sex education, contraception, abortion, pregnancy and maternity leaves, protective legislation, and the status of single mothers and their children with real concern, and who have been critical of past and present policies in these areas. On the other side of the spectrum, we have also witnessed cases of doctors and nurses who give inadequate birth control information, unwilling (or unable) to spend adequate time in answering legitimate women's

concerns about the side-effects of the pill or the IUD. We have also
noted that those who subscribe to the physiological and highly
technological model of childbirth have failed to incorporate few, if
any, social and psychological criteria into their professional perspectives. Finally, there are also doctors who expect large 'tips' from their
patients as additional 'unofficial' payments for treatment of infertility
or for birth attendance which are already covered by the state (in the
form of admittedly low salaries of health care workers).

INDIVIDUAL REPRODUCTIVE RIGHTS AND CHOICES

Where does all of this leave the reproducers themselves? The lack of
broad participation in decision-making on fertility policy has not
meant, for the most part, that women have been unable to exercise
their reproductive rights individually. Despite the adoption of various restrictive guidelines for granting an abortion on non-medical
grounds during the last decade in Czechoslovakia, Hungary, and
Bulgaria (supported by some experts and opposed by others), few
women who persist in their requests are denied termination of their
unwanted pregnancies in these cases. As we noted in Chapter 8,
abortion commissions in Czechoslovakia have, over the years, turned
down only 2–3 per cent of all requests. Moreover, the unsuccessful
requests have often not resulted in childbirth. Of the 555 women who
requested but were denied an abortion in Prague during 1961–3, only
316 (57 per cent) had carried their pregnancy to term. In other words,
239 (43 per cent) of the women managed to avoid giving birth, either
by obtaining a legal abortion from another district abortion commission, or by reapplying in the same district but under an assumed
name and address, or by aborting 'spontaneously'. Twenty-two per
cent, twice the national average for the ratio of miscarriages to
completed pregnancies, 'resolved' their unwanted pregnancy in this
way, either deliberately or by sheer luck.

Even in Romania, almost two decades after abortion was de-
legalised, 60 per cent of the country's pregnancies annually fail to
come to term. Thus, despite the repressive abortion legislation,
abortions have remained very much a part of Romanian women's
lives. The procedure is generally performed illegally and is paid for
on the black-market by barter – notably with food or with Kent
cigarettes. Thus it is clear that, once knowledge of the principal

means of birth avoidance is widespread, effective, long-term 'quantitative' state control of child-bearing is very difficult, even under the
most authoritarian circumstances. The de-legalisation of abortions in
Romania at the end of 1966 was followed by a dramatic increase in
the birth rate, from 14.3 per thousand population in 1966 to 27.3 per
thousand population the following year. But women gradually returned to traditional birth control methods (*coitus interruptus* in
particular), smuggled contraceptives and illegal abortions. By the
mid-1970s, the birth rate was down to less than 20 per thousand
population. However, this particular form of individual management
of reproduction has cost many women their lives – abortion-
associated deaths in Romania increased from 64 in 1965 to 449 in
1978.

We should note, then, that women in contemporary developed
societies take an active part in the management of reproduction.
They do so not only by limiting the number of children they have (by
means of contraception or abortion), but also by speaking out in such
forums as are available. As we noted above, such forums are rather
numerous in the Western liberal democracies, ranging from academia
and critical journalism to the trade unions and the women's health
and reproductive rights movements. We have seen that in Eastern
Europe such forums are much more limited. Critical comments about
specific (as opposed to general and systematic) reproductive issues
(e.g. non-observance or discriminatory application of protective
legislation or maternity leaves in particular enterprises) are typically raised at local trade union meetings or at special national
conferences for women trade union officials. If the criticism is local,
an effort is usually made to remedy the situation. Another area of
women's input into policy changes in Czechoslovakia, discussed in
Chapter 11, concerned the limited consumer involvement in the
introduction of the rooming-in system of newborn care. During the
last few years, several articles and interviews, exalting the virtues of
rooming-in, have appeared in the mass media. However, when
readers of the youth weekly *Mladý svět* were invited in early 1983 to
respond to one such article, their responses were both negative and
positive. Moreover, in some hospitals, pressure from mothers has led
to a faster introduction of this system of care of newborns while in
others, consumers' conservatism, (as well as that of doctors and
nurses), has resulted in only partial implementation of rooming-in,
thus giving mothers slightly more choice about their post-partum

hospital experience. How important then is the exercise of individual reproductive choice? As Rothman (1984, pp. 23, 26) argues for feminists in the United States:

> *choice* and *information* have served as the cornerstones of the women's health and reproductive rights movements. We are, above all, pro-choice. We support the rights of the individual woman to choose, to choose pregnancy or abortion, to choose alternative medical treatments or none at all. And choice, we claim, rests firmly on information: to choose treatment for breast cancer, for example, requires information on the full range of medical treatments, their side effects, and their probability of success. This emphasis on choice and information all sounded very logical at the time, sounded like women were going to get more and more control as first their access to information and then their choices expanded . . . We thought that information would give us power. What we perhaps overlooked is that it is *power* which gives one control over both information and choice.

Moreover, Rothman (1984, p. 30) continues, 'it seems that, in gaining the choice to control the quantity of our children, we may be losing the choice *not* to control the quality, the choice of accepting them as they are'.

We have already noted (in Chapter 11) that, as bonding programmes become more widespread, there is a real danger that they become part of a general conception of what constitutes good 'progressive' parenting, and that this new ideology will in turn be coercively applied to all individuals. Moreover, we also noted that the wholesale adoption of in-hospital programmes to facilitate parental and infant attachment is likely to foreclose the option to regard the home as the best environment for both childbirth and the postpartum interaction of parents and infants. Thus the adoption of particular policies dictated by medical ideology can, and usually does close down the option of choosing others. In a similar vein, we have seen (in Chapter 9) that some 'progressive' policies can have, and often have had, a strong controlling effect on the people whom they have been designed to benefit. While one can generally applaud the provision (largely by the state) of comprehensive medical maternity care in most of the developed world, one must also note that at the same time the widespread provision of this free reproductive service has narrowed, rather than broadened women's choices about their antenatal care. The cultural definition of pregnancy as a 'series of medical encounters, which is characteristic of all the advanced industrial societies, and which is rapidly penetrating also the Third World countries, has become so prevalent, that lack of medical consultation during pregnancy or giving medically-unattended birth at home have become synonymous with deviance. This can easily result in the labelling of the expectant mother as a 'potential risk', subject to the control of the state and its agents, in this case the medical or the social work professions.

The medical control of reproduction is particularly evident in situations when it is possible to label a particular medical procedure as being for the life/death, or simply the well-being of the baby. The birthing mother then has few, if any, real options to choose from, for she is usually in no position to determine whether or not the particular medical diagnosis has a basis in fact. Her lack of choice is limited both at the 'micro-level (by the exercise of medical power in her immediate surroundings) and more generally, at the level of dominant cultural values. As Jordan (1978, p. 88) argues, 'the details of obstetric practices may change in response to societal pressures. What shows no sign of changing is a deep consensus, shared by all of us, that, at least for us, the justification for any way of doing birth must include as its most fundamental concern the issue of medical safety for mother and child.' Thus most mothers who are told by their attending physicians that they need a Caesarean section are likely to agree to have one, since they cannot and for most part would not want to run the risk (medically determined) of harming the baby. Physicians operate in the same way. As we noted in Chapter 10, they are under strong professional pressure to keep lowering the incidence of perinatal mortality, which has become the chief professional as well as political indicator of a good, high quality reproductive care system. While mothers are able to exercise some degree of consumer scepticism with respect to medical advice on such issues as nutrition (their own during pregnancy or that of their babies), physical exercises, sex and alternative birth control methods, this is usually not possible during the medical management of labour and delivery. For in these situations it is very easy for physicians to invoke the drama of 'life and death' during the slightest deviation from the aggregate statistical norm, and the mother then has no option but to follow medical advice.

However, Jordan's comment on safety has to be closely examined. Why should our cultural 'deep consensus, shared by all of us' over the value of the 'medical safety for mother and child' have to change? What would replace it? Some kind of spiritual belief that death is a good thing? While medical *obsession* with safety has to be counter-checked, we also have to be cautious about not 'throwing the baby out with the bathwater'. Thus the dilemma of modern medical management of childbirth is that we must rely on experts and to a large extent also on technology, but at the same time, we want to have some personal control over medical intervention, especially if our bodies or lives (or those of our children) are at stake. The only way out in this situation is to reinforce the other social roles of the people and institutions the doctor has to contend with: parents, social workers, psychologists, the state and so on, so that the medical expert does not find himself/herself occupying the field alone in all his/her professional power.[3]

There is therefore no such thing as an 'absolute' or 'total' reproductive choice or freedom at the individual level. For what individual women want and choose is always bound up with their social position and the processes of socialisation, and thus always the result of either subtle or blatant social manipulation and control. Thus we can conclude with Rothman (1984, p. 33) that 'we have to lift our eyes from the choices of the individual woman, and focus on the control of the social system which structures her choices, which rewards some choices and punishes others, which distributes the rewards and punishments for reproductive choices along class and race lines . . . The next step in the politics of reproductive control is the politics of social control.' Like all other freedoms, there are limits to which the freedom whether, and in what manner, to reproduce may be exercised. As this study has attempted to show, in advanced industrial societies these limits will be socially enforced in varying degrees by the state and the medical profession.

NOTES

1. Illegal movements do not, of course, require state permission. The first *samizdad* feminist almanac, *Women and Russia*, which included moving descriptions of inhuman, assembly-like medical management of abortions and childbirths (without an anaesthetic), was produced without the permission of the Soviet party–state authorities. However, several of the contributors to the almanac were subsequently expelled from the Soviet Union and are now living in exile in the West.

2. As Harding (1984, p. 309) argues, the socialist state regards dissidence and conflict as 'signs of individual morbidity or social malaise, outside, rather than constitutive of, politics'.
3. I am indebted to Maria Victor-Paez for her insights and wording on the issues raised in this paragraph.

Bibliography

Abel-Smith, Brian (1981) 'Foreword', in Maxwell, Robert T. (ed.) *Health and Wealth. An International Study of Health-Care Spending* (Lexington and Toronto: Lexington Books and D.C. Heath).

Acsadi, George and Johnson-Acsadi, Gwendolyn (1980) 'Recent Trends and Determinants of Fertility in Developed Countries', in Arthur Campbell (ed.) *Social, Economic and Health Aspects of Low Fertility*, NIH Publication no. 80–100 (US Department of Health, Education and Welfare) pp. 1–30.

Aleš, Milan (1983) 'Population Development in Czechoslovakia in 1982', *Demosta*, vol. 16, nos. 1–2, pp. 6–8.

Arditti, Rita, Klein, Renate Duelli and Minden, Shelley (eds) (1984) *Test-Tube Women. What Future for Motherhood?* (London: Pandora Press, Routledge & Kegan Paul).

Augustín, J. (1972) 'Problémy s psychoprofylaktickou přípravou těhotných v okrese', *Československá gynekologie*, vol. 37, no. 9 (December), pp. 659–60.

Balák, K. (1972) 'Poznámky ke škodlivosti interrupcí u primigravid', *Československá gynekologie*, vol. 37, no. 7 (September).

Balák, K. (1981) 'Úvod', *Československá gynekologie*, vol. 46, no. 1 (February), pp. 1–2.

Baran, P. (1980) 'Vliv zaměstnanosti těhotných žen na výskyt komplikací v průběhu těhotenství', *Československá gynekologie*, vol. 45, no. 4 (May), pp. 225–8.

Bárdoš, Augustín. (1978) *Žena = Zdravie + Krása. Sprievodca modernej ženy* (Martin: Osveta).

Barron, S.Z. (1979) 'Long-Term Complications of Induced Abortion. WHO Task Force on Sequelae of Abortion', in Gerald T. Zatuchni *et al.* (eds) *Pregnancy Termination Procedures, Safety and New Developments*, (Hagerstown: Harper & Row) pp. 163–5.

Barták, Vladimír (1977) 'Sexuální život', in *Škola pro snoubence a novomanžele* (Praha: Avicenum), pp. 87–242.

Bartošová, Milada (1976) *Výzkum veřejného mínění k otázkám populačního vývoje a populační politiky. Příspěvek k metodice* (Prague: Czechoslovak Research Institute of Work and Social Affairs in Bratislava, Workplace Prague)

Bártová, Eva (1972) 'K práci ženské sestry na obvodě', *Československá gynekologie*, vol. 37, no. 10, pp. 757–8.

Beer, O. (1972) 'Možnosti uplatnění ženských sester v samostatně vedených prenatálních poradnách', *Československá gynekologie*, vol. 37, no. 10, pp. 760–1.

Bell, John D. (1981) 'Giving Birth to the New Soviet Man: Politics and Obstetrics in the USSR', *Slavic Review*, vol. 40, no. 1 (Spring) pp. 1–16.

Belsey, Mark. A. (1979) 'Long Term Sequelae of Induced Abortion: Considerations in Interpretations of Research', in Gerald T. Zatuchni *et al.* (eds) *Pregnancy Termination Procedures, Safety and New Developments*, (Hagerstown: Harper & Row) pp. 156–8.

Berelson, B. (1979) 'Romania's 1966 Anti-Abortion Decree: the Demographic Experience of the First Decade', *Population Studies*, vol. 33, no. 2 (July) pp. 209–22.

Besemeres, J.F. (1980) *Socialist Population Politics* (White Plains, New York: M.E. Sharpe).

Birgus, J. (1979) 'Několik připomínek porodníka k problému těhotenství', *Československá gynekologie*, vol. 44, no. 1, pp. 69–76.

Biryukova, A.P. (1980) 'Special protective legislation and equality of opportunity for women workers in the USSR', *International Labour Review*, vol. 119, no. 1 (January–February) pp. 39–49.

Bittman, Sam and Zalk, Rosenberg, Sue (1978) *Expectant Fathers* (New York: Hawthorne Press).

Bland, Lucy, *et al.* (1978) 'Relations of reproduction: approaches through anthropology', in *Women Take Issue. Aspects of Women's Subordination* (London: Hutchinson in association with the Centre for Contemporary Cultural Studies, University of Birmingham).

Blašková, O. *et al.* (1977) 'Prispěvok k vedeniu porodu pánvovým koncom', *Československá gynekologie*, vol. 42, no. 9, pp. 649–53.

Bogdan, C. (1978) 'Care or Cure? Childbirth Practices in Nineteenth Century America', *Feminist Studies*, vol. 4, no. 2 (June) pp. 92–9.

Bokšajová, Tatiana (1977) 'Úloha žien v rodinách a zdravotná výchova', in *Zdravotná výchova a žena v socialistickej spoločnosti* (Bratislava: Institute for Health Education). pp. 79–81.

Brablcová, Vlasta (ed.) (1977) *Manželství, rodina, rodičovství* (Praha: Horizont).

Breindel, Eric and Eberstadt, Nick (1980) 'Paradoxes of Population', *Commentary*, vol. 70, no. 2 (August) pp. 41–9.

Brodber, Erna (1974) *Abandonment of Children in Jamaica*, Law and Society in the Caribbean, No. 3 (Kingston: Institute of Social and Economic Research, University of West Indies).

Brown, Archie (1984) 'Political Power and the Soviet State: Western and Soviet Perspectives', in Neil Harding (ed.) *The State in Socialist Society* (London: Macmillan in association with St Antony's College, Oxford) pp. 51–103.

Brtníková, Marta (1974) *Výchova k rodičovství. Metodická pomůcka pro učitelé ZDŠ* (Praha: Ústav zdravotní výchovy).

Brucháč, Dušan (1977) 'Zdravotní stav žien na Slovensku a súčasné úlohy preventivnej starostlivosti', in *Zdravotná výchova a žena v socialistickej spoločnosti* (Bratislava: Institute for Health Education) pp. 25–9.

Brucháč, D. and Sochor, J. (1972) 'Súčasné úlohy a riadiaca funkcia oddělenia starostlivosti o novú generáciu pri MZd SSR', *Československá gynekologie*, vol. 37, no. 8 (October) pp. 561–4.

Busfield, Joan (1974) 'Ideologies and Reproduction', in Martin Richards (ed.) *The Integration of a Child into a Social World* (Cambridge University Press) pp. 1–26.

Butler Jr, Julius C. (1979) 'Discussion Summary', in Gerald T. Zattuchni *et al.* (eds) *Pregnancy Termination Procedures, Safety and New Developments*, (Hagerstown: Harper & Row) pp. 82–3.

Cahová, Dagmar (1977) 'Z výzkumu postojů mladých slovenských žen ke zdraví', in *Zdravotná výchova a žena v socialistickej spoločnosti* (Bratislava: Institute for Health Education) pp. 30–3.

Canadian Women and Job Related Laws (1981) (Ottawa: Labour Canada)

Celostátní aktiv k úkolům a podmínkám práce odborářek po IX. všeodborovém sjezdu, 10–11 October 1977 (Praha: Práce).

Cesarean Childbirth (1981) NIH Publication no. 82–2067 (US Department of Health and Human Services).

Chabada, J. *et al.* (1974) 'Interrupcia gravidity ako príčina predčasného porodu', *Československá gynekologie*, vol. 39, no. 5 (June) pp. 329–30.

Chalupa, Miroslav and Friedlanderová, Běla (1965) *Jak připravit ženy k porodu* (Praha: Státní zdravotnické nakladatelství).

Chalupa, M. and Kofroňová, V. (1972) 'Návštěvy u nedělky a kojence', *Československá gynekologie*, vol. 37, no. 10 (December) pp. 761–2.

Chalupský, T. (1984) 'O původu evropské syfilidy', *Výběr*, vol. 17, no. 20 (10 May).

Charles, Nickie and Brown, David (1981) 'Women, Shiftwork and the Sexual Division of Labour', *The Sociological Review*, vol. 29, no. 4 (November) pp. 685–704.

Chenier, Nancy Miller (1982) *Reproductive Hazards. Men, Women and the Fertility Gamble* (Ottawa: Canadian Advisory Council on the Status of Women).

Chodorow, Nancy (1978) *The Reproduction of Mothering* (Berkeley: University of California Press).

Chovanová, Eva (1974) 'Psychosexuálné pozorovania u dospievajících dievčat', *Československá gynekologie*, vol. 39, no. 3, pp. 209–10.

Coale, Ansley T., Anderson, Barbara, Harm, Erna (1979) *Human Fertility in Russia Since the Nineteenth Century* (Princeton University Press).

Comaroff, Jean (1977) 'Conflicting Paradigms of Pregnancy: Managing Ambiguity in Ante-Natal Encounters', in Alan Davis and Gordon Horebin (eds) *Medical Encounters. The Experience of Illness and Treatment* (London: Croom Helm).

Connor, Walter D. (1979) *Socialism, Politics and Equality. Hierarchy and Change in Eastern Europe and the USSR* (New York: Columbia University Press).

Corea, G. (1984) 'Egg Snatchers', in R. Arditti, *et al.* (eds) *Test-Tube Women. What Future for Motherhood?* (London: Pandora Press) pp. 37–41.

Čepelák, J. and Tůmová, Z. (1961) 'Psychologické problémy v ženském lékařství', in *10 let boje za zdraví nové generace 1951-1961. Přehled vědecké činnosti Ústavu pro péči o matku a dítě* (Praha: The Institute for the Care of Mother and Child) pp. 16–19.

Čepický, P. (1984) 'Psychoprofylaktická příprava k porodu', *Československá gynekologie*, vol. 49, no. 2, pp. 119–24.

Čepický, P., Ludvíková, K., Mellanová, A. (1984) 'Současný stav porodnické psychoprofylaxie v Praze. I. Způsob provádění přípravy', *Československá gynekologie*, vol. 49, no. 8, pp. 568–72.

Černoch, Antonín (1980) 'Statistiky perinatální úmrtnosti u nás a jinde', *Československá gynekologie*, vol. 45, no. 5, pp. 319–32.

Černoch, Antonín (1982) 'Úvodní slovo ke konferenci o perinatální úmrtnosti a chorobnosti', *Československá gynekologie*, vol. 47, no. 1, pp. 13–15.

Černoch, Antonín and Uher, J. (1972) 'Posuzování pracovní neschopnosti v gynekologii a porodnictiví', *Československá gynekologie*, vol. 37, no. 9 (December) pp. 695–6.

Černý, Jaroslav, Vogel, Otto and Matějková, Markéta (1977) *Péče o zdraví pracovníků* (Praha: Práce)

Československé zdravotnictví 1979 (1979) (Praha: Ústav pro zdravotnickou statistiku).

Damborská, Marie (1980) 'Co je nefyziologické v přístupu k dítěti nejútlejšího věku', *Psychológia a patapsychológia dieťata*, vol. 15, no. 1, pp. 22–37.

Damborská, Marie (1981) 'Význam prvních týdnů v životě dítěte', *Psychológia a patapsychológia dieťata*, vol. 16, no. 1, pp. 51–5.

David, Henry P. (1972) 'Abortion Seeking in Czechoslovakia, Hungary, and the United States', *International Mental Health Research Newsletter*, vol. 15, no. 4 (Winter).

David, Henry P. (1980) 'The Abortion Decision: National and International Perspectives', in J.T.B. Whitehall (ed.) *Abortion Parley* (Kansas City: Andrews and McMeel) pp. 57–98.

David, Henry P. (1981) 'Unwantedness. Longitudinal Studies of Prague Children Born to Women Twice Denied Abortion for the Same Pregnancy and Matched Control', in Paul Ahmed (ed.) *Coping With Medical Issues: Pregnancy, Childbirth and Parenthood* (New York: Elsevier) pp. 81–102.

David, Henry P. (1982) 'Eastern Europe: Pronatalist Policies and Private Behavior', *Population Bulletin*, vol. 36, no. 6 (February).

David, Henry P. and McIntyre, R.J. (1981) *Reproductive Behavior. Central and Eastern European Experience* (New York: Springer).

David Henry P. and Matějček, Z. (1981) 'Children Born to Women Denied Abortion: An Update', *Family Planning Perspectives*, vol. 13, pp. 32–4.

Deacon, Bob (1983) *Social Policy and Socialism. The Struggle for Socialist Relations of Welfare* (London and Sydney: Pluto Press).

De Kadt, Emanuel (1982) 'Ideology, Social Policy, Health and Health Services: A Field of Complex Interactions', *Social Science and Medicine*, vol. 6, pp. 741–52.

Delaney, Janice, Luxton, Mary Jane and Toth, Emily (1977) *The Curse* (New York: Mentor).

Demko, George T., and Fuchs, Roland T. (1977) 'Demography and Urban and Regional Planning in Northeastern Europe', in Huey Louis Kostanick (ed.) *Population and Migration Trends in Eastern Europe* (Boulder, Colorado: Westview Press) pp. 49–80.

The Determinants and Consequences of Population Trends, (1973) vol. I (New York: United Nations).

284   *Bibliography*

DeVries, Raymond G. (1984) 'Humanizing Childbirth: The Discovery and Implementation of Bonding Theory', *International Journal of Health Services*, vol. 14, no. 1, pp. 89–104.

Dráč, Pavel (1972) 'Úloha a místo gynekologa v plánovaném rodičovstvı', *Československá gynekologie*, vol. 37, no. 7 (September) pp. 489–91.

Dunovský, Jiřı and Zelenková, Marta (1977) 'Nemanželské děti po třech letech', *Populačnı zprávy,*, nos 1–2, pp. 21–6.

Dvořák, Josef (1982a) 'Population Development of Czechoslovakia in 1981', *Demosta*, vol. 15, nos. 1–2, pp. 11–14.

Dvořák, Josef (1982b) 'Projection of the Czechoslovak Population until 2000', *Demosta*, vol. 15, nos. 1–2, pp. 15–17.

Dvořák, Josef (1982c) 'Reproduction Research (1981)', *Demosta*, vol. 15, no. 4, pp. 12–15.

Dytrych, Z. *et al.* (1975) 'Children Born to Women Denied Abortion', *Family Planning Perspectives*, vol. 7, pp. 165–71.

Dytrych, Z. *et al.* (1978) 'Children Born to Women Denied Abortion in Czechoslovakia', in H.P. David (ed.) *Abortion in Psychosocial Perspective: Trends in Transnational Research* (New York: Springer) pp. 201–24.

Edelman, David A. and Berger, Gary S. (1981) 'Menstrual Regulation', in Jane Hodgson (ed.) *Abortion and Sterilization: Medical and Social Aspects* (London: Academic Press) pp. 209–24.

Elkins, Valmai Howe (1980) *The Rights of the Pregnant Parent*, revised edition. (Toronto: Waxwing Productions).

Elkins, Valmai Howe (1983) *The Birth Report* (Toronto: Lester A. Orpen Dennys).

Encyklopedie mladé ženy, (1978) second revised edition (Praha: Avicenum).

Eversley, David E.C. (1980) 'Social Implications of Low Fertility', in Arthur A. Campbell (ed.) *Social Economic and Health Aspects of Low Fertility*, NIH Publication no. 80–100 (US Department of Health, Education and Welfare) pp. 133–85.

'Experiment' (1983) *Mladý svět*, nos. 12, 19 and 25.

Fein, Robert A. (1978) 'Consideration of Men's Experiences and the Birth of a First Child', in Warren B. Miller and Lucille F. Newman (eds) *The First Child and Family Formation*, (Chapel Hill: Carolina Population Center, The University of North Carolina) pp. 327–39.

Felker, Marcia (1982) 'The Political Economy of Sexism in Industrial Health', *Social Science and Medicine*, vol. 16, pp. 3–13.

Ferge, Zsuzsa (1979) *A Society in the Making. Hungarian Social and Societal Policy 1945–75* (White Plains, New York: M.E. Sharpe).

Field, Mark (1957) *Doctor and Patient in Soviet Russia* (Cambridge, Mass.: Harvard University Press).

Field, Mark (1967) *Soviet Socialized Medicine. An Introduction* (New York: The Free Press).

Fielding, A.G. and Portwood, A. (1980) 'Professions and the State – Towards a Typology of Bureaucratic Professions', *The Sociological Review*, vol. 28, no. 1 (February) pp. 23–43.

Fišer, Jan (1981) *Od okouzlení k odpovědnému rodičovstvi* (Praha: Státní pedagogické nakladatelství).

Fišer, Jiří (1977) 'Výchova k rodičovství na školách', in Brablcová, Vlasta (ed.) *Manželství, rodina, rodičovství* (Praha: Horizont).

Folbre, Nancy (1983) 'Of Patriarchy Born: The Political Economy of Fertility Decisions', *Feminist Studies*, vol. 9. no. 2 (Summer) pp. 261–84.

Francome, Colin (1984) *Abortion Freedom. A Worldwide Movement* (London: Allen & Unwin).

Freidson, Eliot (1970) *Professional Dominance: The Social Structure of Medical Care* (New York: Atherton Press).

Frejka, Tomas (1974) 'Which road will population take on the way to the 21st century?', *People*, vol. 1, no. 4, pp. 5–9.

Frejka, Tomas (1980) 'Fertility trends and policies: Czechoslovakia in the 1970s', *Population and Development Review*, vol. 6, no. 1 (March) pp. 65–93.

Fukalová, D. (1974) 'Psychologické aspekty interrupce', *Československá gynekologie*, vol. 39, no. 3, pp. 204–6.

Fukalová, D. (1981) 'Přednosti regulace menstruace z psychologického hlediska', *Československá gynekologie*, vol. 46, no. 6 (July) pp. 490–2.

Fukalová, D. and Uzel, R. (1974) 'Motivace k mateřství u svobodných matek', in *Aktuální problémy v porodnictví*. Proceedings from the 17th inter-county obstetrical seminar of southern and northern Moravian counties, 22–23 April, Uherské Hradiště.

Fukalová, D. and Uzel, R. (1975) 'Postoje k antikoncepci u žen po provedení umělého přerušení těhotenství', *Československá gynekologie*, vol. 40, no. 9.

Galtung, J. (1967) *Theory and Methods of Social Research* (New York: Columbia University Press).

Garfield, Richard (1981) 'Nursing, Health Care and Professionalism in Cuba', *Social Science and Medicine*, vol. 15A, pp. 63–72.

Gazárek, František *et al.* (1982a) 'Cesty ke snížení perinatální úmrtnosti v ČSSR pod 10 promile', *Československá gynekologie*, vol. 47, no. 1 (February) pp. 24–7.

Gazárek, František *et al.* (1982b) 'Císařský řez ze stanoviska současného moderního porodnictví', *Československá gynekologie*, vol. 47, no. 4, pp. 299–303.

Gazárek, František and Křikal, Z. (1972) 'Prevence v prenatální péči', *Československá gynekologie*, vol. 37, no. 8 (October) pp. 613–16.

Geiger, H. Kent (1968) *The Family in Soviet Russia* (Cambridge, Mass.: Harvard University Press).

George, Vic and Manning, Nick (1980) *Socialism, Social Welfare and the Soviet Union* (London, Boston and Henley: Routledge & Kegan Paul).

Giddens, Anthony (1980) *The Class Structure of the Advanced Societies* (London: Hutchinson).

Giláňová, Mária (1977) 'Ženy ako základný pilier výchovy člověka' in *Zdravotná výchova a žena v socialistickej spoločnosti* (Bratislava: Institute for Health Education) pp. 108–10.

Girard, Alain and Roussel, Louis (1982) 'Ideal Family Size, Fertility, and Population Policy in Western Europe', *Population and Development Review*, vol. 8, no. 2 (June) pp. 323–44.

286   *Bibliography*

Glaser, William A. (1971) 'Socialized Medicine in Practice', in R. Elling (ed.) *National Health Care: Issues and Problems in Socialized Medicine* (New York: Atherton) pp. 38–59.

The Globe and Mail (Toronto) 26 October 1982. Interview with Murray Hardie, an executive director of a federal task force on microtechnology.

Glos, Z. (1978) 'Vliv sportu a tělocviku na trvání porodu', *Československá gynekologie*, vol. 43, no. 2 (April) pp. 119–21.

Gold, F. (1981) 'Technika výroby aspiračních kyret k provádění mini-interrupcí', *Československá gynekologie*, vol. 46, no. 6 (July) p. 494.

Gömori, Edith (1980) 'Special protective legislation and equality of employment opportunity for women in Hungary', *International Labour Review*, vol. 119, no. 1 (January–February) pp. 67–77.

Gordon, Linda (1976) *Woman's Body, Woman's Right. A Social History of Birth Control in America* (New York: Grossman Publishers).

Graham, Hilary (1977) 'Images of Pregnancy in Antenatal Literature', in R. Dingwald (ed.) *Health Care and Health Knowledge*, (London: Croom Helm).

Graham, Hilary and Oakley, Ann (1981) 'Competing Ideologies of Reproduction: Medical and Maternal Perspectives on Pregnancy and Childbirth', in H. Roberts (ed.) *Women and Health Care* (London: Routledge & Kegan Paul).

Greenglass, Esther (1981) 'A Canadian Study of Psychological Adjustment After Abortion', in Paul Sachdev (ed). *Abortion: Readings and Research* (Toronto: Butterworth) pp. 76–90.

Greer, Germaine (1984) *Sex and Destiny: The Politics of Human Fertility* (London: Secker & Warburg).

Gronský, L. (1972) 'Prevence v prenatální péči', *Československá gynekologie*, vol. 37, no. 9 (December).

Haire, Doris (1973) 'The Cultural Warping of Childbirth', *Environmental Child Health*, June (Special Issue).

Hajná, Zdeňka (1980) 'Výchova k manželství a odpovědnému rodičovství', *Sociální politika*, vol. 6, no. 2 (February).

Hall, M.H., Ching, P.K., MacGillivray, I. (1980) 'Is Routine Antenatal Care Worth While?' *The Lancet* (12 July) pp. 78–80.

Hanmer, J. (1981) 'Sex predetermination, artifical insemination and the maintenance of male-dominated culture'. in H. Roberts (ed.) *Women, Health and Reproduction* (London: Routledge & Kegan Paul) pp. 163–90.

Hanmer, J. and Allen P. (1980) 'Reproductive Engineering – The Final Solution', in L. Birke and S. Best (eds) *Alice Through the Microscope: The Power of Science Over Women's Lives*, (London: Virago).

Hansluwka, Harold (1980) 'Needed Research' in Arthur A. Campbell (ed.) *Social, Economic and Health Aspects of Low Fertility*, NIH Publication no. 80–100, (US Department of Health, Education and Welfare) pp. 299–319.

Hansson, Carola and Lidén, Karin (1983) *Moscow Women. Thirteen Interviews*, translated by Gerry Bothmer, George Blecher and Lane Blecher. Introduction by Gail Warshofsky Lapidus (New York: Pantheon).

Harding, Neil (1984) 'Conclusion' in Neil Harding (ed.) *The State in Socialist Society* (London: Macmillan in association with St Antony's College, Oxford) pp. 299–311.

Harris, Jeffrey E. (1982) 'Prenatal Medical Care and Infant Mortality', in Victor R. Fuchs (ed.) *Economic Aspects of Health* (University of Chicago Press) pp. 15–52.

Havelka, Jaroslav (1972) 'Hlavní směry naší populačni politiky', in *Děti, naše budoucnost*, pamphlet published by the Government Population Committee and the Central Committee of the National Front, Prague.

Havelka, Jaroslav (1978) 'Social policy and population development in Czechoslovakia', *Demosta*, vol. 11, no. 1, pp. 9–14.

Havelka, Jaroslav (1979) 'Výsledky a úkoly společenské pomoci rodinám s dětmi', *Sociální politika*, vol. 15, no. 6 (June).

Havelka, Jaroslav (1981) 'Population Policy', in *The Family in Socialist Czechoslovakia* (Prague: Orbis) pp. 7–18.

Havelka, Jaroslav and Ottomanský, J. (1983) 'Position of Young Generation in Czechoslovakia', *Demosta*, vol. 16, nos. 3–4, pp. 12–17.

Haverkamp, Albert D. and Orleans, Miriam (1983) 'An Assessment of Electronic Fetal Monitoring', *Women and Health*, vol. 7, nos. 3/4, pp. 115–34.

Havlík, I. *et al.* (1978) 'Výsledky psychoprofylaktické přípravy k porodu', *Československá gynekologie*, vol. 43, no. 10 (December) pp. 776–9.

Havránek, František (1975) 'Umělé přerušení raných stádií těhotenství (regulace menstruace, mini-interrupce)', *Československá gynekologie*, vol. 44, no. 5 (June) pp. 374–8.

Havránek, František (1978) 'Antikoncepce a umělé přerušení těhotenství, jejich role při regulaci porodnosti', *Demografie*, vol. 20, no. 4, pp. 356–8.

Havránek, František (1979a) 'Možnosti medicíny při regulaci porodnosti', *Populační zprávy*, nos. 1–3, pp. 51–5.

Havránek, František (1979b) 'Fertilita a možnosti antikoncepce v adolescenci', *Československá gynekologie*, vol. 44, no. 4 (May).

Havránek, František (1981) 'Význam mini-interrupce (regulace menstruace) jako metody regulace porodnosti', *Československá gynekologie*, vol. 46, no. 6 (July) pp. 481–5.

Havránek, František and Šmeral, P. (1979) 'Přerušení raných stádií těhotenství (regulace menstruace, mini-interrupce) v praxi', *Československá gynekologie*, vol. 44, no. 8 (September) pp. 561–6.

Hay, John (1982) 'Canada's leaking immigration lifeboat', *Macleans*, vol. 95, no. 45 (8 November) p. 56.

Health United States 1980, DHHS Publication no. (PHS) 81–1232.

Heczko, P. *et al.* (1970) 'Vliv interrupce první gravidity na gestaci' *Československá gynekologie*, vol. 35, no. 6, pp. 333–4.

Heer, David (1968) 'The Childbearing Functions of the Soviet Family', in D.R. Brown (ed.) *The Role and Status of Women in the Soviet Union* (New York: Teachers College Press) pp. 125–9.

Heer, David (1981) 'Soviet Population Policy: Four Model Futures', in Helen Desfosses (ed.) *Soviet Population Policy. Conflicts and Constraints* (New York: Pergamon Press) pp. 124–54.

Heitlinger, Alena (1975) 'Births in East Europe', *New Society*, 3 July, p. 20.

Heitlinger, Alena (1976) 'Pro-Natalist Population Policies in Czechoslovakia', *Population Studies*, vol. 30, no. 1 (March) pp. 123–35.

Heitlinger, Alena (1979) *Women and State Socialism. Sex Inequality in the*

Soviet Union and Czechoslovakia (London, Montreal: Macmillan/McGill
    –Queen's University Press).
Hejda, Stanislav (1979) 'Nutrition and nutrition state of the population in the
    Czechoslovak Socialist Republic', *Demosta*, vol. 12, no. 4, pp. 110–14.
Hepner, Vladimír (1980) *Postoje české veřejnosti k problematice k manželství
    a rodičovství* (Praha: Institute for Research of Culture).
Herinková, Libuše *et al.* (1981) 'Psychologické aspekty týmového vyšetření
    dětí porozených koncem pánevním', *Psychológia i patopsychológia dieťata*,
    vol. 16, no. 1, pp. 45–9.
Hinšt, J. and Brucháč, D. (1981) 'Vplyv dopravného letectva na reprodukčný
    systém ženy', *Československá gynekologie*, vol. 46, no. 6, pp. 456–9.
Hirschman, Charles (1979) *Trends in Breast Feeding Among American
    Women*, DHEW Publication (PHS) 79–1979 (November).
*Hlavní směry a opatření k dalšímu rozvoji výchovy k manželství a rodičovství
    v ČSR do roku 1990* (1977) December (Praha: Ministry of Labour and
    Social Affairs).
Hluchy, Patricia (1983) 'Of human bonding', *Macleans* (10 October).
Hodanová, Zdenka (1977) 'Zdravotní výchova jako profese ženy-SZP', in
    Zdravotná výchova a žena v socialistickej spoločnosti (Bratislava: Institute
    for Health Education) pp. 56–9.
Hodgson, Jane E. (1981a) 'Editor's addendum', in Jane Hodgson (ed.)
    Abortion and Sterilization: Medical and Social Aspects (London:
    Academic Press) p. 224.
Hodgson, Jane E. (1981b) 'Abortion by vacuum aspiration', in Jane Hodg-
    son (ed.) *Abortion and Sterilization: Medical and Social Aspects* (London:
    Academic Press) pp. 215–9.
Holland, Barbara, and McKevitt, Teresa (1985) 'Maternity care in the Soviet
    Union', in B. Holland (ed.) *Soviet Sisterhood* (Bloomington: Indiana
    University Press) pp. 145–76.
Holmes, Helen B., Hoskins, Betty B., and Gross, Michael (eds) (1981) *The
    Custom-Made Child? Women-Centered Perspectives* (Clifton, New Jersey:
    The Humana Press).
Holubová, V. (1981) 'Předcházejme konfliktům na pracovišti', *Zdravotnická
    pracovnice*, vol. 31, no. 11.
Horáková, M. (1982) 'Psychologicko-výchovné aspekty v práci ženskej se-
    stry', *Zdravotnická pracovnice*, vol. 32, no. 1, pp. 44–8.
Horanská, E. (1982) 'Trend dojčenia', *Československá pediatrie*, vol. 37, no.
    2 (February) pp. 90–1.
Houštek, Josef (1978) 'Význam kojení pro zdravý vývoj dítěte', *Populační
    zprávy*, nos. 1–2, pp. 42–4.
Houštek, Josef and Syrovátka, A. (1982) 'Výzkum v oblasti reprodukce a
    pediatrie v 6. pětiletce', *Československá pediatrie*, vol. 37, no. 1 (January)
    pp. 3–8.
Hrabětová, M. *et al.* (1975) *Práca odborov medzi ženami* (Bratislava: Práca).
Hrdá, Milada (1977) 'Sociálně právní ochrana ženy v pracovněprávních
    vztazích a její hmotné zabezpečení v době těhotenství a mateřství', in
    Vlasta Brablcová (ed.) *Manželství, rodina, rodičovství* (Praha: Horizont)
    pp. 80–104.

Bibliography 289

Hyde, Gordon (1974) *The Soviet Health Service. A Historical and Comparative Study* (London: Lawrence and Wishart).
Hynie, Josef (1977) 'Příprava na manželství a rodičovství', in Vlasta Brablcová (ed.) *Manželství, rodina, rodičovství* (Praha: Horizont) pp. 105–6.
Ispa, Jean (1983) 'Soviet and American Childbearing Experiences and Attitudes: A Comparison', *Slavic Review* vol. 42, no. 1 (Spring) pp. 1–13.
J. K. (1978) 'Poznámky teratologa k činnosti prenatálních poraden', *Československá gynekologie*, vol. 43, no. 9, pp. 660–7.
Jancar, Barbara Wolfe (1978) *Women Under Communism* (Baltimore: Johns Hopkins University Press).
Janovský, M. and Procházková, E. (1981) 'Některé fyziologické předpoklady úspěšné laktace', *Československá pediatrie*, vol. 36, no. 1 (January) pp. 27–9.
Janssen-Jurreit, Marielouise (1982) *Sexism. The Male Monopoly on History and Thought*. Translated from the German by Verne Moberg (New York: Farrar, Straus and Giroux).
Jarolímek I. (1980) 'Obsahová přestavba lékařského studia', *Československé zdravotnictví*, vol. 28, no. 10 (October) pp. 431–4.
Jarolímek I. (1982) 'Učebnice pro lékařské fakulty a zásady jejich tvorby', *Československé zdravotnictví*, vol. 30, no. 1 (January) pp. 39–42.
Jellife, D.B. and Jellife, E.P.P. (1978) *Human Milk in the Modern World* (Oxford University Press).
Jeník, Pavel (1980) *The Czechoslovak Educational System* (Prague: Orbis).
Jerrie, J. (1958) *Uvolnění potratu v našem státě* (Praha: Ministerstvo zdravotnictví).
Jerrie, J. et al. (1961) *Organizace a metodika péče o ženu v ČSSR (v oboru porodnictví a gynekologie)* (Praha: Státní zdravotnické nakladatelství).
Jersáková, L. (1972) 'Aktivní ošetřování rodíčích žen na porodním sále', *Československá gynekologie*, vol. 37, no. 10 (December) pp. 750–3.
Johnson, Terence J. (1972) *Professions and Power* (London: Macmillan).
Jones, R.A.K. and Belsy, E.M. (1977) 'Breast Feeding in an Inner London Borough – A Study of Cultural Factors', *Social Science and Medicine*, vol. 11, pp. 175–9.
Jordan, Brigitte (1980) *Birth in Four Cultures. A Crosscultural Investigation of Childbirth in Yucatan, Holland, Sweden and the United States* (St Albans, Vermont and Montreal, Quebec: Eden Press).
Kadlecová, Zdeňka (ed.) (1974) *Z průzkumu mezi mladými ženami* (Praha: Organizační a tiskové oddělení ministerstva práce a sociálních věcí ČSR).
Kadlecová, Zdeňka and Brtníková, Marta (1977) 'Manželství, rodina a rodičovství ve světle sociálních průzkumů v ČSSR', in Vlasta Brablcová (ed.) *Manželství rodina, rodičovství* (Praha: Horizont) pp. 107–14.
Kadrnková, M. (1981) 'Nežádoucí účinky steroidní antikoncepce', *Československá gynekologie*, vol. 46, no. 6 (July) pp. 473–4.
Kaloyanova, Fina (1976) 'Women at Work', *World Health* (August–September) pp. 32–5.
Kaser, Michael (1976) *Health Care in the Soviet Union and Eastern Europe* (London: Croom Helm).
Kazda, S. et al. (1961) 'Lékařské vedení porodu', in *10 let boje za zdraví nové*

generace 1951–1961. Přehled vědecké činnosti Ústavu pro péči o matku a dítě (Praha: ÚPMD) pp. 43–53.

Kemény, István (1982) 'The Unregistered Economy in Hungary', *Soviet Studies*, vol. 34, no. 3 (July) pp. 349–66.

Kitzinger, Sheila (1962) *The Experience of Childbirth* (Harmondsworth: Penguin).

Kitzinger, Sheila (1980) *The Experience of Breastfeeding* (Harmondsworth: Penguin).

Klaus, Marshall H. and Kennell, John H. (1976) *Maternal–infant bonding. The impact of early separation or loss on family development* (Saint Louis: C.V. Mosby).

Kliment, Peter *et al.* (1977) 'Žena a zdravotné informácie', in *Zdravotná výchova a žena v socialistickej spoločnosti* (Bratislava: Institute for Health Education) pp. 85–8.

Kliment, V. (1973) 'Poznámky k pracovnej neschopnosti žien pri ambulantnej liečbe' *Československá gynekologie*, vol. 38, no. 7 (August) pp. 527–8.

Kliment, V. (1977) 'K niektorým otázkam LTV v gynekológii a porodnictve', *Československá gynekologie*, vol. 47, no. 3.

Kliment, V. *et al.* (1972a) 'Je správný názov DANA?' *Československá gynekologie*, vol. 37, no. 7 (September) pp. 496–7.

Kliment, V. *et al.* (1972b) 'K problému dalších možností využitia kvalifikácie ženskej sestry na oddelení polikniky a na obvodě', *Československá gynekologie*, vol. 37, no. 10 (December) p. 756.

Kliment, V. *et al.* (1974) 'Psychosociálne aspekty predčasných pôrodov', *Československanska gynekologie*, vol. 39, no. 3 (April) pp. 197–8.

Klinger, A. (1977) 'Hungary', in Bernard Berelson (ed.) *Population Policy in Developed Countries* (New York: McGraw-Hill) pp. 225–69.

Knaus, William A. (1981) *Inside Russian Medicine: An American Doctor's First-Hand Report* (New York: Everest House).

Koch, Jaroslav (1977) *Výchova kojence v rodině* (Praha: Avicenum).

Koch, Jaroslav (1978) *Total Baby Development* (New Jersey: (Wallaby).

Koch, Jaroslav (1982) *Superbaby* (Prague: Orbis).

'Koordinační porada o výzkumných úkolech s populační problematikou Žďáň, February 21–25' (1978) *Demografie*, vol. 20, no. 2, pp. 160–4.

Kops, Jaromír (1981) 'Výskum mienky pacientov o pobyte v nemocnici', *Sociológia*, vol. 13, no. 14, pp. 452–8.

Kotásek, Alfred (1970) 'Následky po umělém přerušení těhotenství', *Československá gynekologie*, vol. 35, no. 6, pp. 325–8.

Kotásek, Alfred (1975) 'Péče o ženu v ČSR z hlediska porodníka a gynekologa', in *Rok ženy. Unesco 1975. Podkladové materiály* (Praha: Ministerstvo zdravotnictví, Ústav zdravotní výchovy) pp. 19–30.

Kotzmanova, Jiřina (1979) 'Hlavní úkoly naší zdravotní péče o ženu k Mezinárodnímu roku dítěte', *Československá gynekologie*, vol. 44, no. 1 (February).

Koubek, Josef (1974) *Populační politika evropských socialistických států v letech 1945-1972* (Praha: Vysoká škola ekonomická).

Koubek, Josef (1981) 'Populační politika Československé republiky v letech 1945-1980', *Demografie*, vol. 23, no. 1, pp. 32–50.

Kováčová, L. and Kováč, R. (1974) 'Sexuálný život mladých žien a dievčat po interrupcii', *Československá gynekologie*, vol. 39, no. 3 (April) pp. 218–9.

Kramer, John M. (1983) 'The Environmental Crisis in Eastern Europe: The Price for Progress', *Slavic Review*, vol. 42, no. 2 (Summer) pp. 204–20.

Křesťan, Rudolf (1985) 'Místo narození: Brno', *Mladý svět*, vol. 27, no. 22, May 22–27.

Kříšťová, Zdena (1977) *Ako pracuje komisia žien základnej organizácie ROH* (Bratislava: Práca).

Kubica, M. et al, (1978) 'Postpartálná sterilizácia', *Československá gynekologie*, vol. 43, no. 8 (September) pp. 607–8.

Kučera, Z. (1981) 'Názory na přípravu k manželství a rodičovství', *Československá pediatrie*, vol. 36, no. 7 (July) pp. 441–4.

Kutěj, B. and Hejná, D. (1972) 'Struktura pracovního času zdravotních sester gynekologického oddělení okresní nemocnice', *Československá gynekologie*, vol. 37, no. 10, pp. 763–4.

Květoň, J. and Vojta, M. (1972) 'Postoje žen k umělému přerušení těhotenství a úkoly gynekologa', *Československá gynekologie*, vol. 37, no. 7 (September) pp. 533–4.

Kvíčalová, Vlasta and Zemanová, Jana (1978) *Společenská péče o rodinu a děti. Odpovědi na otázky z nemocenského pojištění pracovníků* (Praha: Práce).

Kvíz, D. (1972) 'Duplicity v dokumentaci ženských středisek', *Československá gynekologie*, vol. 37, no. 8 (October).

Kvíz, D. (1978) 'Zamyšlení nad dvaceti lety platnosti zákona č. 68/57 Sb', *Československá gynekologie*, vol. 43, no. 6 (July) pp. 452–3.

Kvíz, D. (1982) 'Příspěvek k historii vývoje pracovní psychologie gynekologů', *Československá gynekologie*, vol. 47, no. 3 (April) pp. 187–91.

Laně, Václav (1967) *Kapitoly o zdraví a hygieně ženy* (Plzeň: Západočeské nakladatelství).

Laufe, Leonard E. (1979) 'Menstrual Regulation – International Perspectives', in Gerald Zatuchni, et al. (eds) *Pregnancy Termination Procedures, Safety and New Developments* (Hagerstown: Harper & Row) pp. 78–81.

Lavigne, Yves (1983) 'Abortion: an issue around the world', *The Globe and Mail*, 3 February.

Leavitt, Judith and Walton, Whitney (1981) 'Down to Death's Door: Women's Perception of Childbirth', in *Childbirth: The Beginning of Motherhood*. Proceedings of the Second Motherhood Symposium of the Women's Studies Research Center, University of Wisconsin, Madison, 9 and 10 April, pp. 113–30.

Leboyer, Frederic (1975) *Birth Without Violence* (London: Wildwood House).

Lédr, J. (1972) 'Samostatné ordinace ženských sester', *Československá gynekologie*, vol. 37, no. 10, pp. 758–9.

Lesný, Ivan (1978) 'Plodnost poválečných kohort v ČSR', *Demografie*, vol. 20, no. 2, pp. 106–16.

Lewis, Jane (1980) *The Politics of Motherhood: Child and Maternal Welfare in England 1900–1939* (London and Montreal: Croom Helm and McGill–Queen's University Press).

Lindner, E. *et al.* (1977) 'Vývoj vaginálních porodnických operací na gynek.-porod. klinice v Olomouci za 15 let', *Československá gynekologie*, vol. 42, no. 7 (August) pp. 511–3.

Lipson, Juliene (1981) 'Cesarean Support Groups: Mutual Help and Education', *Women & Health*, vol. 6, nos. 3–4 (Fall/Winter) pp. 27–39.

Lozoff, Betsy (1981) 'What is "Natural" in Childbirth', in *Childbirth: The Beginning of Motherhood*. Proceedings of the Second Motherhood Symposium of the Women's Studies Research Center, University of Wisconsin, Madison, 9 and 10 April, pp. 137–44.

Luker, Kristin (1975) *Taking Chances: Abortion and the Decision not to Contracept* (Berkeley: University of California Press).

Luker, Kristin (1984) *Abortion and the Politics of Motherhood*. California Series on Social Choice and Political Economy (Berkeley: University of California).

Lumley, Judith and Astbury, Jill (1980) *Birth Rites Birth Rights. Childbirth Alternatives for Australian Parents* (Melbourne: Sphere Books).

McAuley, Alastair (1981) *Women's Work and Wages in the Soviet Union* (London: Allen & Unwin).

McDonnell, Kathleen (1984) *Not An Easy Choice. A Feminist Re-Examines Abortion* (Toronto: The Women's Press).

McIntosh, Alison C. (1981) 'Low Fertility and Liberal Democracy in Western Europe', *Population and Development Review*, vol. 7, no. 2, pp. 181–207.

McIntyre, Robert T. (1981) 'Demographic Policy and Sexual Equality: Value Conflicts and Policy Appraisal in Hungary and Romania', in Sharon Wolchik and A. Meyer (eds) *Women, State and Party in Eastern Europe* (Duke University Press).

Macintyre Sally (1976) 'Who Wants Babies: The Social Construction of "Instincts"', in Diana Leonard Barker and Sheila Allen (eds) *Sexual Divisions and Society, Process and Change* (London: Tavistock Publications).

Macintyre, Sally (1977) 'Childbirth: the Myth of the Golden Age', *World Medicine*, vol. 12, no. 17.

Mackŭ, F. *et al* (1978) Umělé přerušení těhotenství primigravid jako rizikový faktor dalšího těhotenství', *Československá gynekologie*, vol. 43, no. 5 (June) pp. 340–2.

Macura, Miloš (1980) 'Low Fertility and the Labor Force,' in A. Campbell (ed.) *Social Economy and Health Aspects of Low Fertility*. NIH Publication No. 80–100.

Macura, Miloš (1981) 'Evolving Population Policies', in Henry P. David and Robert T. McIntyre, *Reproductive Behavior: Central and Eastern European Experience* (New York: Springer) pp. 30–52.

Maine, Deborah (1979) 'Does Abortion Affect Later Pregnancies?' *International Family Planning Perspectives*, vol. 5, no. 1 (March) pp. 22–5.

Makovický, E. and collective (1981) *Sociálne lekárstvo a organizácia zdravotníctva*: *Compendium*, second revised edition (Martin: Osveta).

Málek, Prokop (1982) 'Boj proti přežitkŭm v lékařské vědě, *Časopis lékařŭ českých*, vol. 121, no. 19 (May) pp. 577–9.

Bibliography 293

Mamonova, Tatyana and Matilsky, Sarah (eds) (1984) *Women and Russia : Feminist Writings from the Soviet Union* (Boston: Beacon Press).
Mareš, Josef and Brtníková, Marta (1976) *Výchova k rodičovství pro pracovníky ženského lékařství* (Praha: Ústav zdravotní výchovy).
Masterman, Sue (1984) 'A War on Abortions', *Macleans*, (23 April) p. 12.
Matějček, Z., Dytrych, Z. and Schüller, V. (1978) 'Children from Unwanted Pregnancies', *Acta Psychiatrica Scandinavia*, vol. 57, pp. 67–90.
Matějček, Z., Dytrych, Z. and Schüller, V. (1979) "The Prague Study of Children Born from Unwanted Pregnancies', *International Journal of Mental Health*, vol. 7, pp. 63–77.
Matějček, Z., Dytrych, Z. and Schüller, V. (1980) 'Follow-up Study of Children Born from Unwanted Pregnancies', *International Journal of Behavioral Development*, vol. 3, pp. 243–51.
Maternity and Child Care Leave in Canada (1983) (Ottawa: Labour Canada).
Matoušek, Miroslav (1980) *První rok dítěte* (Praha: Avicenum).
Maxwell, Robert T. (1981) *Health and Wealth. An International Study of Health-Care Spending* (Lexington: Lexington Books and D. C. Heath).
Měcíř, M. (1961) 'Problémy výživy novorozenců, kojenců a batolat', in *10 let boje za zdraví nové generace 1951–1961. Přehled vědecké činnosti ústavu pro péči o matku a dítě* (Praha: ÚPMD) pp. 85–7.
Mendl, V. *et al.* (1982) 'Zkušenosti s ošetřováním matky a novorozence', *Československá pediatrie*, vol. 37, no. 2 (February) pp. 88–89.
Meszárová, A. *et al.* (1973) 'Práceschopnost pre komplikácie po zavedení IUD', *Československá gynekologie*, vol. 38, no. 7, pp. 541–2.
Michlíček, J. (1976) 'Příspěvek k retrospektivnímu porodnickému sledování dětí s psychomotorickou retardací', in *Aktuální problémy v porodnictví.* Proceedings from the 17th inter-county obstetrical seminar of southern and northern Moravian counties, 22–23 April. Uherské Hradiště.
Michlíček, J. (1978) 'Příspěvek k problematice převádění žen na jinou práci v graviditě a mateřství v praxi obvodního a závodního gynekologa', *Československá gynekologie*, vol. 43, no. 5 (June) pp. 397–8.
Mieczkowski, Bogdan (1982) *Social Services for Women in Eastern Europe* (Charlestown, Illinois: The Association for the Study of Nationalities (USSR and East Europe)).
Millard, Frances L. (1981) 'The Health of the Polish Health Service', *Critique*, no. 15, pp. 57–67.
Millard, Frances L. (1982) 'Health Care in Poland: From Crisis to Crisis', *International Journal of Health Services*, vol. 12, no. 13, pp. 497–515.
Moen, Elizabeth W. (1979) 'What Does Control over Our Bodies Really Mean?' *International Journal of Women's Studies*, vol. 2, no. 2, pp. 129–43.
Mohapl, M. and Dobešová, B. (1978) 'Problematika žen s nežádoucím těhotenstvím', *Československá gynekologie*, vol. 43, no. 8 (September) pp. 605–7.
Molyneux, Maxine (1981) 'Women in Socialist Societies: Problems of Theory and Practice', in Kate Young, Carol Wolkowitz and Roslyn McCullagh (eds) *Of Marriage and the Market: women's subordination in international perspective* (London: CSE Books) pp. 167–202.

Morokvasić, Mirjana (1981) 'Sexuality and Control of Procreation', in Kate Young, Carol Wolkowitz and Roslyn McCullagh (eds) *Of Marriage and the Market: women's subordination in international perspective* (London: CSE Books) pp. 127–43.

Mosher, William D. (1981) *Contraceptive Utilization, United States 1976*, DHHS Publication no. 81–1983 (March).

Mrkvička, Jiří (1977) 'Psychologie soužití, in *Škola pro snoubence a novomanžele* (Praha: Avicenum) pp. 15–85.

Müller, C. (1971) 'Sociální problematika v ženském lékařství', *Československá gynekologie*, vol. 36, no. 5 (June) pp. 271–3.

Müller, C., Šturma, J. and Zelenková, M. (1972) 'Problémy sociální gynekologie', *Československá gynekologie*, vol. 37, no. 8 (October) pp. 568–71.

Muresan, Petre and Copil, Ioan (1974) 'Romania' in Bernard Berelson (ed.) *Population Policy in Developed Countries*, (New York: McGraw-Hill) pp. 355–81.

Murphy, Julie (1984) 'Egg Farming and Women's Future', in R. Arditti, R. Duelli Klein and S. Minden (eds) *Test-Tube Women. What Future for Motherhood?* (London: Pandora Press) pp. 68–75.

National Health Care Expenditures in Canada, 1970–1982 (no date) (Ottawa: Health and Welfare Canada).

Navarro, Vicente (1977) *Social Security and Medicine in the USSR. A Marxist Critique* (Lexington and Toronto: D. C. Heath).

Němcová, J. and Langrová, J. (1977) 'Domov pro osamělé matky', *Populační zprávy*, nos. 1–2, pp. 49–52.

Nentvichová, Božena (1982) 'Children and Young People in Czechoslovakia', *Demosta*, vol. 15, no. 3, pp. 3–6.

Niederle, Petr (1982) 'Rozvoj společenské péče o rodinu a děti a zvláštní skupiny obyvatelstva v sedmé pětiletce', *Sociální politika*, vol. 8, no. 4 (April), pp. 74–5.

Oakley, Ann (1979a) *From Here to Maternity. Becoming a Mother* (Oxford: Martin Robertson).

Oakley, Ann (1979b) 'A Case of Maternity: Paradigms of Women as Maternity Cases', *Signs*, vol. 4, no. 4 (Summer) pp. 607–31.

Oakley, Ann (1980) *Women Confined: Toward a Sociology of Childbirth* (Oxford: Martin Robertson).

Oakley, Ann (1982) 'The Relevance of the History of Medicine to an Understanding of Current Change: Some Comments from the Domain of Antenatal Care', *Social Science and Medicine*, vol. 16, no. 6, pp. 667–74.

Oakley, Ann (1983) *The Captured Womb. A History of Medical Care of Pregnant Women* (Oxford: Martin Robertson).

O'Brien, Mary (1981) *The Politics of Reproduction* (London: Routledge & Kegan Paul).

Ouřadová, Dagmar (1981) 'Aby se děti nerodily dvakrát (aneb co je to rooming-in)', *Mladá fronta*, 13 June.

Oxorn, Harry and Foote, William R. (1975) *Human Labor and Birth*, third edition (New York: Appleton-Century-Crofts).

Pancurák, J. (1973) 'Vývoj pracovní neschopnosti v českých zemích a její gynekologické příčiny, *Československá gynekologie*, vol. 38, no. 7 (August) pp. 527–8.

Paoli, Chantal (1982) 'Women workers and maternity: some examples from Western Europe', *International Labour Review*, vol. 121, no. 1, pp. 1–16.

Parmeggiani, L. (1982) 'State of the art: recent legislation on workers' health and safety', *International Labour Review*, vol. 121, no. 3 (May–June)pp. 271–85.

Parmelee, Donna, Henderson, Gail and Cohen, Myron S. (1982) 'Medicine Under Socialism: Some Observations on Yugoslavia and China', *Social Science and Medicine*, vol. 16, pp. 1389–96.

Parsons, Jacquelynne Eccles (1983) 'Sexual Socialization and Gender Roles in Childhood', in Elizabeth Rice Allgeier and Naomi B. McCormick (eds) *Changing Boundaries. Gender Roles and Sexual Behavior* (Palo Alto: Mayfield), pp. 19–48.

Pávek, František *et al.* (1979) *Manželská čítanka* (Praha: Mladá fronta).

Pavlík Zdeněk (1978) 'Baby Boom in Czechoslovakia', *Intercom*, vol. 6, no. 6, pp. 8–9.

Pavlík, Zdeněk (1982) 'Interview', *Rudé právo*, 12 June.

Pavlík Zdeněk and Wynnyczuk, Vladimír (1974) 'Czechoslovakia', in Bernard Berelson (ed.) *Population Policy in Developed Countries* (New York: McGraw-Hill).

Pavlík Zdeněk and Zbořilová, J. (1978) 'Changes in Czechoslovak Marital Fertility', in M. Niphins-Nell (ed.) *Demographic Aspects of the Changing Status of Women* (Leiden: Nijhoff).

Pavlusová, J. (1980) 'Význam sociálního lékařství pro teorii prevence rozvinuté socialistické společnosti', *Československé zdravotnictví*, vol. 28, no. 6 (June) pp. 243–50.

Petro, Mikuláš (1980) *Cesta k socialistickému zdravotnictví* (Praha: Avicenum).

Petchesky Pollack, Rosalind (1980) 'Reproductive Freedom: Beyond A Woman's Right to Choose', *Signs*, vol. 5 no. 4 (Summer) pp. 661–85.

Petchesky Pollack, Rosalind (1984) *Abortion and Woman's Choice. The State, Sexuality and Reproductive Freedom* (Boston: Northeastern University Press).

Píschová, Zelmíra (1977) 'Vplyv pohyblovej aktivity na telesnú zdatnosť a zdravie žien', in *Zdravotná výchova a žena v socialistickej spoločnosti* (Bratislava: Institute for Health Education) pp. 34–8.

Pokorný, Jaroslav (1972) 'Pracující žena v lehkém průmyslu', in *Péče ženského lékaře o pracující ženu, zejména ve vztahu k pracovní neschopnosti.* Proceedings from the 13th inter-county seminar of southern and northern Moravian counties, 26 May 1972, Razula in Velké Karlovice, pp. 19–21.

Poliaková, Eva (1977) 'Príklad využitia programovej výučby v zdravotnej výchove medzi mladými dievčaty', in *Zdravotná výchova a žena v socialistickej spoločnosti* (Bratislava: Institute for Health Education) pp. 89–91.

Poradovský, Karol (1977a) 'Úlohy krajských a okresných odborníkov pre starostlivosť' o ženu v porodnickej prevencii', *Československá gynekologie*, vol. 42, no. 8, pp. 590–1.

Poradovský, Karol (1977b) 'Problematika porodnosti a potratovosti v socialistickej spoločnosti dneška,' in *Zdravotná výchova a žena v socialistickej spoločnosti* (Bratislava: Institute for Health Education) pp. 60–3.

Poradovský, Karol (1979) 'Názory, postoje a chovanie mládeže vo vztahu k rodičovství', *Československá gynekologie*, vol. 44, no. 6 (July) pp. 428–49.

Poradovský, Karol *et al.* (1981) 'Nové zásady pri vedení pôrodov koncom pánvovym a ich dopad na perinatálnu úmrtnosť', *Československá gynekologie*, vol. 46, no. 3 (April) pp. 163–9.

Poradovský, J. Poradovský, K., and Frič, D. (1977) 'Naše skúsenosti so sterilizačnými operáciami', *Československà gynekologie*, vol. 42, no. 3 pp. 191–2.

Pouťuch, A. *et al.* (1965) *Duševná a tělesná príprava těhotnej ženy na pôrod.* (Bratislava: Slovenský ústav zdravotnickej osvěty).

Pouťuch, A., *et al.* (1972) 'Náplň gynekóloga v ambulantní praxi', *Československá gynekologie*, vol. 37, no. 8 (October) pp. 607–9.

Presl, J. (1977) 'Vývoj spotřeby perorálních steroidních kontraceptiv v ČSR a SSR', *Československá gynekologie*, vol. 42, no. 7 (August) pp. 543–4.

Presl, J. *et al.* (1982) 'Reprodukční medicína a biologie v gynekologii', *Československá gynekologie*, vol. 47, no. 2, pp. 89–91.

Procházka, J., and Černoch, A. (1970) 'Pohlavní styk v těhotenství', *Československá gynekologie*, vol. 35, no. 5 (June) pp. 282–6.

Prokopec, Jaroslav (1975) *Zdraví a společnost* (Praha: Avicenum).

Prokopec, Jiří and Mikšík, Oldřich (1978) 'Pražský výzkum psychické zátěže zaměstnaných žen-matek', *Demografie*, vol. 20, no. 1.

Prokopová, J. (1974) 'Struktūra pracovního času sester pracujících na ženských odděleních nemocnic', *Československá gynekologie*, vol. 39, no. 7 (August) pp. 544–8.

Průcha, Miroslav (1981) 'Social Security Measures', in *The Family in Socialist Czechoslovakia* (Prague: Orbis) pp. 19–30.

Pudlák, Pavel (1978) 'Editorial' *Czechoslovak Medicine*, vol. 1, no. 1.

Reid, M. E. and McIlwaine, G. M. (1980) 'Consumer Opinion of a Hospital Antenatal Clinic', *Social Science and Medicine*, vol. 14A, pp. 363–8.

Rich, Adrienne (1976) *Of Woman Born. Motherhood as Experience and Institution* (New York: W. W. Norton).

Riessman, Catherine Kohler (1983) 'Women and Medicalization: A New Perspective', *Social Policy*, vol. 14, no. 1 (Summer) pp. 3–18.

Riska, Elianne (1982) 'Health Education and its Ideological Content', *Acta Sociologica*, vol. 25, Supplement, pp. 41–6.

Robinson, David (1981) 'Self-help groups in primary health care', *World Health Forum*, vol. 2, no. 2, pp. 185–91.

Rödling, Jiří (1980) *Další vzdělávání lékařů v ČSSR* (Praha: Avicenum).

Romalis, Coleman (1981) 'Taking Care of the Little Woman: Father–Physician Relations during Pregnancy and Childbirth', in Shelly Romalis (ed.) *Childbirth Alternatives to Medical Control* (Austin: University of Texas Press) pp. 92–121.

Rose, Hilary and Hanmer, Jalna (1976) 'Women's Liberation, Reproduction and the Technological Fix', in D. L. Barker and S. Allen (eds) *Sexual Divisions and Society: Process and Change* (London: Tavistock) pp. 199–223.

Rothenberg, P. B. (1980) 'Communication about sex and birth control between mothers and their adolescent children', *Population and Environment*, vol. 3, pp. 35–50.

Rothman, Barbara (1982) *In Labour. Women and Power in the Birthplace* (London: Junction Books).

Rothman, Barbara (1984) 'The Meanings of Choice in Reproductive Technology', in R. Arditti, R. Duelli Klein and S. Minden (eds) *Test-Tube Women. What Future for Motherhood?* (London: Pandora Press) pp. 23–34.

Russo, Nancy Felipe (1979) 'Overview: Sex Roles, Fertility and the Motherhood Mandate', *Psychology of Women Quarterly*, vol. 4, no. 1 (Fall) pp. 7–15.

Ruzek, Sheryl Burt (1979) *The Women's Health Movement. Feminist Alternatives to Medical Control* (New York: Praeger).

Ryan, Michael (1978) *The Organisation of Soviet Medical Care* (Oxford: Blackwell/Martin Robertson).

Rychtaříková, Jitka (1982) 'Vývoj kojenecké úmrtnosti', *Demografie*, vol. 24, no. 1, pp. 21–4.

Rydell, Lars H. (1976) 'Trends in Infant Mortality: Medical Advances or Socioeconomic Changes', *Acta Sociologica*, vol. 19, no. 2, pp. 47–68.

Ryder, Norman B. (1974) 'The Family in Developed Countries', *Scientific American*, vol. 231, no. 3 (September) pp. 123–30.

Rýdl, Drahomír (1982) '1981 Microcensus and Its Basic Results', *Demosta*, vol. 15, no. 3, pp. 16–24.

Říčan, P. (1980) 'Ke vztahu mezi lékařem a pacientami', *Československé zdravotnictví*, vol. 28, nos. 8–9 (September) pp. 372–8.

Sayers, Janet (1982) *Biological Politics. Feminist and Anti-Feminist Perspectives* (London and New York: Tavistock Publications).

Schiff, Gary S. (1978) 'The Politics of Population Policy in Israel', *Forum*, nos. 28–29 (Winter) pp. 173–92.

Schmidt, K. and Tarina, F. (1972) 'Poznámky k problémom nášho populáčneho vývoja a praxa zákona o UPT', *Československá gynekologie*, vol. 37, no. 7 (September).

Schvarcová, Mária (1973) *Systém populačných dávok v ČSSR*, (Bratislava: Výzkumný ústav životnej úrovne).

Schvarcová, Mária (1978) 'Životné a pracovné podmienky matiek,' in *Pracovné podmienky žien ve výrobnej sfére* (Bratislava: Dom techniky CSVTS) pp. 71–112.

Schvarcová, Mária (1979) 'Niektore poznatky o prognózách v oblasti populačnej klimy v ČSSR z hladiska vydatých ekonomicky činných žien s nezaopatrenými detmi (výsledky empirického výzkumu)', *Populační zprávy*, nos. 1–2.

Schwarz, Karl (1980) 'Implications for Public Health of Stationary and Declining Populations, in Arthur A. Campbell (ed.) *Social, Economic and Health Aspects of Low Fertility*, NIH Publication no. 80–100 (US Department of Health Education and Welfare).

Scott, Hilda (1974) *Does Socialism Liberate Women? Experiences from Eastern Europe* (Boston: Beacon Press).

Scott, Hilda (1978) 'Eastern European Women in Theory and Practice', *Women's Studies International Quarterly*, vol. 1, pp. 180–99.

'Serena: An Alternative Approach to Family Planning in Canada' (1974) in Benjamin Schlesinger (ed.) *Family Planning in Canada. A Source Book* (University of Toronto Press).

Shusterman, Lisa Roseman (1979) 'Predicting the Psychological Consequences of Abortion', *Social Science and Medicine*, vol. 13A, pp. 683–89.

Shuval, Judith T (1983) *Newcomers and Colleagues: Soviet Immigrant Physicians in Israel*, with a Foreword by Mark G. Field (Houston: Cap and
Gown).

Sittková, B. (1979) 'Úkoly péče o ženu na závodech ve světle XV. sjezdu
KSČ', *Československá gynekologie*, vol. 44, no. 9 (November).

Sládek, M., Bártová, D., Kalužík, M. (1976) 'Psychologické a sociologické
problémy můžu a žen žádajících o umělou inseminaci', *Československá
gynekologie*, vol. 41, no. 1, pp. 41–3.

Slunský, Rudolf (1965) *Žena a porod. Psychoprofylaktická příprava k porodu. Tělocvik pro těhotné* (Ostrava: Společnost pro šíření politických a
vědeckých znalostí).

Snowden, R. and Mitchell, G. D. (1981) *The Artificial Family. A Consideration of Artificial Insemination by Donor* (London: Allen & Unwin).

Snowden, R., Mitchell, G. D. and Snowden E. M. (1983) *Artificial Reproduction: A Social Investigation* (London: Allen & Unwin).

Sochor, T. (1971) 'Správa z poradného zboru hlavneho odborníka pre
gynekológiu a pôrodnictvo pri Ministerstve zdravotnictva SSR',
Československá gynekologie vol. 36, no. 3 (April) pp. 188–9.

Social and Labour Bulletin (1982) nos. 2–3, IL0.

Soderstrom, Richard M. (1979) 'Menstrual Regulation Technology', in Gerald T. Zatuchni *et al.* (eds) *Pregnancy Termination Procedures, Safety and
New Developments* (Hagerstown: Harper & Row).

Sokolík, L. and Lipenský, S. (1973) 'Pracovná neschopnost' po legálnom
prerušení tehotenstva u slobodných žien', *Československá gynekologie*,
vol. 37, no. 7 (August) pp. 523–4.

Sommerová, Jaroslava (1978a) 'Výroba sušené kojenecké a dětské mléčné
výživy v ČSSR', *Populační zprávy*, pp. 48–50.

Sommerová, Jaroslava (1978b) 'Dětská výživa, dětské průmyslové zboží a
racionalizace práce v domácnosti', *Populační zprávy*, pp. 51–4.

Soukup, O. (1980) 'Sociální lékařství a ekonomika zdravotnictví' *Československá zdravotnictví*, vol. 28, no. 2 (February) pp. 52–4.

Srb, Vladimir (1979a) 'Šetření plodnosti (1977)', *Demografié*, vol. 21, nos. 1,
2, 3, 4.

Srb, Vladimir (1979b) 'Šetření plodnosti žen v ČSSR (1977)', *Populační
zprávy* , nos. 1–2, pp. 21–8.

Srb, Vladimir (1981a) 'Nové projekce obyvatelstva ČSSR do roku 2000',
Československá pediatrie, vol. 36, no. 1 (January) pp. 30–2.

Srb, Vladimir (1981b) 'Woman's Fertility in Czechoslovakia During
1970–1979', *Demosta*, vol. 14, no. 2, pp. 44–9.

Srb, Vladimir and Konečná A. (1977) 'Plodnost žen v ČSSR a její struktura v
letech 1960–1976', *Demografie*, vol. 19, no. 4, pp. 357–61.

Srp, B. *et al.* (1978) 'Intenzivní porodní péče z hlediska současných
požadavků', *Československá gynekologie*, vol. 43, no. 10, pp. 752–7.

Stacey, Margaret (1982) 'Comment on the Paper "The Political Economy of
Sexism in Industrial Health' by Marcia Felker', *Social Science and Medicine*, vol. 16, pp. 15–18.

Stach, J. *et al.* (1977) 'Vývoj potratů podle věků ženy', *Populační zprávy*,
nos. 1–2, pp. 33–5.

'Stále s matkou. Zaznamenávají příznivé výsledky', (1982) *Rudé právo*, 6 October.

Statistická ročenka ČSSR 1960 to 1984 (Praha).

Stetson, Dorothy M. (1973) 'Population Policy and the Limits of Government Capability in the United States' in Richard L. Clinton (ed.) *Population and Politics, New Directions in Political Science Research* (Lexington, Mass.: Lexington Books, and D.C. Heath) pp. 247–71.

Strong, P. M. (1979) 'Sociological Imperialism and the Profession of Medicine. A Critical Examination of the Thesis of Medical Imperialism', *Social Science and Medicine*, vol. 13A, pp. 199–215.

Suchá, Hana and Chlubnová, Božena (1979) *Rehabilitace v práci ženské sestry* (Brno: Institute for further education of middle-level health care workers).

Suchá, Helena (1981) 'Direct and Indirect Forms of Aid to Families with Children in Czechoslovakia', *Demosta*, vol. 14, no. 1, pp. 19–22.

Suk, V. (1979) 'Technizace v porodnictví', *Československá gynekologie*, vol. 44, no. 7 (August) pp. 477–80.

Suller, John. (1984) 'The Role of Ideology in Self-Help Groups', *Social Policy* (Winter) pp. 29–36.

Svobodová, Alena (1981) 'Zkušenosti dětí školního věku s kouřením cigaret', *Československá pediatrie*, vol. 36, no. 7 (July) pp. 400–2.

Svobodová Alena and Vodrážka, Rudolf (1977) *Výchova k rodičovství na základní škole*. Metodicky text pro učitele 1.–4. ročníku (Praha: Státní pedagogické nakladatelství).

Syrovátka, Augustín (1975) 'Žena a zdraví dítěte', in *Žena a rodina v socialistickej spoločnosti*. Collection of papers given at a scientific conference in Bratislava, 15–19 December 1975. (Slovak Union of Women) pp. 184–9.

Szalai, Julia (1981) 'Use and Abuse of Social Services and Benefits', *New Hungarian Quarterly* no. 84, pp. 148–53.

Šabata, Vladimír and Fišerová, Zdeňka (1974) *Výživa těhotné a kojící ženy* (Praha: Avicenum).

Šalda, Vladimír (1978) 'K současné potratovosti v ČSSR', *Populační zprávy*, nos. 1–2, pp. 19–24.

Šebek, V. (1977) 'Je ženská léčebná tělovýchova zanedbávána?' *Ceskoslovenská gynekologié*, vol. 47, no. 3.

Šipr, Květoslav (1972) 'Možnost širšího využívání teplotní metody regulace početí', *Československá gynekologie*, vol. 37, no. 7 (September) pp. 526–8.

Šipr, Květoslav (1975) *Přirozené plánované rodičovství* (Praha: Avicenum).

Šipr, Květoslav (1981) *Hovory o lásce* (Praha: Avicenum).

Škola pro snoubence a novomanžele (Praha: Avicenum, 1977).

Šráček, Jiří (1977) 'Antikoncepce', in Vlasta Brablcová (ed.) *Manželství, rodina, rodičovstvi* (Praha: Horizont) pp. 70–9.

Šráček, Jiří (1981) 'Některé trendy v současném porodnictví ve vztahu matka-dítě', *Československá gynekologié*, vol. 46, no. 3 (April) pp. 191–2.

Šráčková, D. (1981) 'K problematice řešení vztahu matka-dítě v neonatálním období', *Československá pediatrie*, vol. 36, no. 12 (December) pp. 689–92.

Šráčková, D. *et al.* (1975) 'Přiložení novorozence k prsu bezprostředně po narození', *Československá gynekologie*, vol. 40, no. 1, pp. 56–7.

300   *Bibliography*

Šrám, R. J. (1978) 'Current State and Future Trends in the Estimation of Human Genetic Risk from Environmental Chemicals in the Czech Socialist Republic', *Czechoslovak Medicine*, vol. 1.
Šteker, Antonín (1977) 'Populační politika státu', in Vlasta Brablcová (ed.) *Manželství, rodina, rodičovství* (Praha: Horizont), pp. 70–9.
Šteker, Antonín (1979) 'Průzkum populačních tendencí mladých rodin v ČSR', *Sociální politika*, vol. 5, no. 7 (July) pp. 150–1.
Štembera, Zdeněk (1977) 'Směry socialistické soutěže a komplexní socialistické racionalizace na gynekologicko – porodnických odděleních', *Československá gynekologie*, vol. 42, no. 6, pp. 401–4.
Štembera, Zdeněk (1979) 'Screening Early Diagnosis and Prevention of Prematurity and Placental Insufficiency', *Czechoslovak Medicine*, vol. 2, nos. 1–2, pp. 23–7.
Štembera, Zdeněk (1981) 'Development of maternal and child health-care in Czechoslovakia' *World Health Forum*, vol. 2, no. 4, pp. 516–20.
Štembera, Zdeněk (1982) 'Ohrození plodu při rizikovém těhotenství', *Československá gynekologie*, vol. 47, no. 2, pp. 96–9.
Štembera, Zdenek *et al.* (1979) *Rizikové těhotenství a dítě*, second revised edition (Praha: Avicenum).
Štěpán, J. (1981a) 'Právní aspekty výzkumu a praxe na úseku regulace porodnictví', *Československá gynekologie*, vol. 46 no. 3, pp. 212–6.
Štěpán, J. (1981b) 'K právním aspektům výzkumu a praxe na úseku porodnictví', *Československá gynekologie*, vol. 46, no. 6, pp. 493–4.
Štěpán, J. (1984) 'K etickoprávním problémům moderního porodnictví', *Československá gynekologie*, vol. 49, no. 2, pp. 125–35.
Štěpánková, J. (1983) 'Antikoncepce – Ano, či Ne?' an interview with Dr Jiří Šráček, *Rudé Právo, Haló sobota*, 17 December, p. 4.
Štipal, B. (1972) 'Perspektivy a úkoly zdravotní péče v pětiletém plánu v letech 1971–1975', *Československá gynekologie*, vol. 37, no. 8 (October) pp. 553–7.
Švancarová, Lea (1981) 'Psychologická problematika v péči o novorozence', *Psychológia i patopsychológia dieťata*, vol. 26, no. 1, pp. 74–6.
Švarcová, H. (1970) 'Vztahy společensko-ekonomické působící na reprodukci', *Československá gynekologie* vol. 35, no. 3, pp. 182–4.
Švejcar, Josef (1980) 'Výživa kojence kojením', *Československá pediatrie*, vol. 35, no. 10 (October) pp. 542–52.
Švejcar, Josef (1981) 'Interview', *Mladý svět*, vol. 23, no. 17, (1159), 21–27.4.
Švejcar, Josef (1982) 'Interview', *Rudé právo* 15 May.
Taufrová, M. (1981) 'Odraz stavu a změn společenského prostředí na hospitalizovaného pacienta', *Československé zdravotnictví*, vol. 29, no. 4 (April) pp. 166–71.
Taylor, Rex (1979) 'Conference Report: Polish–British Symposium on Medical Sociology, Jablonna/Warsaw, May 1978', *Social Science and Medicine*, vol. 13A, pp. 293–6.
Tekse, Kalman (1980) 'Demographic Implications of Low Fertility', in Arthur A. Campbell (ed.) *Social, Economic and Health Aspects of Low Fertility*, NIH Publication no. 80–100, (US Department of Health, Education and Welfare) pp. 59–78.

Tenčl, Ladislav (1980) 'Medical and Para Medical Schools in Czechoslovakia', *Demosta*, vol. 13, no. 3, pp. 95–8.

Thompson, Arlene B. and Wilson, Audrey M. (1981) 'Quantity First Then Quality. A hospital looks at cost-effective staff utilization', *The Canadian Nurse*, vol. 24 (May).

Tietze, Christopher (1981) *Induced Abortion. A World Review, 1981*, fourth edition (New York: The Population Council).

Tilly, Louise A. and Scott, Joan W. (1978) *Women, Work and Family* (New York: Holt, Rinehart & Winston).

Tošovská, Z. *et al.* (1974) 'Sexuální život žen žádající antikoncepci', *Československá gynekologie*, vol. 39, no. 3, pp. 217–8.

Trča, Stanislav (1965) *Zdravotní výchova žen* (Praha: Institute of Health Education).

Trča, Stanislav (1971) 'Ve kterém období života ženy je propagace antikoncepce nejúčinější', *Československá gynekologie*, vol. 36, no. 1 (February).

Trča, Stanislav (1975) 'Péče státu o ženu, zvláště o těhotnou ženu a matku, in *Rok zeny. Unesco 1975. Podkladové materialy* (Praha: Ministerstvo zdravotnictvi, Ústav zdravotní výchovy).

Trča, Stanislav (1977) 'Kolik žen přestává v těhotenství kouřit', *Československá gynekologie*, vol. 42, no. 10 (December).

Trča, Stanislav (1978) 'Příprava těhotných žen na porod', in *Populační zprávy*, nos. 1–2, pp. 38–41.

Trča, Stanislav (1979) *Budeme mit děťátko*, third revised edition (Praha: Avicenum).

Trča, Stanislav (1980) *Umění zdravě žít. Kniha pro ženy* (Praha: Avicenum).

Trča, Stanislav and Rejmanová, E. (1974) 'Kolik žen je uspokojivě informováno o sexuálních otázkách', *Československá gynekologie*, vol. 39, no. 3, pp. 212–3.

Trnka, V. *et al.* (1981) 'Vývoj perinatální úmrtnosti v hlavním městě Praze', *Československá gynekologie*, vol. 46, no. 9 (November) pp. 722–5.

Trnka V. and Doležal, A. (1978) 'Vaginální porody po císařských řezech a operacích na děloze,' *Československá gynekologie*, vol. 43, no. 4 (May) pp. 254–7.

Tyndale, Eleanor (1980) 'The Birth-Control Decision-Making Process', *Resources for Feminist Research*, Special Publication 8 (Fall) pp. 70–3.

'U matky je dítěti nejlépe' (1982) *Rudé právo*, 6 November.

Uhlíř, M. and Čupr, Z. (1982) 'Indikace k císařskému řezu', *Československá gynekologie*, vol. 47, no. 4, pp. 304–6.

Uhlíř, M., Ždímalová, M., Dráč, P. (1974) 'Psychosomatické faktory sterility', *Československá gynekologié*, vol. 39, no. 3 (April) pp. 189–91.

Urbanová, Hedviga (1977) 'Vedomosti matiek o starostlivosti o deti do jednoho roka', in *Zdravotná výchova a žena v socialistickej spoločnosti* (Bratislava: Institute for Health Education) pp. 71–9.

Vaessan, Martin (1978) 'World Fertility Survey: The Current Situation', *International Family Planning Perspectives and Digest*, vol. 4, no. 3 (Fall) pp. 73–4.

Vaněk, Antonín (1971) *Příznaky krize manželské rodiny* (Praha: Státní pedogogicke nakladatelství).

Veevers, Jean E. (1980) *Childless by Choice* (Toronto: Butterworths).

Velvovskii, I. Z. (ed.) (1960) *Painless Childbirth through Psychoprophylaxis* (Moscow: Progress Publishers).

Víšek, Petr (1979) 'Výsledky šetření o příjemcích přídavků na děti v roce 1978', *Socialni politika*, vol. 5, no. 6 (June).

Vodák, Pavel (1968) *Adoptivní dítě a jeho rodiče. O jistotách a pochybnostech rodičovského svazku* (Praha: Státní zdravotnické nakladatelství).

Vojta, Miroslav (1961a) 'Psychoprofylaxe a tělocvik – příprava na porod', in *10 let boje za zdraví nové generace 1951–1961. Přehled vědecké činnosti Ústavu pro péči o matku a dítě.* (Praha: The Institute for Care of Mother and Child) pp. 31–35.

Vojta, Miroslav (1961b) 'Boj proti mateřské úmrtnosti', in *10 let boje za zdraví nové generace 1951–1961. Přehled vědecké činnosti Ústavu pro péči o matku a dítě.* (Praha: The Institute for Care of Mother and Child) pp. 47–50.

Vojta, Miroslav (1971) 'Aktuální možnosti zlepšit péči o ženy v našem socialistickém zdravotnictví', in Mirko Horak (ed.) *Sborník prací* (Ostrava), pp. 73–9.

Vojta, Miroslav (1974) 'Výsledky populační politiky', *Československá gynekologie*, vol. 39, no. 5 (June).

Vojta, Miroslav and Poláček, K. (1961) 'Uvod', in *10 let boje za zdraví nové generace 1951–1961. Přehled vědecké činnosti Ústavu pro péči o matku a dítě.* (Praha: The Institute for Care of Mother and Child) pp. 8–11.

Vorlová, M. and Němec, M. (1976) 'UPT a jeho vliv na předčasnou porodnost', in *Aktualní problémy v porodnictví*, proceedings from the 17th inter-county obstetrical seminar of the southern and northern Moravian counties, 22–23 April, Uherské Hradište, pp. 94–103.

'Výsledky sociologického průzkumu "Rodina a děti"' (1978) *Populační zprávy*, pp. 65–78.

'Vztah porodnosti a potratovosti v ČSSR' (1979) *Demografie*, vol. 21, no. 2.

Wertz, Richard W. and Wertz, Dorothy C. (1977) *Lying In: History of Childbirth in America* (New York: Schocken Books).

Wolchik, Sharon L. (1979) 'The Status of Women in a Socialist Order: Czechoslovakia, 1948–1978', *Slavic Review*, vol. 38, no. 4 (December) pp. 583–602.

Wolchik, Sharon L. (1981) 'Elite Strategy toward Women in Czechoslovakia: Liberation or Mobilization?' *Studies in Comparative Communism*, vol. 15, nos. 2–3 (Summer/Autumn) pp. 123–42.

Wolchik, Sharon L. (1983) 'The Scientific–Technological Revolution and the Role of Specialist Elites in Policy-making in Czechoslovakia', in Michael J. Sodaro and Sharon L. Wolchik (eds.) *Foreign and Domestic Policy in Eastern Europe in the 1980s: Trends and Prospects* (London: Macmillan) pp. 111–32.

Woodhouse, Ann (1982) 'Sexuality, Femininity and Fertility Control', *Women's Studies International Forum*, vol. 5, no. 1, pp. 1–15.

Working Women in Czechoslovakia (1975) (Prague: Práce).

Wulf, Deirdre (1979) 'WFS: Hungary's Population Decline Will Continue Unless More Women Stay Home, Bear More Children', *International Family Perspectives*, vol. 5, no. 4 (December) pp. 167–8.

Wulf, Deirdre (1982) 'Low Fertility in Europe: A Report from the 1981 IUSSP Meeting', *International Family Planning Perspectives*, vol. 8, no. 2 (June) pp. 63–9.

Wynnyczuk, Vladimir (1981) 'Education to Marriage and Parenthood', in *The Socialist Family in Czechoslovakia* (Prague: Orbis) pp. 69–78.

Wynnyczuk, Vladimir and Faktorová, Františka (1980) 'Mezinárodní srovnání populačních opatření v Evropě (1978)', *Demografie*, vol. 22, no. 1, pp. 1–15.

Wynnyczuková, Helena (1979) 'Umělé přerušení těhotenství mladých žen v ČSSR (1958–1977)', *Demografie*, vol. 21, no. 3, pp. 218–22.

Závadská, Elena (1983) 'Zákon o rodine po novom', *Sociální politika*, vol. 9, no. 11 (November) pp. 246–7.

Zdravotnictví a populace (1971) (Praha: Ministry of Health ČSR).

Zdravotnictví ČSR, 1945–1980 (1980) (Praha: Ministry of Health ČSR).

Zellman, Gail L. and Goodchilds, Jacqueline D. (1983) 'Becoming Sexual in Adolescence', in Elizabeth Rice Allgeier and Naomi B. McCormick (eds) *Changing Boundaries. Gender Roles and Sexual Behavior* (Palo Alto: Mayfield Publishing) pp. 49–63.

Zeman, L. (1982) 'Péče o nezletilé a mladistvé matky v kojeneckém ústavu', *Československá pediatrie*, vol. 37, no. 4 (April) pp. 215–9.

Ziolkowski, J. A. (1974) 'Poland', in Bernard B. Berelson (ed.) *Population Policy in Developed Countries*, (New York: McGraw-Hill) pp. 445–88.

Zollinger, Richard (1980) 'The Economic Position of Young Couples', in Arthur A. Campbell (ed.) in *Aspects of Low Fertility* NIH Publication no. 80–100 (US Department of Health Education and Welfare) pp. 121–9.

Židovský, J. (1978) 'Pomoc a úkoly výzkumu v oblasti péče o ženu matku a novorozence', *Československá gynekologie*, vol. 43, no. 7 (August) pp. 485–9.

Židovský, J. (1982) 'Třicet let výzkumu v péči o matku a dítě', *Československá gynekologie*, vol. 47, no. 2, pp. 83–9.

Index

sterilisation in, 139; 'unwanted'
children in, 169
House of the Unmarried Woman and
Child, 243
Households, *see* Housing; Family size
Housework, *see* Domestic work
Housing, 6, 24, 25, 28, 35, 56, 84, 87,
131, 165, 166, 168, 237, 240–1, 243–4,
250t, 252t, 256, 257, 258, 259, 260t,
263, 264n, 268
Hungary, 7, 20, 24, 32, 35n, 44, 68, 69,
76, 81, 101, 102–4, 135–6, 137, 144n,
149–50, 152–7, 159, 174n, 267, 274
Hynie, J., 46
Husbands, 7, 10, 129–31, 142, 166,
185–6, 187, 189, 201, 218, 220n,
231–2, 241, 248, 250t, 259; *see also*
Couples; Fathers; Marriage; Men
Hypertension, 98, 99

Ideologies, *see* Cultural norms
Illness, *see* Morbidity
Income, as reproductive variable, 3,
258–60, 263; during pregnancy, 60, 64,
70n; equalisation of, xiii, 70; loss of,
6, 61, 66, 68, 70, 88, 197n, 259; low,
243, 259, 269; of health care workers,
94, 95, 96, 103, 121, 170, 274; rise in,
59, 257, 259–60; women's, 63, 66,
70, 256, 260, 269; *see also* Birth
grants; Couples, loans for; Family
allowances; Fiscal incentives,
Maternity allowance and leave;
Sickness benefits
Incubators, 5, 208, 213; *see also* Birth
technology; Foetal monitoring
Individualism, 4–5
Induction, *see* Childbirth, medical
management; Labour and delivery
Industrial development in Eastern
Europe, *see* Economic growth
Infanticide, 2
Infecundity, 251
Infections, 63, 216, 222–3, 245n
Infertility, 2, 81, 128, 142, 195n, 274;
see also Sterility; Sterilisation
Institute for Czech language, 223
Institute for Further Education of
Middle-level Health Care Workers,
118
Institute for the Care of Mother and
Child, 144–5n, 160–1, 163, 164, 180,
190–1, 213, 233, 262

Institute for Research of Public
Opinion, 193
Institute of Health Education, 40, 43,
48, 138
Institute of Hygiene and Epidemiology,
62–3
Insurance schemes, *see* Sickness leave,
certificates and benefits; Social
welfare (security) policies
Inter-Professional conflicts, 30, 39,
44–8, 225, 233
Ireland, 212, 246n, 250, 267
Ispa, J., 196n, 219, 220n, 240–1
Israel, 21, 82, 107n, 108n, 209
Italy, 69, 94, 109n, 209

J. K., 180–4
Jamaica, 179
Jancar, B., 57, 62
Japan, 66, 152–5, 209, 212
Jerrie, J., 91, 147, 157
Johnson, T., 111n
Jones, R., 235, 236, 246n
Jordan, B., 198, 277–8
Jurisdictional conflicts, *see*
Inter-professional conflicts

Kadlecová, Z., 49, 134
Kadrnková, M., 127, 135
Kaloynova, F., 56–7, 62
Kaser, M., 88, 94, 106–7n, 108n, 114
Kemény, I., 103–4
Kindergartens, 35, 39, 66, 113
Kitzinger, S., 189, 196n, 237
Klaus, M. and Kennell, J., 217, 224,
225
Klement Gottwald Iron and Steel
Works, 63
Kliment, P., 51
Kliment, V., 118, 135, 188–9
Knaus, W., 95, 106n
Koch, J., 53, 242, 246n
Kollontai, A., 27
Kops, J., 101–2, 200
Korea, 174n
Košice, 205
Kotásek, A., 28, 84, 85, 107n, 148, 158,
166, 207–8
Kramer, J., 239
Koubek, J., 21, 23–4, 256
Kučera, Z., 43–4, 45, 50
Kvíz, D., 82, 182, 262

312 *Index*

Soviet Union, 5, 27, 76, 77, 78, 108n, 175, 190, 219n, 220n; industrial, 77, 87–90, 108n, 109n; power and dominance of, 75, 96–7, 106, 109n, 266, 272, 273, 276–8; *see also* Abortion; Bonding; Clinics; Doctors; Education of doctors; Health care services; Maternity care; Obstetrics/gynaecology; Paediatrics; Perinatal morbidity and mortality; Social gynaecology

Men, 7, 9, 10, 61–3, 67, 146, 165, 192, 194, 196n, 218–9, 219n, 232, 248t, 260; *see also* Husbands; Fathers

Mendl, V., 229, 233

Menstruation, 2, 3, 57, 62, 66, 128–9, 144n, 157, 161–3, 164, 273

Methodological considerations, xiii, xiv, 6, 9, 48–50, 149–50, 251, 263–4n

Michlíček, J., 60–1, 69, 214

Midwives, 79t, 112, 176, 183, 185, 186, 198, 200, 272

Mieckowski, B., xiii, 178, 197n

Migration, 21–2, 35n, 196n, 236, 219n

Military, doctors, 108n; clinics, 88, 106n, 233; service, 39, 40, 67

Milk, breast, 2, 227, 228, 236, 239, 240; formula (artificial), 222, 234–9, 246n; *see also* Breastfeeding

Millard, F., 77, 81–2, 92–3, 100–1, 104–5, 106n

Ministry of Culture, 43, 44

Ministry of Education, 40, 41, 43, 96–7

Ministry of Health, 26, 29, 30, 41, 43, 44, 76, 90–1, 93, 102, 108–9n, 121, 144n, 164, 168, 178, 190

Ministry of Justice, 26, 43

Ministry of Work (Labour) and Social Affairs, 30, 43, 244

Miscarriage, 1, 2, 3, 24, 36n, 59, 62, 63, 148, 157, 158, 169, 176, 187, 213, 274; *see also* Abortion

Mladá Boleslav, 163

Mladá fronta, 230, 245n

Mladý svět, 230–2, 245n, 246n, 275

Moen, E., 15, 25–6, 266

Molyneux, M., xiv, xvn, 71

Montreal, 205

Moravia, 75, 120, 134, 139, 142, 191, 199, 213, 226

Morbidity, abortion, 40, 42, 84–5, 150, 157–60, 166, 173, 213; children, 59, 64, 88–9, 169, 181–2, 215, 216; contraceptive, 127, 135; frequency

and structure of, 15–16, 83, 84–5, 94, 111n; gynaecological, 79, 83, 84–5, 113, 276; infant, 53, 207, 217, 222; infections, 63, 216, 218, 222–31, 245n; male, 52, 185, 219, 220n; maternal, 89, 163, 203, 207, 262; neonatal, 16, 202, 203, 213; obstetrical, 2–3, 16, 62, 65, 81, 82, 157–60, 163, 173, 175–7, 180–2, 183, 187, 216, 243, 262; perinatal, 3, 157, 187, 203–4, 206–17, 262; tumours and cancer, 78, 81, 83, 113, 276; venereal disease, 80, 107–8n; *see also* Breech presentation, Caesarean births

Morokvasić, M., 8, 141, 143, 161

Mortality, abortion, 147–8, 275; infant, 6, 16–17, 96, 139, 174n, 178, 179, 180, 207, 208, 210, 219n; maternal, 24, 78, 79, 148, 163, 203, 207, 209, 211, 219n, 262; neonatal, 35n, 65, 79, 183, 203–4, 210; perinatal, 24, 35n, 78, 79, 82, 139, 157, 158, 178, 183, 200, 202–4, 206, 208–17, 262, 271, 277; statistics, 15, 17, 198, 208–17; *see also* Miscarriage; Stillbirth

Mosher, W., 135, 137

Most, 229–30, 233, 246n

Motherhood, experience of, 3, 18, 31, 66–7, 225–6, 230–3, 240–5, 246n, 259; ideologies of, 3, 10, 24, 30, 37, 38, 40, 52–8, 68–9, 71n, 98, 167, 195n, 215, 222–7, 234, 245n, 246n, 268, 269–70, 276; transition to, 1–2, 4, 125–226; *see also* Bonding; Breastfeeding; Child care; Children; Expert advice; Maternity allowance and leave; Post-partum; Rooming-in

Mothers, and child development, 53, 84–5; and knowledge of parenting, 51–3; of abortion applicants, 168; of adolescents, 46, 49, 50; of newborns, 66–7, 217–18, 221–6; single (parents), 32, 64, 89, 100, 195n, 243–4, 273; teenage, 244; *see also* Bonding; Breastfeeding; Child care; Expert advice; Family; Marriage; Post-partum; Pregnancy; Rooming-in

Mrkvička, J., 38, 127

Müller, C., 84–5

Nappies, *see* Diapers
National Institute of Child Health and Human Development (NICHD), 159